FROM WHAT I HEAR, MACS ARE, LIKE, TOTALLY *THE BOMB.*
WHAT ABOUT WHAT YOU JUST WROTE?! OR WERE YOU ONLY PRETENDING TO BE CHEERFUL?

和月伸宏

NOBUHIRO WATSUKI

NAME DIVINATION

BEFORE I WAS PUBLISHED, I HAD A FRIEND OF MINE DO A "READING" ON MY NAME. BOTH MY REAL NAME AND MY PEN NAME CAME OUT TO THE EFFECT, "WILL ACHIEVE A PORTION OF SUCCESS, BUT WILL ALSO BE FOREVER LONELY." THESE DAYS, I'VE BEGUN TO THINK THEY WEREN'T TOO FAR FROM THE MARK. AS WATSUKI HAS NEVER PLACED THAT HIGH A PREMIUM ON HIS PERSONAL RELATIONSHIPS (BLAMING THE BUSINESS), PERHAPS HE'S BROUGHT IT UPON HIMSELF. STILL, I'M GOING TO DO WHAT I CAN, MEANING THAT I'LL KEEP NEEDING YOUR SUPPORT, NOW MORE THAN EVER....

Rurouni Kenshin, which has found fans not only in Japan but around the world, first made its appearance in 1992, as an original short story in ***Weekly Shonen Jump Special***. Later rewritten and published as a regular, continuing ***Jump*** series in 1994, ***Rurouni Kenshin*** ended serialization in 1999 but continued in popularity, as evidenced by the 2000 publication of ***Yahiko no Sakabatô*** ("Yahiko's Reversed-Edge Sword") in ***Weekly Shonen Jump***. His most current work, ***Busô Renkin*** ("Armored Alchemist"), began publication in June 2003, also in ***Jump***.

RUROUNI KENSHIN
VOL. 12: THE GREAT KYOTO FIRE
The SHONEN JUMP Graphic Novel Edition

STORY AND ART BY
NOBUHIRO WATSUKI

English Adaptation/Gerard Jones
Translation/Kenichiro Yagi
Touch-Up Art & Lettering/Steve Dutro
Cover, Graphics & Layout/Sean Lee
Editor/Avery Gotoh

Supervising Editor/Kit Fox
Managing Editor/Elizabeth Kawasaki
Director of Production/Noboru Watanabe
Editorial Director/Alvin Lu
Executive Vice President & Editor in Chief/Hyoe Narita
Sr. Director of Acquisitions/Rika Inouye
Vice President of Sales & Marketing/Liza Coppola
Vice President of Strategic Development/Yumi Hoashi
Publisher/Seiji Horibuchi

Printed in the U.S.A.

Published by VIZ, LLC
P.O. Box 77010
San Francisco, CA 94107

SHONEN JUMP Graphic Novel Edition
10 9 8 7 6 5 4 3 2 1
First printing, February 2005

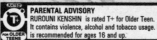

www.viz.com

THE WORLD'S
MOST POPULAR MANGA

SHONEN JUMP
GRAPHIC NOVEL
www.shonenjump.com

SHONEN JUMP GRAPHIC NOVEL

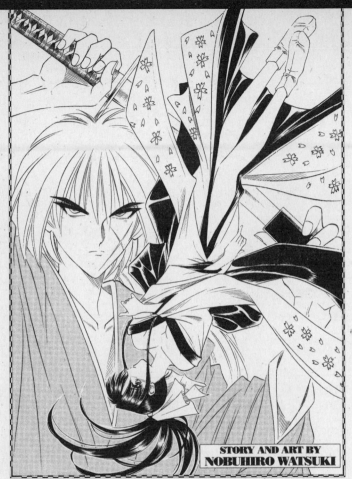

STORY AND ART BY
NOBUHIRO WATSUKI

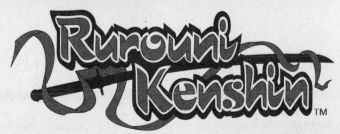

Rurouni Kenshin™

MEIJI SWORDSMAN ROMANTIC STORY
Vol. 12: THE GREAT KYOTO FIRE

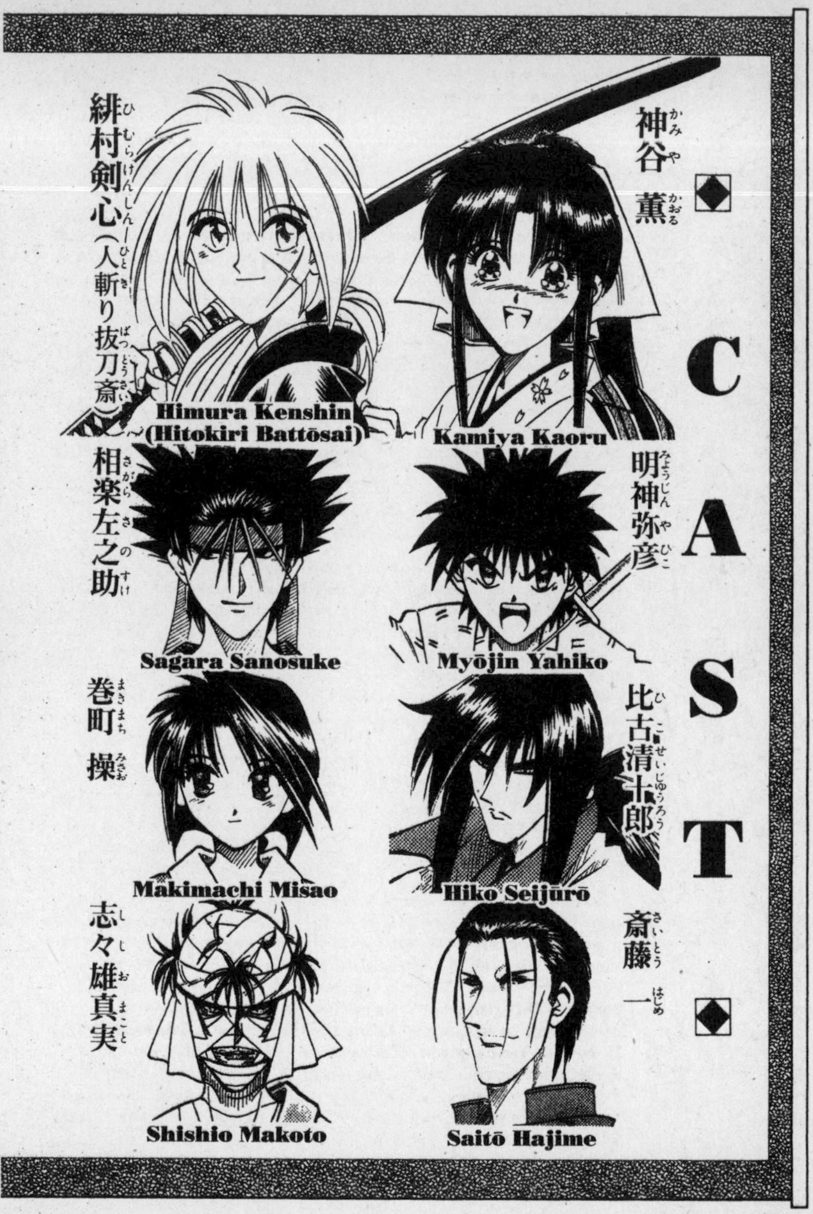
CAST
神谷薫
Kamiya Kaoru
緋村剣心（人斬り抜刀斎）
Himura Kenshin (Hitokiri Battōsai)
明神弥彦
Myōjin Yahiko
相楽左之助
Sagara Sanosuke
比古清十郎
Hiko Seijūrō
巻町操
Makimachi Misao
斎藤一
Saitō Hajime
志々雄真実
Shishio Makoto

Once he was *hitokiri*, an assassin, called Battōsai. His name was legend among the *Ishin Shishi* pro-Imperialist or "patriot" warriors who launched the Meiji Era. Now, Himura Kenshin is *rurouni*, a wanderer, and carries a reversed-edge *sakabatō* to prohibit himself from killing.

Ōkubo Toshimichi, head of the government's "Internal Affairs," tries to hire Kenshin to assassinate Shishio Makoto, the successor to "Hitokiri Battōsai." But it is Ōkubo who is assassinated, and Kenshin sets out for Kyoto to find his killers. On the East Sea Road, Kenshin meets a girl named Misao and travels with her to a village occupied by Shishio's men—where he reconnects with fellow swordsman Saitō Hajime. There, they encounter Shishio himself, but the assassin refuses to fight Kenshin (because he is no longer *hitokiri*) and vanishes. Instead, Kenshin fights Sōjirō... shattering his *sakabatō*.

T H U S F A R

In Kyoto, Kenshin stays at Aoi-Ya—an inn run by Okina, Misao's ex-Oniwabanshū surrogate father—and, to save Seikū (son of late swordsmith Arai Shakkū) and his family, is forced to battle Chō, a *Juppongatana* or "Ten Swords" assassin. Having been given the new *sakabatō* "Shinuchi," Kenshin goes to see Hiko Seijūrō, current master of his school of swordsmanship. But Seijūrō refuses to teach Kenshin the ultimate Hiten Mitsurugi move, saying, "One who sides with any powers or parties does not deserve the secret." Just then, Misao leads in Yahiko and Kaoru... and Seijūrō, having been convinced by Kaoru that Kenshin *has* internalized the principles of Hiten Mitsurugi on his own, decides that he will teach him the secret.

Meanwhile, Shinomori Aoshi—spurned by Okina as a prospective spy—decides to take his information on Kenshin to Shishio. Okina tries to stop him, but Aoshi has rid himself of compassion and has turned into a kind of demon. With Okina's death, Misao proclaims herself *Okashira* or "head" of the Oniwabanshū, swearing to defeat Shishio and his men... including her beloved Aoshi-sama. Elsewhere, at the police department, Sanosuke has contacted Saitō and together the two interrogate Chō, learning that Shishio is about to launch his grand scheme, which begins with the burning of Kyoto....

CONTENTS

RUROUNI KENSHIN

Meiji Swordsman Romantic Story

BOOK TWELVE: THE GREAT KYOTO FIRE

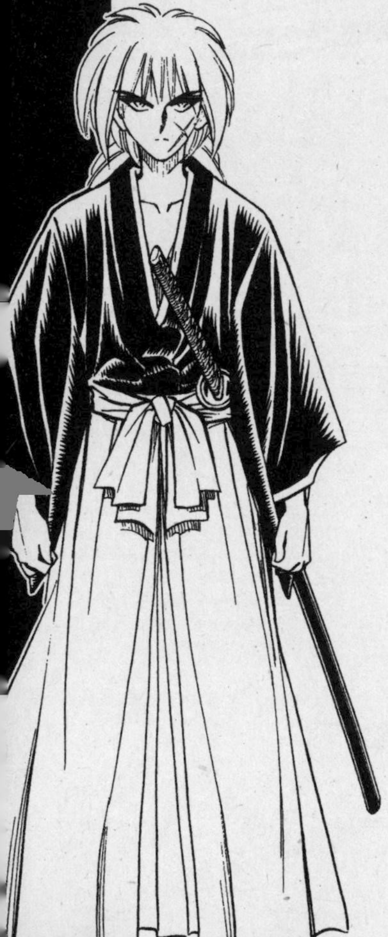

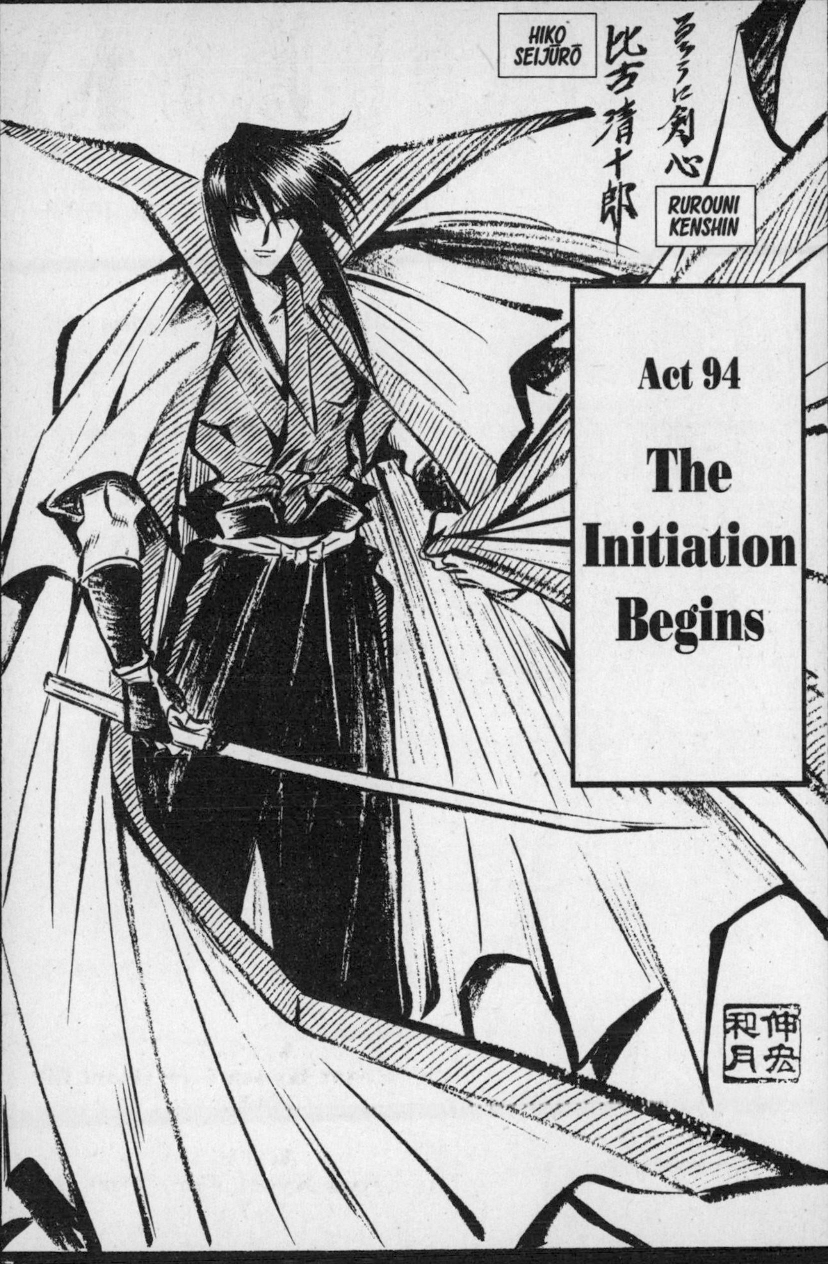
るろうに剣心
RUROUNI KENSHIN
比古清十郎
HIKO SEIJŪRŌ
Act 94
The Initiation Begins
伸宏 和月

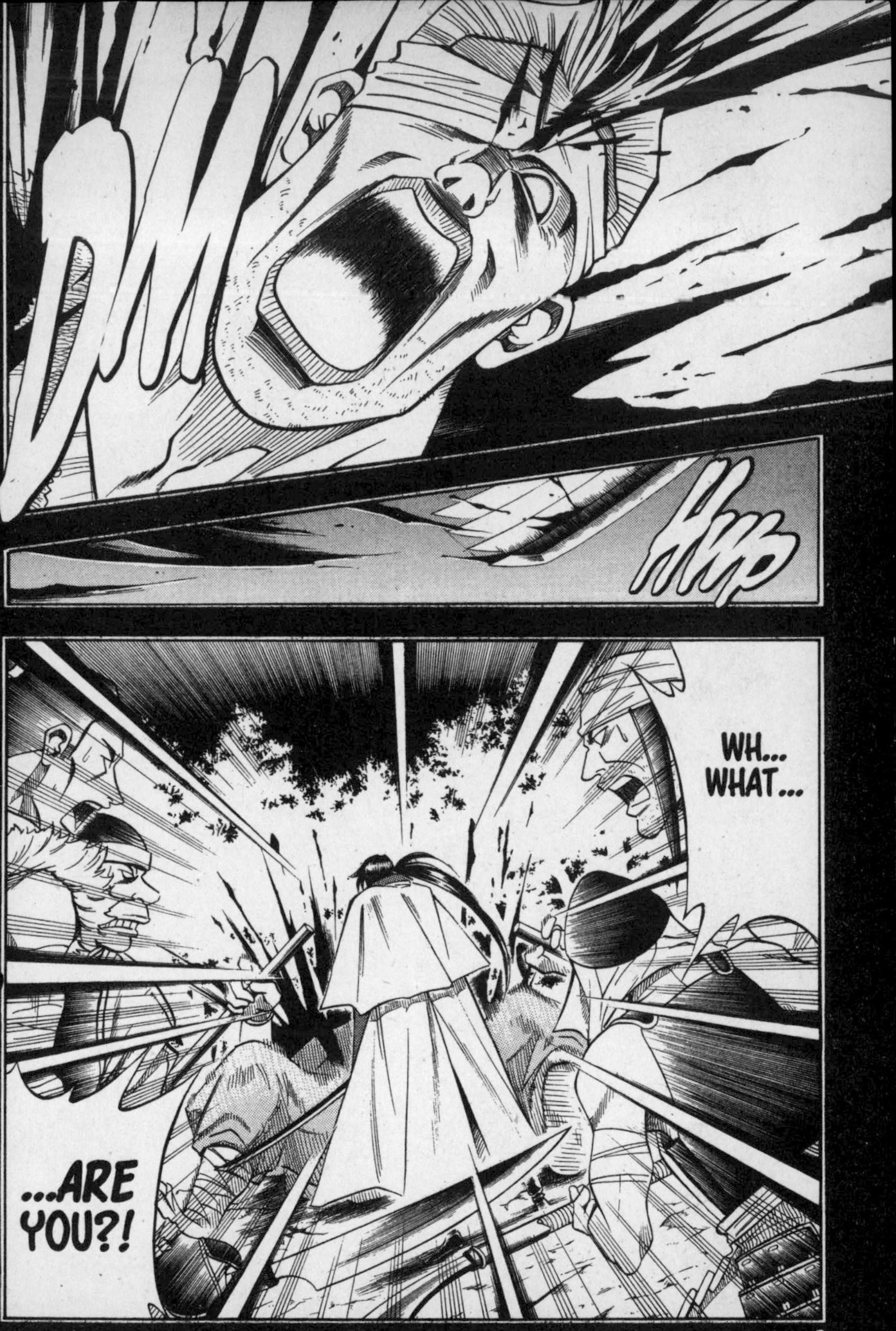
Hup
WH...
WHAT...
...ARE
YOU?!

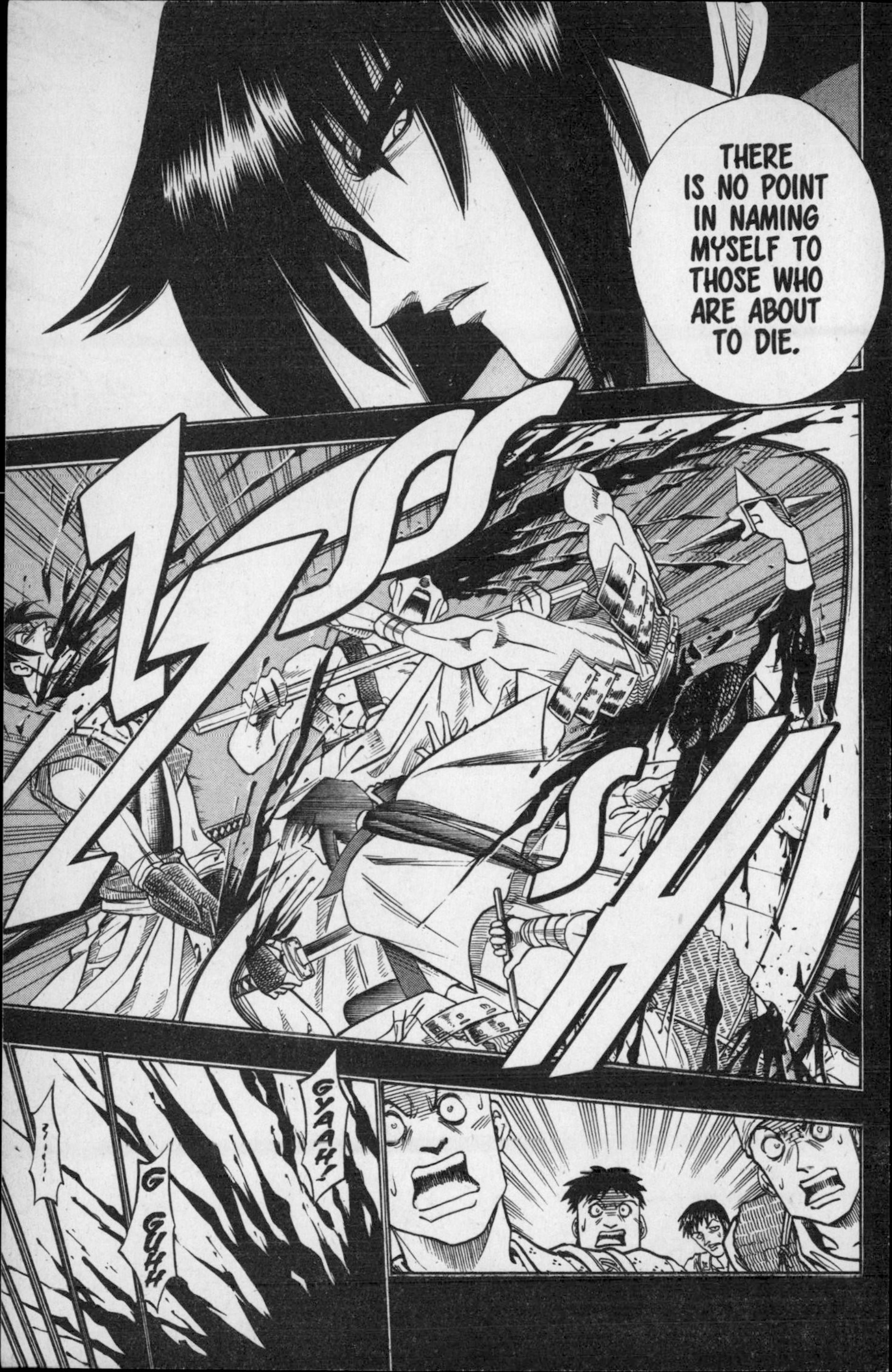
THERE IS NO POINT IN NAMING MYSELF TO THOSE WHO ARE ABOUT TO DIE.
GYAAAH!
G GUHH

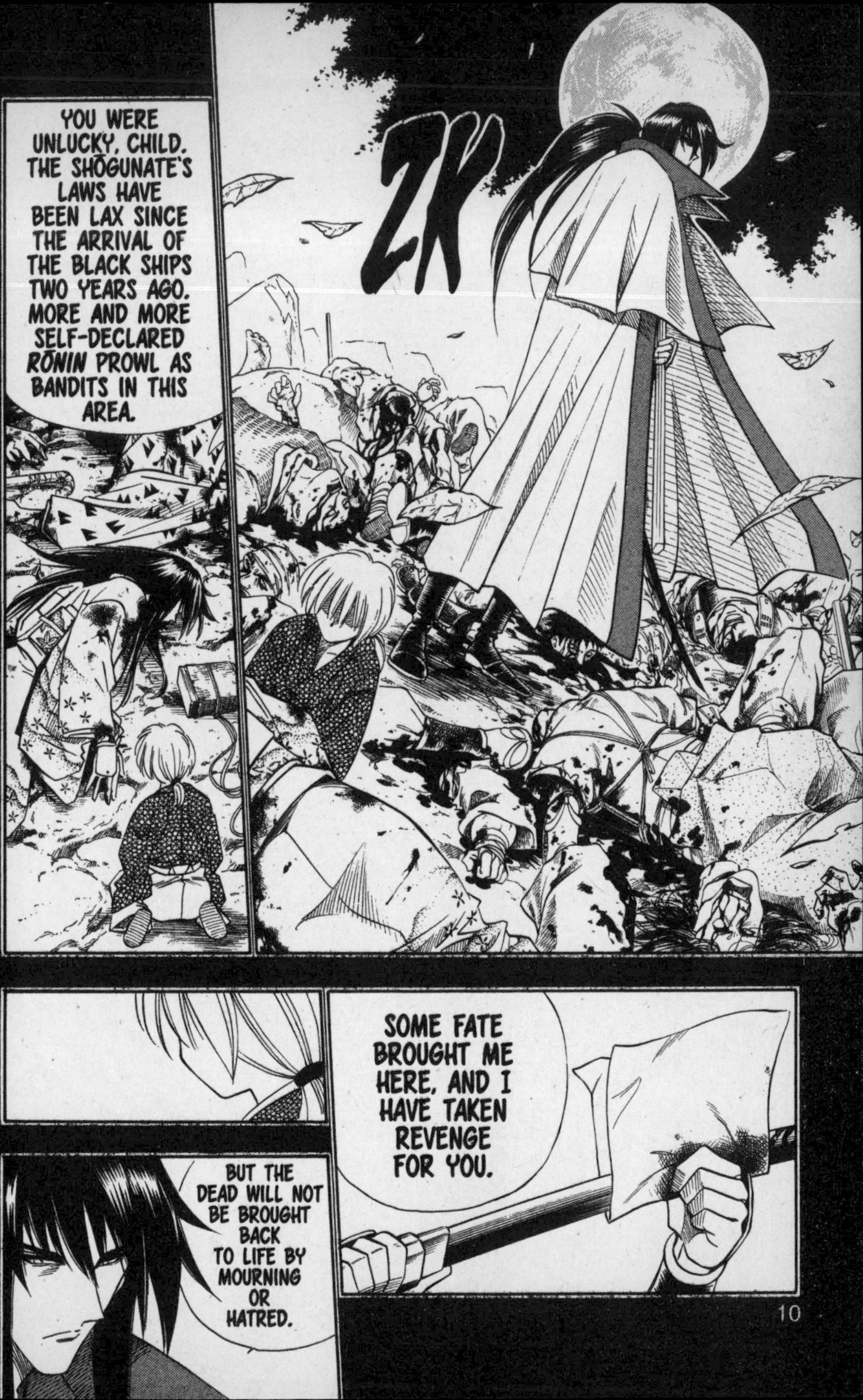
ZK
YOU WERE UNLUCKY, CHILD. THE SHŌGUNATE'S LAWS HAVE BEEN LAX SINCE THE ARRIVAL OF THE BLACK SHIPS TWO YEARS AGO. MORE AND MORE SELF-DECLARED *RŌNIN* PROWL AS BANDITS IN THIS AREA.
SOME FATE BROUGHT ME HERE, AND I HAVE TAKEN REVENGE FOR YOU.
BUT THE DEAD WILL NOT BE BROUGHT BACK TO LIFE BY MOURNING OR HATRED.

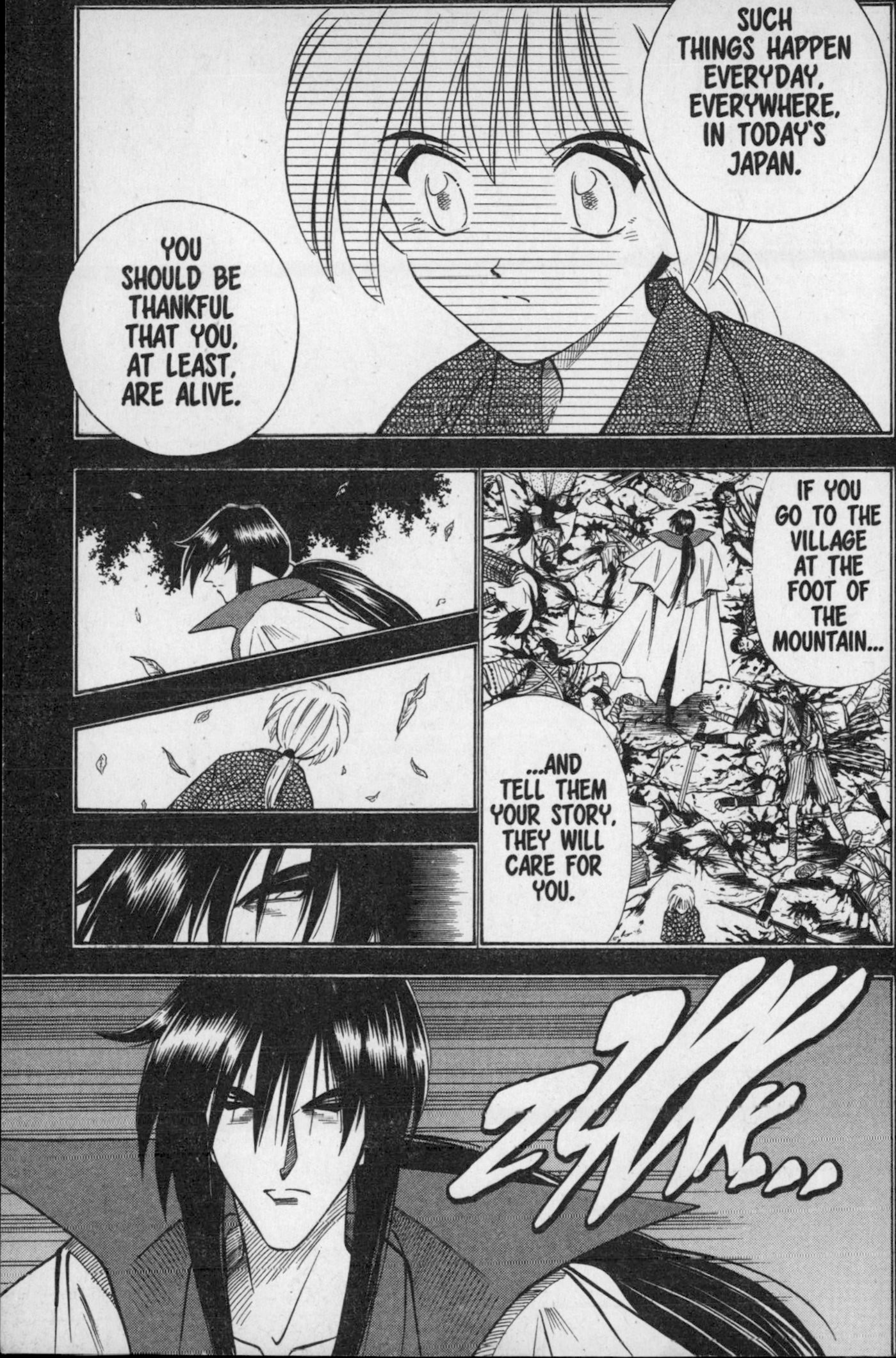
SUCH THINGS HAPPEN EVERYDAY, EVERYWHERE, IN TODAY'S JAPAN.
YOU SHOULD BE THANKFUL THAT YOU, AT LEAST, ARE ALIVE.
IF YOU GO TO THE VILLAGE AT THE FOOT OF THE MOUNTAIN...
...AND TELL THEM YOUR STORY, THEY WILL CARE FOR YOU.

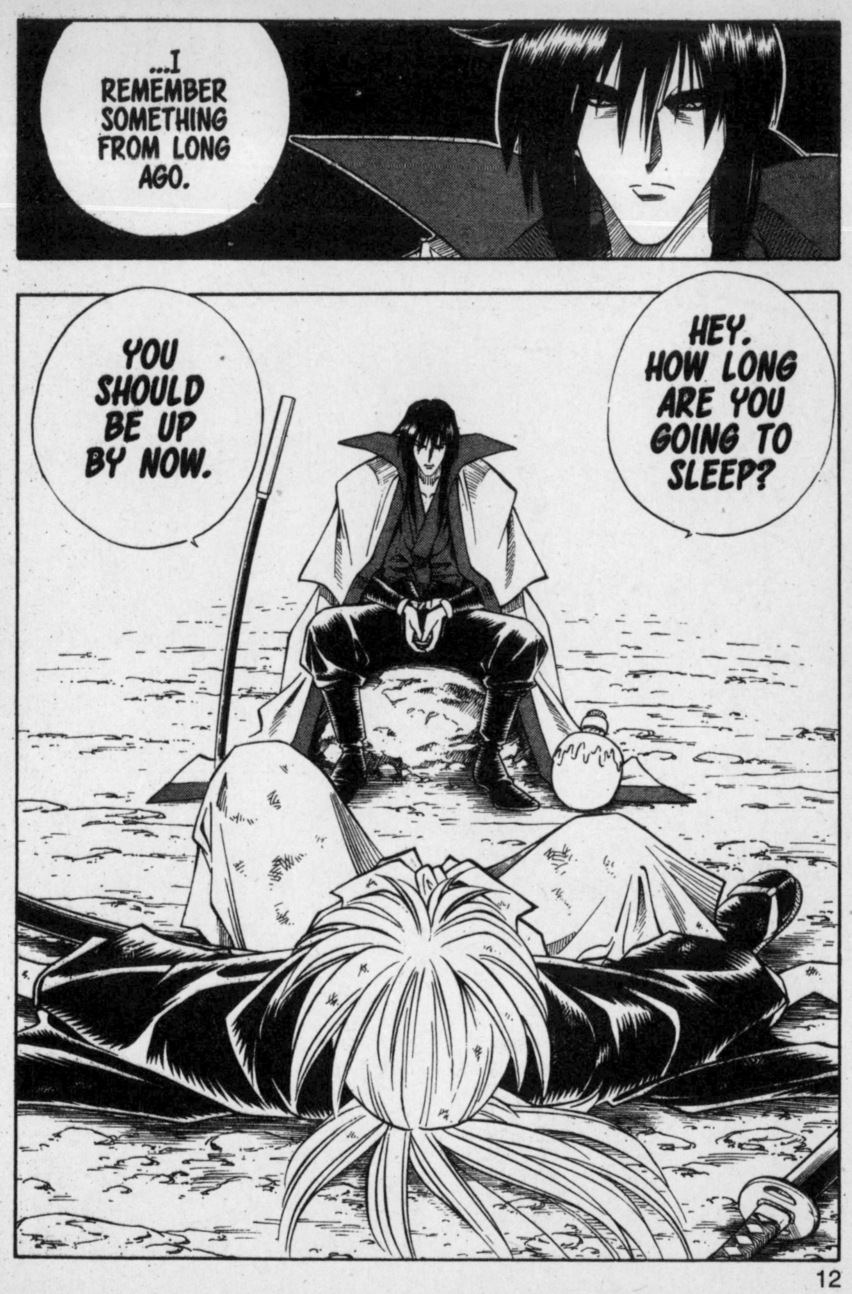
...I REMEMBER SOMETHING FROM LONG AGO.
HEY. HOW LONG ARE YOU GOING TO SLEEP?
YOU SHOULD BE UP BY NOW.

READ THIS WAY

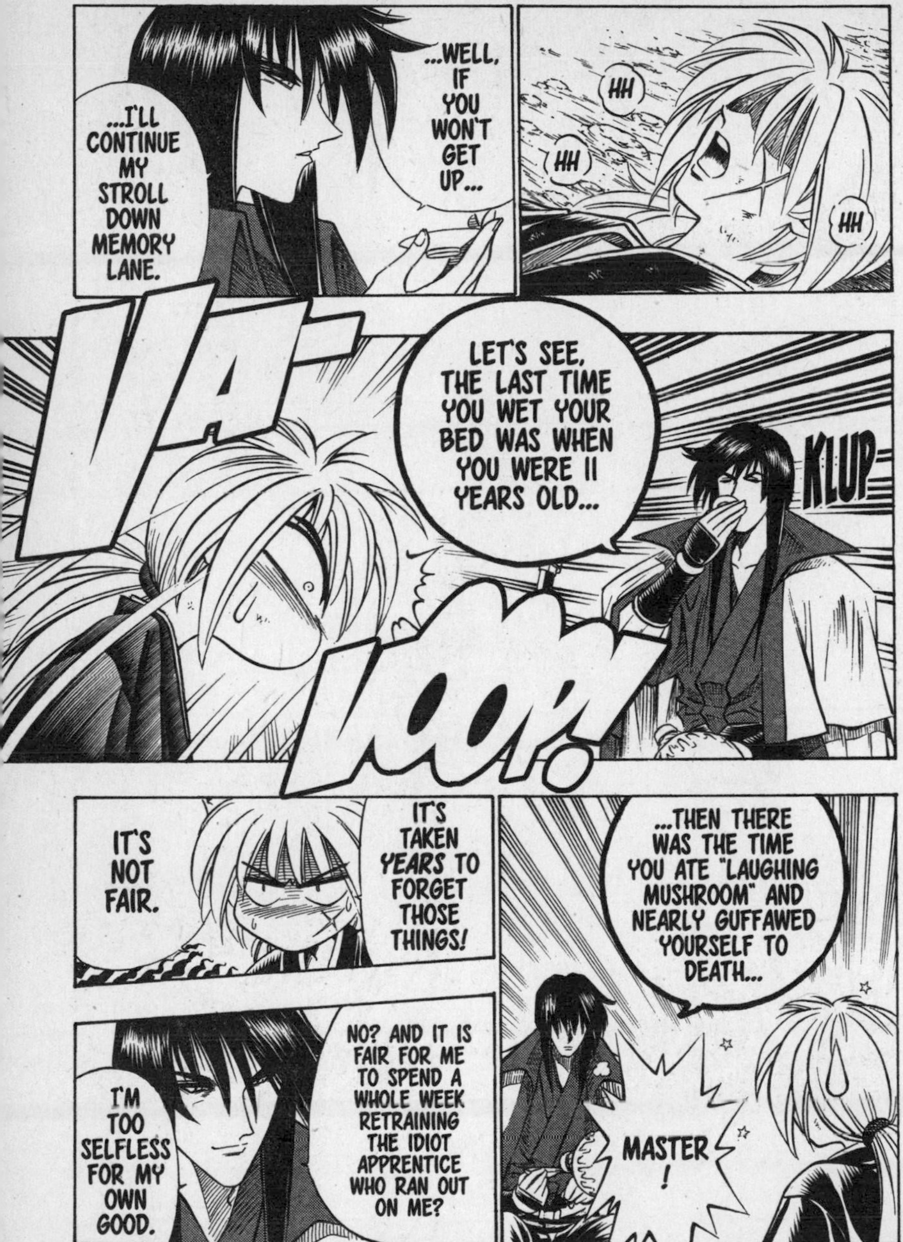
HH
HH
HH
...WELL, IF YOU WON'T GET UP...
...I'LL CONTINUE MY STROLL DOWN MEMORY LANE.
LET'S SEE, THE LAST TIME YOU WET YOUR BED WAS WHEN YOU WERE 11 YEARS OLD...
KLUP
VA-
VOOP!
...THEN THERE WAS THE TIME YOU ATE "LAUGHING MUSHROOM" AND NEARLY GUFFAWED YOURSELF TO DEATH...
MASTER!
IT'S TAKEN *YEARS* TO FORGET THOSE THINGS!
IT'S NOT FAIR.
NO? AND IT IS FAIR FOR ME TO SPEND A WHOLE WEEK RETRAINING THE IDIOT APPRENTICE WHO RAN OUT ON ME?
I'M TOO SELFLESS FOR MY OWN GOOD.

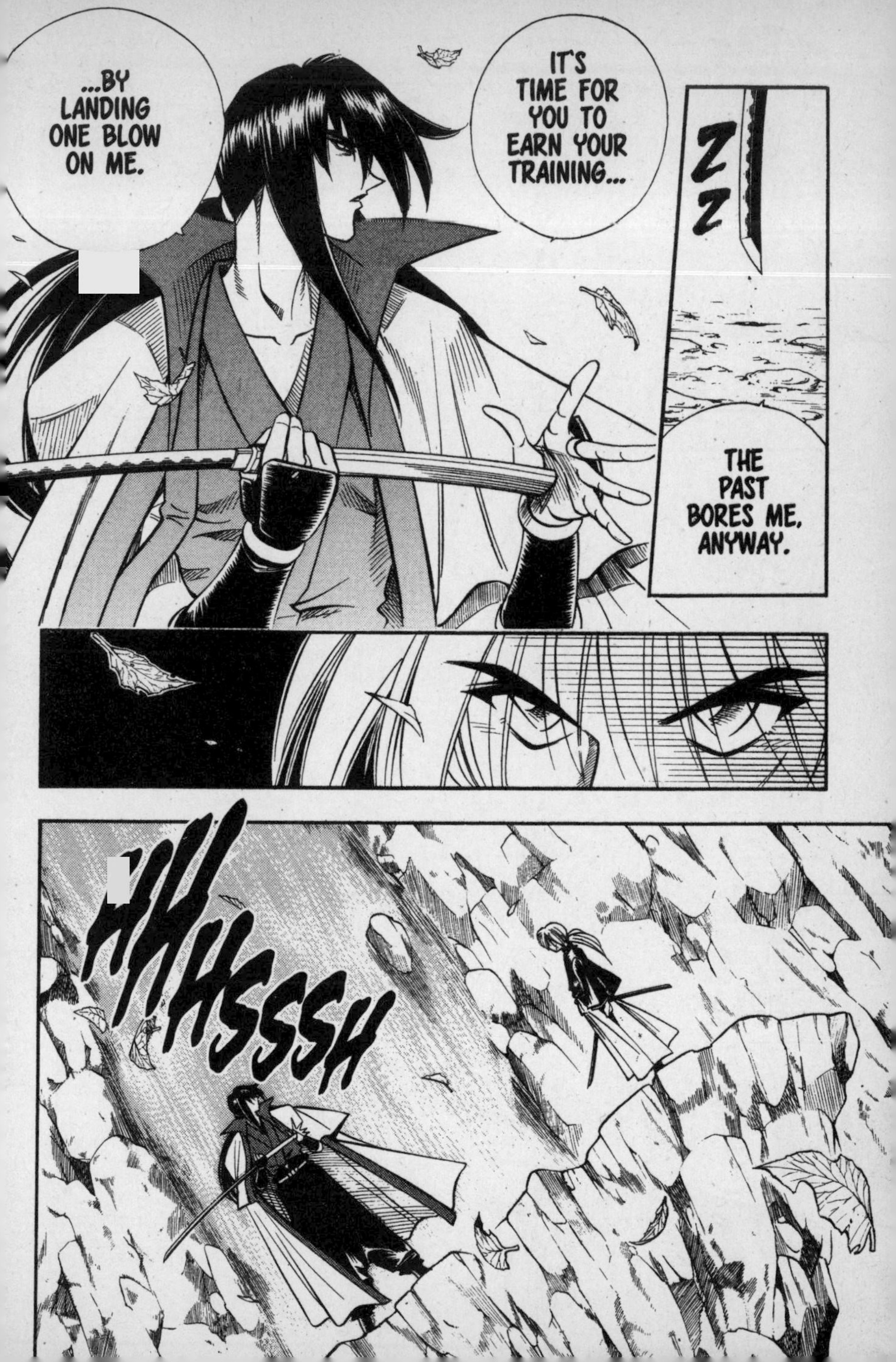
ZZ
THE PAST BORES ME, ANYWAY.
IT'S TIME FOR YOU TO EARN YOUR TRAINING...
...BY LANDING ONE BLOW ON ME.
HHSSSH

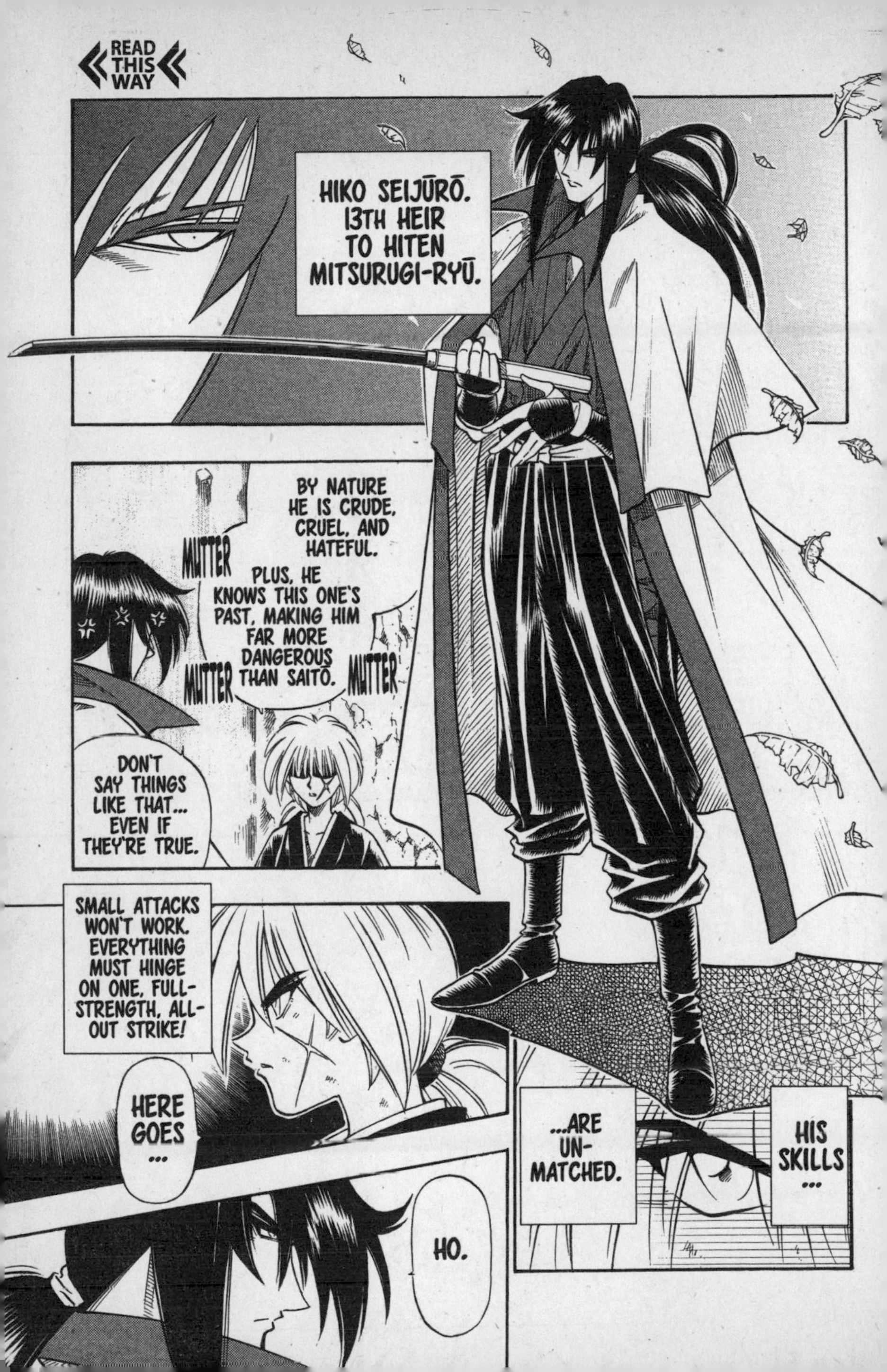
READ THIS WAY
HIKO SEIJŪRŌ. 13TH HEIR TO HITEN MITSURUGI-RYŪ.
BY NATURE HE IS CRUDE, CRUEL, AND HATEFUL.
PLUS, HE KNOWS THIS ONE'S PAST, MAKING HIM FAR MORE DANGEROUS THAN SAITŌ.
MUTTER
MUTTER
MUTTER
DON'T SAY THINGS LIKE THAT... EVEN IF THEY'RE TRUE.
HIS SKILLS...
...ARE UN-MATCHED.
SMALL ATTACKS WON'T WORK. EVERYTHING MUST HINGE ON ONE, FULL-STRENGTH, ALL-OUT STRIKE!
HERE GOES...
HO.

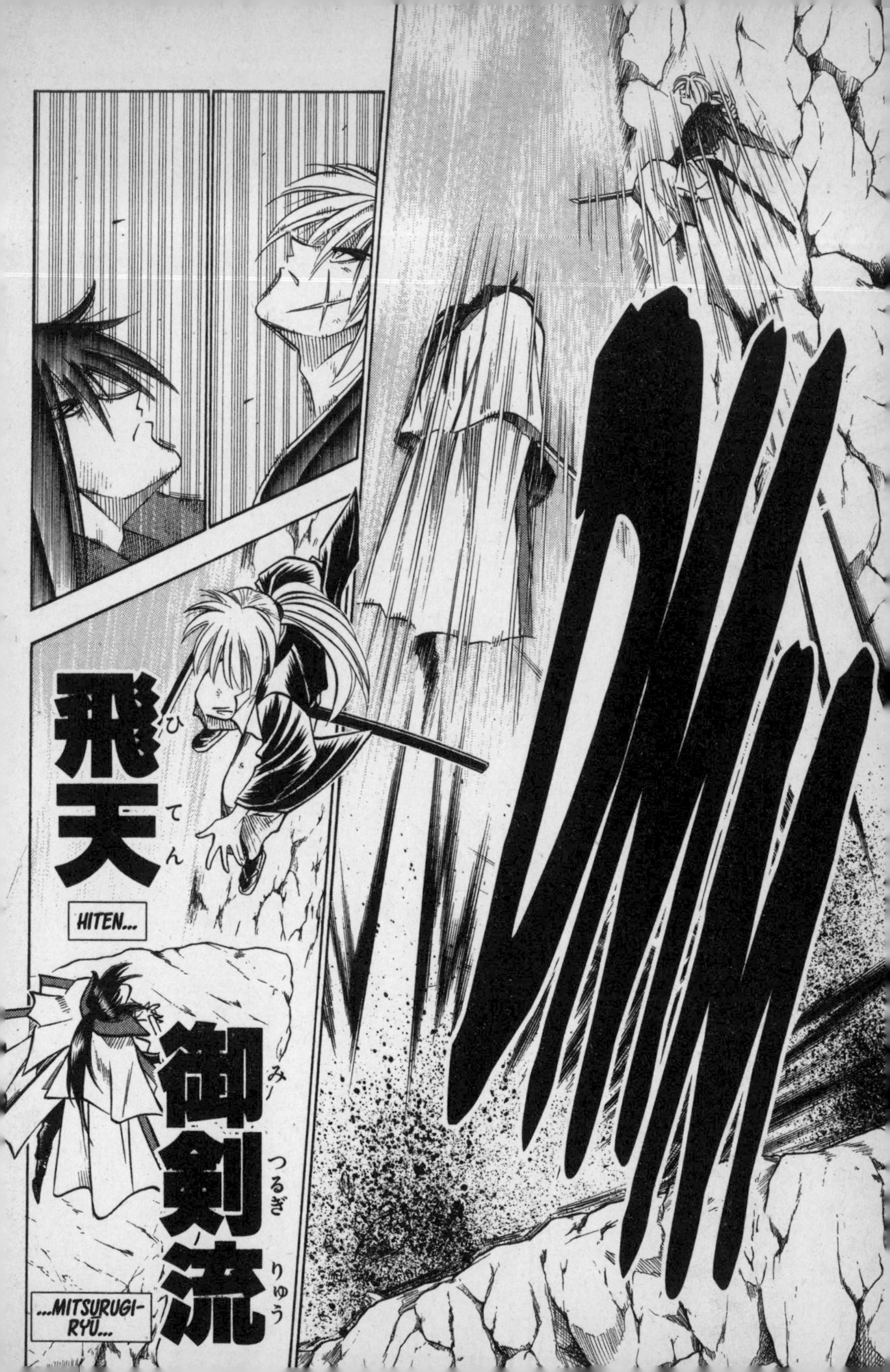
飛天
HITEN...
御剣流
...MITSURUGI-RYŪ...

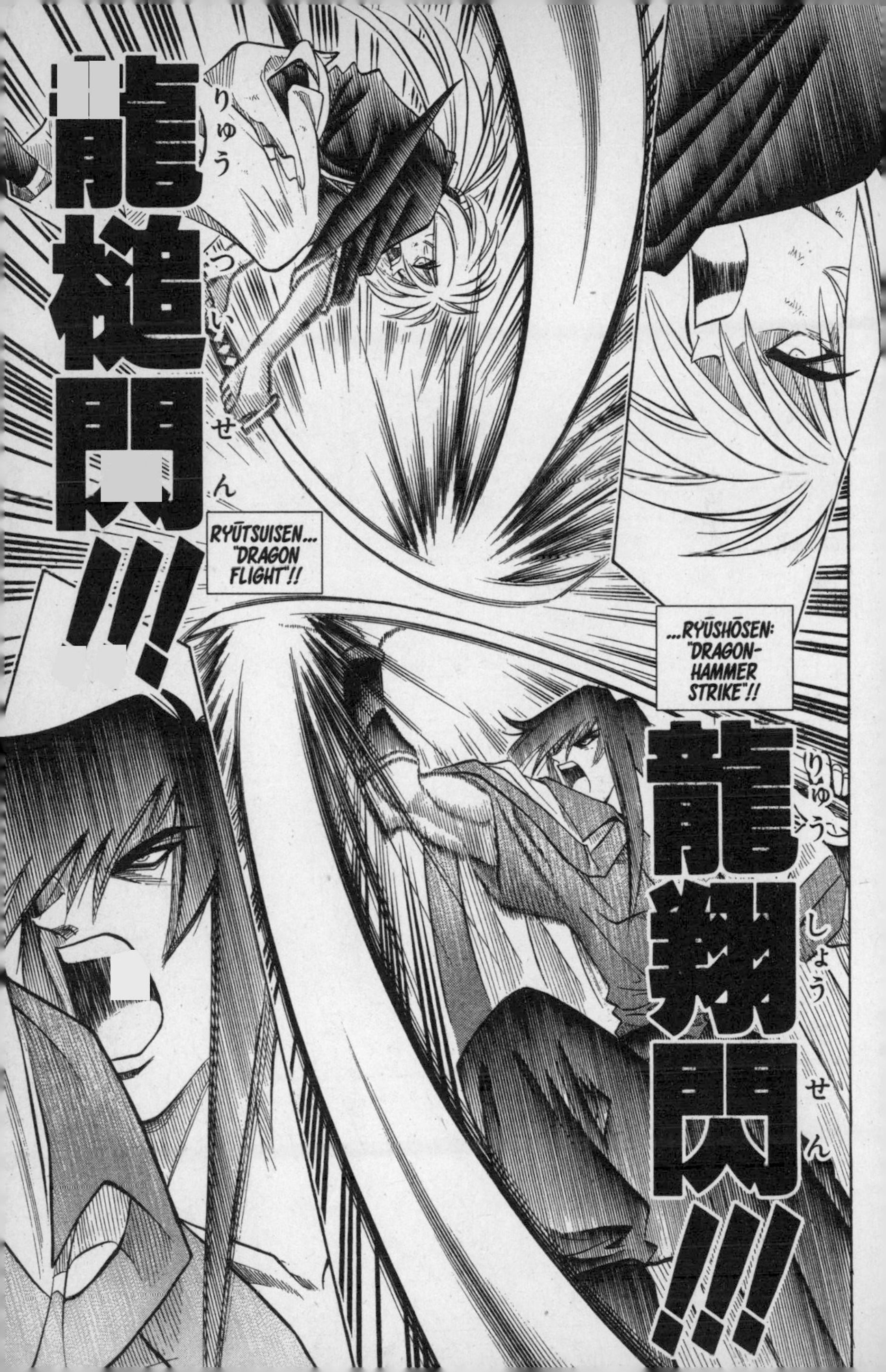

龍槌閃!!
りゅうついせん
RYŪTSUISEN... "DRAGON FLIGHT"!!
...RYŪSHŌSEN: "DRAGON-HAMMER STRIKE"!!
龍翔閃!!
りゅうしょうせん

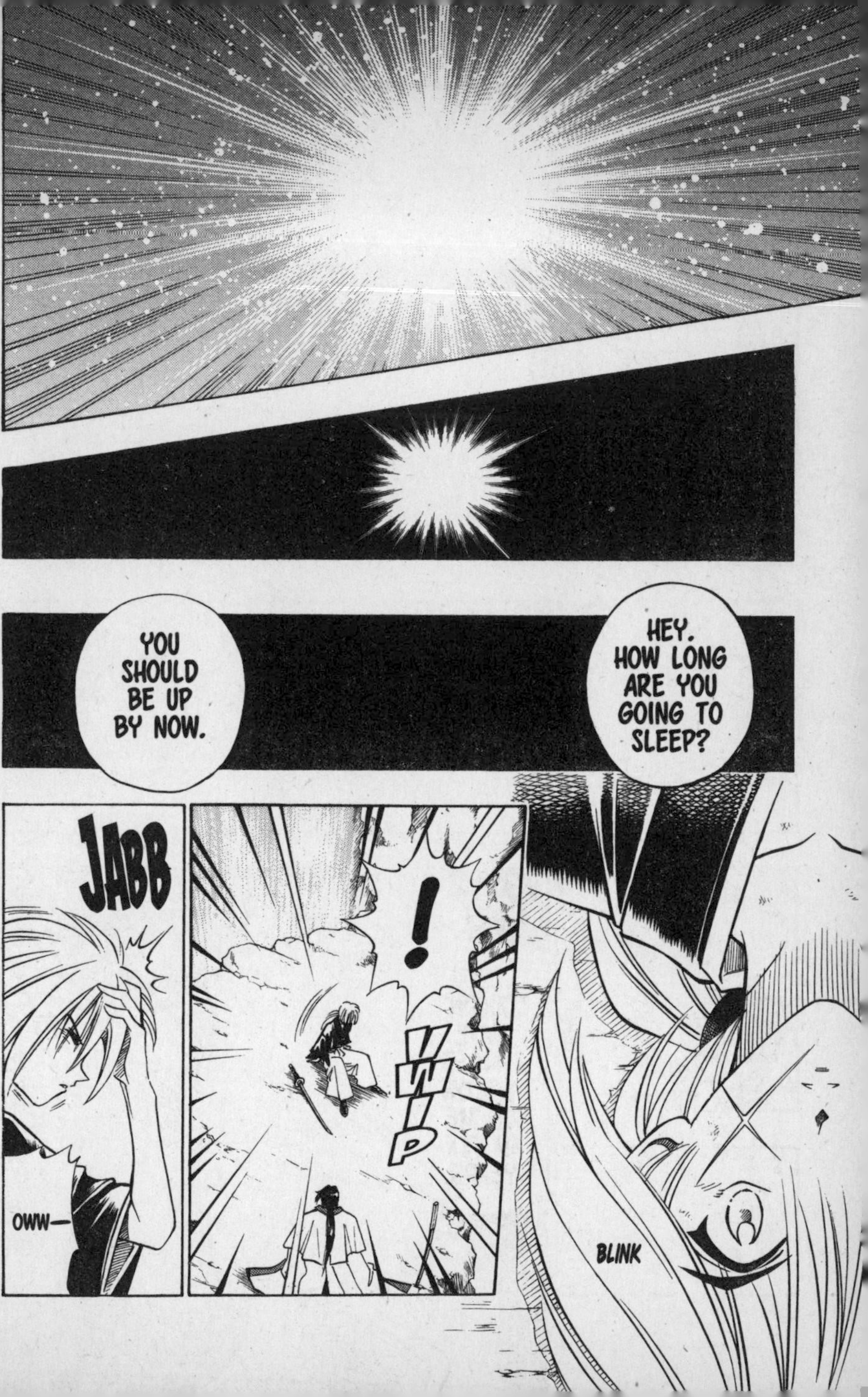
HEY. HOW LONG ARE YOU GOING TO SLEEP?
YOU SHOULD BE UP BY NOW.
BLINK
!
WHIP
JABB
OWW—

READ THIS WAY

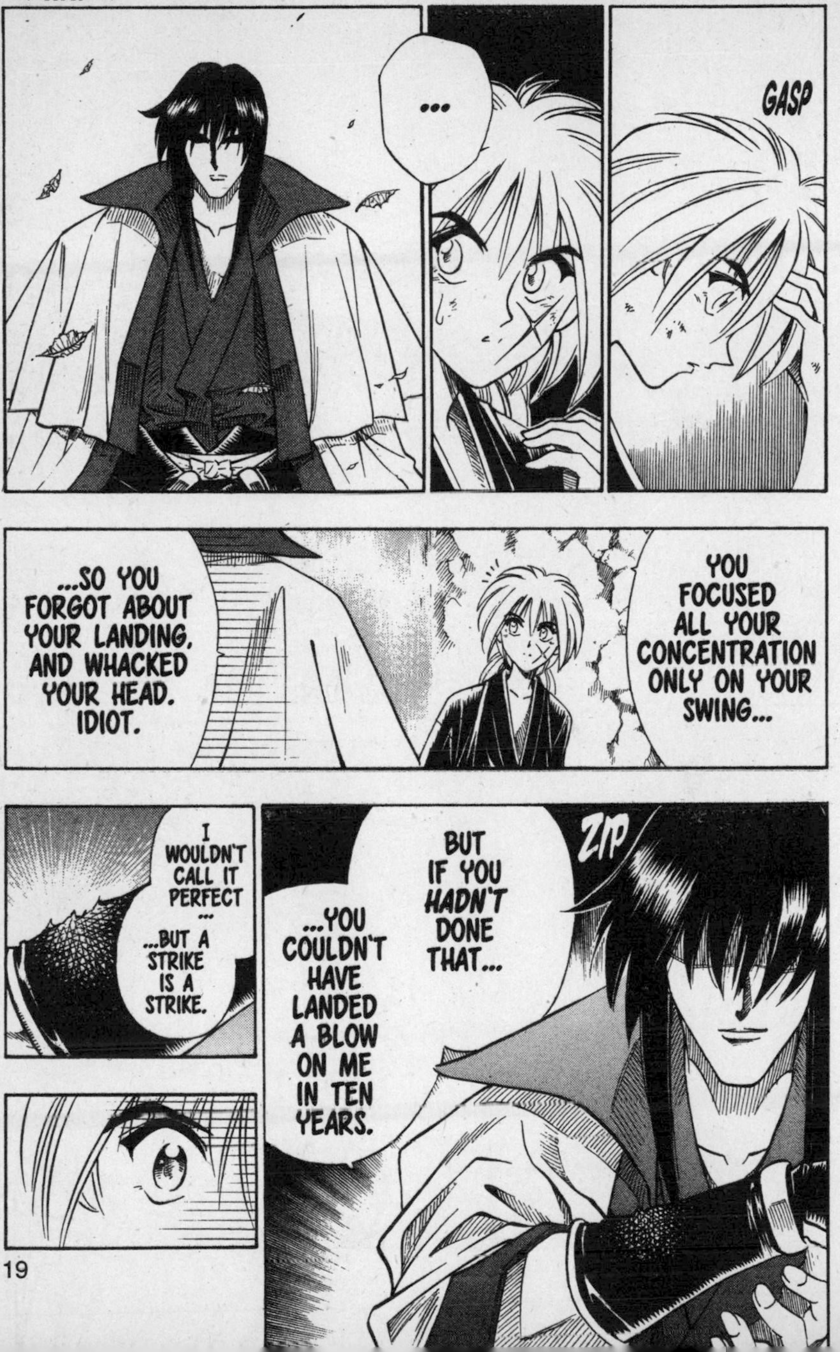
GASP
...
YOU FOCUSED ALL YOUR CONCENTRATION ONLY ON YOUR SWING...
...SO YOU FORGOT ABOUT YOUR LANDING, AND WHACKED YOUR HEAD. IDIOT.
ZIP
BUT IF YOU HADN'T DONE THAT...
...YOU COULDN'T HAVE LANDED A BLOW ON ME IN TEN YEARS.
I WOULDN'T CALL IT PERFECT...
...BUT A STRIKE IS A STRIKE.

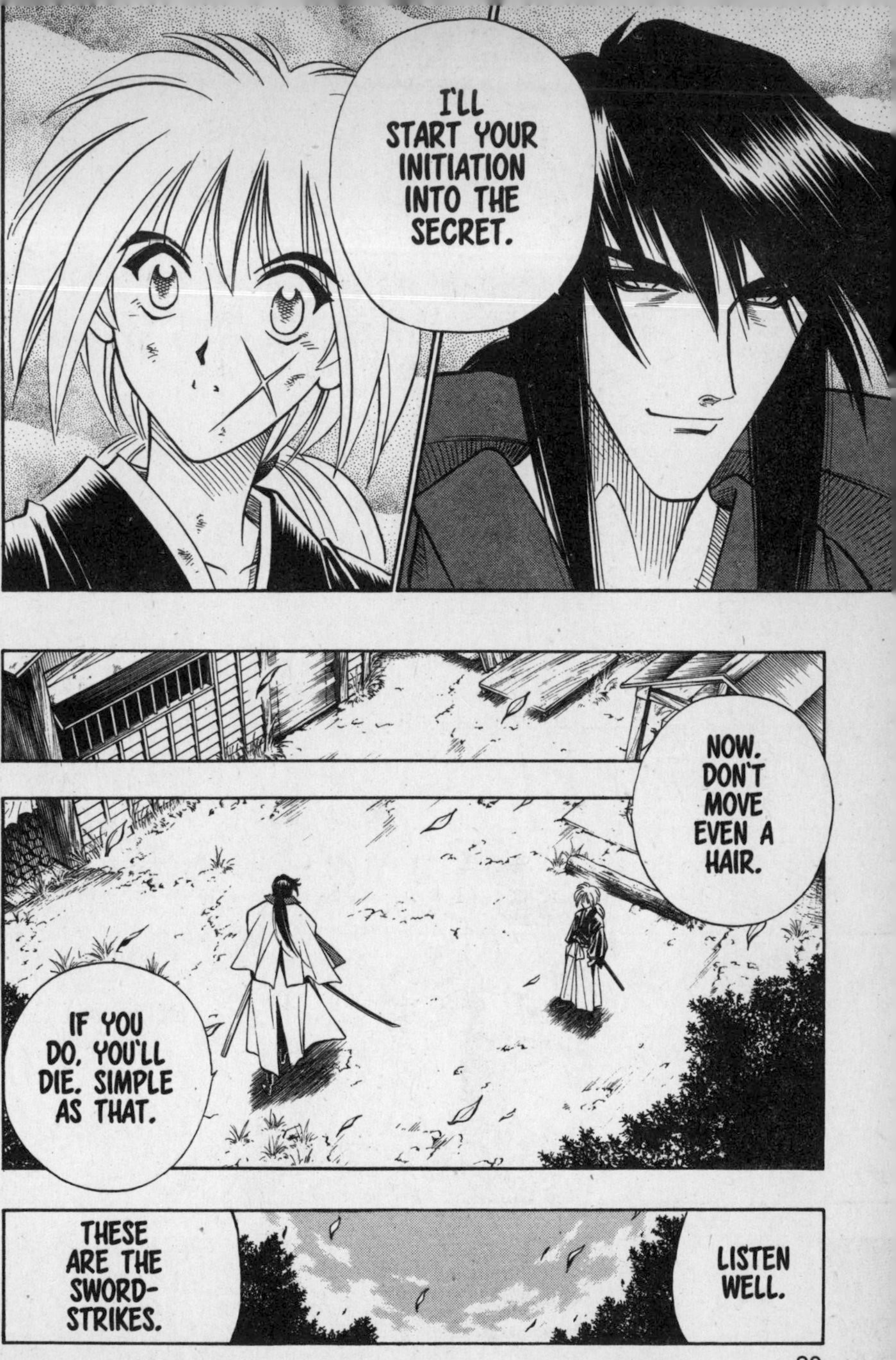
I'LL START YOUR INITIATION INTO THE SECRET.
NOW. DON'T MOVE EVEN A HAIR.
IF YOU DO, YOU'LL DIE. SIMPLE AS THAT.
LISTEN WELL.
THESE ARE THE SWORD-STRIKES.

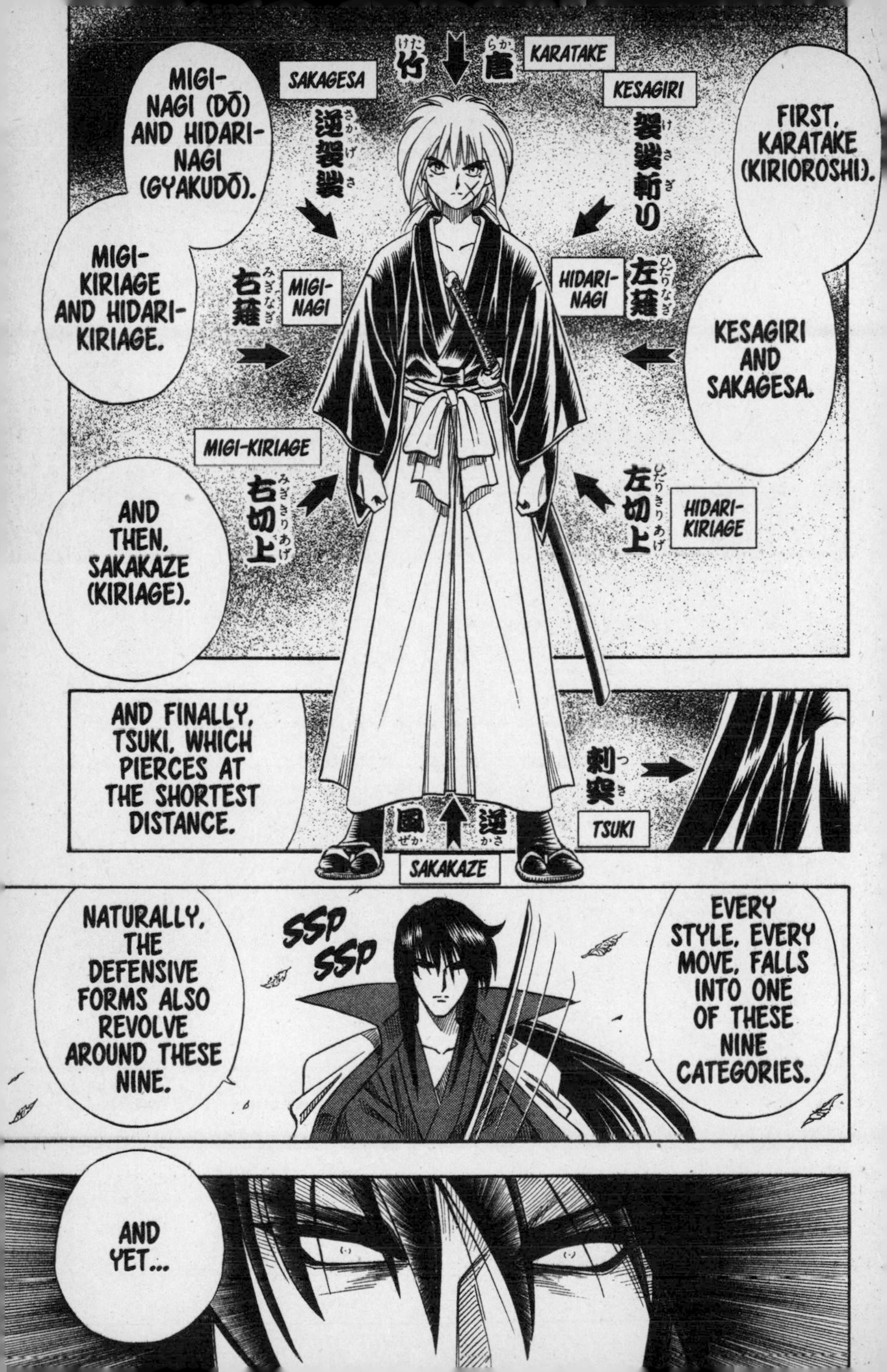
FIRST, KARATAKE (KIRIOROSHI).
KESAGIRI AND SAKAGESA.
MIGI-NAGI (DŌ) AND HIDARI-NAGI (GYAKUDŌ).
MIGI-KIRIAGE AND HIDARI-KIRIAGE.
AND THEN, SAKAKAZE (KIRIAGE).
唐竹
KARATAKE
袈裟斬り
KESAGIRI
逆袈裟
SAKAGESA
左薙
HIDARI-NAGI
右薙
MIGI-NAGI
左切上
HIDARI-KIRIAGE
右切上
MIGI-KIRIAGE
刺突
TSUKI
逆風
SAKAKAZE
AND FINALLY, TSUKI, WHICH PIERCES AT THE SHORTEST DISTANCE.
EVERY STYLE, EVERY MOVE, FALLS INTO ONE OF THESE NINE CATEGORIES.
SSP SSP
NATURALLY, THE DEFENSIVE FORMS ALSO REVOLVE AROUND THESE NINE.
AND YET...

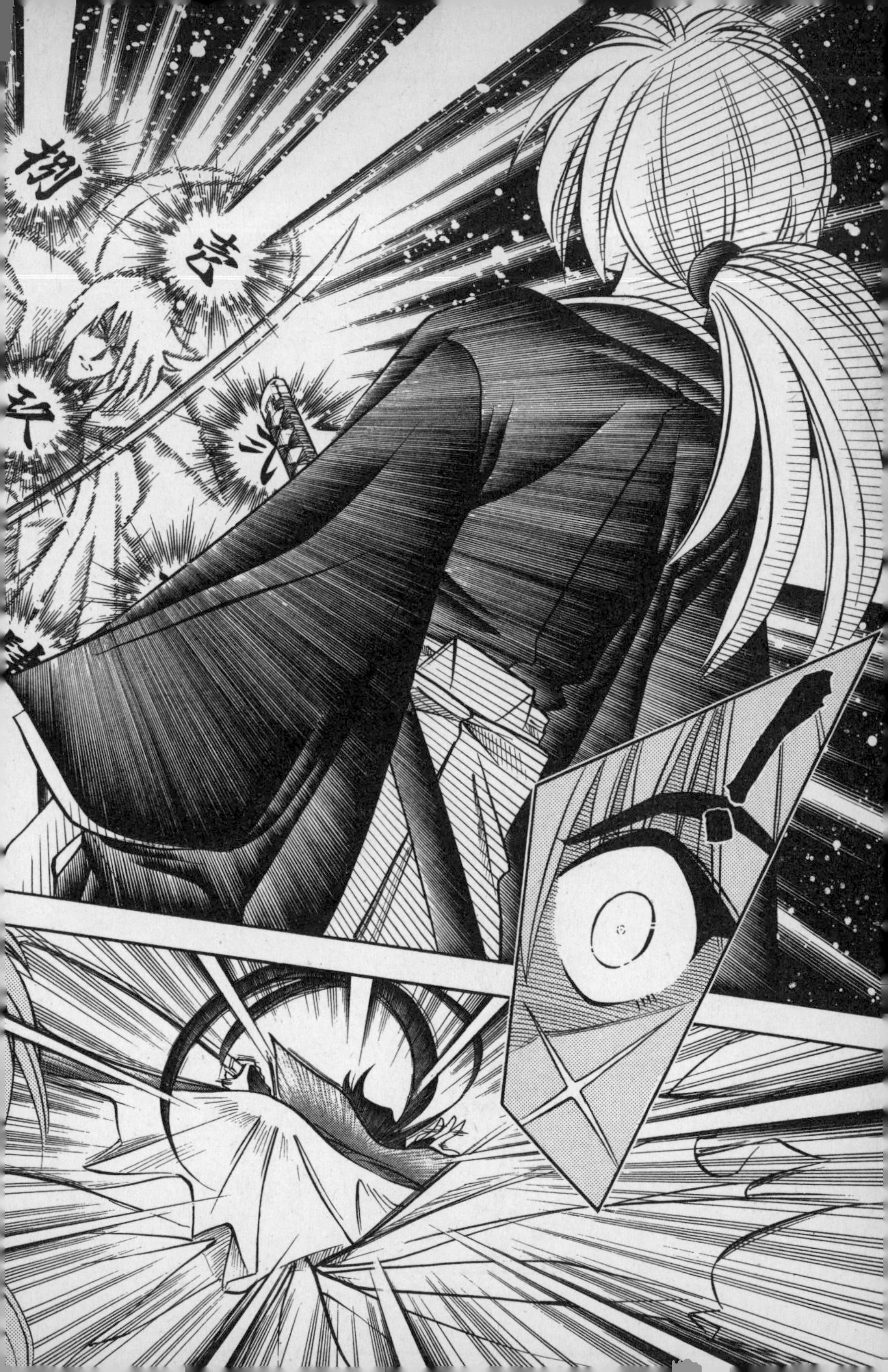

READ THIS WAY

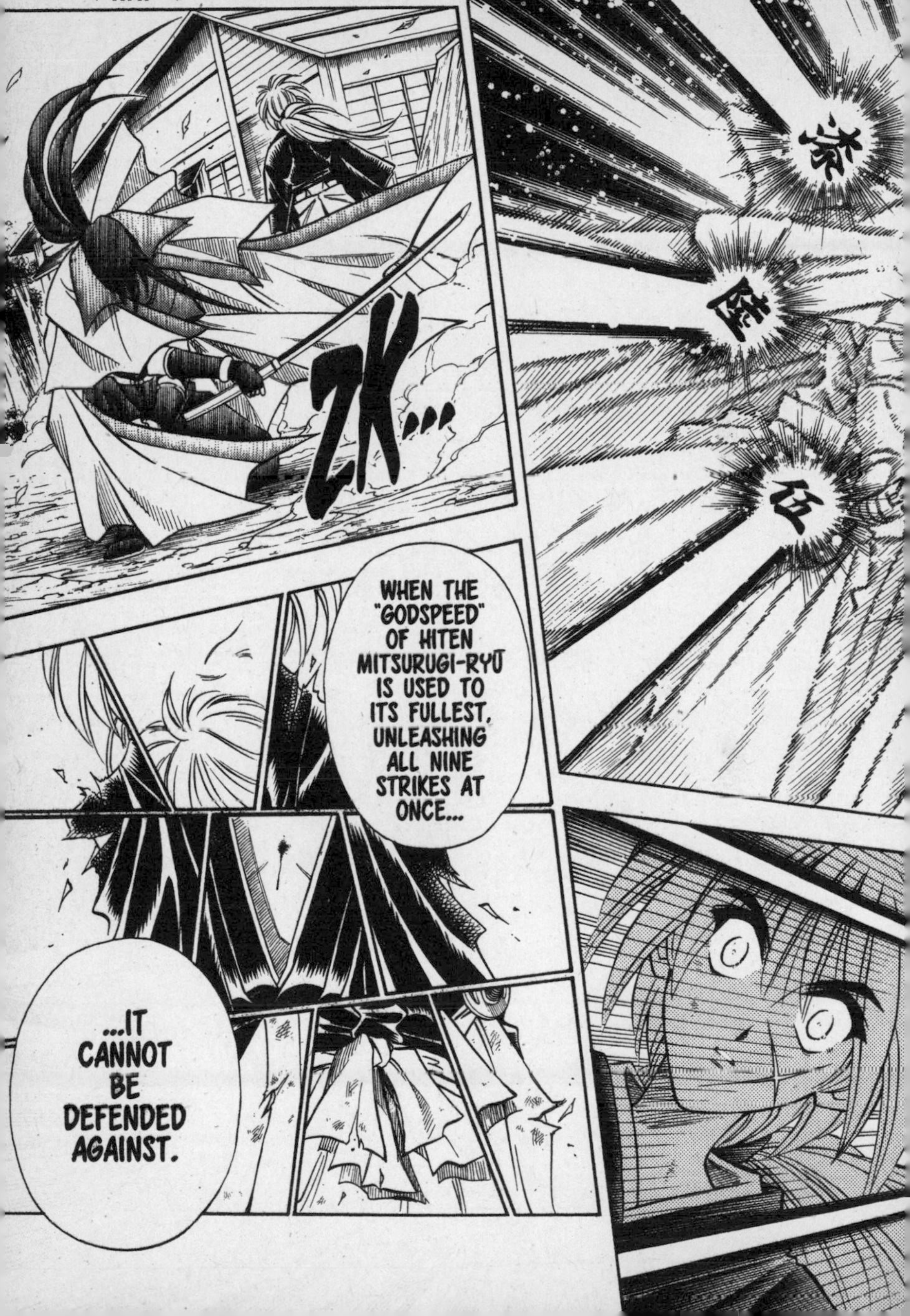

ZK...
WHEN THE "GODSPEED" OF HITEN MITSURUGI-RYU IS USED TO ITS FULLEST, UNLEASHING ALL NINE STRIKES AT ONCE...
...IT CANNOT BE DEFENDED AGAINST.

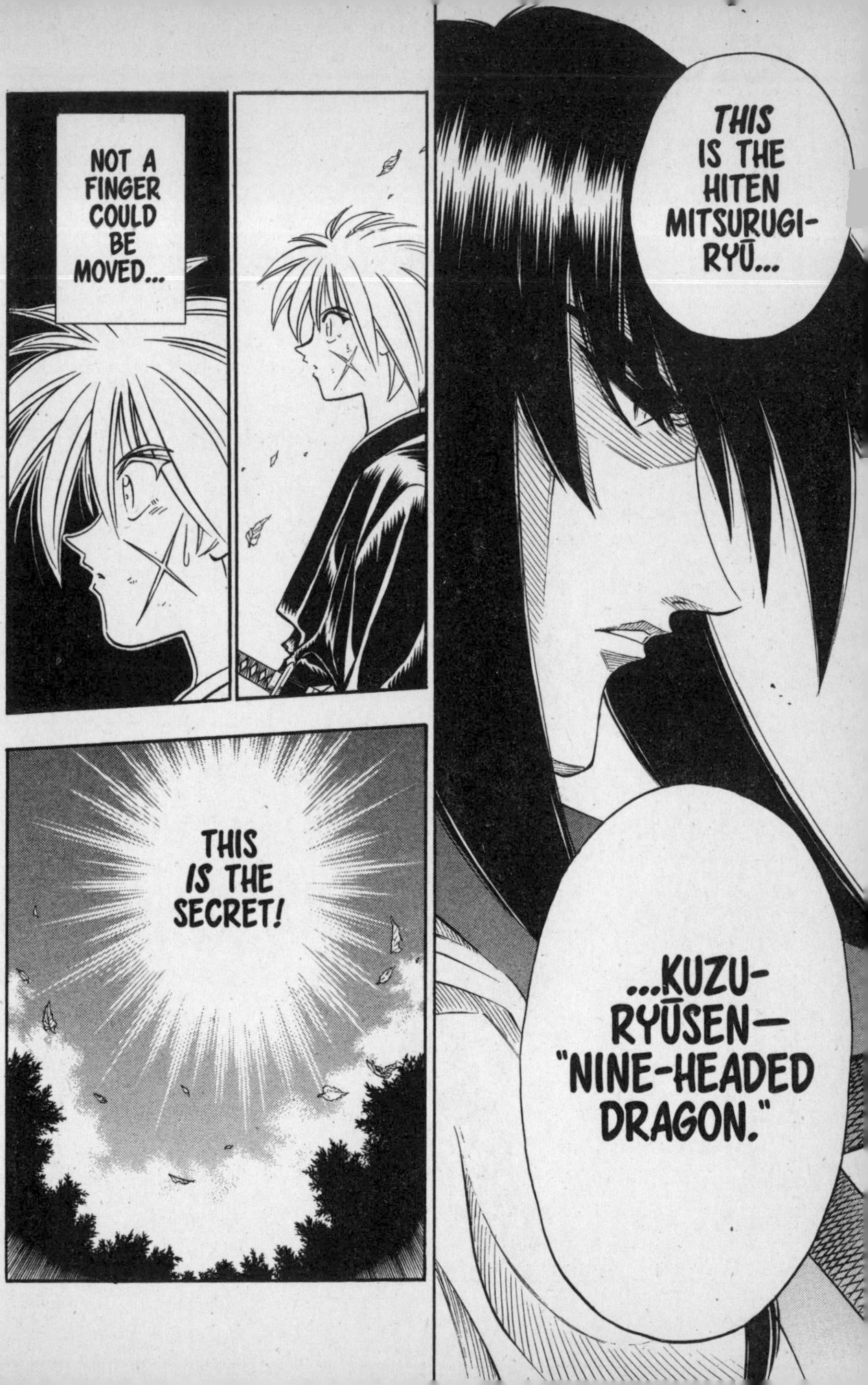
THIS IS THE HITEN MITSURUGI-RYŪ...
...KUZU-RYŪSEN— "NINE-HEADED DRAGON."
NOT A FINGER COULD BE MOVED...
THIS IS THE SECRET!

READ THIS WAY

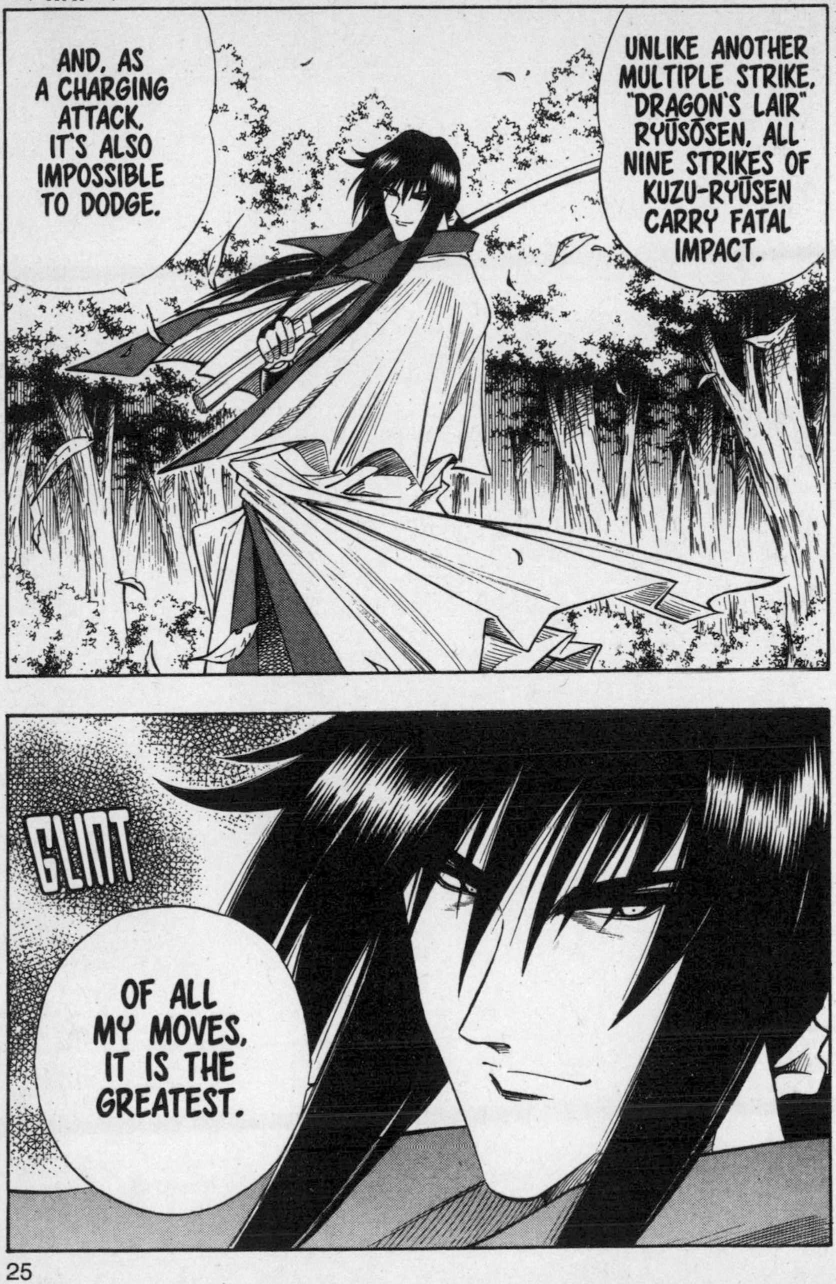
UNLIKE ANOTHER MULTIPLE STRIKE, "DRAGON'S LAIR" RYŪSŌSEN, ALL NINE STRIKES OF KUZU-RYŪSEN CARRY FATAL IMPACT.
AND, AS A CHARGING ATTACK, IT'S ALSO IMPOSSIBLE TO DODGE.
GLINT
OF ALL MY MOVES, IT IS THE GREATEST.

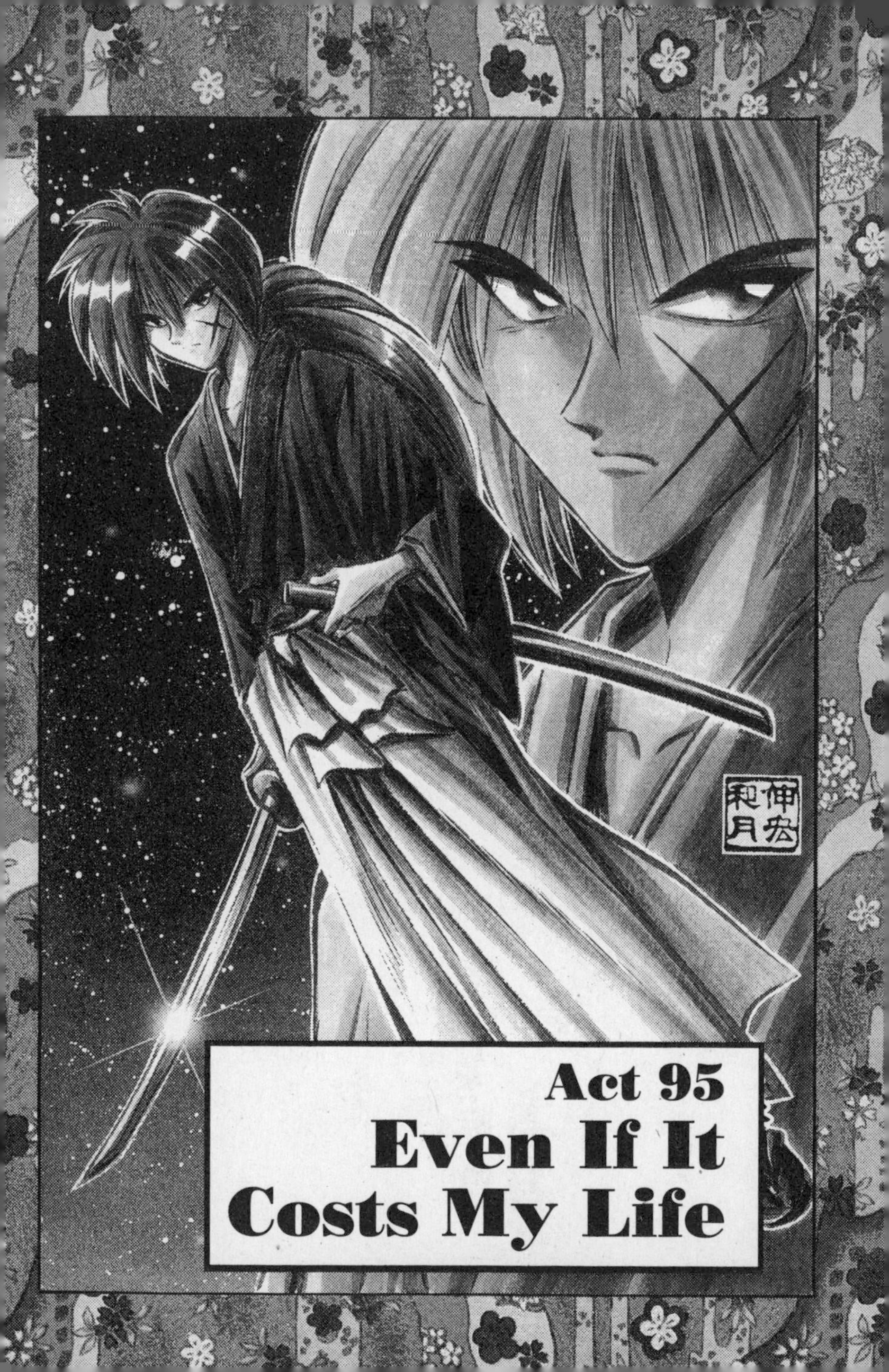
Act 95
Even If It Costs My Life
伸宏
和月

READ THIS WAY

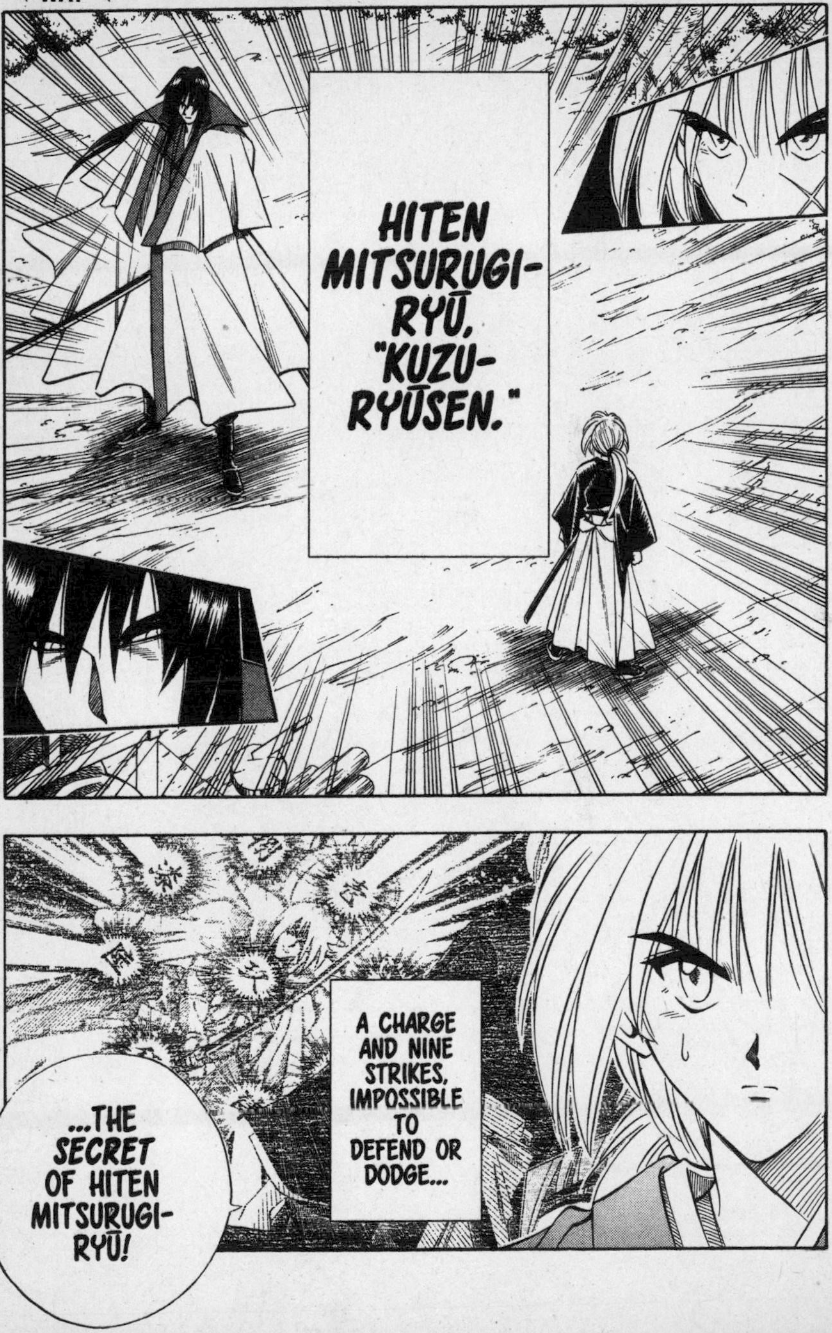

HITEN MITSURUGI-RYŪ, "KUZU-RYŪSEN."
A CHARGE AND NINE STRIKES, IMPOSSIBLE TO DEFEND OR DODGE...
...THE *SECRET* OF HITEN MITSURUGI-RYŪ!

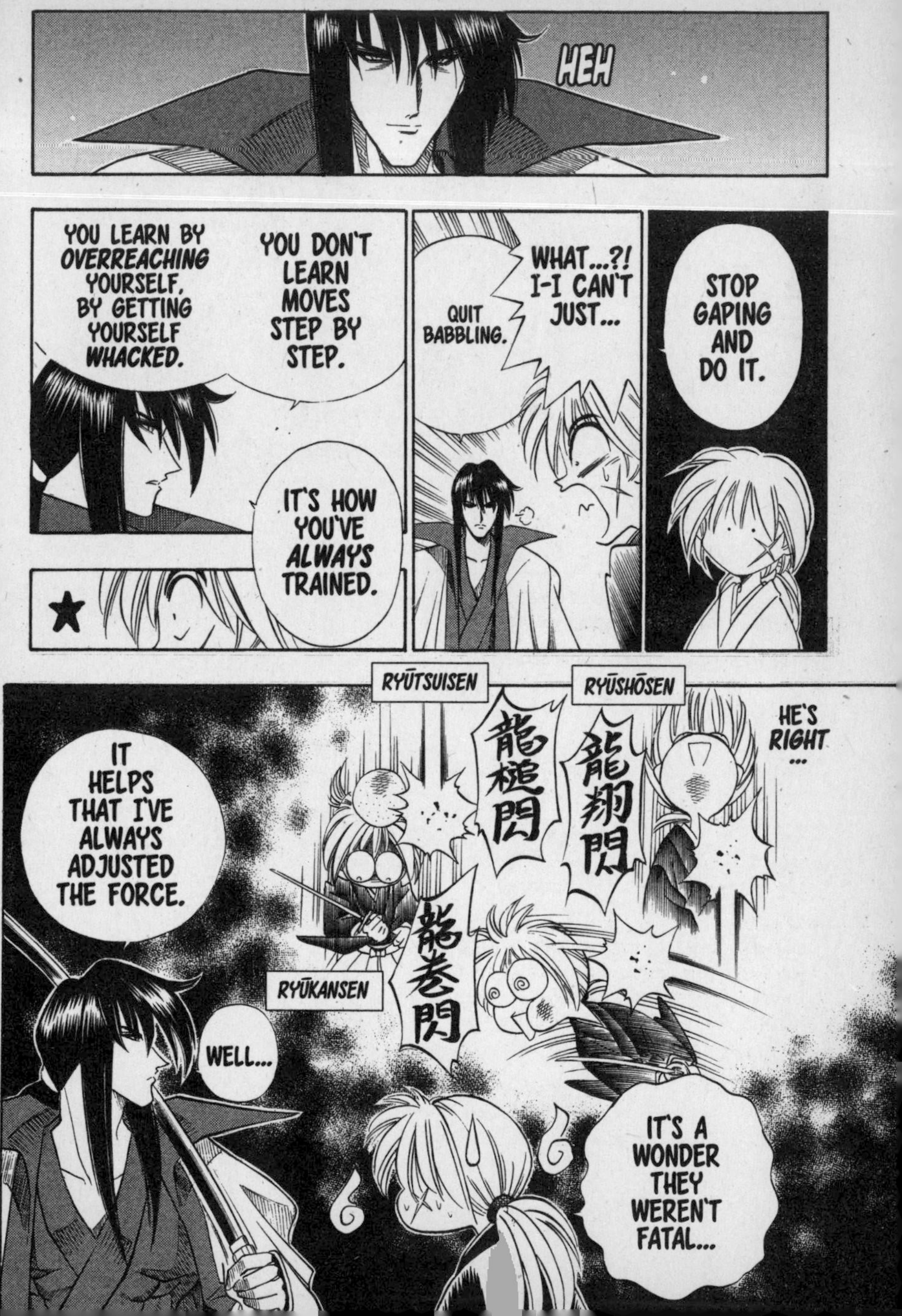
HEH
STOP GAPING AND DO IT.
WHAT...?! I-I CAN'T JUST...
QUIT BABBLING.
YOU DON'T LEARN MOVES STEP BY STEP.
YOU LEARN BY OVERREACHING YOURSELF, BY GETTING YOURSELF WHACKED.
IT'S HOW YOU'VE ALWAYS TRAINED.
HE'S RIGHT...
RYŪSHŌSEN
龍翔閃
RYŪTSUISEN
龍槌閃
IT HELPS THAT I'VE ALWAYS ADJUSTED THE FORCE.
RYŪKANSEN
龍巻閃
IT'S A WONDER THEY WEREN'T FATAL...
WELL...

READ THIS WAY

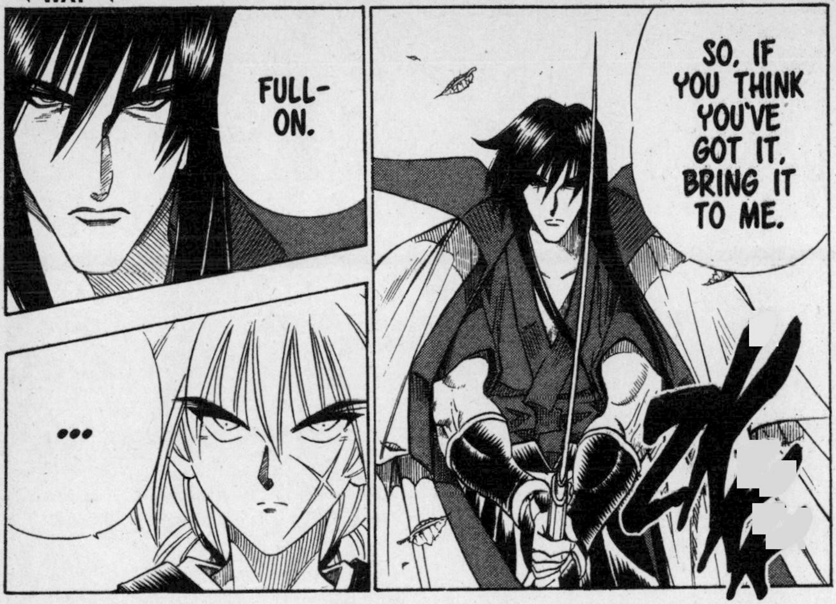
SO, IF YOU THINK YOU'VE GOT IT, BRING IT TO ME.
FULL-ON.
...

Long time no see! Watsuki here. Since here is the only space we've got this time, let's get the usual nonsense out of the way:

- "*Samurai Spirits: Zankurō Musōken*"...my friend showed me it. I'm totally into "rasetsu-mode" Genjūrō!! Throwing-weapons ricocheting...triple spins in mid-air! I'm crazy about "SamuSupi." I can't get enough.
- I read the American comic, "*Silver Surfer*." I never thought it was for me, but it turns out it's a really deep story!! The Surfer is so classy...and so lonely. Everyone at work's passed it around. Give it a try if you have the chance.
- The "*Spawn*" toys from the American comic series are so far out there, they're great... especially the 13-inch figure. That one's so cool, I keep it on my desk, rather than on the display shelf. I hope McFarlane Toys can keep it up. Hurray for the toy biz!
- A serious topic for a change. My personal relationships lately have been pretty unstable. Usually, the problem's with me, but sometimes it's the other person, and that depresses me. I've started thinking about responsibility—it's hard to explain what I'm getting at, bu I think about AIDS being spread by medication, or a cult like Aum [Shinri-kyō]. People don't take responsibility for what they do. I can't fix other people, but as an individual, I'm trying to be as aware as I can.
- My replies to your fan letters have ground to a complete halt. I'm so sorry about that. I am reading them, at least, so I hope you'll hang in there with me (and here I was just going on about responsibility, too).

See you next volume! 伸宏和月

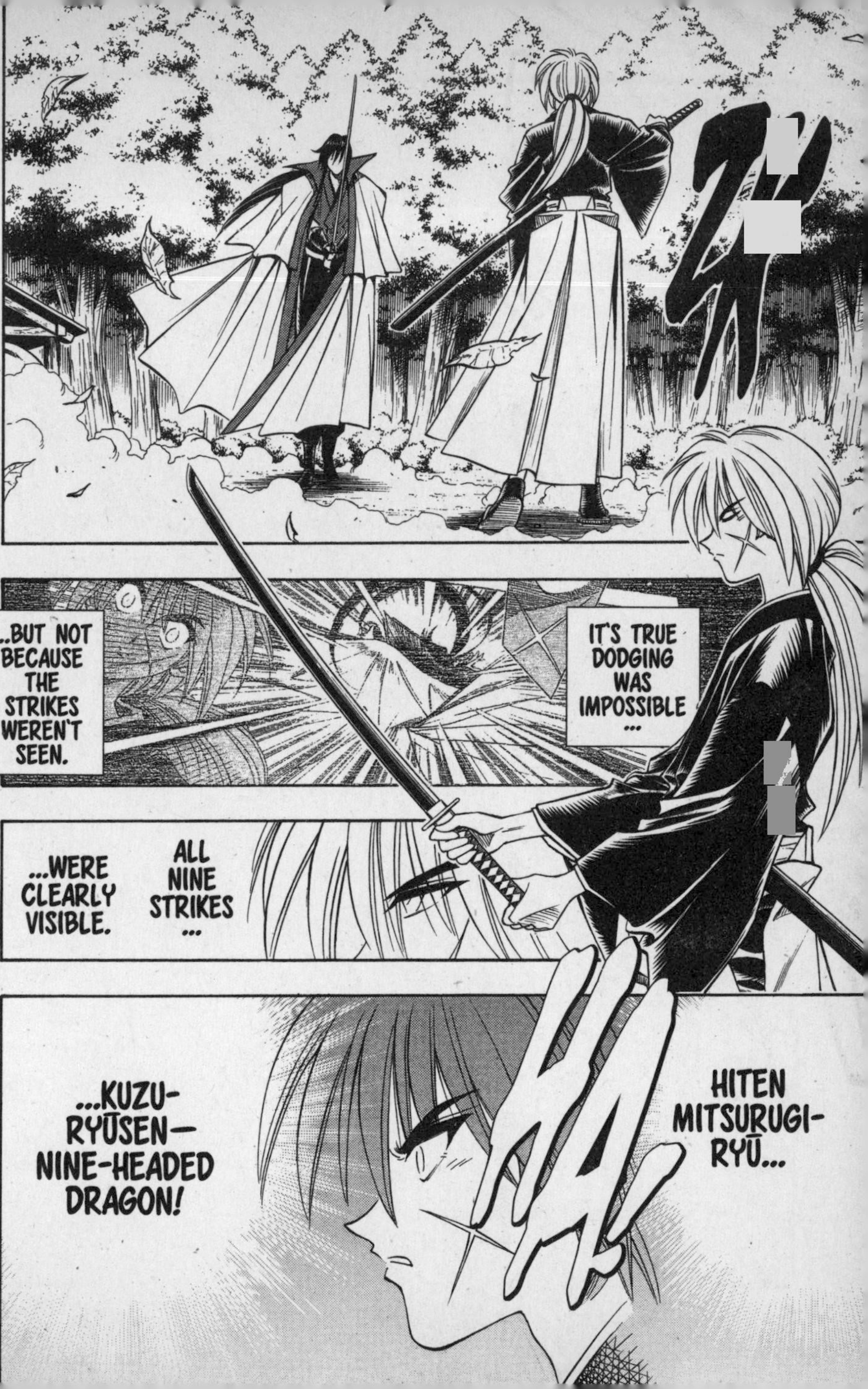
IT'S TRUE DODGING WAS IMPOSSIBLE ...
...BUT NOT BECAUSE THE STRIKES WEREN'T SEEN.
ALL NINE STRIKES ...
...WERE CLEARLY VISIBLE.
HITEN MITSURUGI-RYŪ...
...KUZU-RYŪSEN—NINE-HEADED DRAGON!

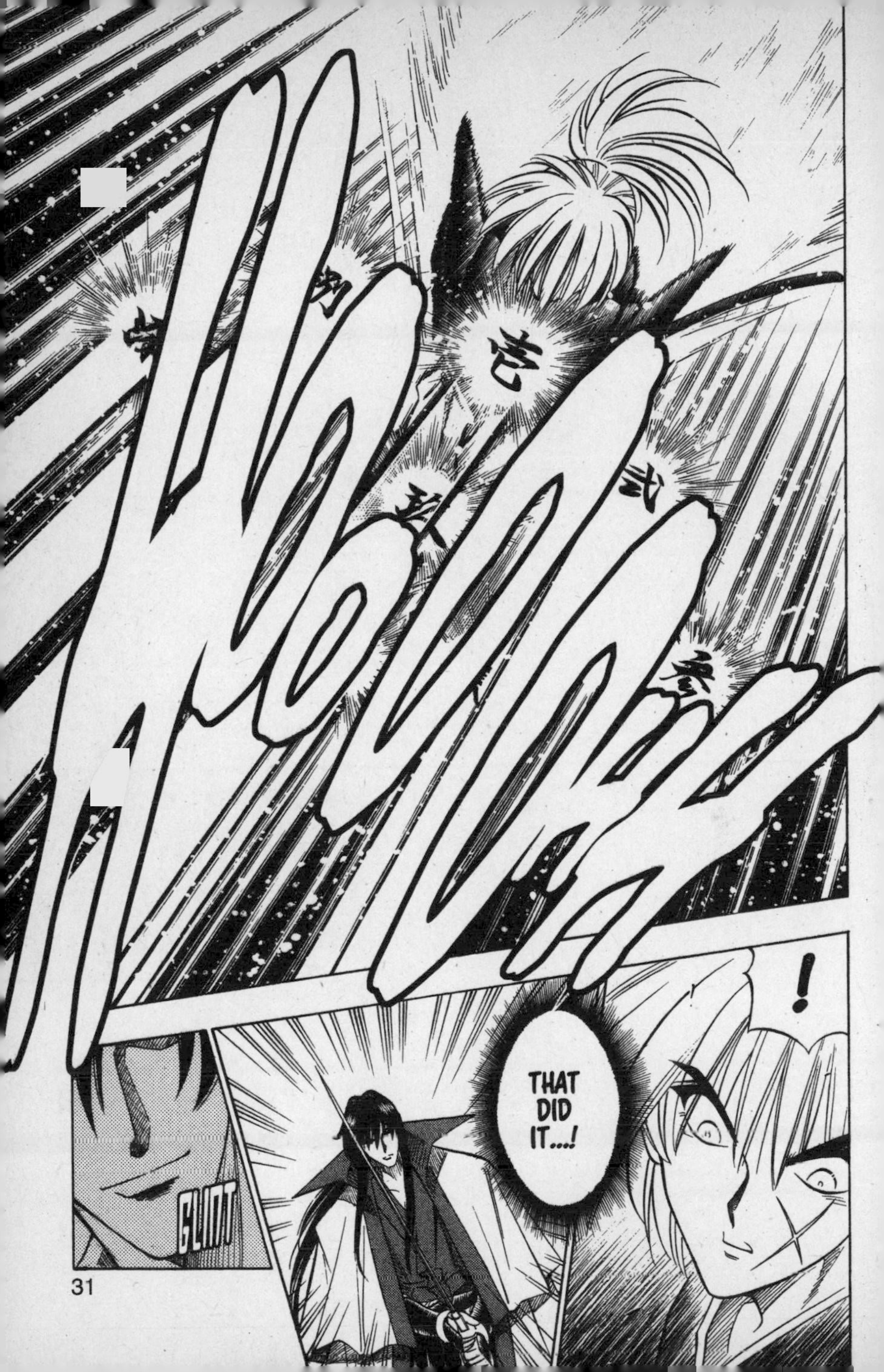
壱
弐
参
!
THAT DID IT...!
GLINT

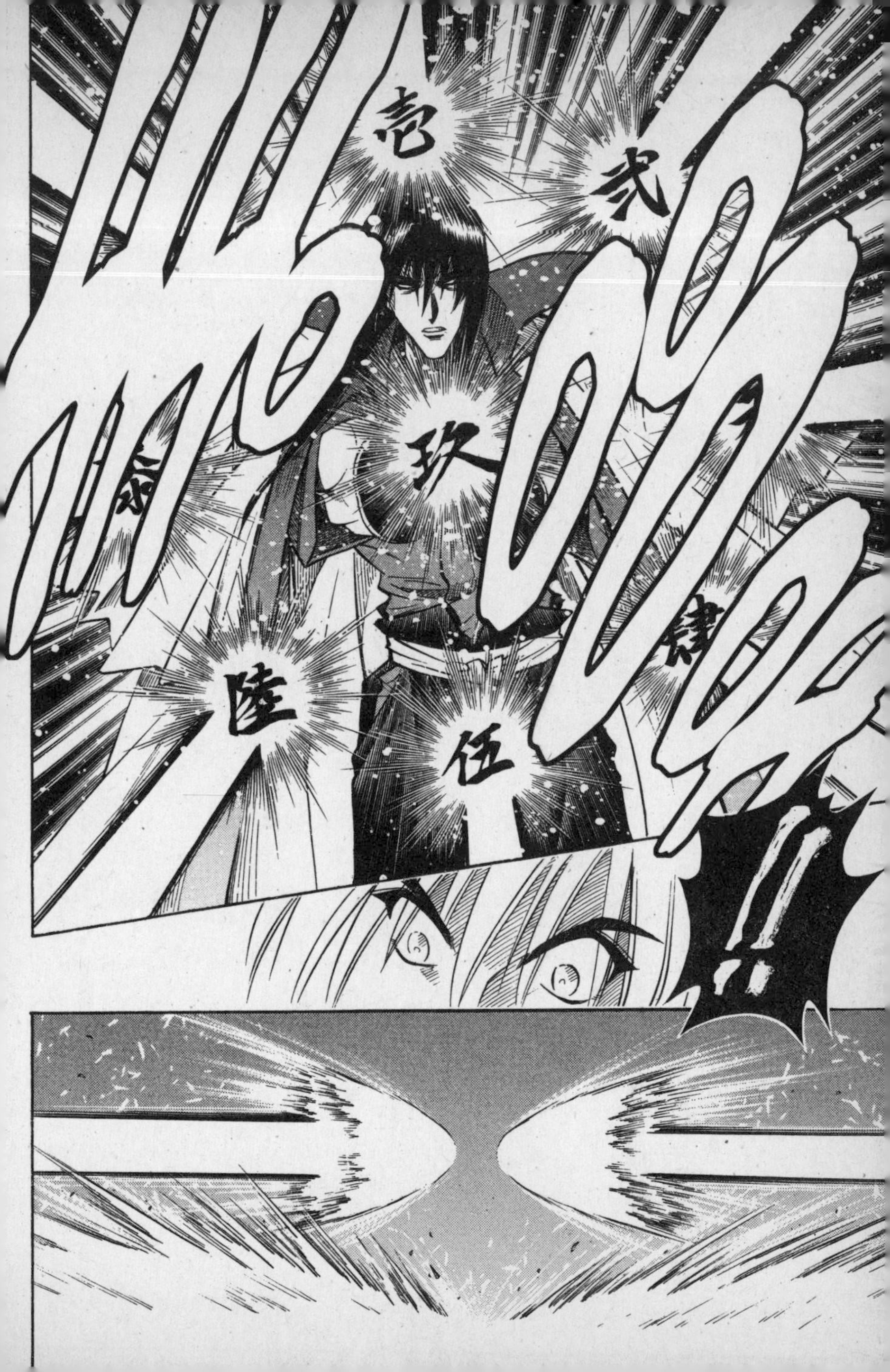
弐
壱
肆
玖
伍
陸
!!

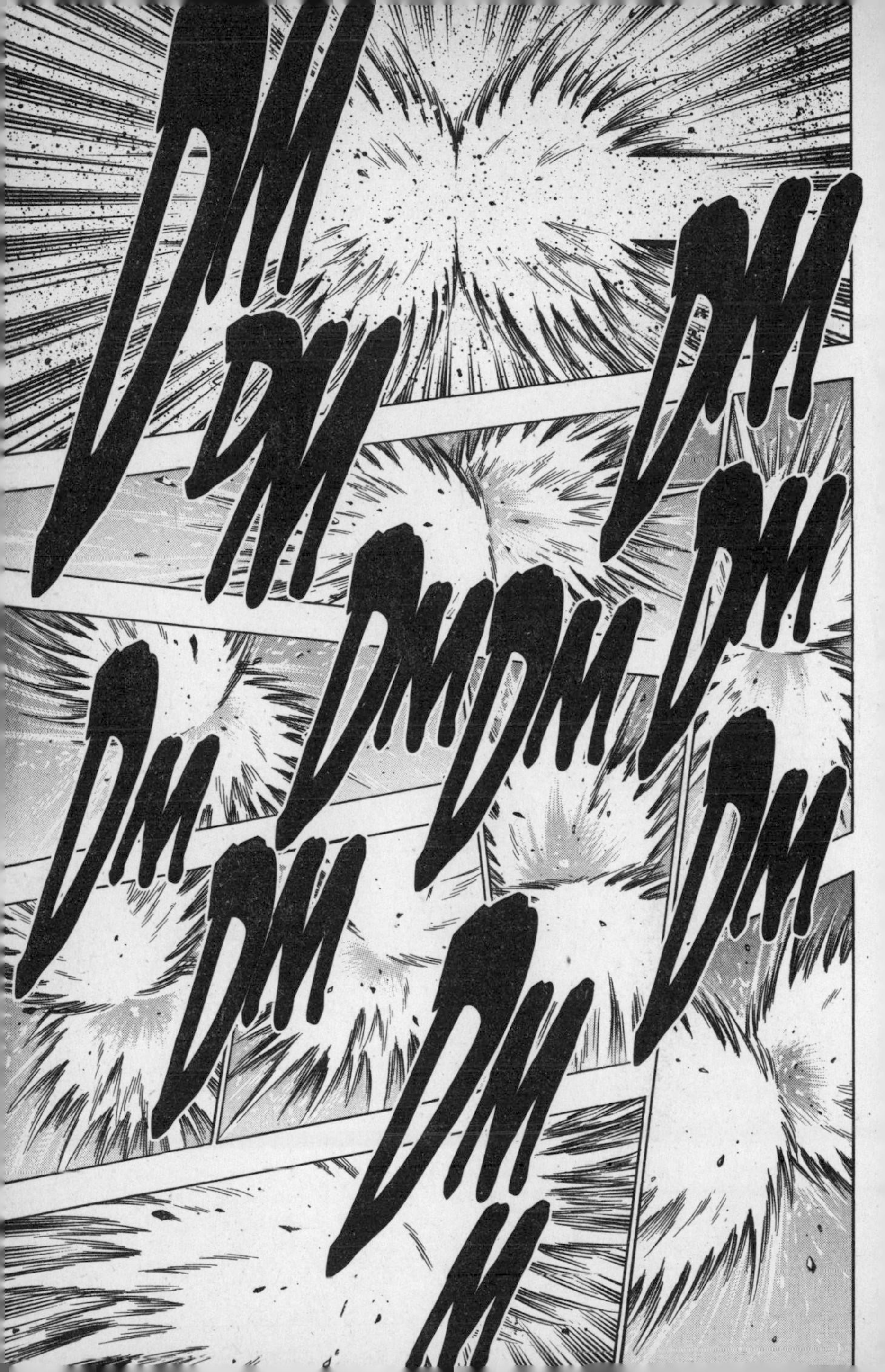
DM
DM
DM
DM
DMDM
DM
DM
DM
DM
DM
DM

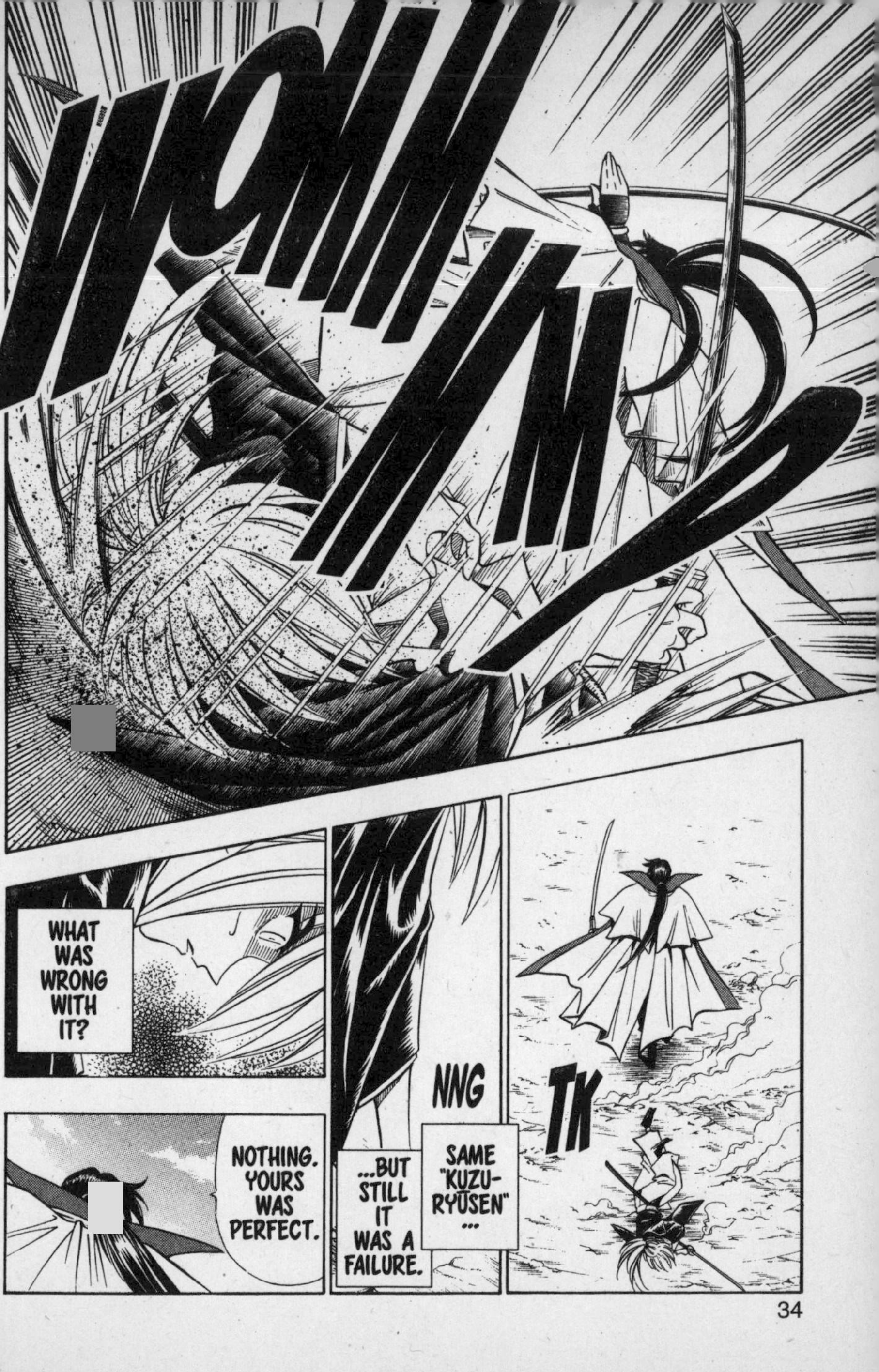
TK
SAME "KUZU-RYŪSEN" ...
NNG
...BUT STILL IT WAS A FAILURE.
WHAT WAS WRONG WITH IT?
NOTHING. YOURS WAS PERFECT.

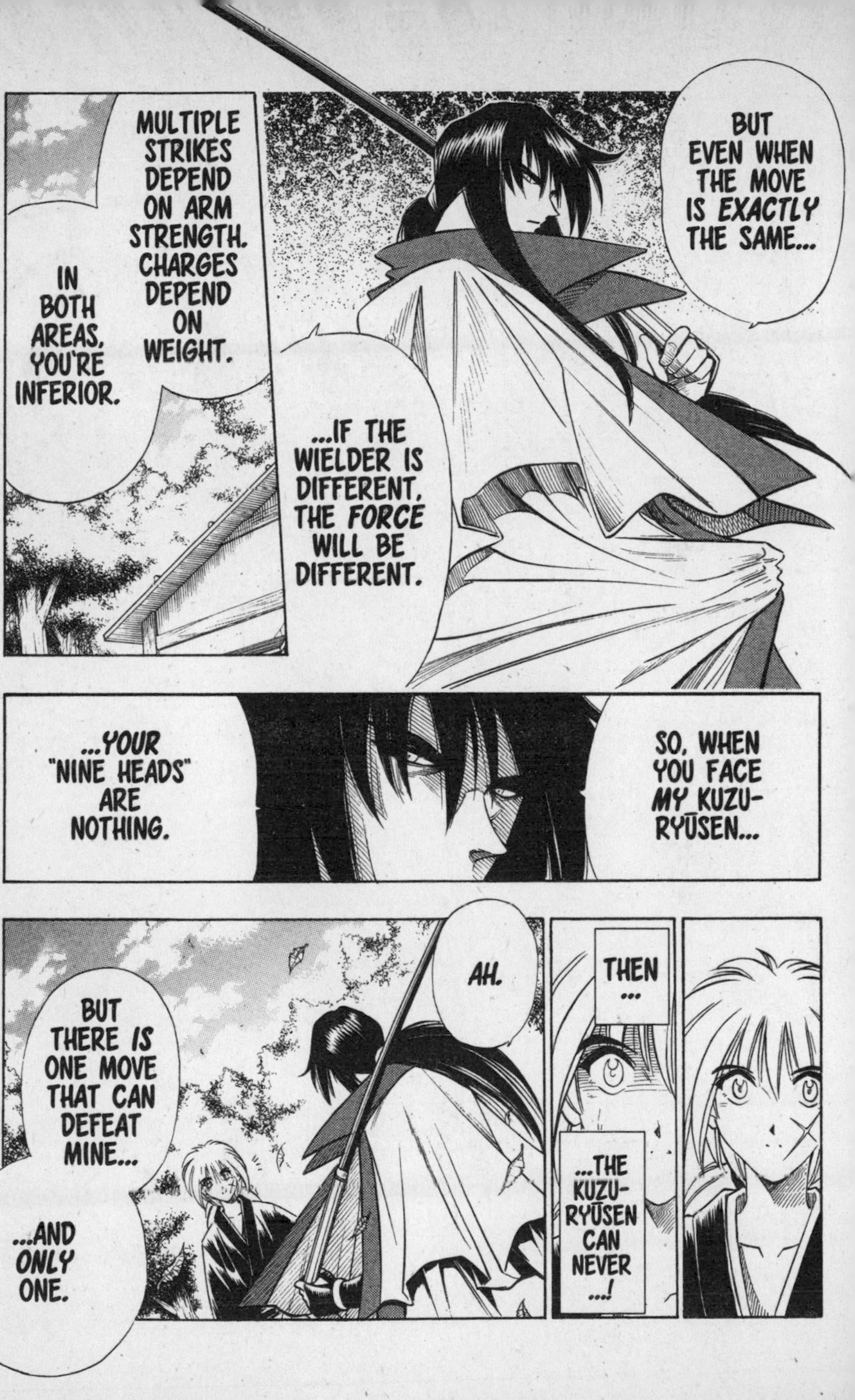
BUT EVEN WHEN THE MOVE IS *EXACTLY* THE SAME...
...IF THE WIELDER IS DIFFERENT, THE *FORCE* WILL BE DIFFERENT.
MULTIPLE STRIKES DEPEND ON ARM STRENGTH. CHARGES DEPEND ON WEIGHT.
IN BOTH AREAS, YOU'RE INFERIOR.
SO, WHEN YOU FACE *MY* KUZU-RYŪSEN...
...*YOUR* "NINE HEADS" ARE NOTHING.
THEN...
...THE KUZU-RYŪSEN CAN NEVER ...!
AH.
BUT THERE *IS* ONE MOVE THAT CAN DEFEAT MINE...
...AND *ONLY* ONE.

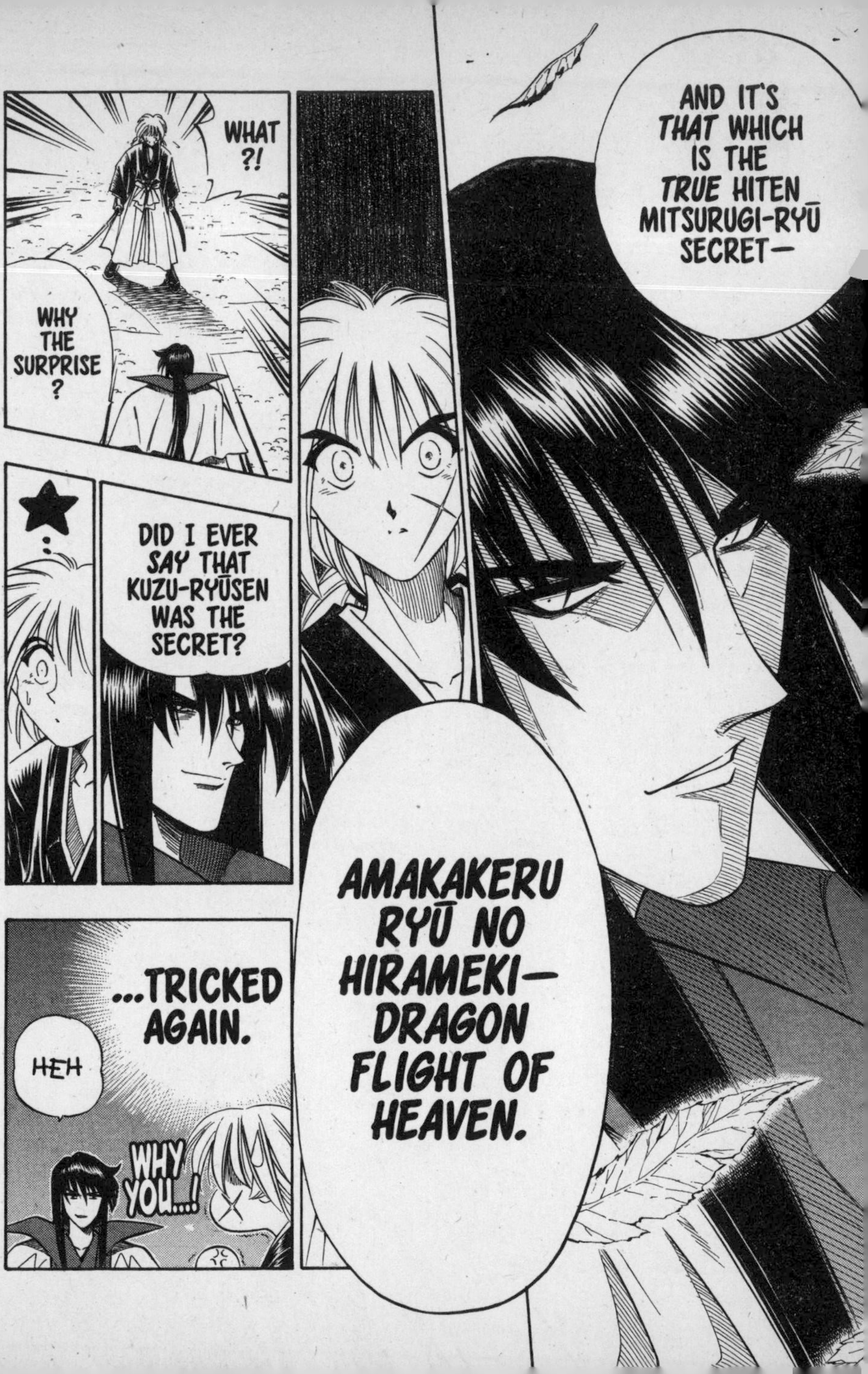
AND IT'S THAT WHICH IS THE TRUE HITEN MITSURUGI-RYŪ SECRET—
AMAKAKERU RYŪ NO HIRAMEKI— DRAGON FLIGHT OF HEAVEN.
WHAT?!
WHY THE SURPRISE?
DID I EVER SAY THAT KUZU-RYŪSEN WAS THE SECRET?
...TRICKED AGAIN.
HEH
WHY YOU...!

READ THIS WAY

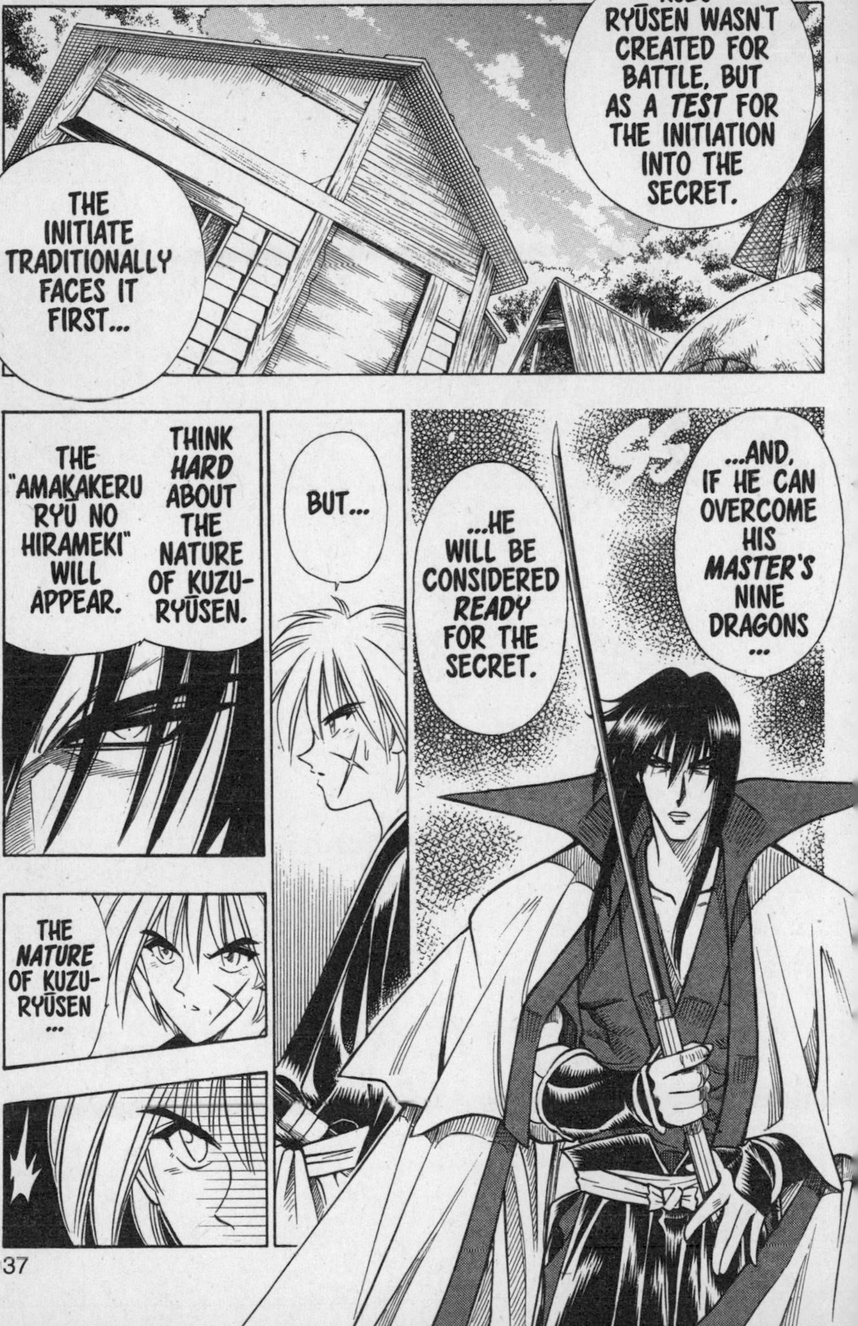
KUZU-RYŪSEN WASN'T CREATED FOR BATTLE, BUT AS A *TEST* FOR THE INITIATION INTO THE SECRET.
THE INITIATE TRADITIONALLY FACES IT FIRST...
SS
...AND, IF HE CAN OVERCOME HIS *MASTER'S* NINE DRAGONS...
...HE WILL BE CONSIDERED *READY* FOR THE SECRET.
BUT...
THINK *HARD* ABOUT THE NATURE OF KUZU-RYŪSEN.
THE "AMAKAKERU RYŪ NO HIRAMEKI" WILL APPEAR.
THE *NATURE* OF KUZU-RYŪSEN...

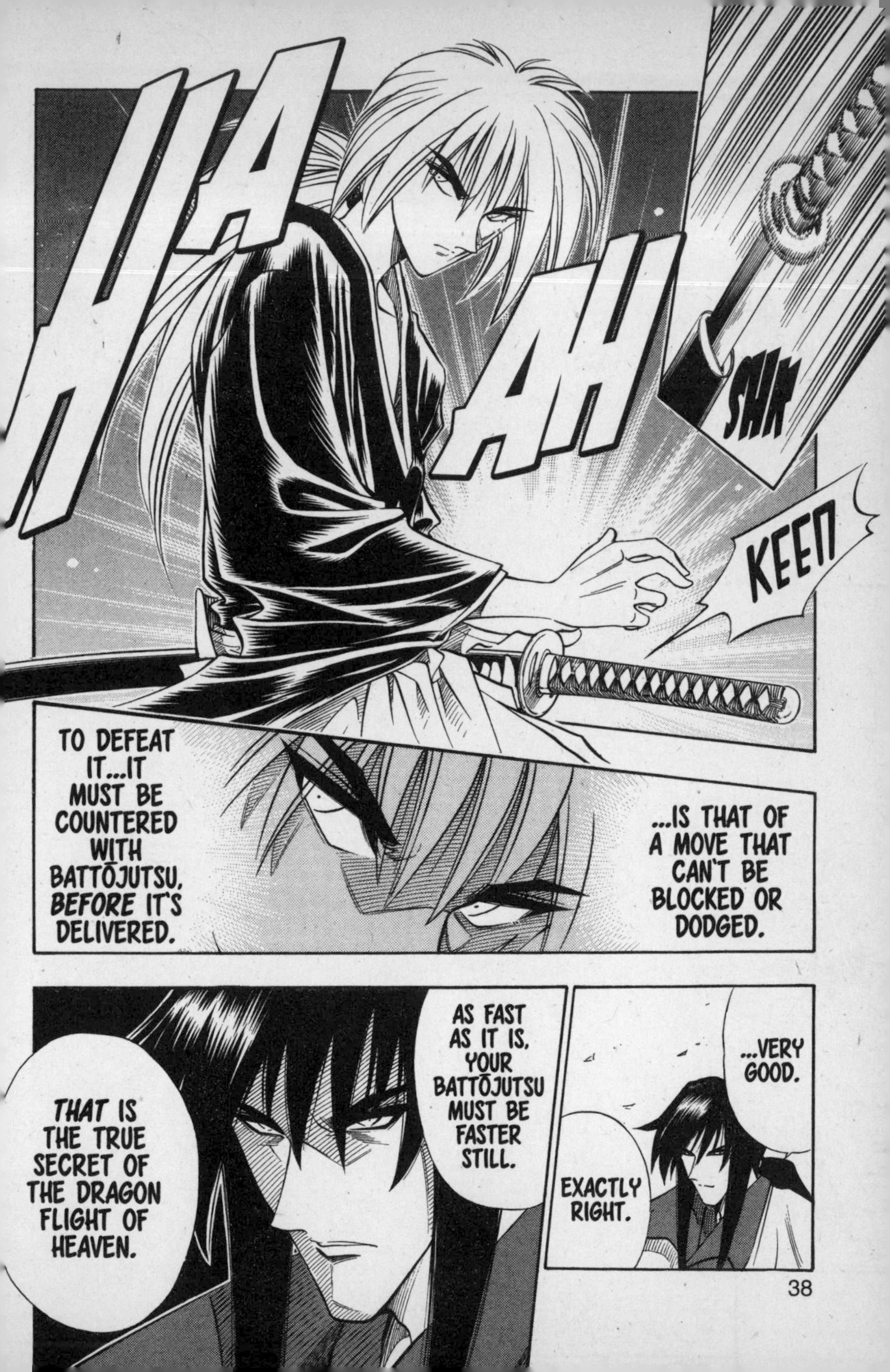
SHK
KEEN
HA-AH
...IS THAT OF A MOVE THAT CAN'T BE BLOCKED OR DODGED.
TO DEFEAT IT...IT MUST BE COUNTERED WITH BATTŌJUTSU, *BEFORE* IT'S DELIVERED.
...VERY GOOD.
EXACTLY RIGHT.
AS FAST AS IT IS, YOUR BATTŌJUTSU MUST BE FASTER STILL.
THAT IS THE TRUE SECRET OF THE DRAGON FLIGHT OF HEAVEN.

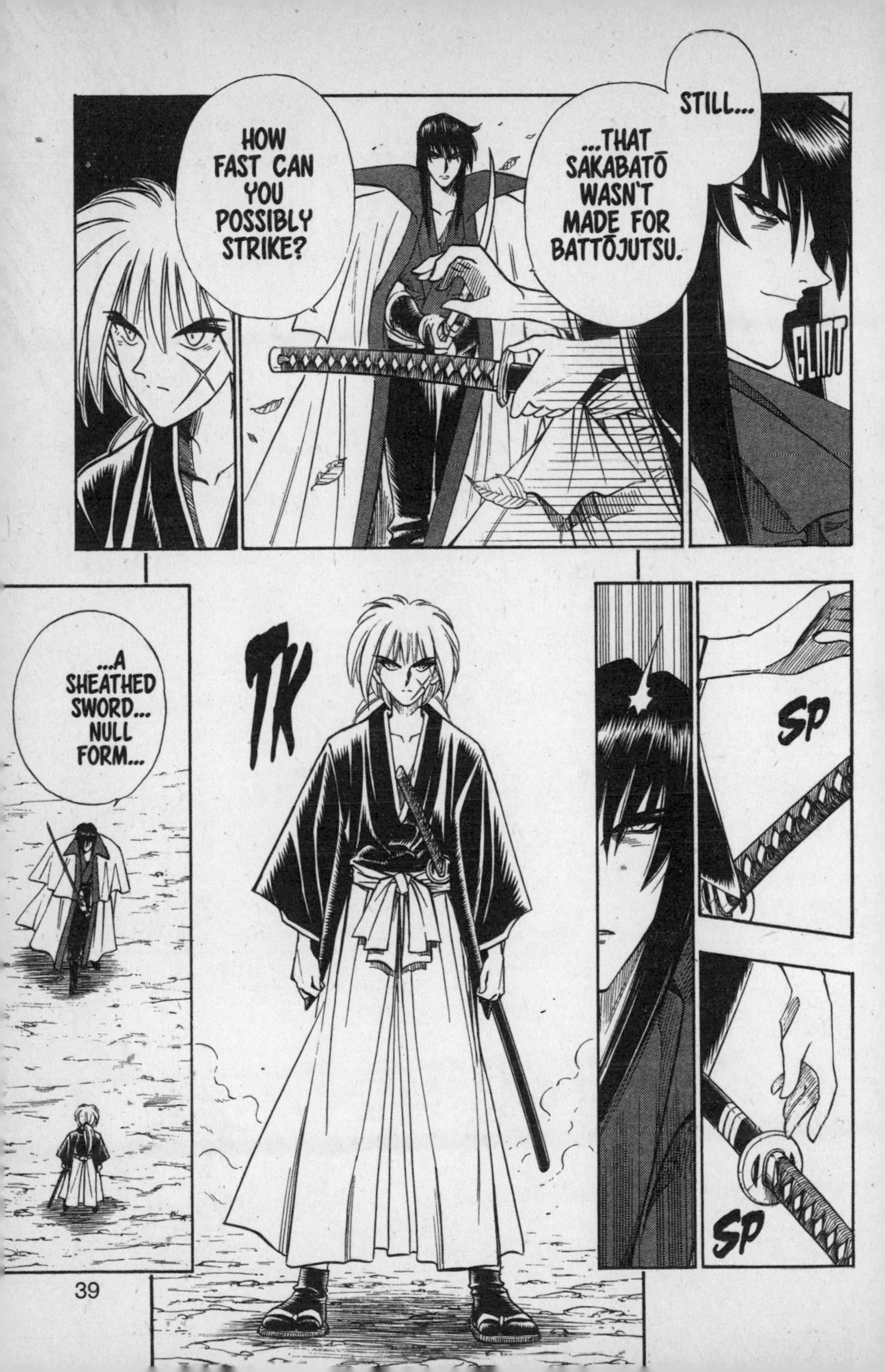
STILL...
...THAT SAKABATŌ WASN'T MADE FOR BATTŌJUTSU.
GLINT
HOW FAST CAN YOU POSSIBLY STRIKE?
SP
SP
TK
...A SHEATHED SWORD... NULL FORM...

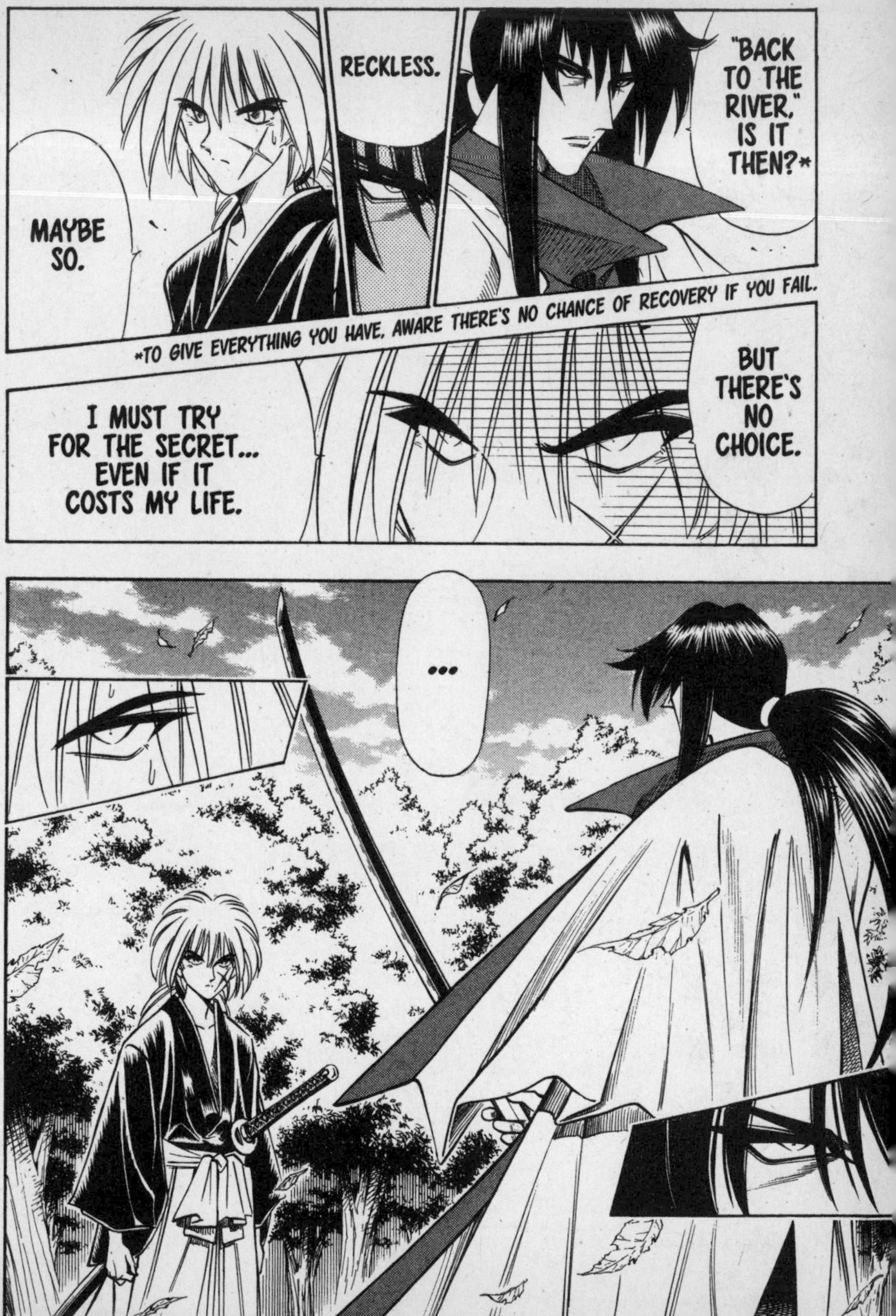
"BACK TO THE RIVER," IS IT THEN?*
RECKLESS.
MAYBE SO.
*TO GIVE EVERYTHING YOU HAVE, AWARE THERE'S NO CHANCE OF RECOVERY IF YOU FAIL.
BUT THERE'S NO CHOICE.
I MUST TRY FOR THE SECRET... EVEN IF IT COSTS MY LIFE.
...

WHAT?

YOU ARE MY IDIOT PUPIL.

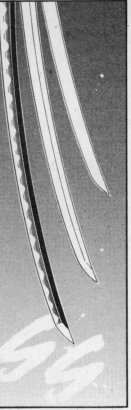

MASTER...

WHEN IT COMES DOWN TO IT, YOU DON'T UNDERSTAND A THING.

TP

I GIVE YOU ONE NIGHT.

SEARCH YOUR SOUL AND FIND WHAT'S LACKING IN YOU BEFORE SUNRISE.

SS

IF YOU CANNOT DO THAT, YOU WILL NOT ONLY FAIL TO OBTAIN THE SECRET...

...BUT HERE WILL ALSO BE WHERE YOU LOSE YOUR LIFE.

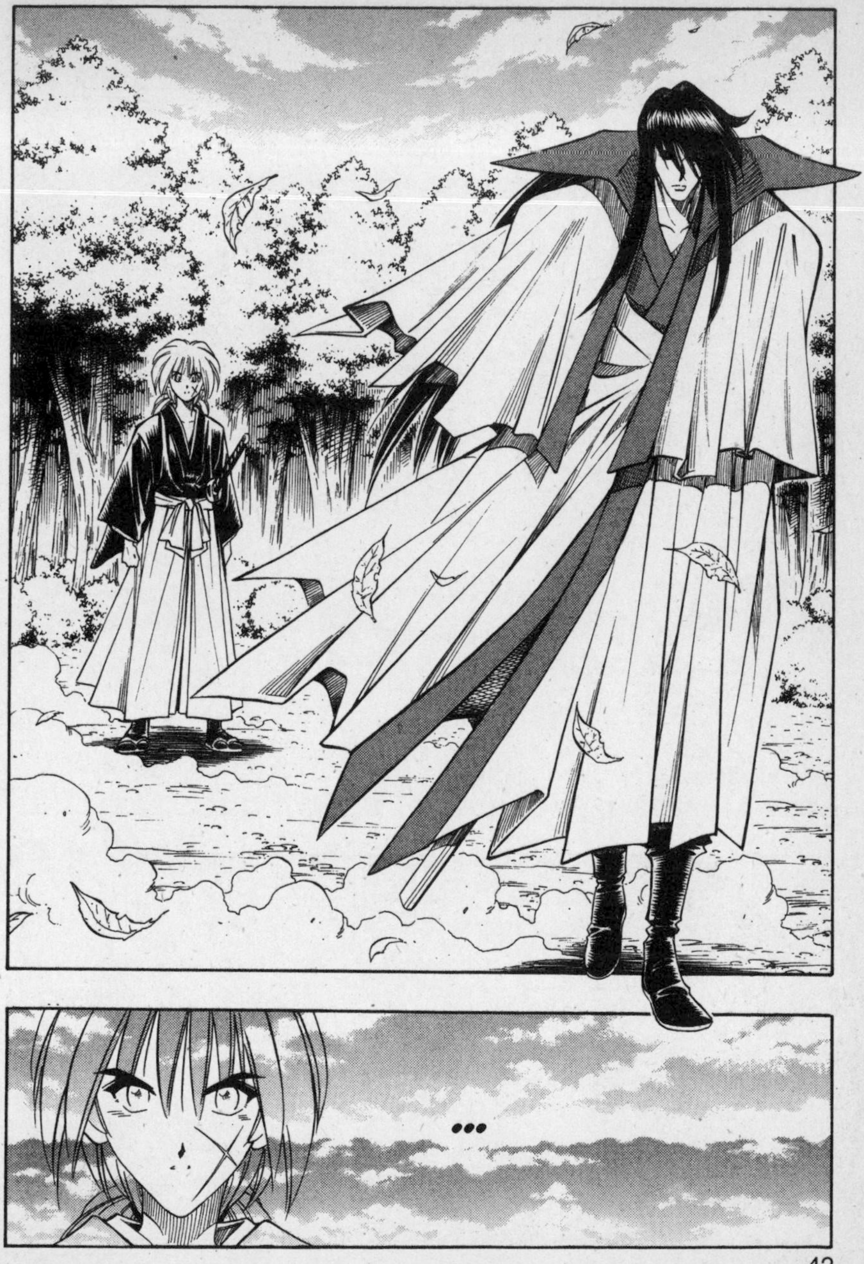
...

READ THIS WAY

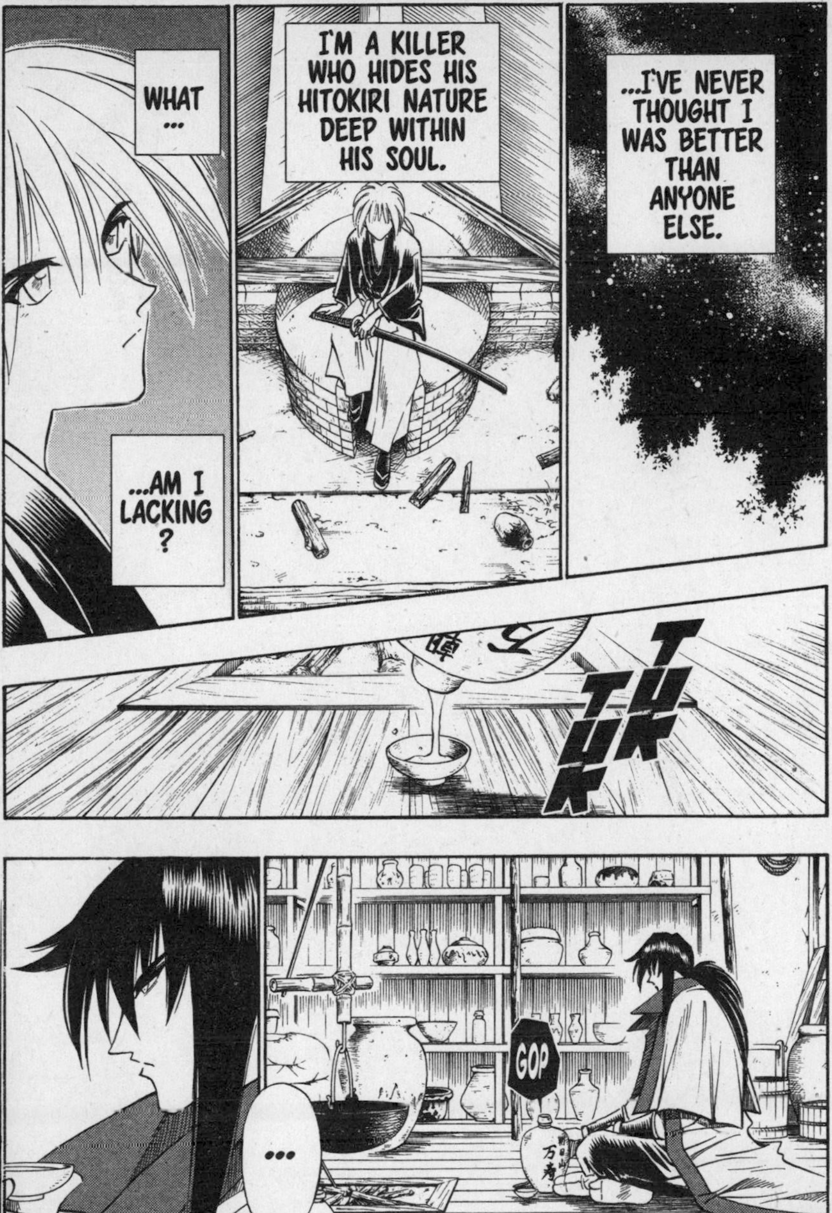

...I'VE NEVER THOUGHT I WAS BETTER THAN ANYONE ELSE.
I'M A KILLER WHO HIDES HIS HITOKIRI NATURE DEEP WITHIN HIS SOUL.
WHAT ...
...AM I LACKING ?
THUNK
GOP
...

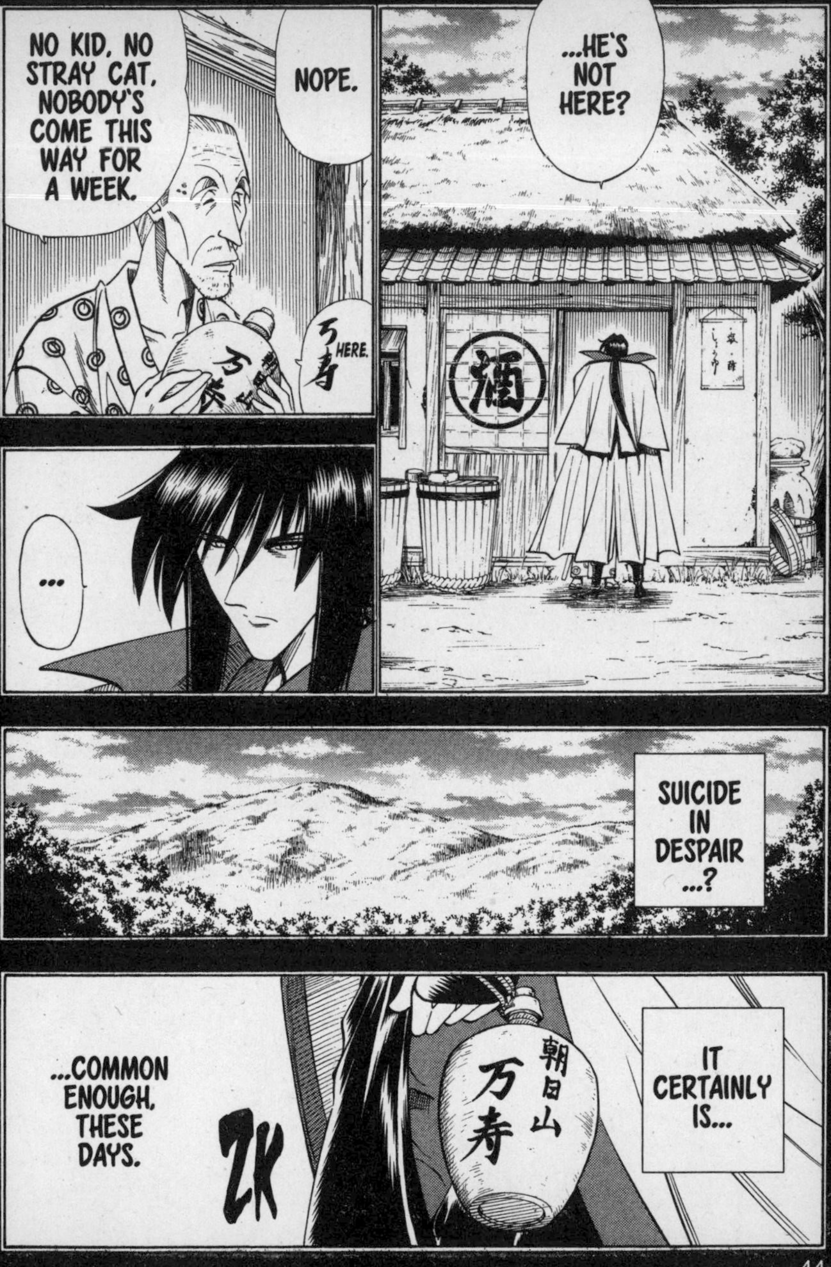
...HE'S NOT HERE?
NOPE.
NO KID, NO STRAY CAT, NOBODY'S COME THIS WAY FOR A WEEK.
万寿
HERE.
...
SUICIDE IN DESPAIR ...?
IT CERTAINLY IS...
朝日山
万寿
ZK
...COMMON ENOUGH, THESE DAYS.

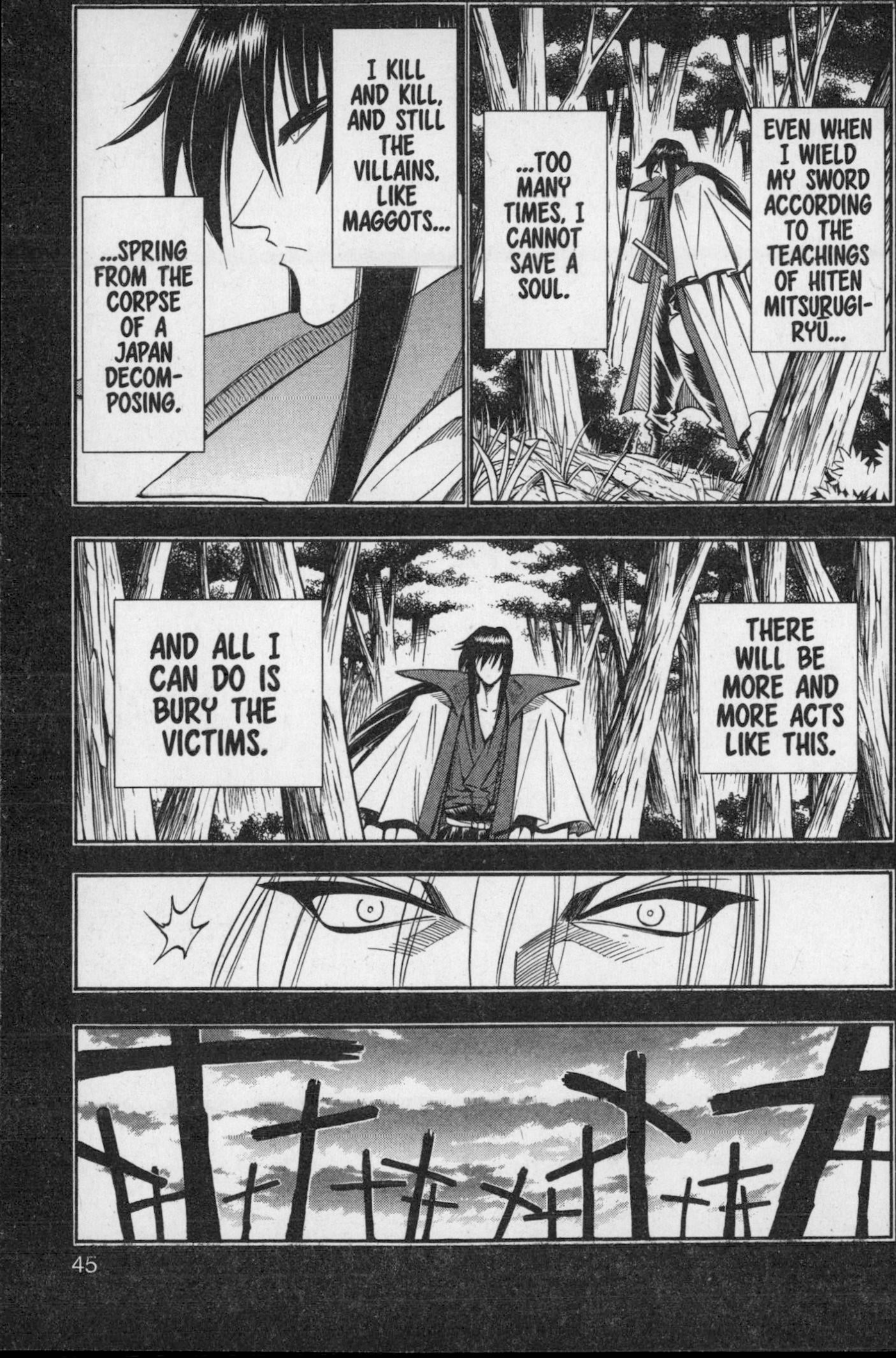
EVEN WHEN I WIELD MY SWORD ACCORDING TO THE TEACHINGS OF HITEN MITSURUGI-RYŪ...
...TOO MANY TIMES, I CANNOT SAVE A SOUL.
I KILL AND KILL, AND STILL THE VILLAINS, LIKE MAGGOTS...
...SPRING FROM THE CORPSE OF A JAPAN DECOMPOSING.
THERE WILL BE MORE AND MORE ACTS LIKE THIS.
AND ALL I CAN DO IS BURY THE VICTIMS.

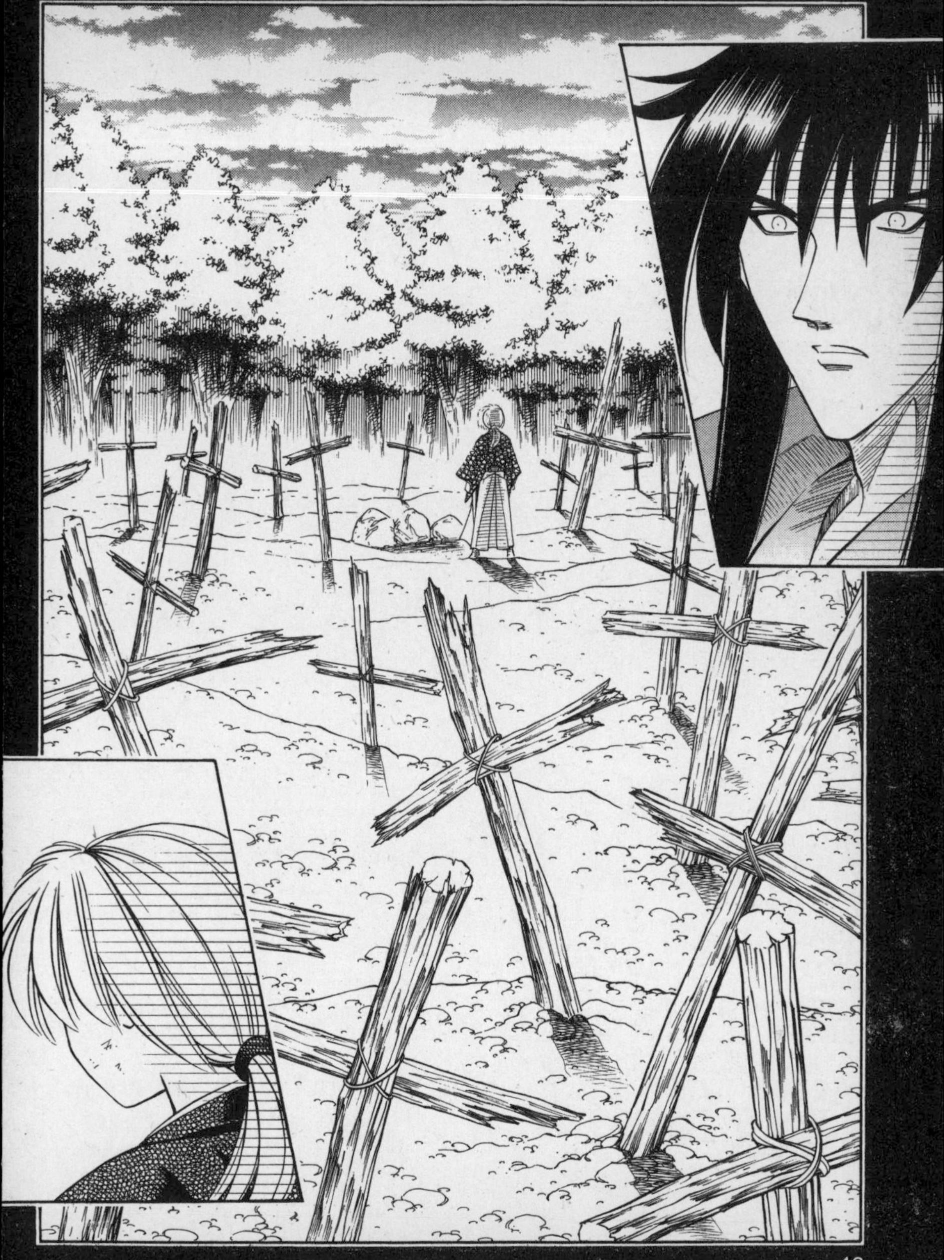

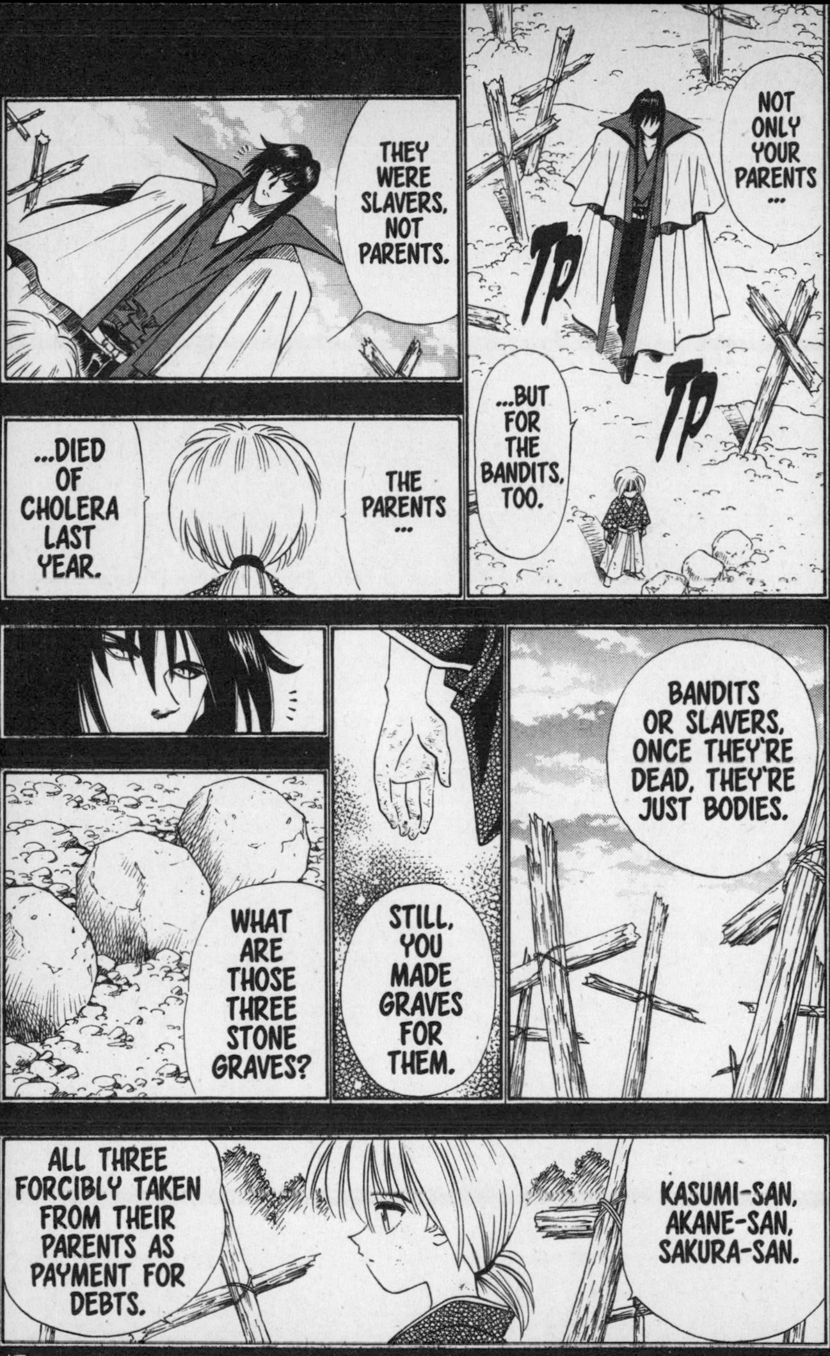
NOT ONLY YOUR PARENTS...
TP
TP
...BUT FOR THE BANDITS, TOO.
THEY WERE SLAVERS, NOT PARENTS.
THE PARENTS...
...DIED OF CHOLERA LAST YEAR.
BANDITS OR SLAVERS, ONCE THEY'RE DEAD, THEY'RE JUST BODIES.
STILL, YOU MADE GRAVES FOR THEM.
WHAT ARE THOSE THREE STONE GRAVES?
KASUMI-SAN, AKANE-SAN, SAKURA-SAN.
ALL THREE FORCIBLY TAKEN FROM THEIR PARENTS AS PAYMENT FOR DEBTS.

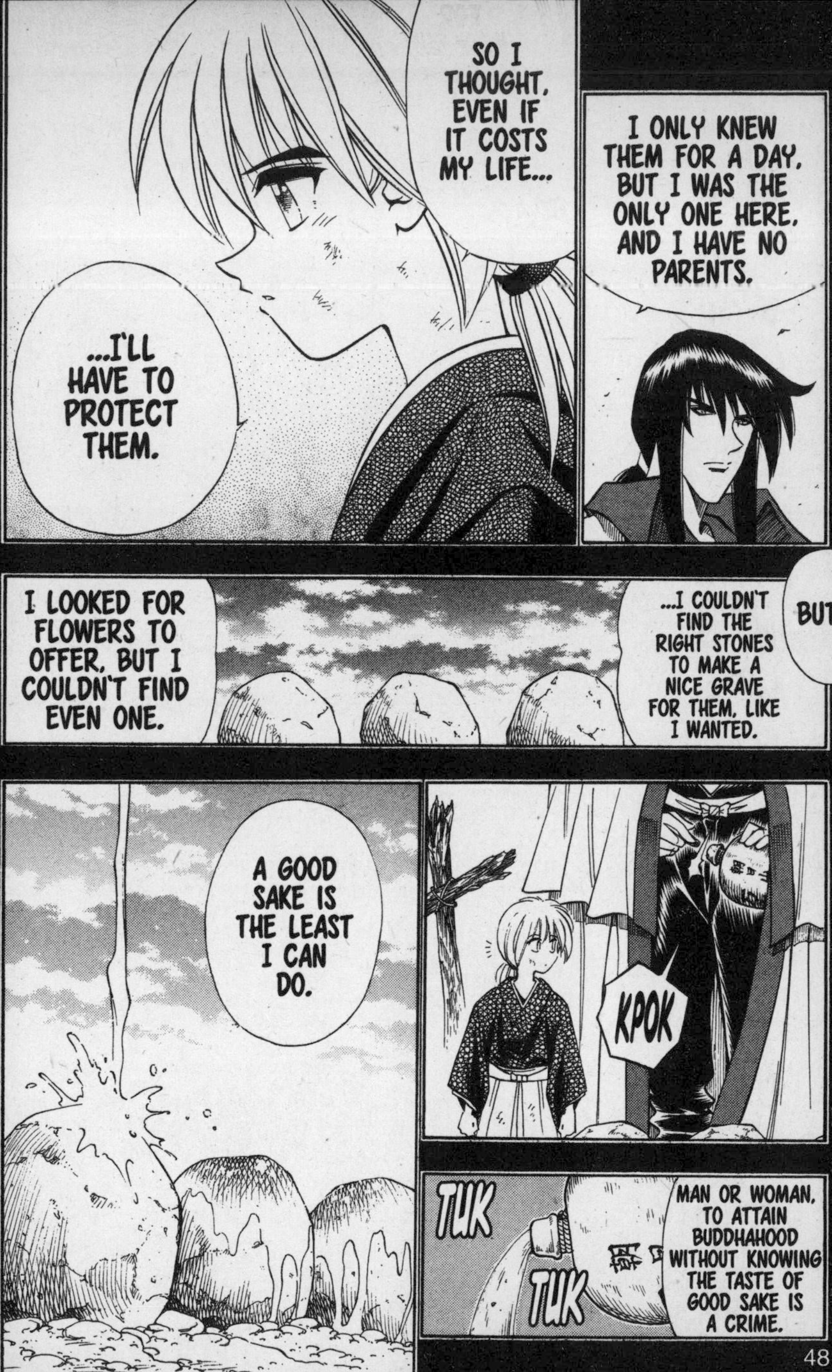
I ONLY KNEW THEM FOR A DAY, BUT I WAS THE ONLY ONE HERE, AND I HAVE NO PARENTS.
SO I THOUGHT, EVEN IF IT COSTS MY LIFE...
...I'LL HAVE TO PROTECT THEM.
BUT...
...I COULDN'T FIND THE RIGHT STONES TO MAKE A NICE GRAVE FOR THEM, LIKE I WANTED.
I LOOKED FOR FLOWERS TO OFFER, BUT I COULDN'T FIND EVEN ONE.
KPOK
TUK
TUK
MAN OR WOMAN, TO ATTAIN BUDDHAHOOD WITHOUT KNOWING THE TASTE OF GOOD SAKE IS A CRIME.
A GOOD SAKE IS THE LEAST I CAN DO.

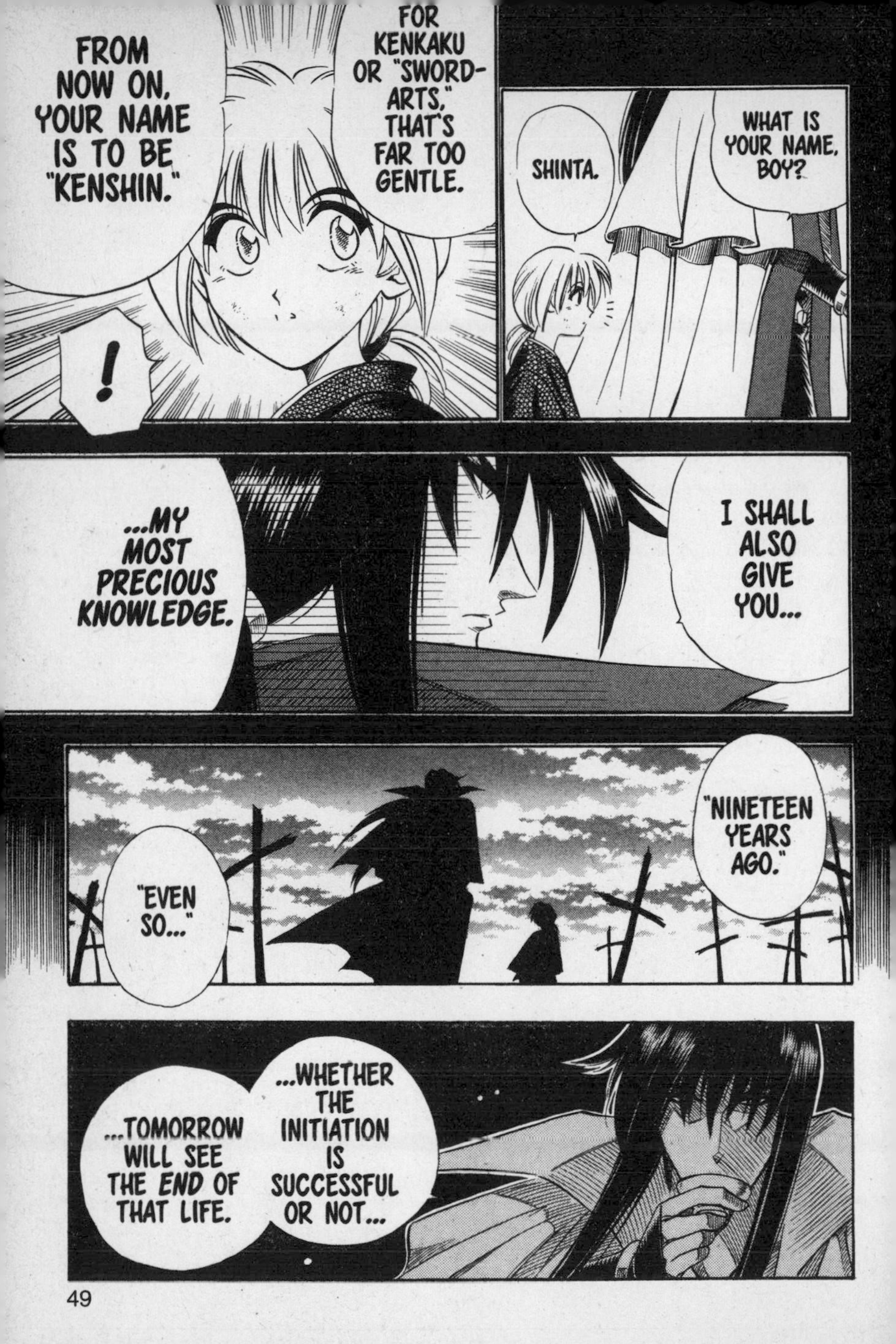
WHAT IS YOUR NAME, BOY?
SHINTA.
FOR KENKAKU OR "SWORD-ARTS," THAT'S FAR TOO GENTLE.
FROM NOW ON, YOUR NAME IS TO BE "KENSHIN."
!
I SHALL ALSO GIVE YOU...
...MY MOST PRECIOUS KNOWLEDGE.
"NINETEEN YEARS AGO."
"EVEN SO..."
...WHETHER THE INITIATION IS SUCCESSFUL OR NOT...
...TOMORROW WILL SEE THE *END* OF THAT LIFE.

Rurouni Kenshin

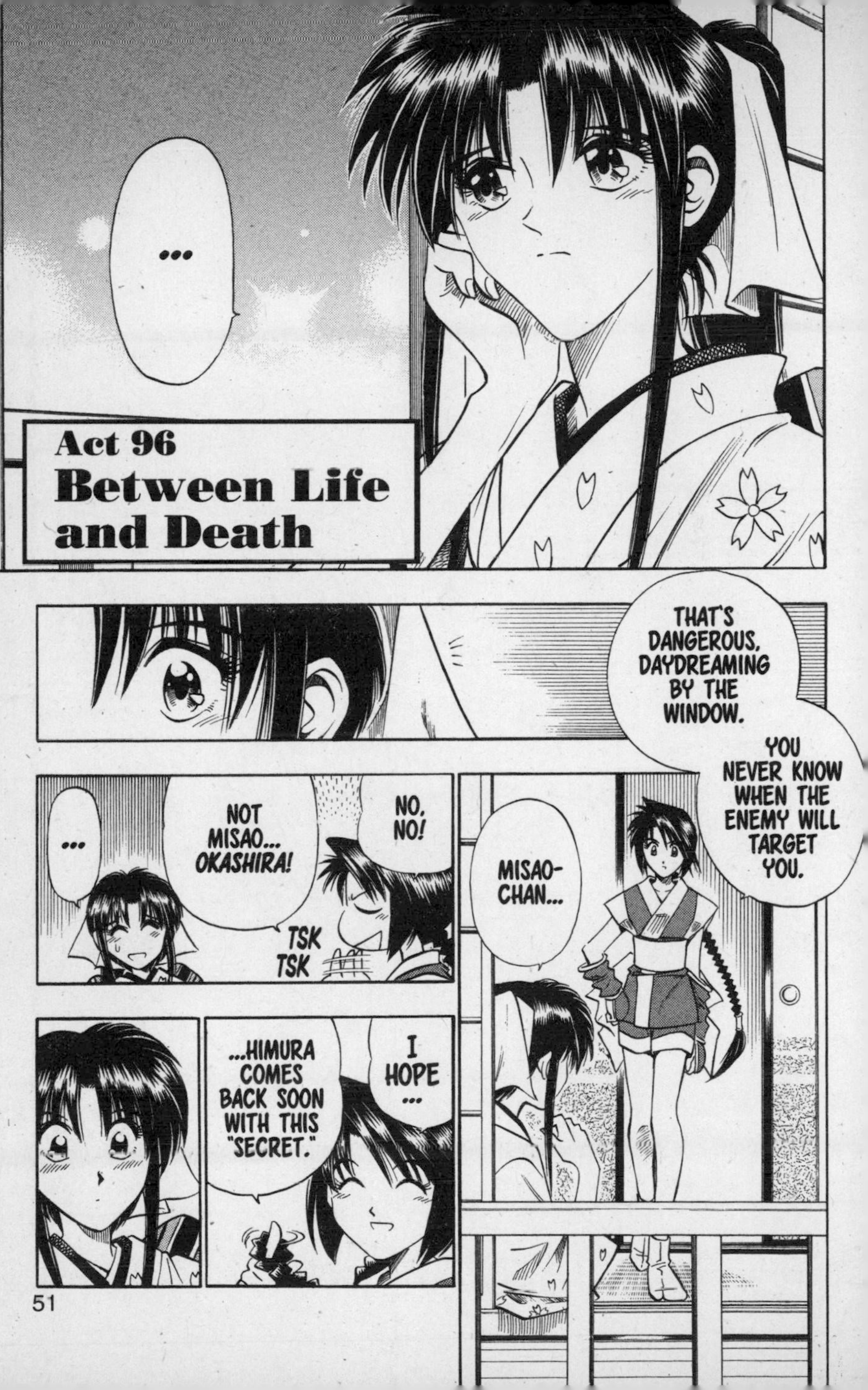
...
Act 96
Between Life and Death
THAT'S DANGEROUS, DAYDREAMING BY THE WINDOW.
YOU NEVER KNOW WHEN THE ENEMY WILL TARGET YOU.
MISAO-CHAN...
NO, NO!
NOT MISAO... OKASHIRA!
TSK TSK
...
I HOPE...
...HIMURA COMES BACK SOON WITH THIS "SECRET."

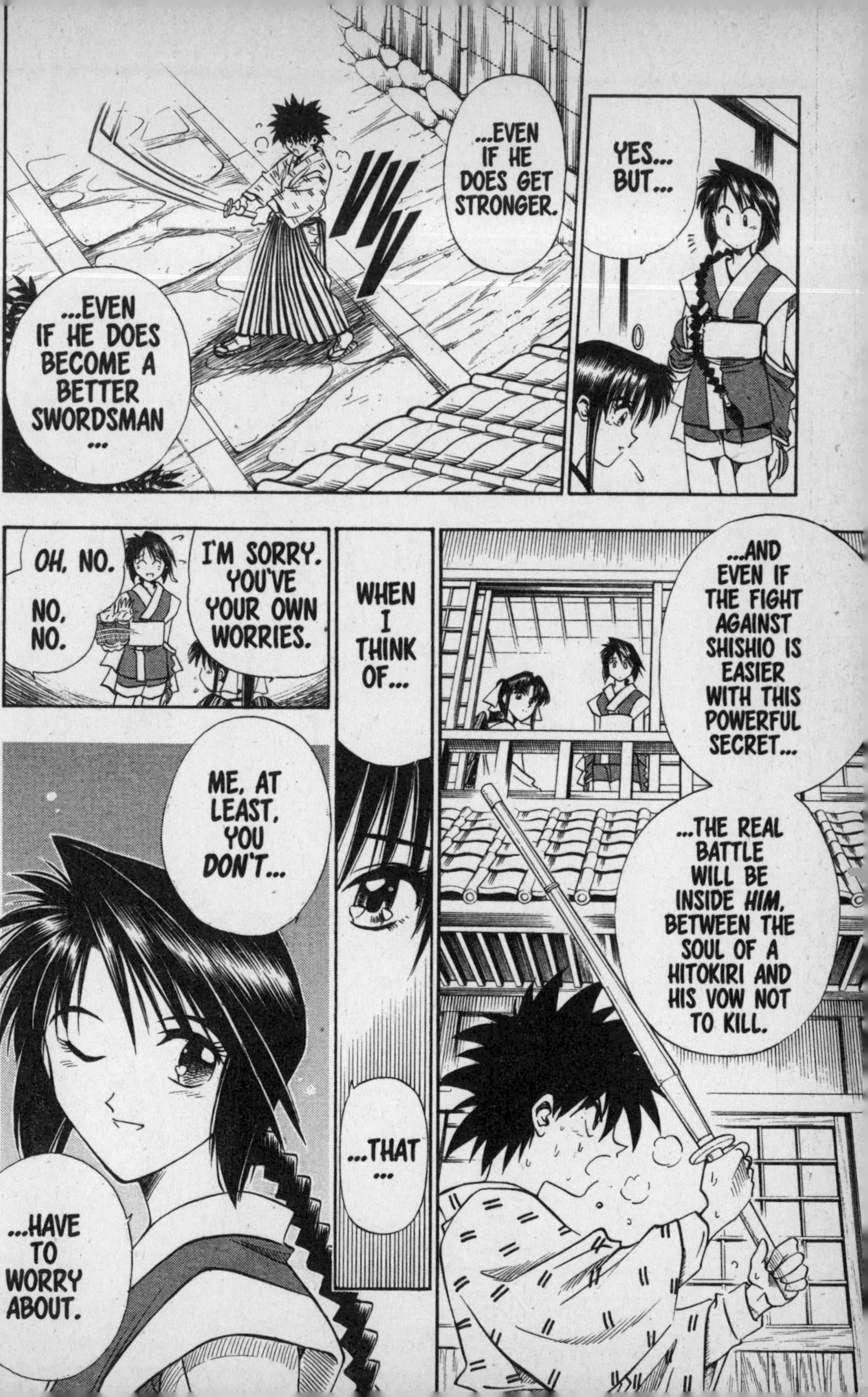
YES... BUT...
...EVEN IF HE DOES GET STRONGER.
...EVEN IF HE DOES BECOME A BETTER SWORDSMAN ...
...AND EVEN IF THE FIGHT AGAINST SHISHIO IS EASIER WITH THIS POWERFUL SECRET...
...THE REAL BATTLE WILL BE INSIDE *HIM*, BETWEEN THE SOUL OF A HITOKIRI AND HIS VOW NOT TO KILL.
WHEN I THINK OF...
...THAT ...
I'M SORRY. YOU'VE YOUR OWN WORRIES.
OH, NO.
NO, NO.
ME, AT LEAST, YOU *DON'T*...
...HAVE TO WORRY ABOUT.

Act 96
Between Life and Death

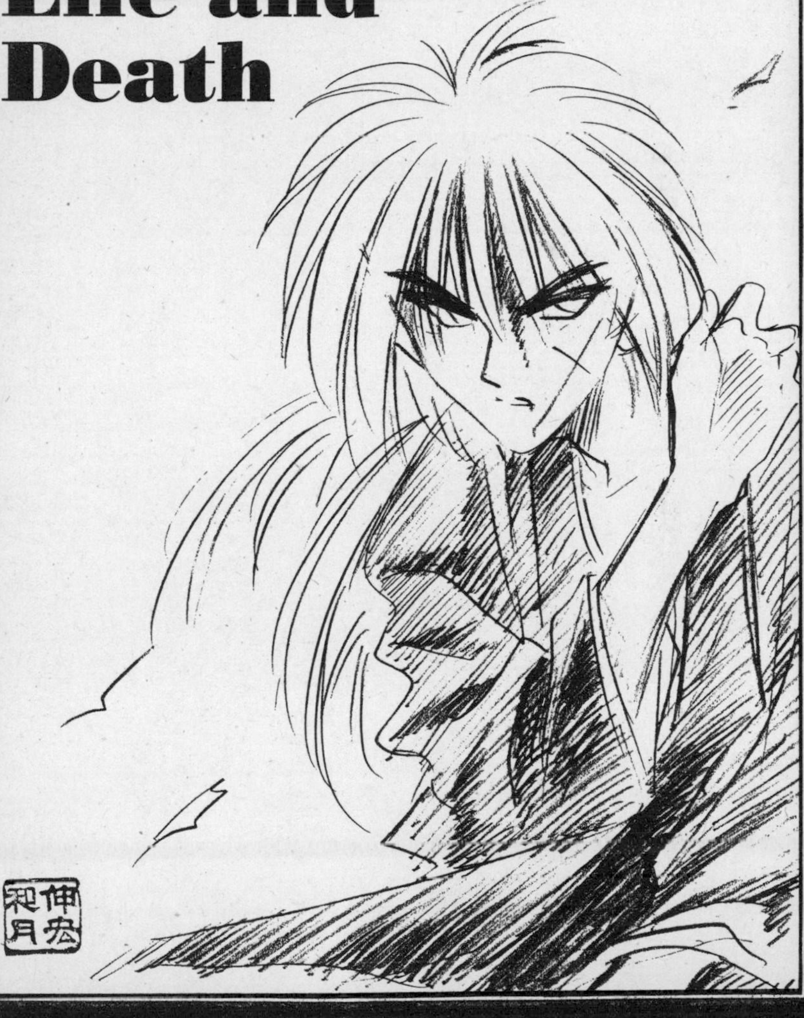
伸宏和月

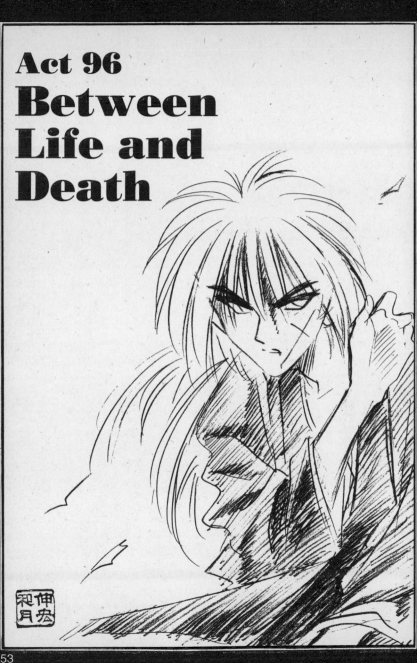

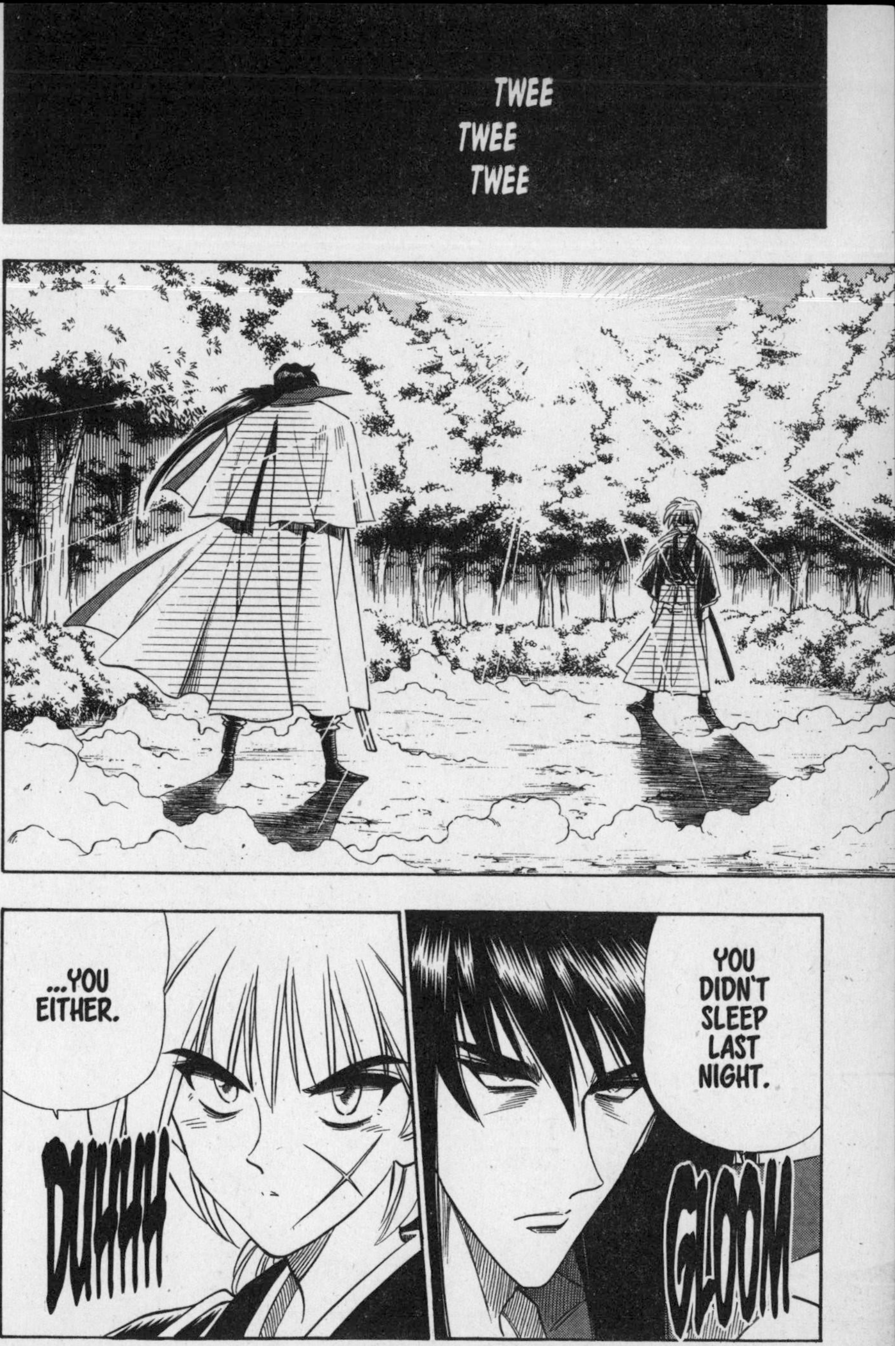
TWEE
TWEE
TWEE
YOU DIDN'T SLEEP LAST NIGHT.
GLOOM
...YOU EITHER.
DUHHH

READ THIS WAY

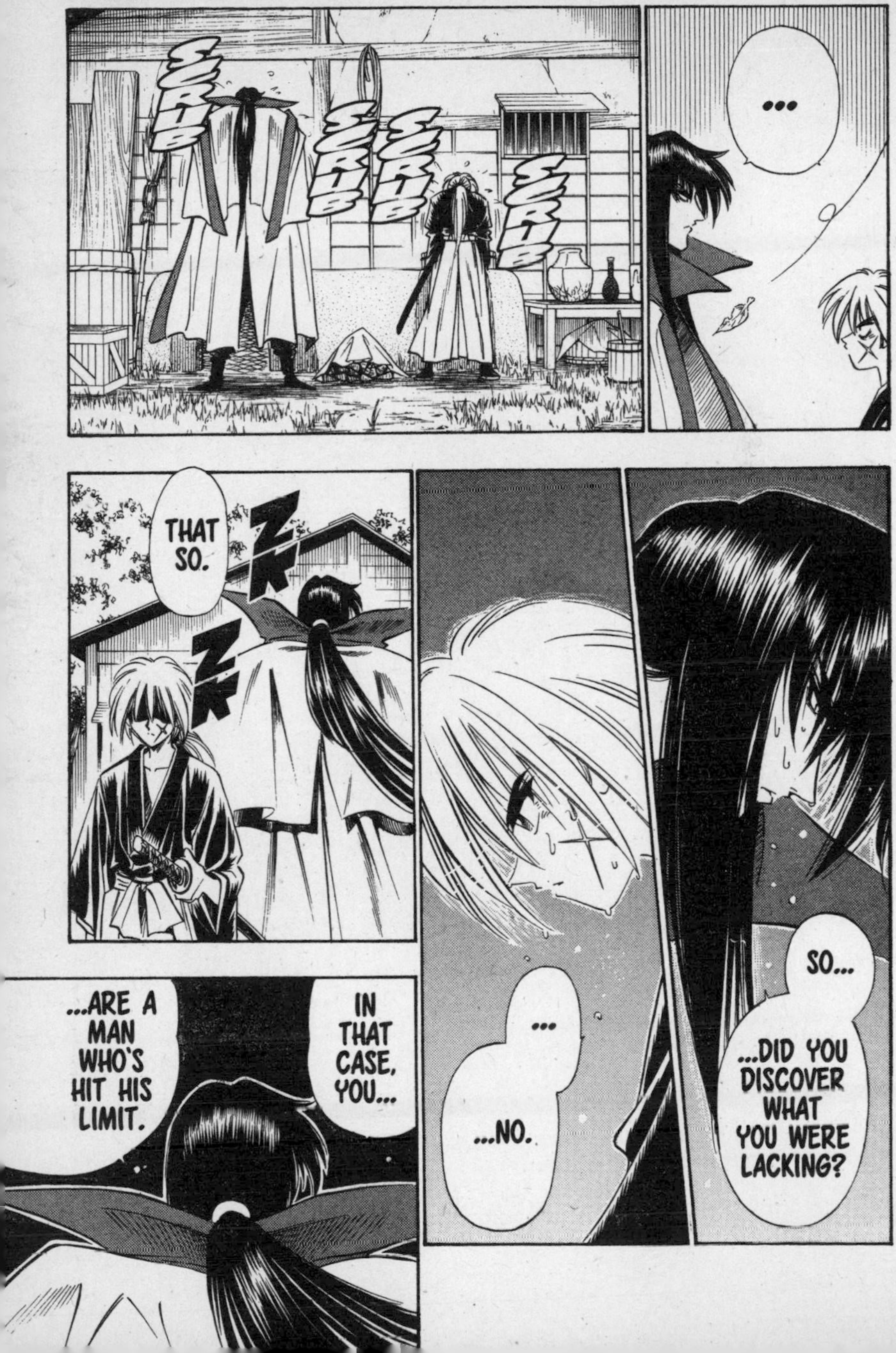
...
SCRUB SCRUB SCRUB SCRUB
SO...
...DID YOU DISCOVER WHAT YOU WERE LACKING?
...
...NO.
THAT SO.
ZK ZK
IN THAT CASE, YOU...
...ARE A MAN WHO'S HIT HIS LIMIT.

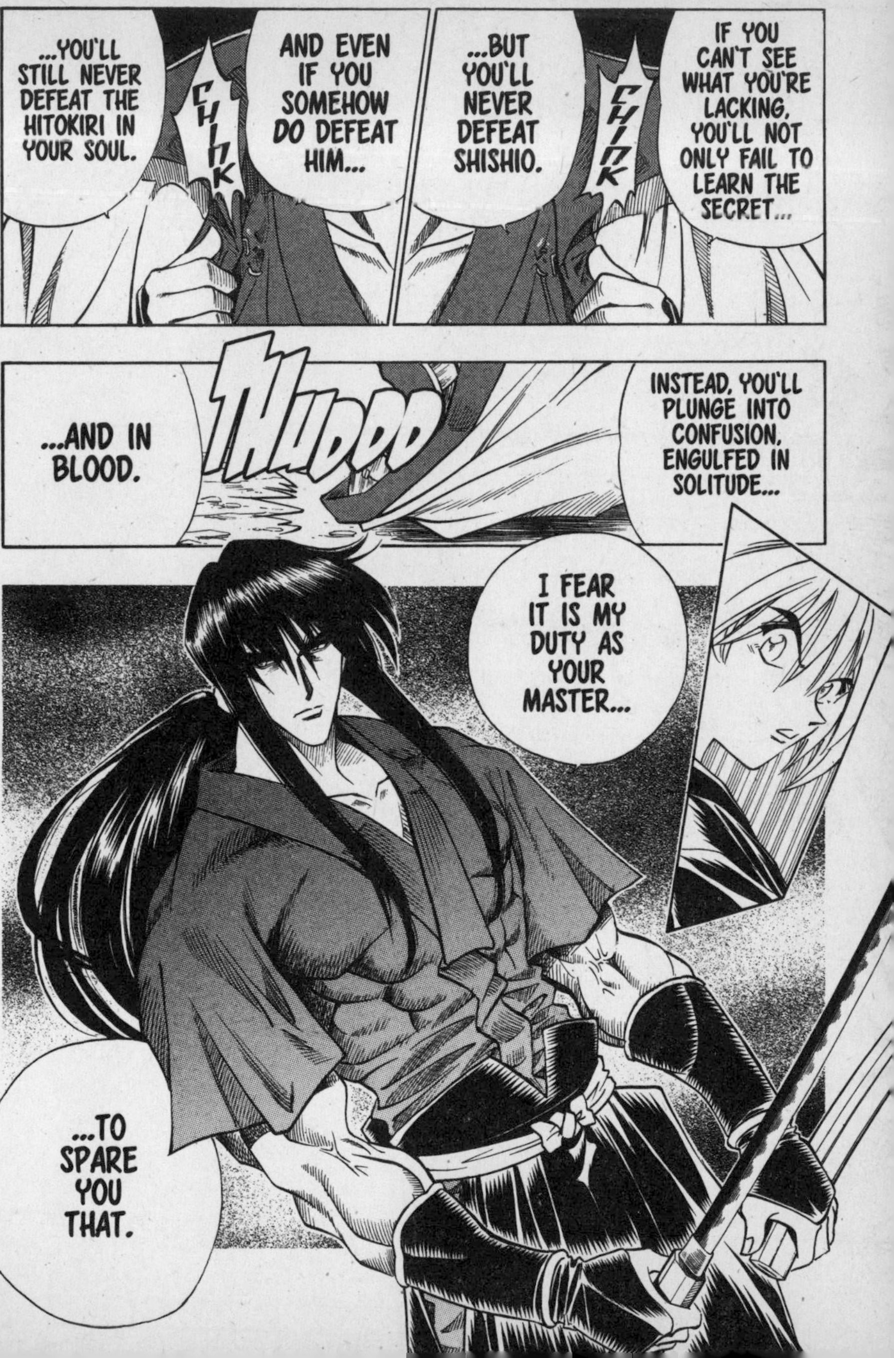
IF YOU CAN'T SEE WHAT YOU'RE LACKING, YOU'LL NOT ONLY FAIL TO LEARN THE SECRET...
CHINK
...BUT YOU'LL NEVER DEFEAT SHISHIO.
AND EVEN IF YOU SOMEHOW DO DEFEAT HIM...
CHINK
...YOU'LL STILL NEVER DEFEAT THE HITOKIRI IN YOUR SOUL.
INSTEAD, YOU'LL PLUNGE INTO CONFUSION, ENGULFED IN SOLITUDE...
THUDDD
...AND IN BLOOD.
I FEAR IT IS MY DUTY AS YOUR MASTER...
...TO SPARE YOU THAT.

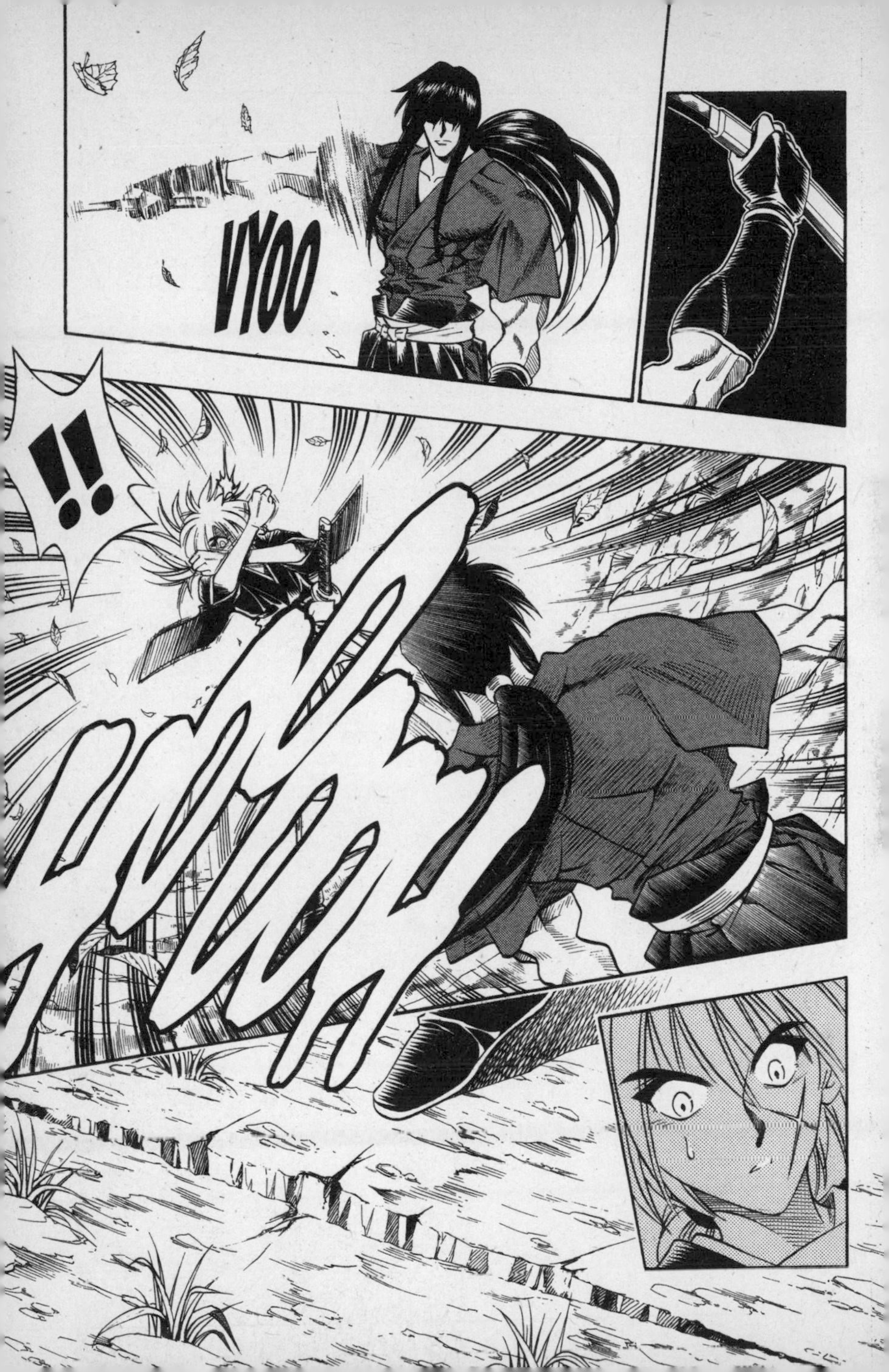
VYOO
!!

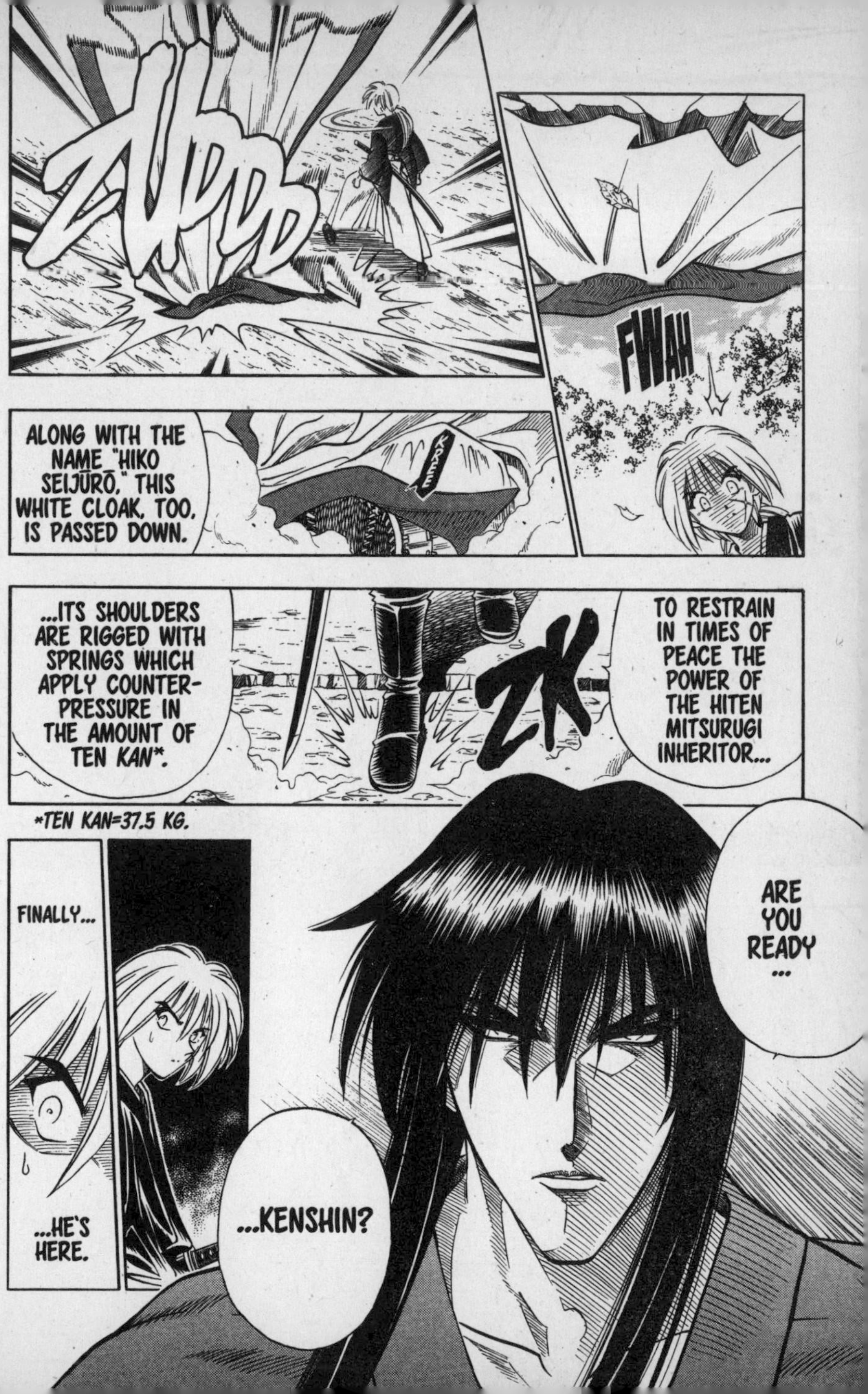
FWAH
KREE
ALONG WITH THE NAME "HIKO SEIJŪRŌ," THIS WHITE CLOAK, TOO, IS PASSED DOWN.
TO RESTRAIN IN TIMES OF PEACE THE POWER OF THE HITEN MITSURUGI INHERITOR...
ZK
...ITS SHOULDERS ARE RIGGED WITH SPRINGS WHICH APPLY COUNTER-PRESSURE IN THE AMOUNT OF TEN KAN*.
*TEN KAN=37.5 KG.
ARE YOU READY...
...KENSHIN?
FINALLY...
...HE'S HERE.

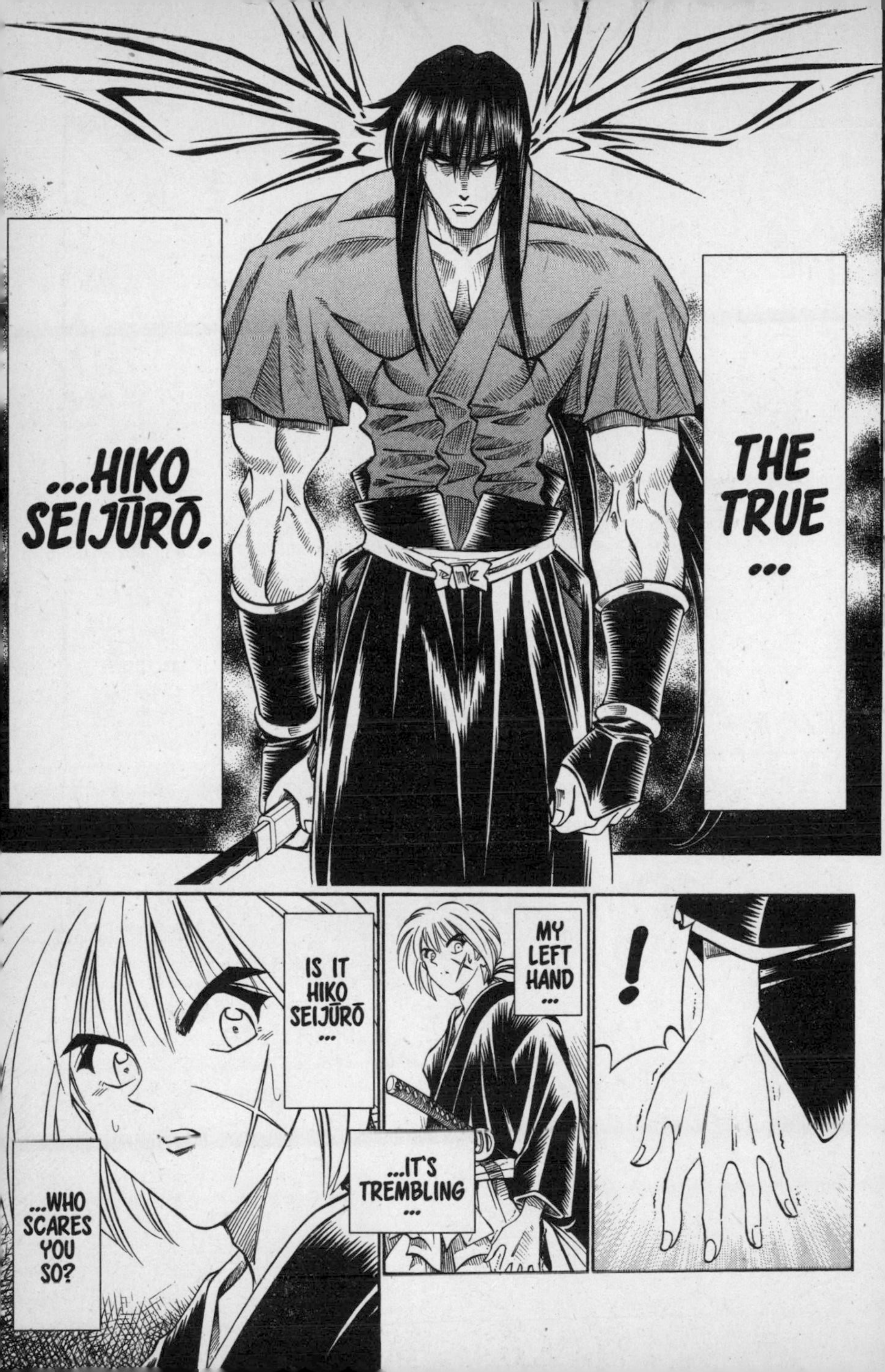
THE TRUE ...
...HIKO SEIJŪRŌ.
!
MY LEFT HAND ...
...IT'S TREMBLING ...
IS IT HIKO SEIJŪRŌ ...
...WHO SCARES YOU SO?

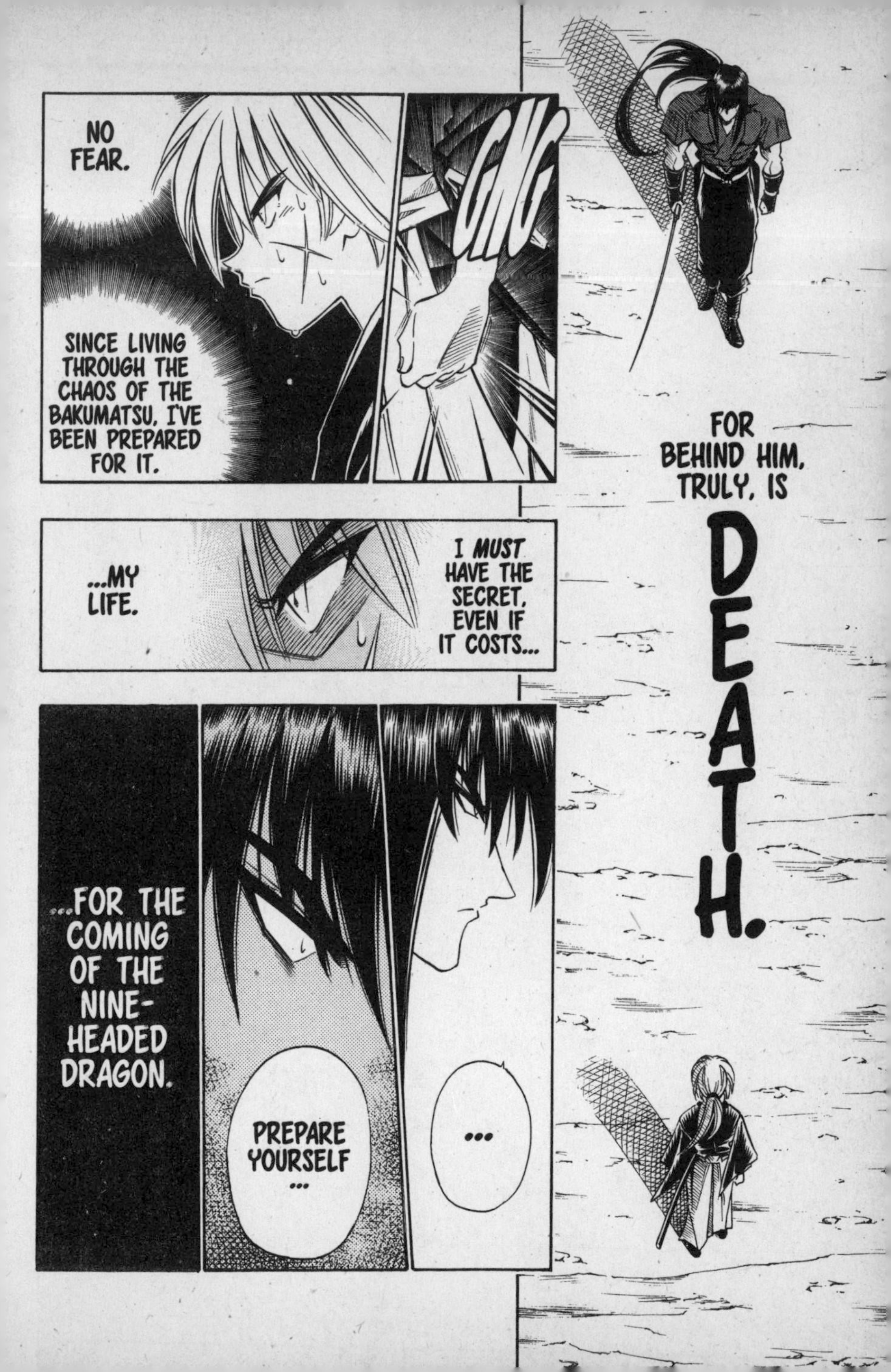
FOR BEHIND HIM, TRULY, IS
DEATH.
NO FEAR.
SINCE LIVING THROUGH THE CHAOS OF THE BAKUMATSU, I'VE BEEN PREPARED FOR IT.
I MUST HAVE THE SECRET, EVEN IF IT COSTS...
...MY LIFE.
...
PREPARE YOURSELF ...
...FOR THE COMING OF THE NINE-HEADED DRAGON.

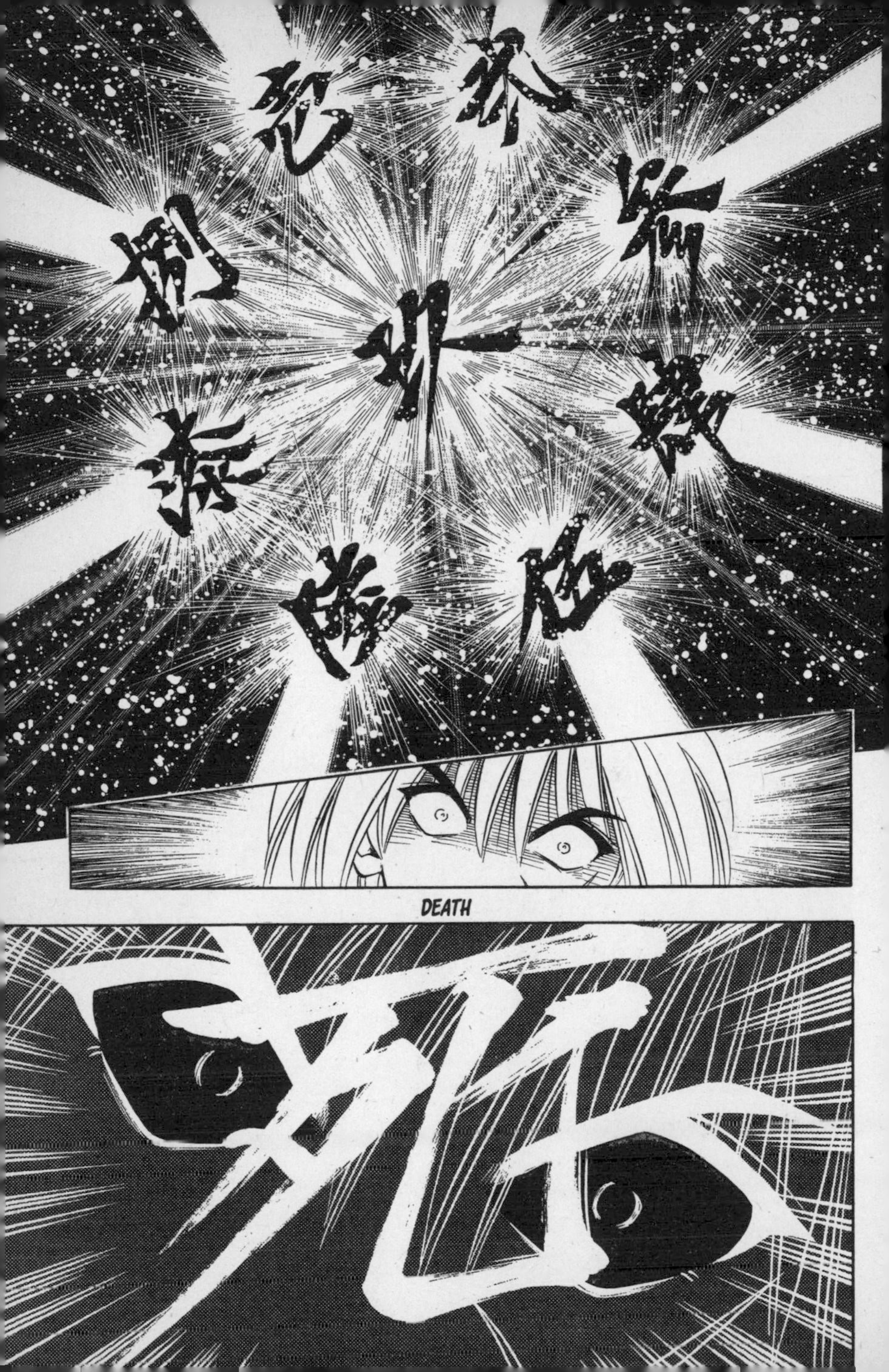
DEATH

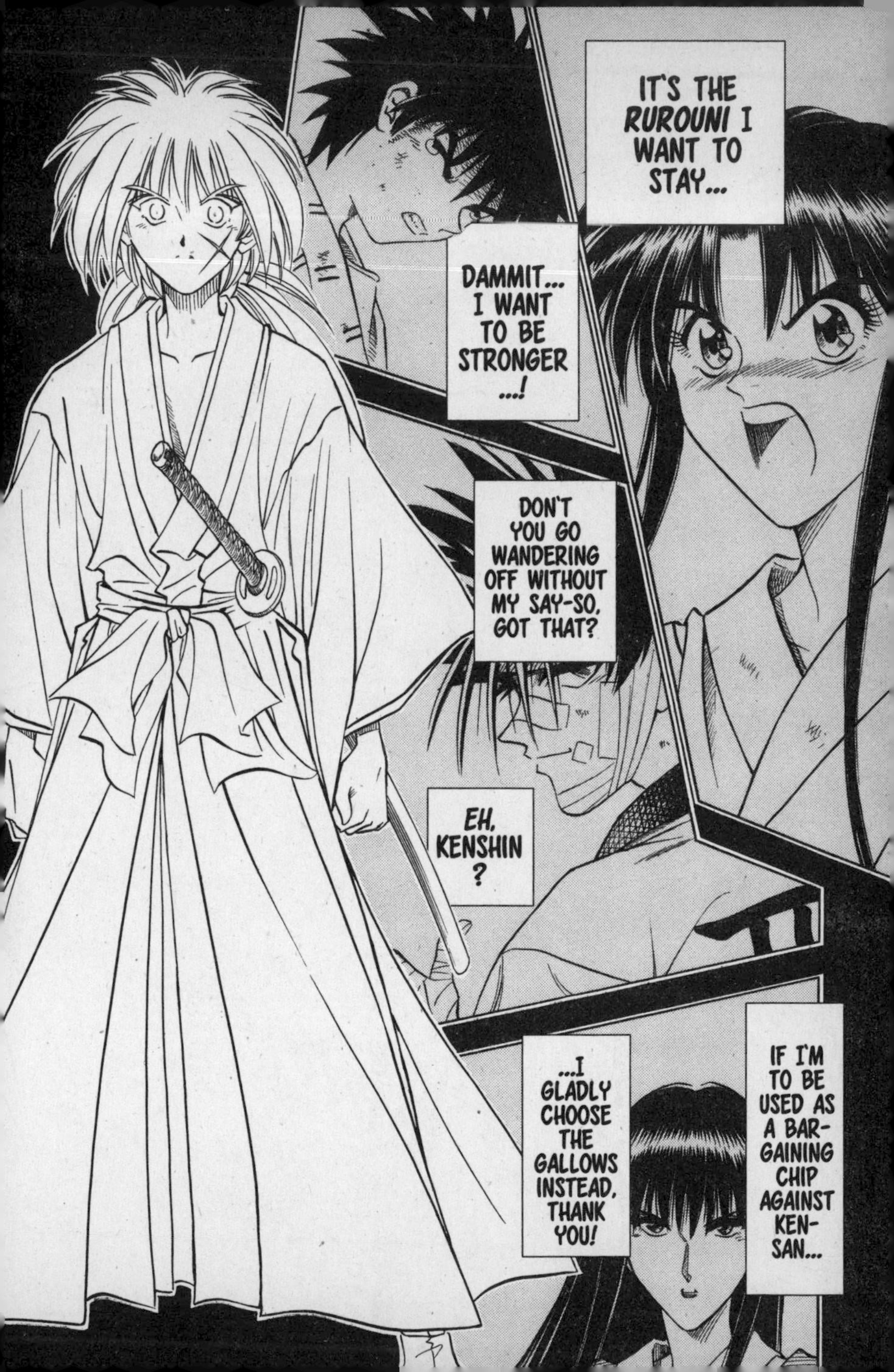
IT'S THE *RUROUNI* I WANT TO STAY...
DAMMIT... I WANT TO BE STRONGER ...!
DON'T YOU GO WANDERING OFF WITHOUT MY SAY-SO, GOT THAT?
EH, KENSHIN?
IF I'M TO BE USED AS A BAR-GAINING CHIP AGAINST KEN-SAN...
...I GLADLY CHOOSE THE GALLOWS INSTEAD, THANK YOU!

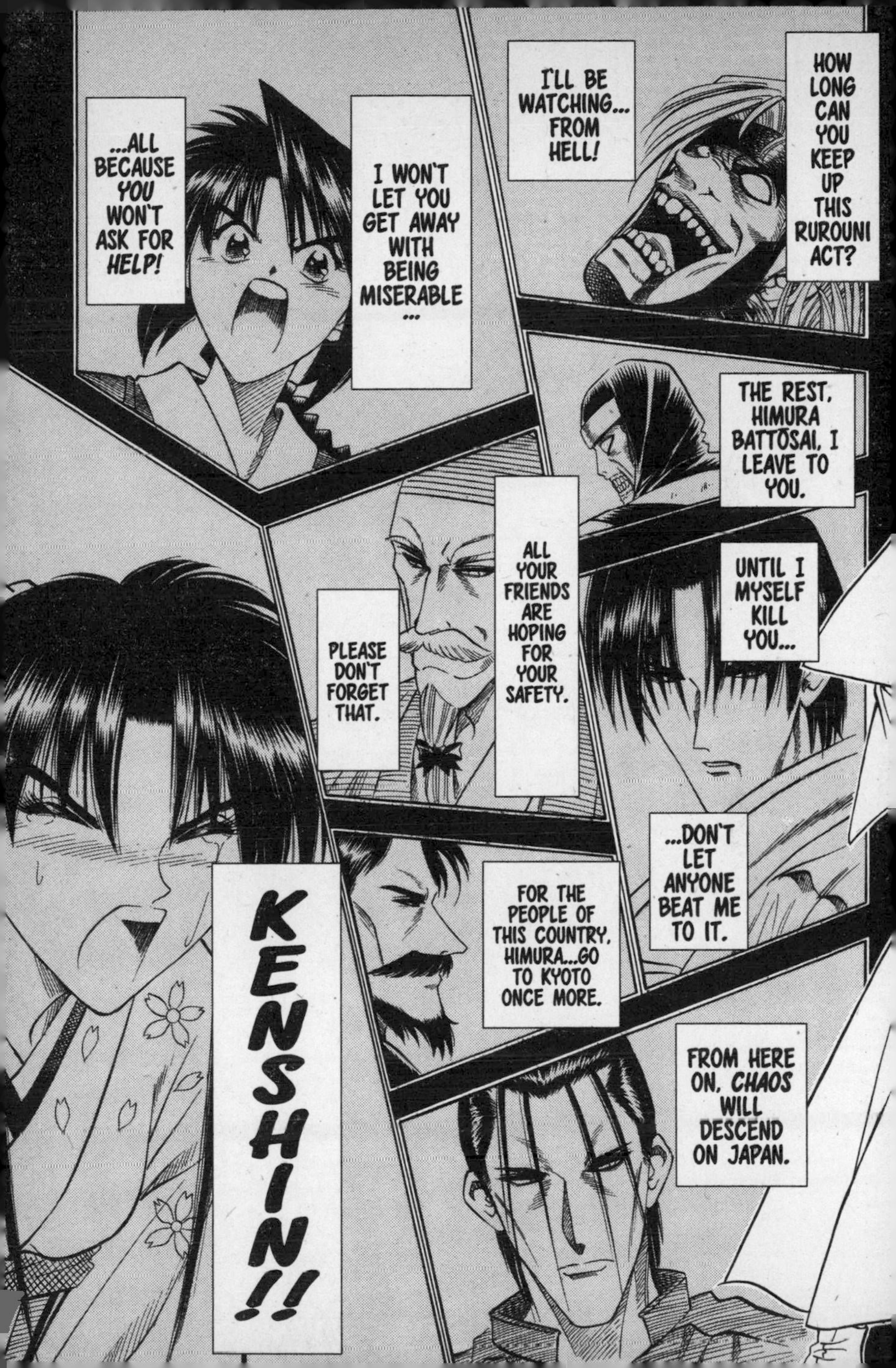
HOW LONG CAN YOU KEEP UP THIS RUROUNI ACT?
I'LL BE WATCHING... FROM HELL!
I WON'T LET YOU GET AWAY WITH BEING MISERABLE...
...ALL BECAUSE YOU WON'T ASK FOR HELP!
THE REST, HIMURA BATTŌSAI, I LEAVE TO YOU.
UNTIL I MYSELF KILL YOU...
...DON'T LET ANYONE BEAT ME TO IT.
ALL YOUR FRIENDS ARE HOPING FOR YOUR SAFETY.
PLEASE DON'T FORGET THAT.
FOR THE PEOPLE OF THIS COUNTRY, HIMURA...GO TO KYOTO ONCE MORE.
FROM HERE ON, CHAOS WILL DESCEND ON JAPAN.
KENSHIN!!

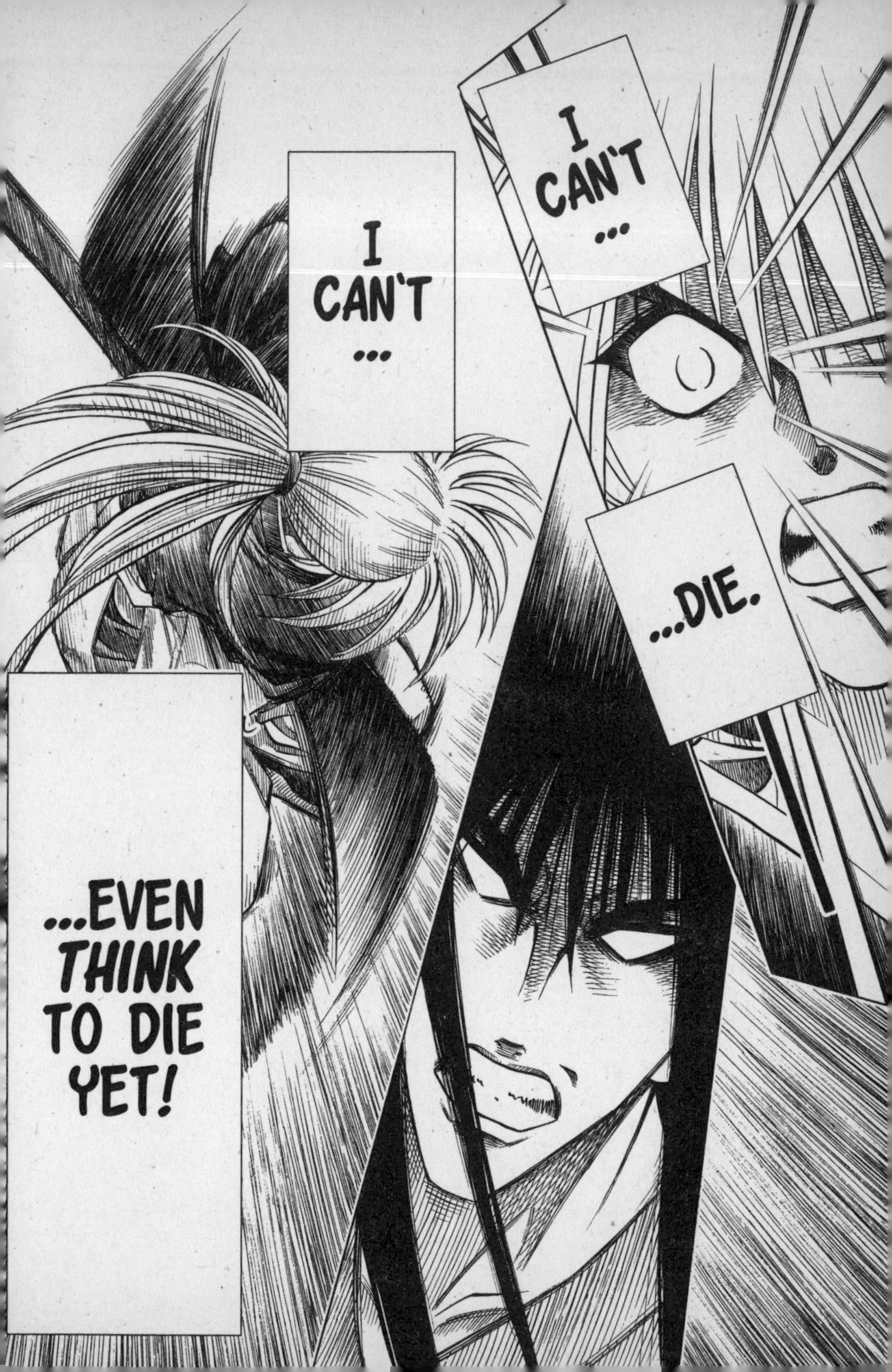
I CAN'T ...
I CAN'T ...
...DIE.
...EVEN THINK TO DIE YET!

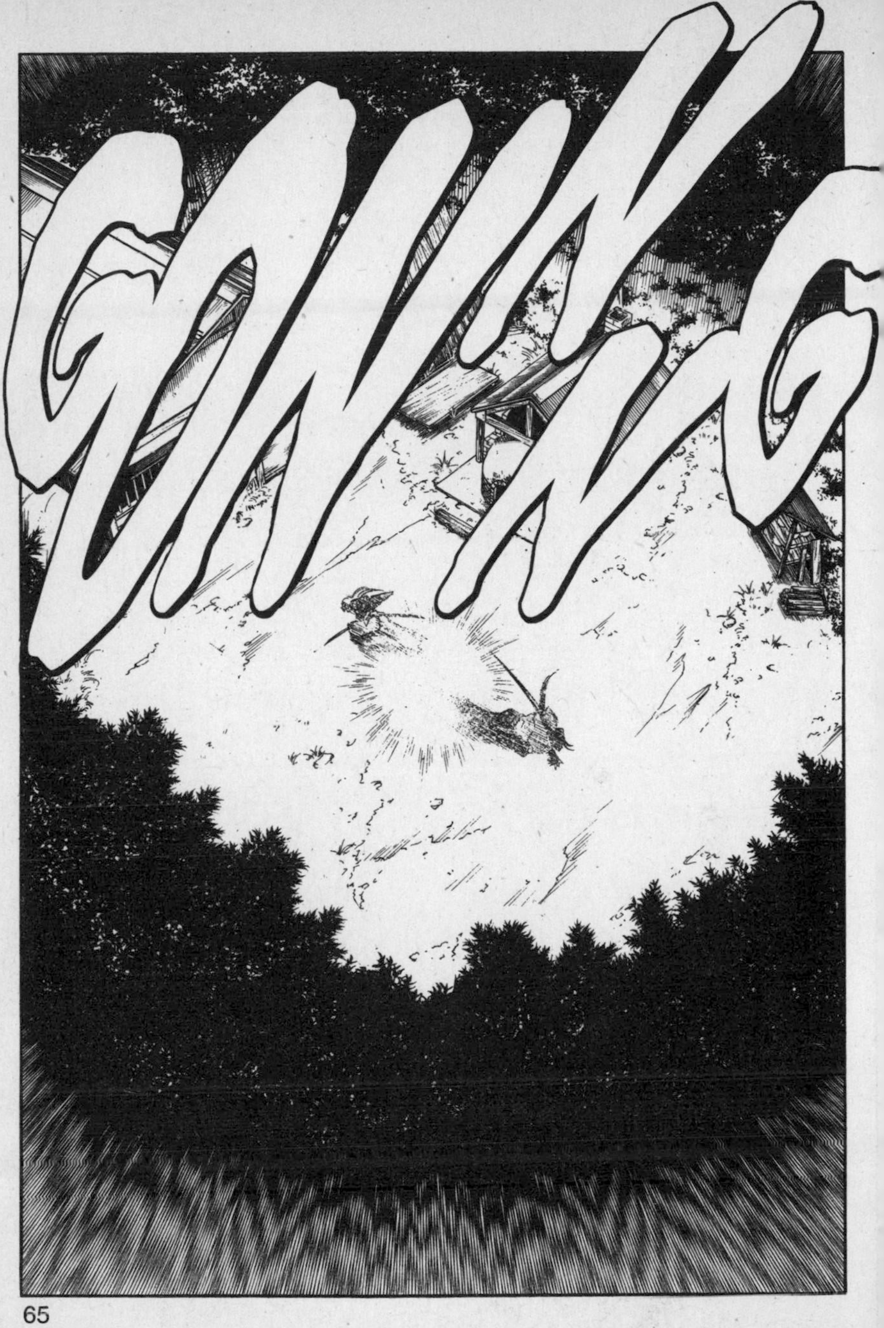

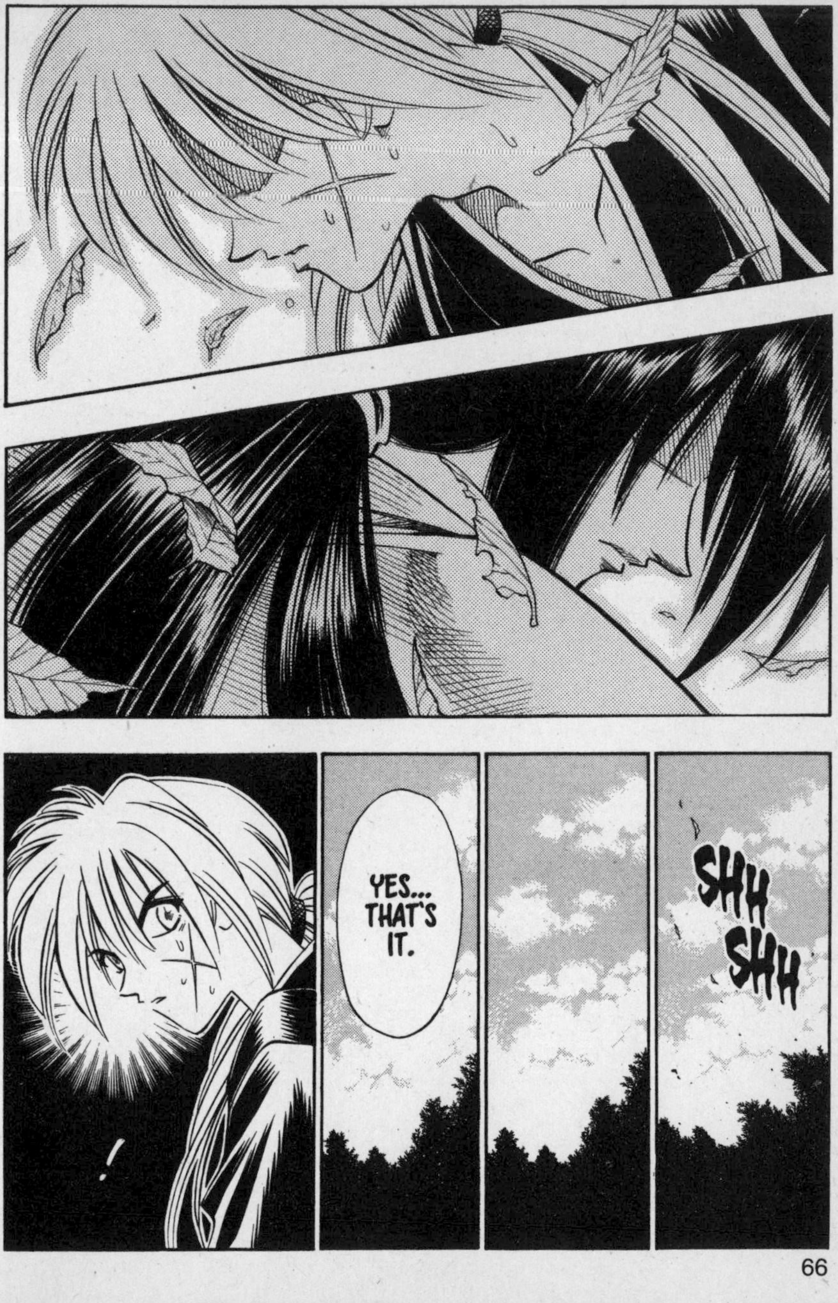
SHH SHH
YES... THAT'S IT.
!

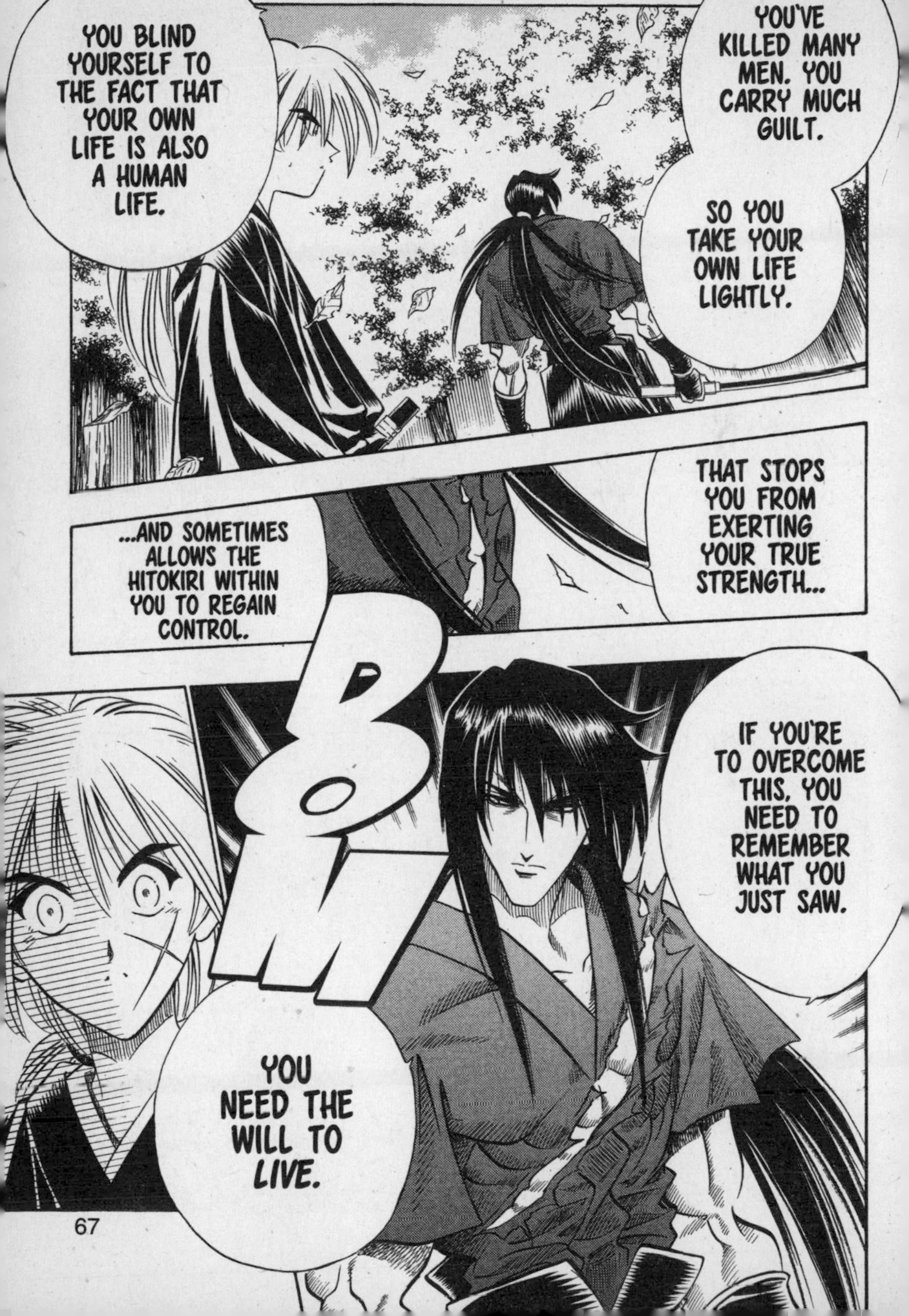
YOU'VE KILLED MANY MEN. YOU CARRY MUCH GUILT.
SO YOU TAKE YOUR OWN LIFE LIGHTLY.
YOU BLIND YOURSELF TO THE FACT THAT YOUR OWN LIFE IS ALSO A HUMAN LIFE.
THAT STOPS YOU FROM EXERTING YOUR TRUE STRENGTH...
...AND SOMETIMES ALLOWS THE HITOKIRI WITHIN YOU TO REGAIN CONTROL.
IF YOU'RE TO OVERCOME THIS, YOU NEED TO REMEMBER WHAT YOU JUST SAW.
BOM
YOU NEED THE WILL TO *LIVE.*

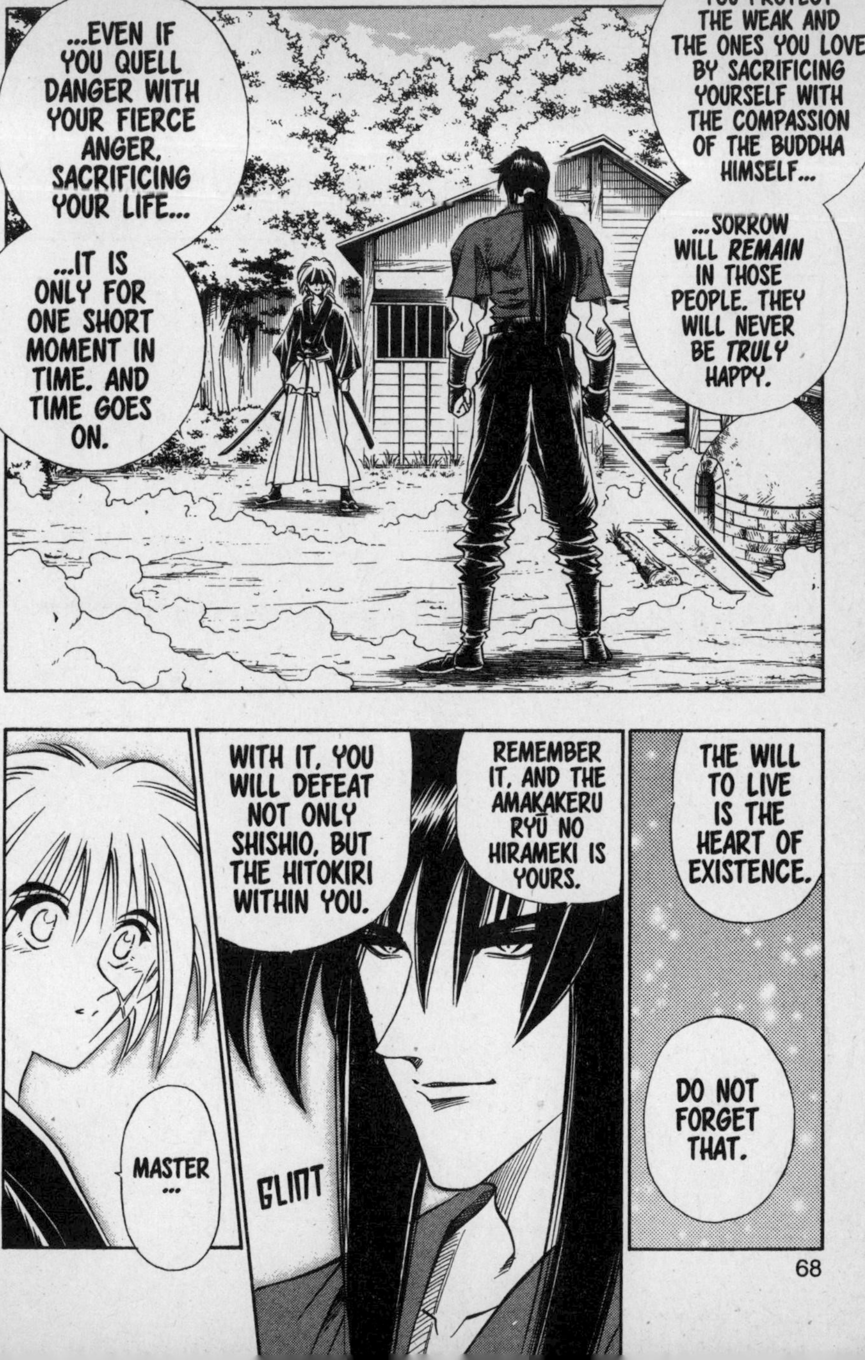
EVEN IF YOU PROTECT THE WEAK AND THE ONES YOU LOVE BY SACRIFICING YOURSELF WITH THE COMPASSION OF THE BUDDHA HIMSELF...
...SORROW WILL *REMAIN* IN THOSE PEOPLE. THEY WILL NEVER BE *TRULY* HAPPY.
...EVEN IF YOU QUELL DANGER WITH YOUR FIERCE ANGER, SACRIFICING YOUR LIFE...
...IT IS ONLY FOR ONE SHORT MOMENT IN TIME. AND TIME GOES ON.
THE WILL TO LIVE IS THE HEART OF EXISTENCE.
DO NOT FORGET THAT.
REMEMBER IT, AND THE AMAKAKERU RYŪ NO HIRAMEKI IS YOURS.
WITH IT, YOU WILL DEFEAT NOT ONLY SHISHIO, BUT THE HITOKIRI WITHIN YOU.
GLINT
MASTER...

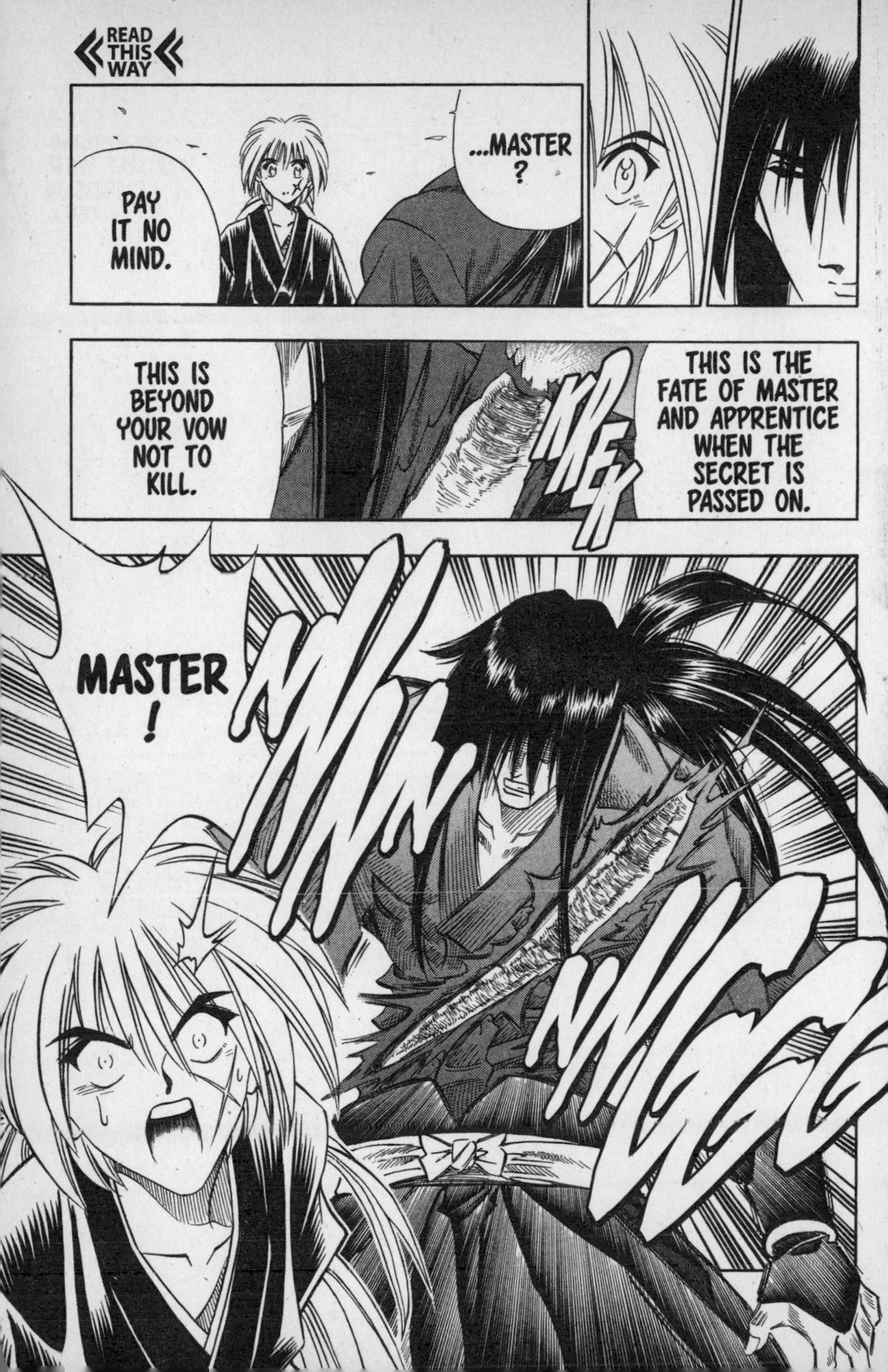
READ THIS WAY
...MASTER ?
PAY IT NO MIND.
THIS IS THE FATE OF MASTER AND APPRENTICE WHEN THE SECRET IS PASSED ON.
THIS IS BEYOND YOUR VOW NOT TO KILL.
MASTER !

Rurouni Kenshin

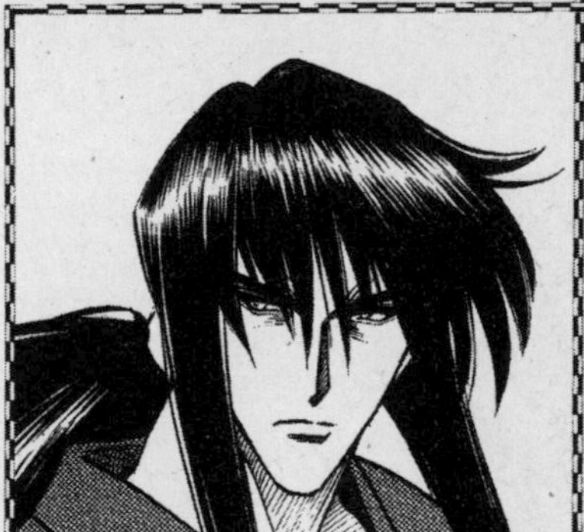

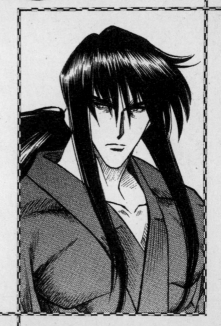

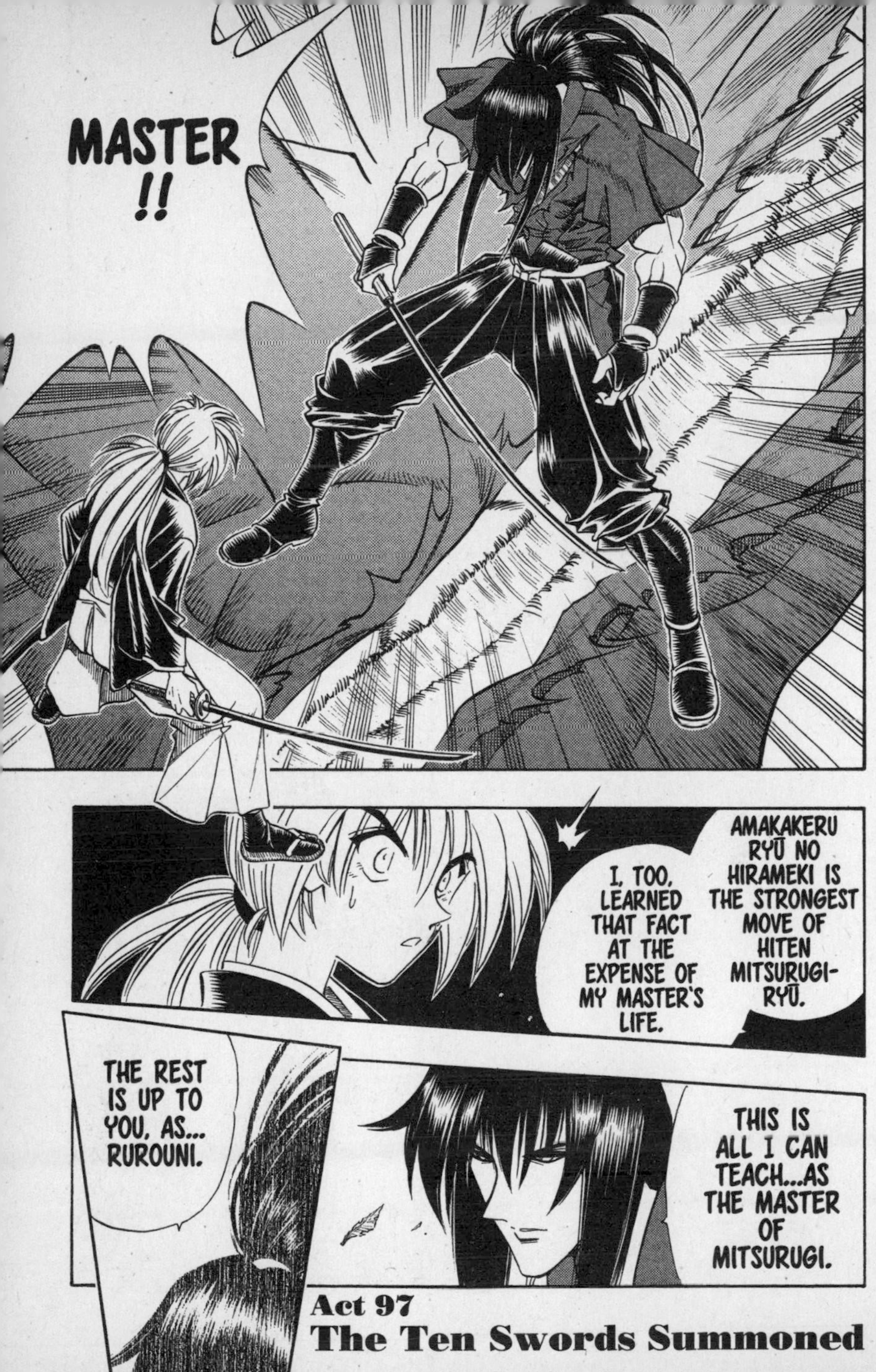

MASTER !!
AMAKAKERU RYŪ NO HIRAMEKI IS THE STRONGEST MOVE OF HITEN MITSURUGI-RYŪ.
I, TOO, LEARNED THAT FACT AT THE EXPENSE OF MY MASTER'S LIFE.
THIS IS ALL I CAN TEACH...AS THE MASTER OF MITSURUGI.
THE REST IS UP TO YOU, AS... RUROUNI.

Act 97
The Ten Swords Summoned

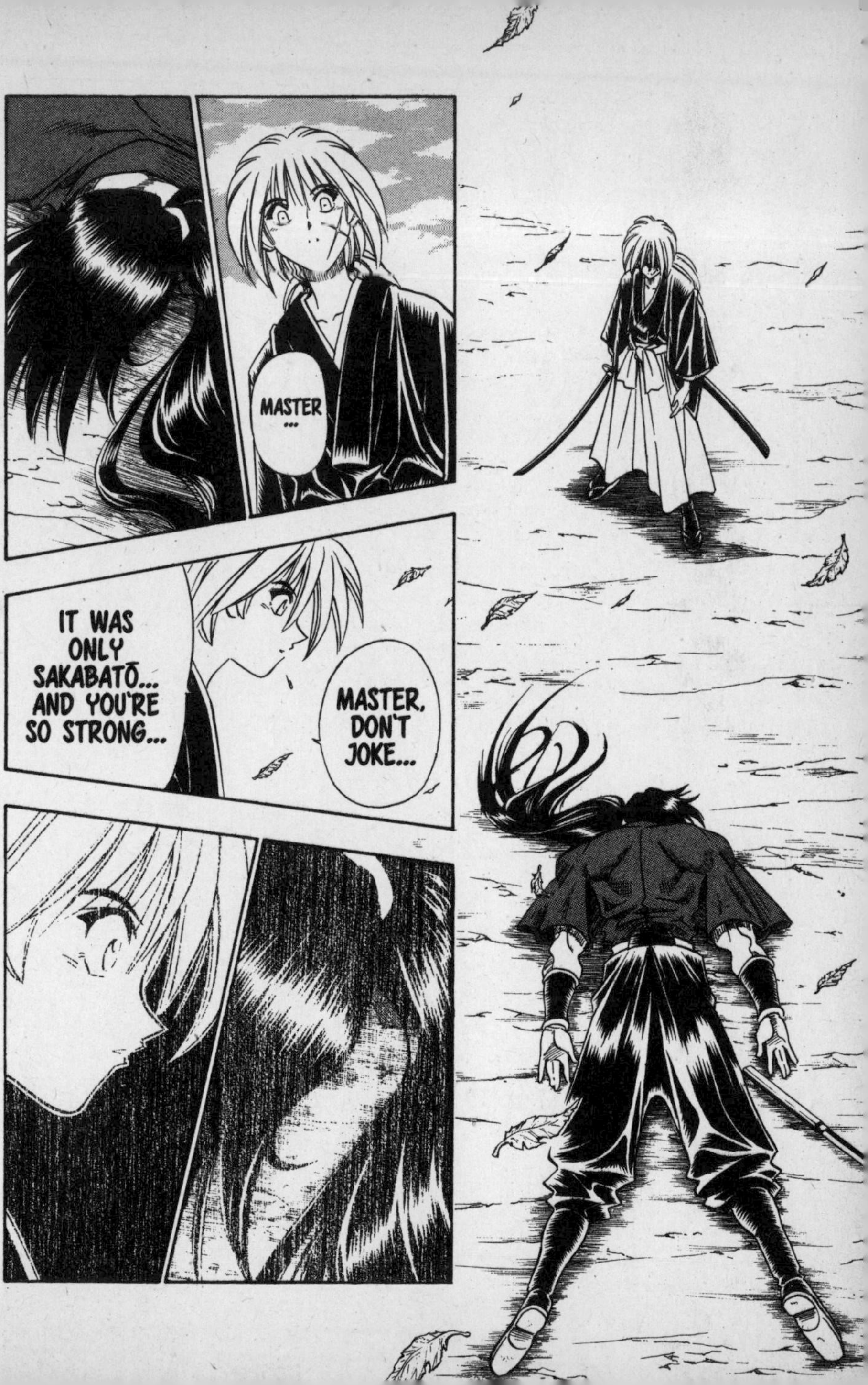
MASTER...
MASTER, DON'T JOKE...
IT WAS ONLY SAKABATŌ... AND YOU'RE SO STRONG...

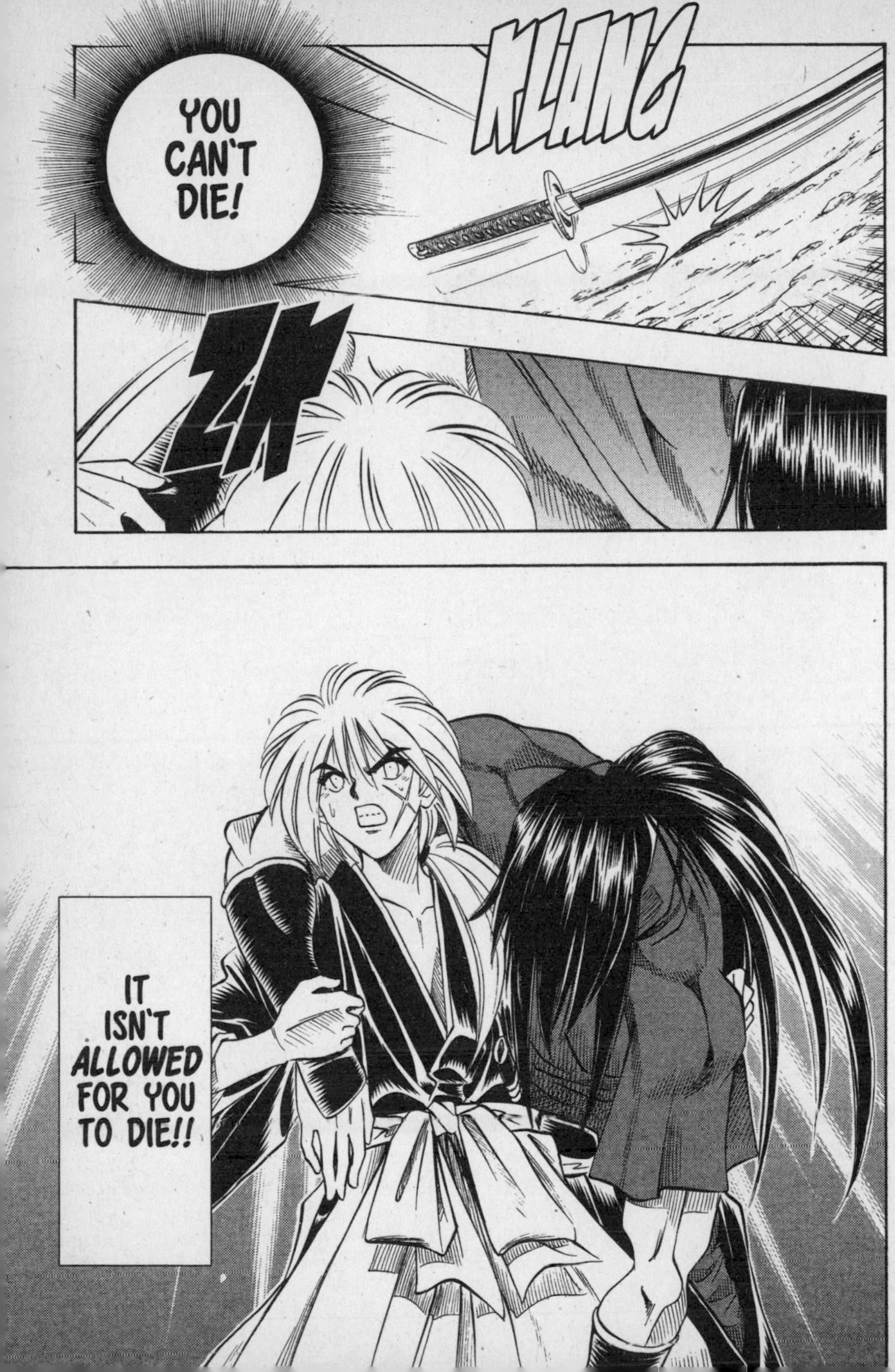
KLANG
YOU CAN'T DIE!
IT ISN'T ALLOWED FOR YOU TO DIE!!

Act 97
The Ten Swords Summoned

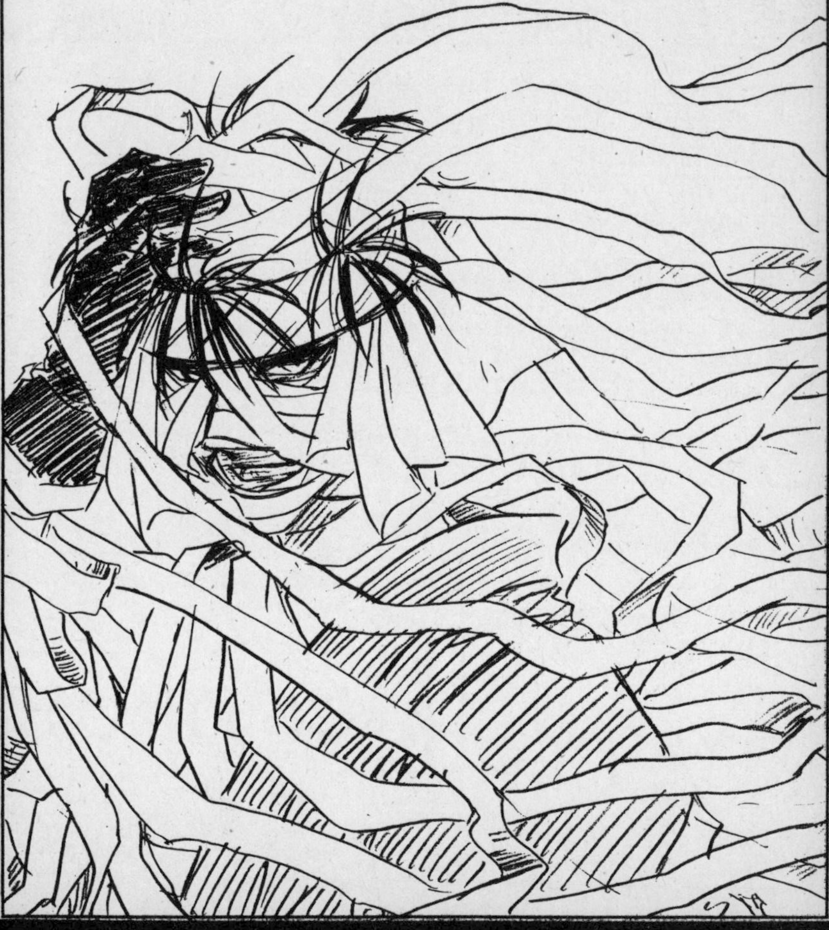

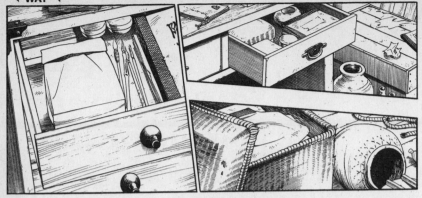

READ THIS WAY

IT'S HERE...
HH
HH
...THE HEART MEDICATION MASTER MADE, BACK DURING THE TIME OF THE POISON MUSHROOMS!
IT'S TOO LATE TO GO DOWN THE MOUNTAIN AND FIND A DOCTOR.
IT'S A LONG SHOT, BUT WITH THIS MEDICINE...
...AND WITH HIS TOUGHNESS... MAYBE...
MASTER!!

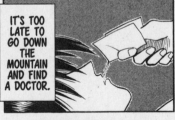

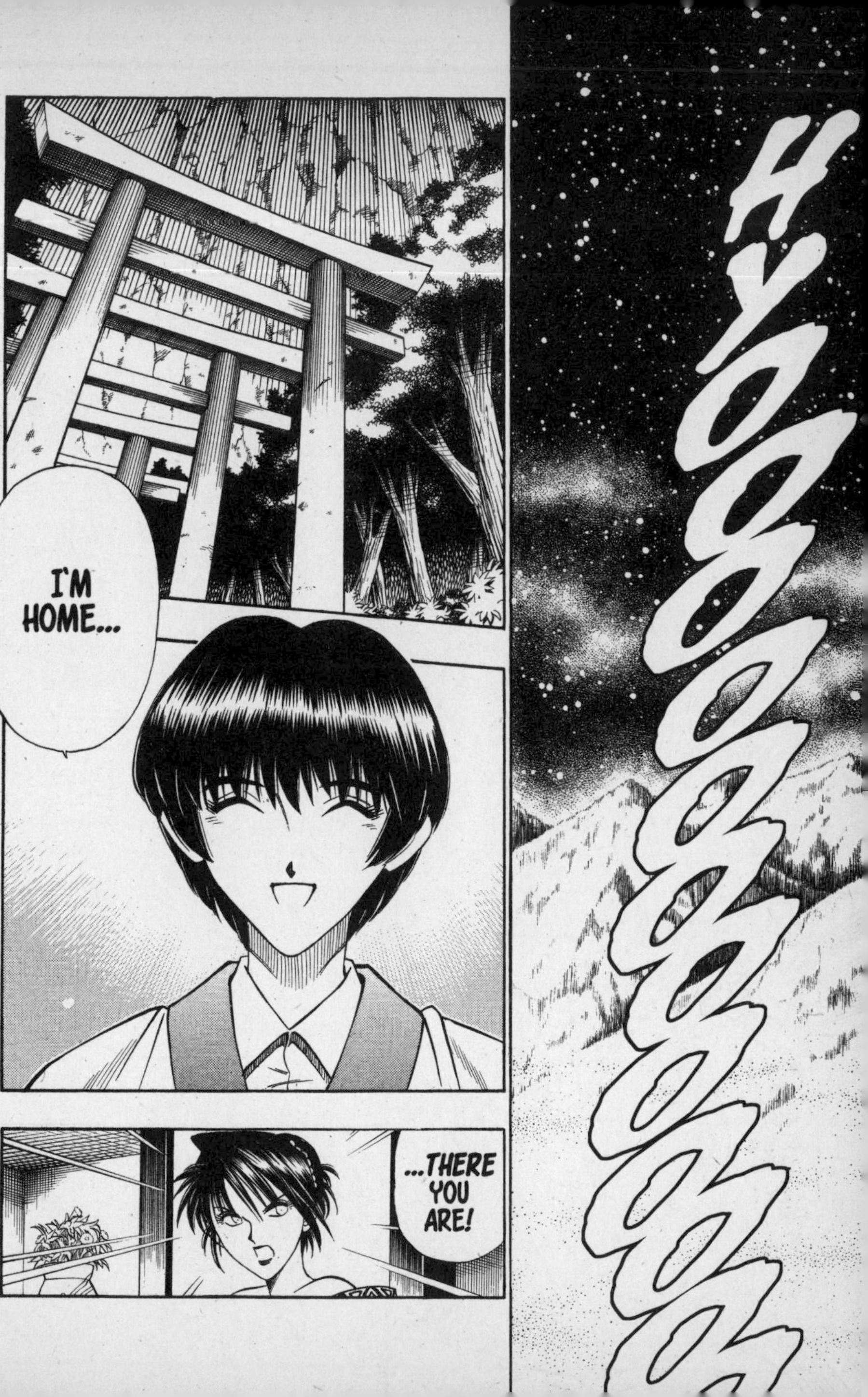
HYOOOOOOOOOOOOOO
I'M HOME...
...THERE YOU ARE!

READ THIS WAY

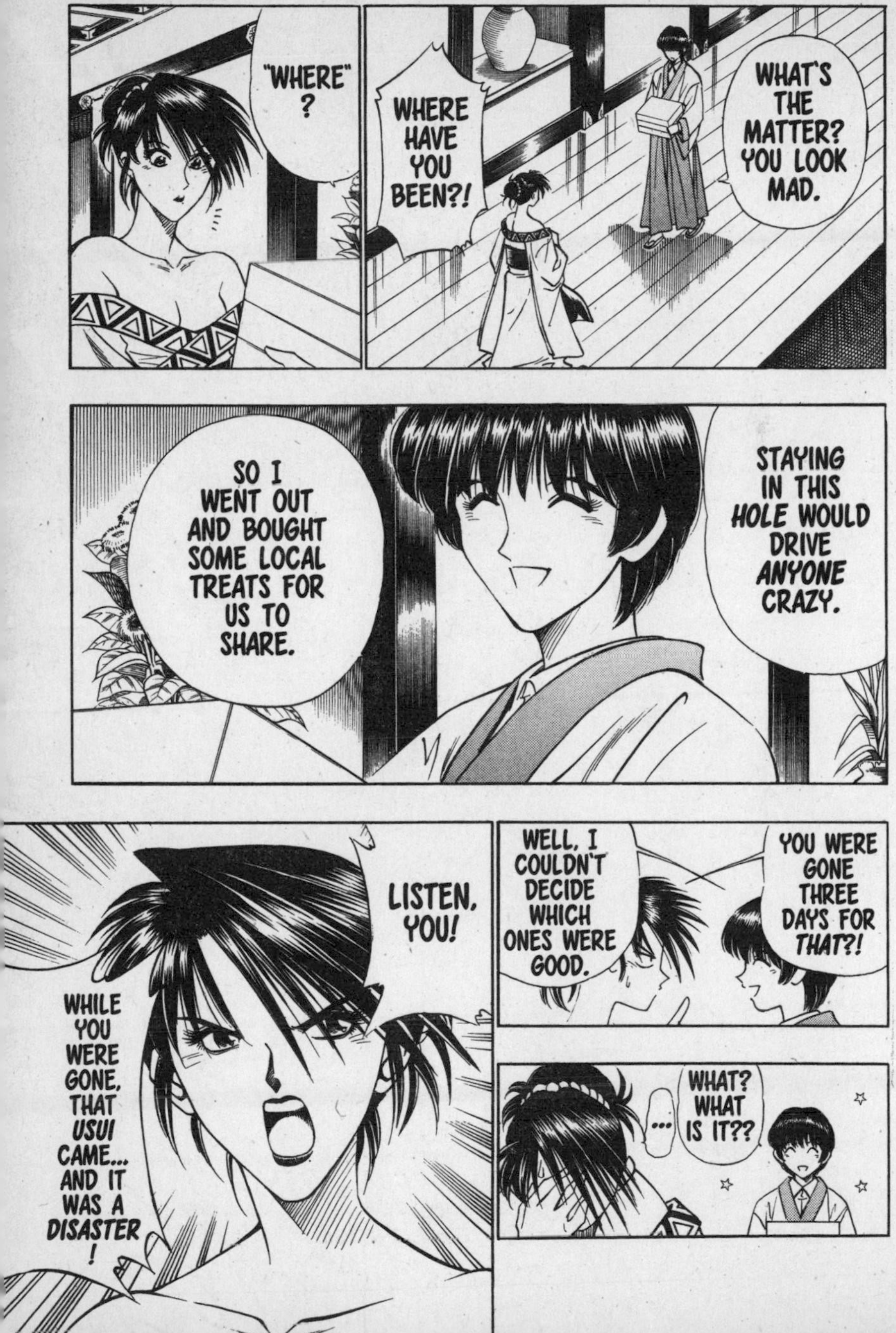
WHAT'S THE MATTER? YOU LOOK MAD.
WHERE HAVE YOU BEEN?!
"WHERE"?
STAYING IN THIS *HOLE* WOULD DRIVE *ANYONE* CRAZY.
SO I WENT OUT AND BOUGHT SOME LOCAL TREATS FOR US TO SHARE.
YOU WERE GONE THREE DAYS FOR *THAT*?!
WELL, I COULDN'T DECIDE WHICH ONES WERE GOOD.
WHAT? WHAT IS IT??
...
LISTEN, YOU!
WHILE YOU WERE GONE, THAT *USUI* CAME... AND IT WAS A *DISASTER*!

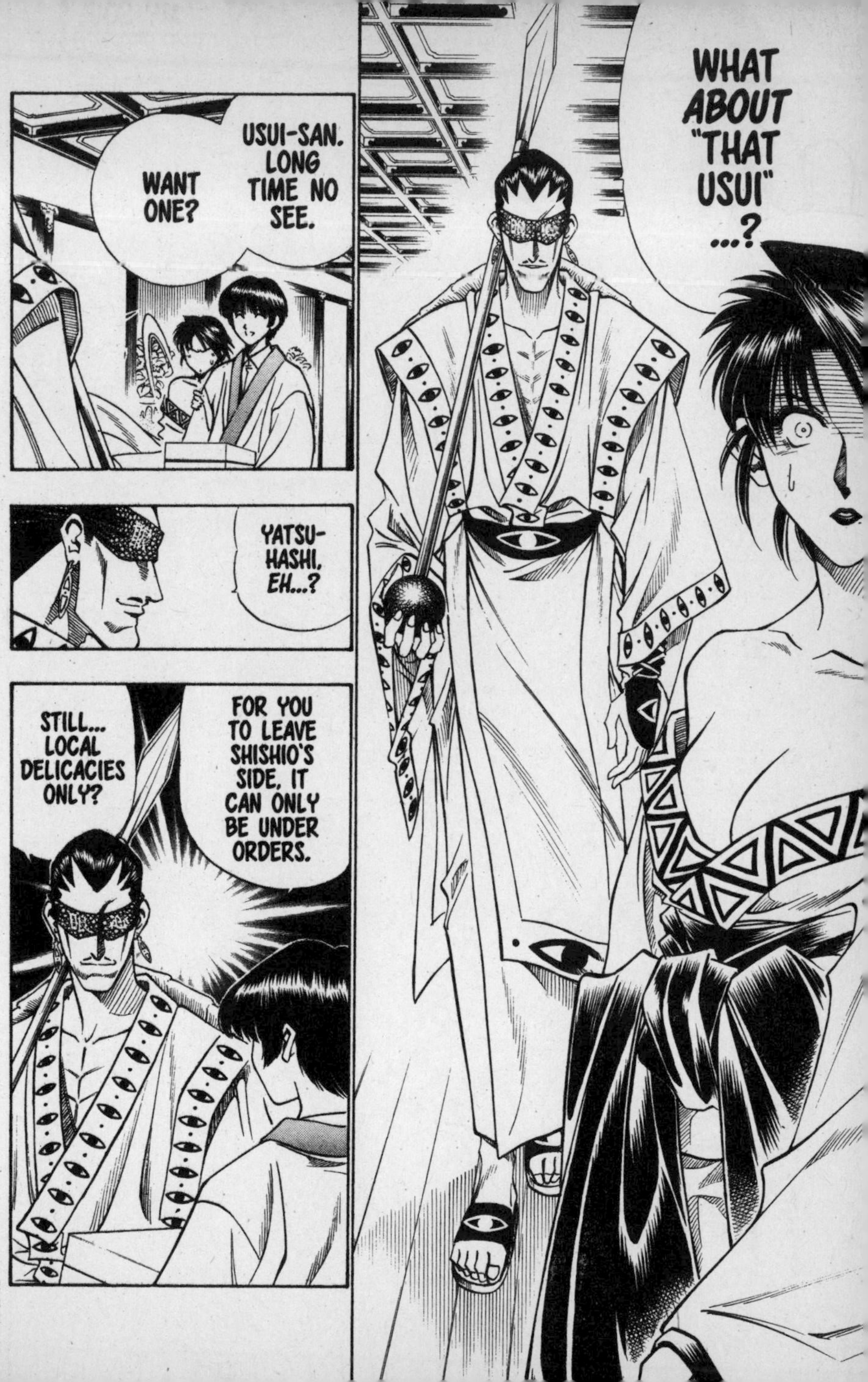
WHAT ABOUT "THAT USUI" ...?
USUI-SAN. LONG TIME NO SEE.
WANT ONE?
YATSU-HASHI, EH...?
FOR YOU TO LEAVE SHISHIO'S SIDE, IT CAN ONLY BE UNDER ORDERS.
STILL... LOCAL DELICACIES ONLY?

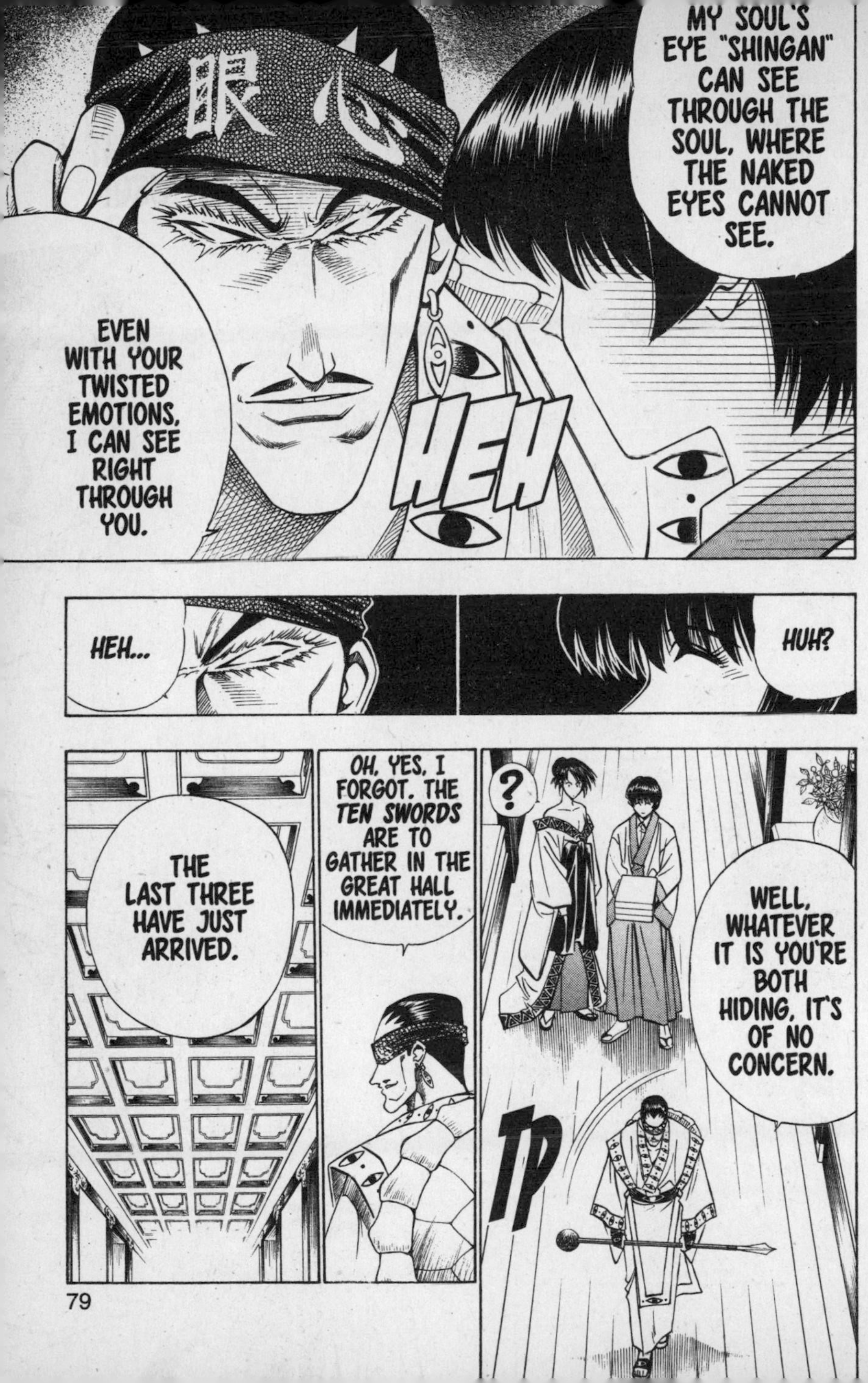

MY SOUL'S EYE "SHINGAN" CAN SEE THROUGH THE SOUL, WHERE THE NAKED EYES CANNOT SEE.
EVEN WITH YOUR TWISTED EMOTIONS, I CAN SEE RIGHT THROUGH YOU.
HEH
HUH?
HEH...
?
WELL, WHATEVER IT IS YOU'RE BOTH HIDING, IT'S OF NO CONCERN.
TP
OH, YES, I FORGOT. THE *TEN SWORDS* ARE TO GATHER IN THE GREAT HALL IMMEDIATELY.
THE LAST THREE HAVE JUST ARRIVED.

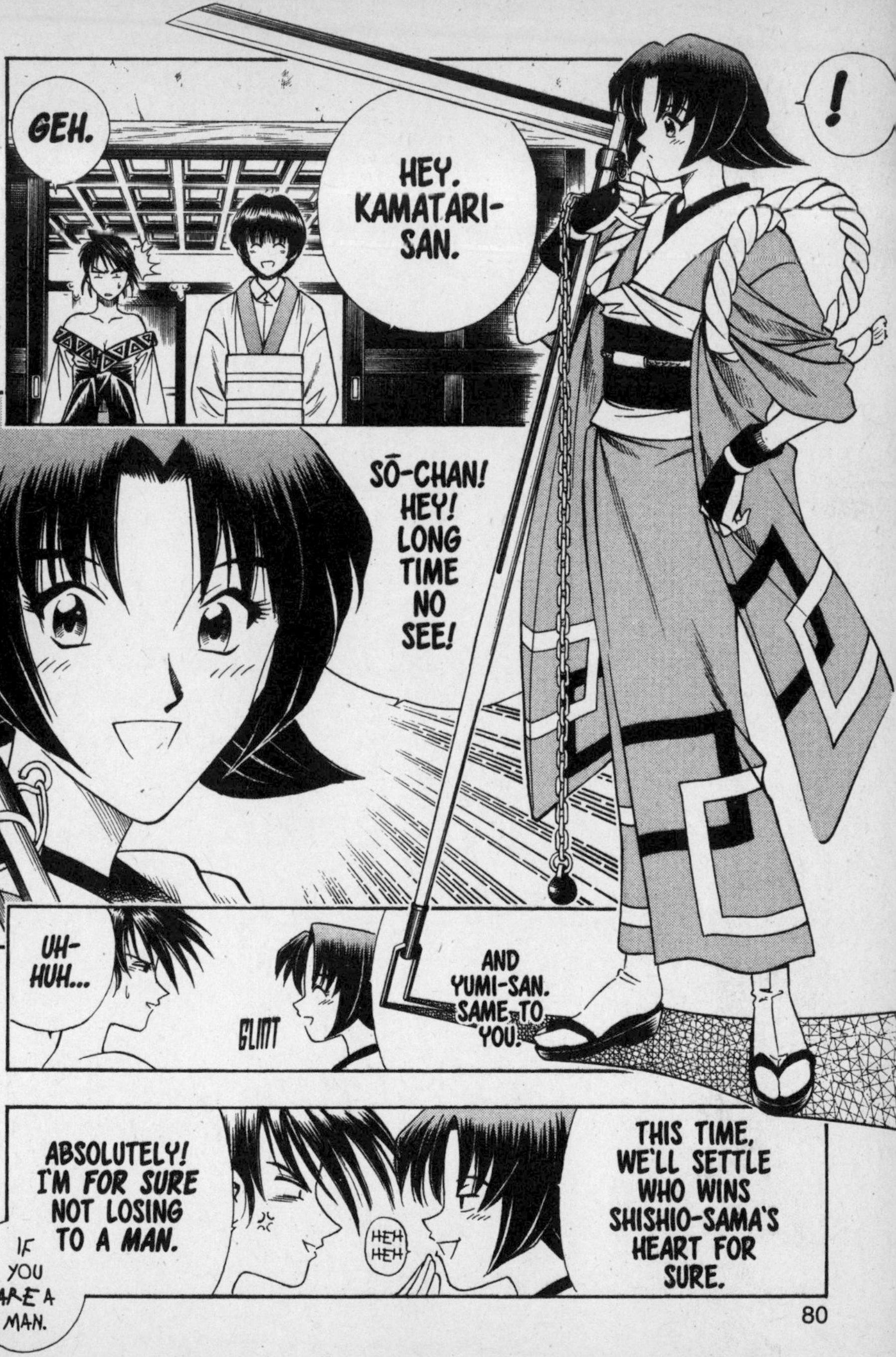
!
HEY. KAMATARI-SAN.
GEH.
SŌ-CHAN! HEY! LONG TIME NO SEE!
AND YUMI-SAN. SAME TO YOU.
GLINT
UH-HUH...
THIS TIME, WE'LL SETTLE WHO WINS SHISHIO-SAMA'S HEART FOR SURE.
HEH HEH
ABSOLUTELY! I'M *FOR SURE* NOT LOSING TO A *MAN*.
IF YOU ARE A MAN.

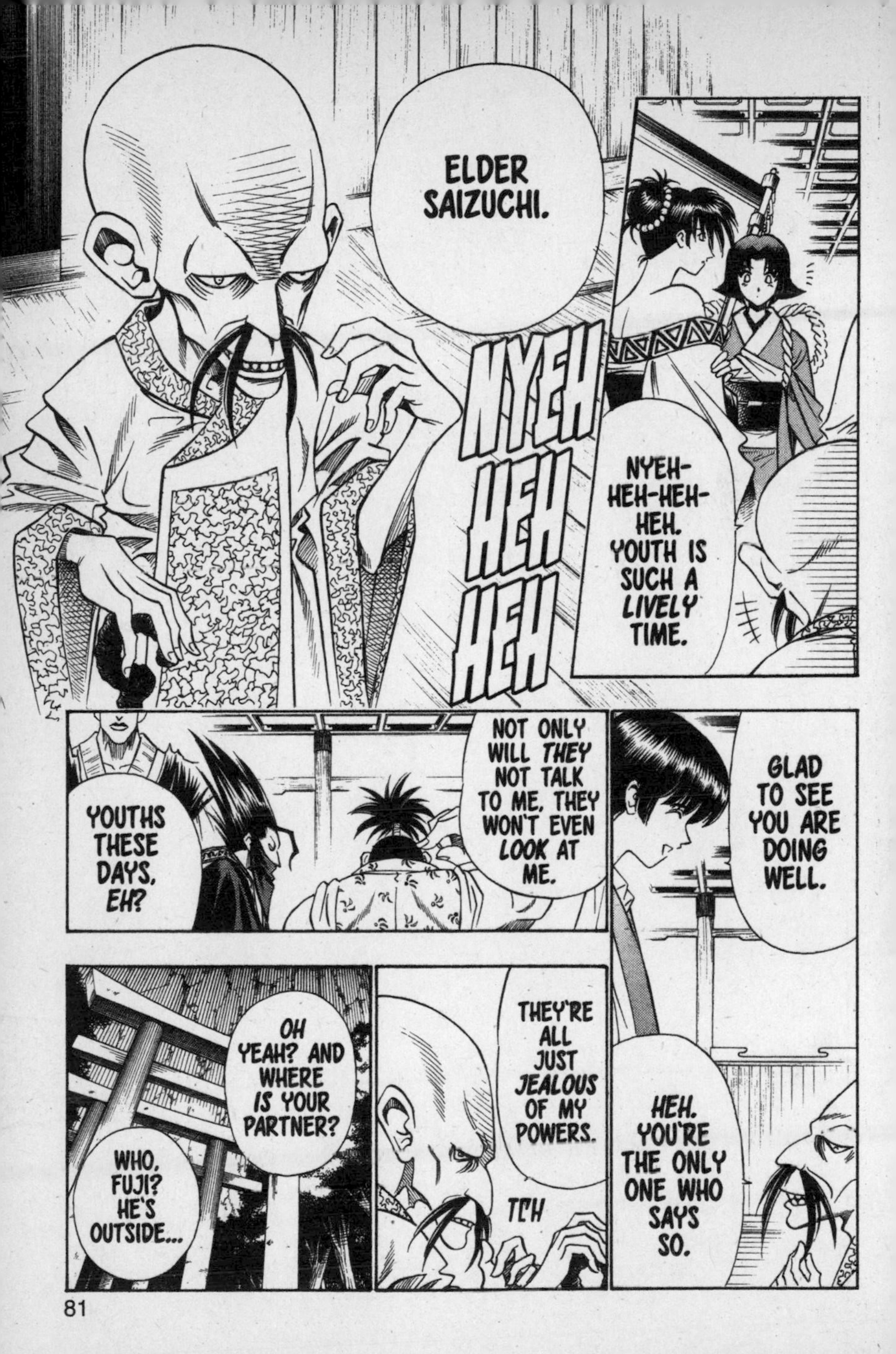
NYEH-HEH-HEH-HEH. YOUTH IS SUCH A *LIVELY* TIME.
ELDER SAIZUCHI.
NYEH HEH HEH HEH
GLAD TO SEE YOU ARE DOING WELL.
NOT ONLY WILL *THEY* NOT TALK TO ME, THEY WON'T EVEN *LOOK* AT ME.
YOUTHS THESE DAYS, *EH?*
HEH. YOU'RE THE ONLY ONE WHO SAYS SO.
THEY'RE ALL JUST *JEALOUS* OF MY POWERS.
TCH
OH YEAH? AND WHERE *IS* YOUR PARTNER?
WHO, FUJI? HE'S OUTSIDE...

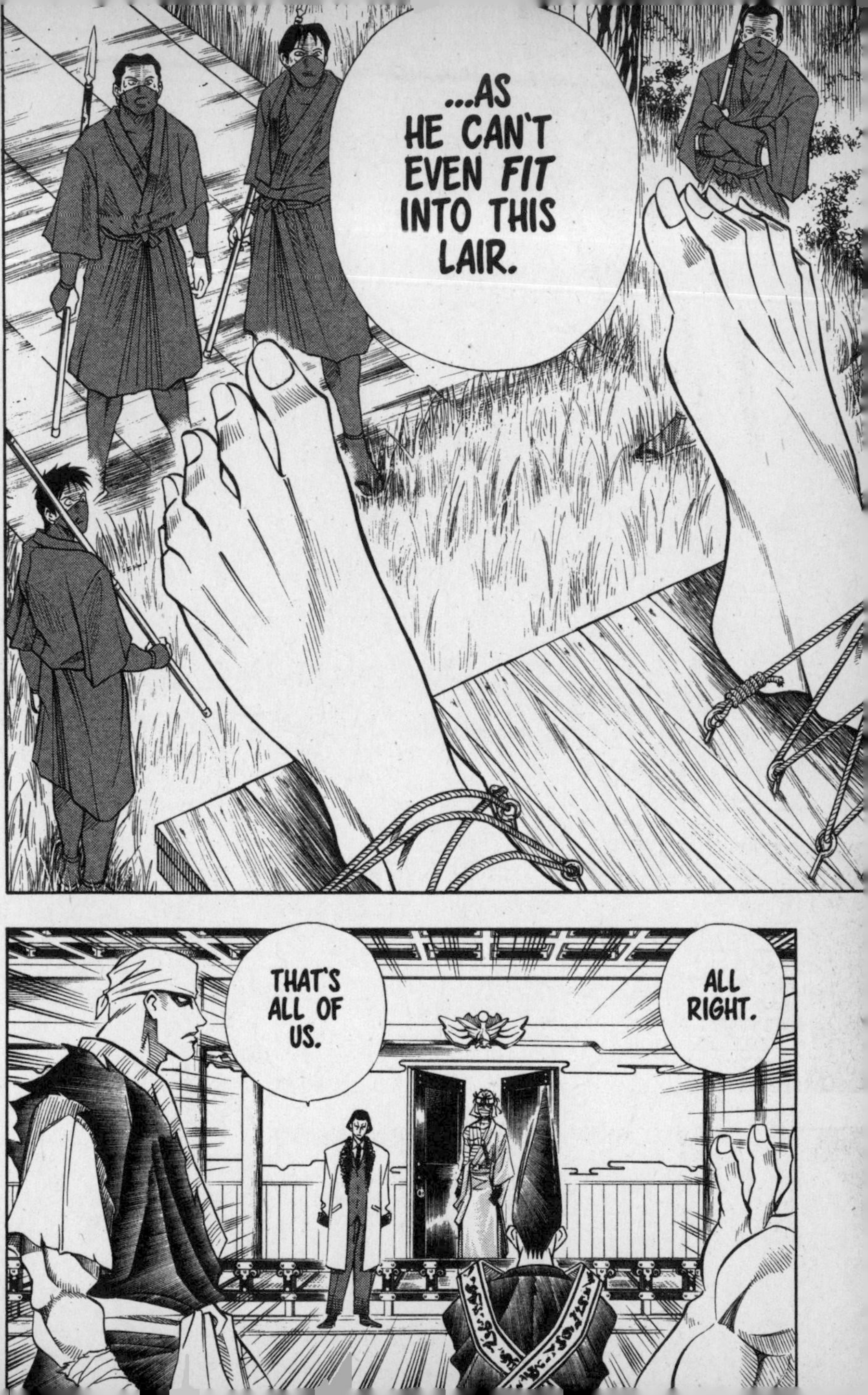
...AS HE CAN'T EVEN FIT INTO THIS LAIR.
ALL RIGHT.
THAT'S ALL OF US.

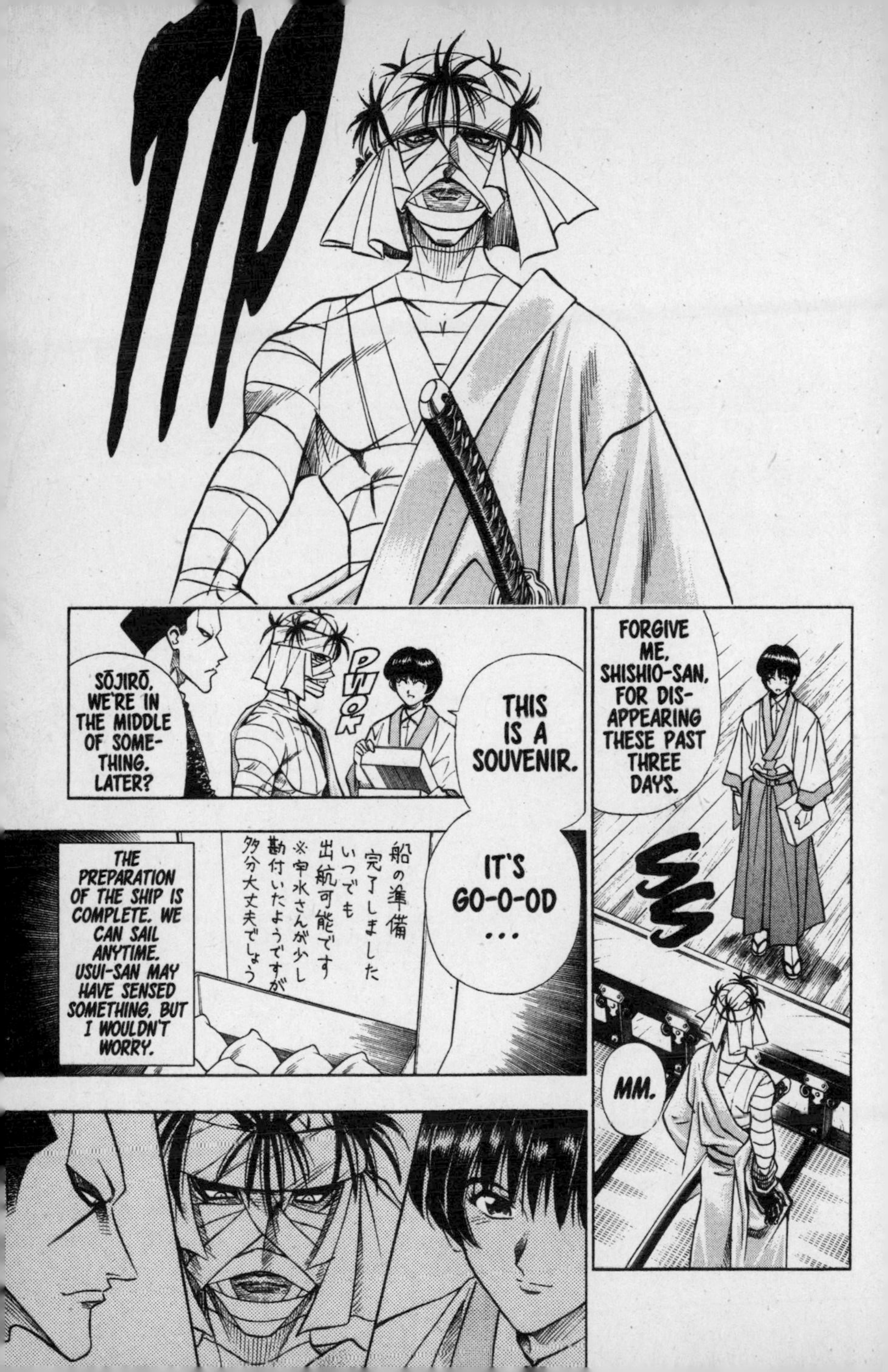
FORGIVE ME, SHISHIO-SAN, FOR DIS-APPEARING THESE PAST THREE DAYS.
SS
MM.
THIS IS A SOUVENIR.
PWOK
SŌJIRŌ, WE'RE IN THE MIDDLE OF SOME-THING. LATER?
IT'S GO-O-OD ...
船の準備完了しました いつでも出航可能です ※宇水さんが少し勘付いたようですが 多分大丈夫でしょう
THE PREPARATION OF THE SHIP IS COMPLETE. WE CAN SAIL ANYTIME. USUI-SAN MAY HAVE SENSED SOMETHING, BUT I WOULDN'T WORRY.

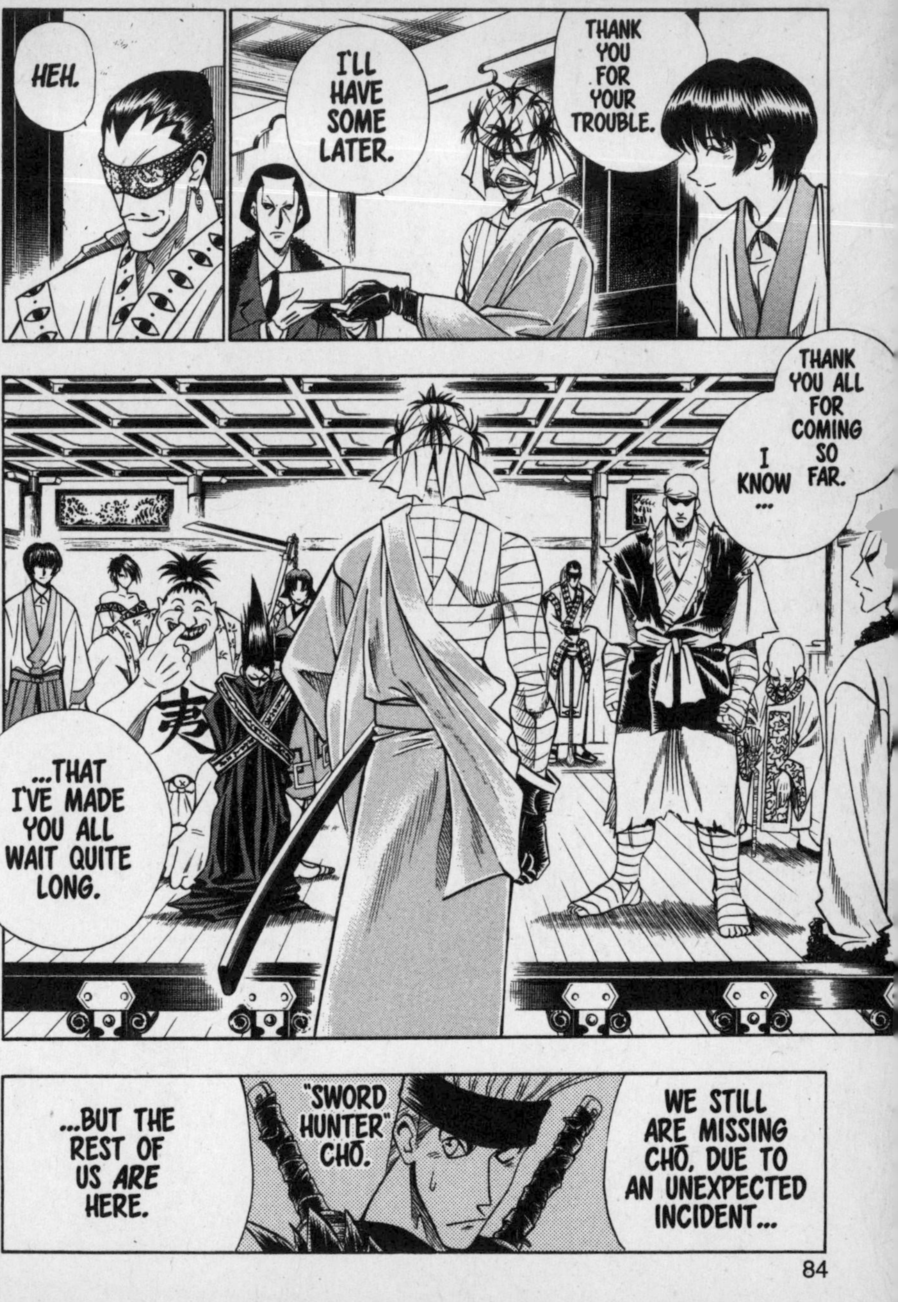
THANK YOU FOR YOUR TROUBLE.
I'LL HAVE SOME LATER.
HEH.
THANK YOU ALL FOR COMING SO FAR.
I KNOW...
...THAT I'VE MADE YOU ALL WAIT QUITE LONG.
WE STILL ARE MISSING CHŌ, DUE TO AN UNEXPECTED INCIDENT...
"SWORD HUNTER" CHŌ.
...BUT THE REST OF US *ARE* HERE.

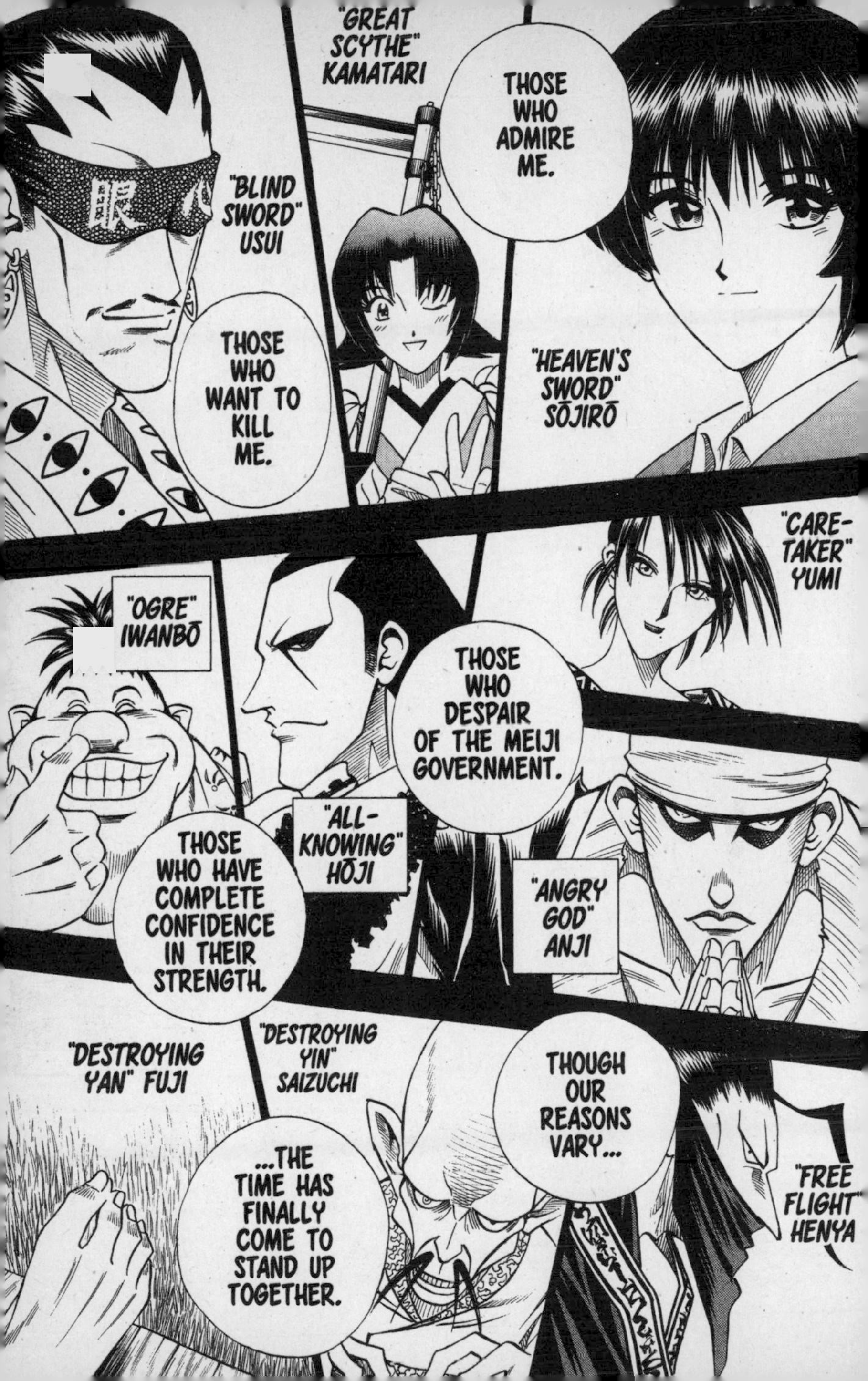
"HEAVEN'S SWORD" SŌJIRŌ
"GREAT SCYTHE" KAMATARI
THOSE WHO ADMIRE ME.
"BLIND SWORD" USUI
THOSE WHO WANT TO KILL ME.
"CARE-TAKER" YUMI
THOSE WHO DESPAIR OF THE MEIJI GOVERNMENT.
"ANGRY GOD" ANJI
"ALL-KNOWING" HŌJI
THOSE WHO HAVE COMPLETE CONFIDENCE IN THEIR STRENGTH.
"OGRE" IWANBŌ
"FREE FLIGHT" HENYA
THOUGH OUR REASONS VARY...
"DESTROYING YIN" SAIZUCHI
...THE TIME HAS FINALLY COME TO STAND UP TOGETHER.
"DESTROYING YAN" FUJI

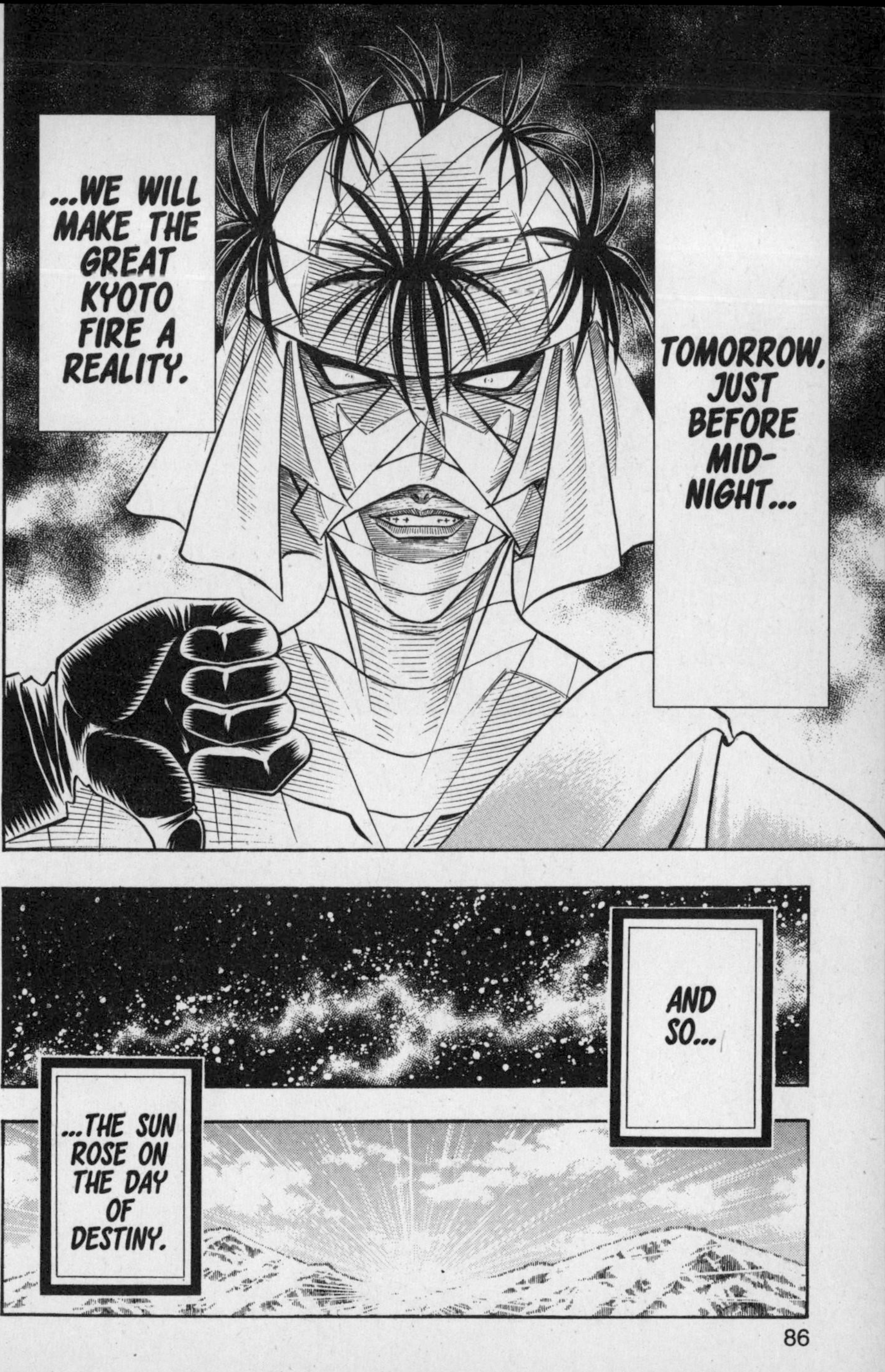
TOMORROW, JUST BEFORE MID-NIGHT...
...WE WILL MAKE THE GREAT KYOTO FIRE A REALITY.
AND SO...
...THE SUN ROSE ON THE DAY OF DESTINY.

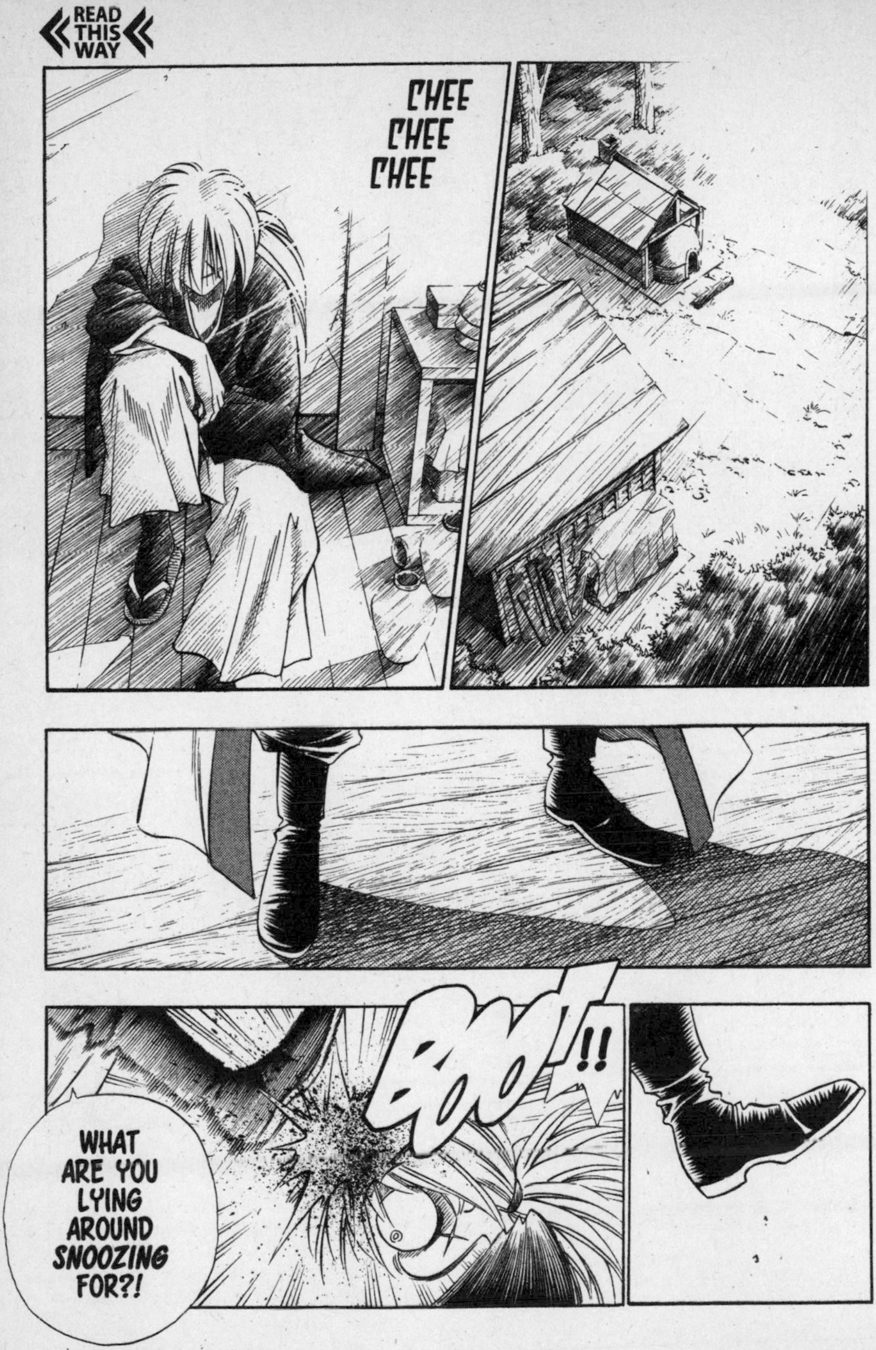
READ THIS WAY
CHEE CHEE CHEE
BOOT!!
WHAT ARE YOU LYING AROUND SNOOZING FOR?!

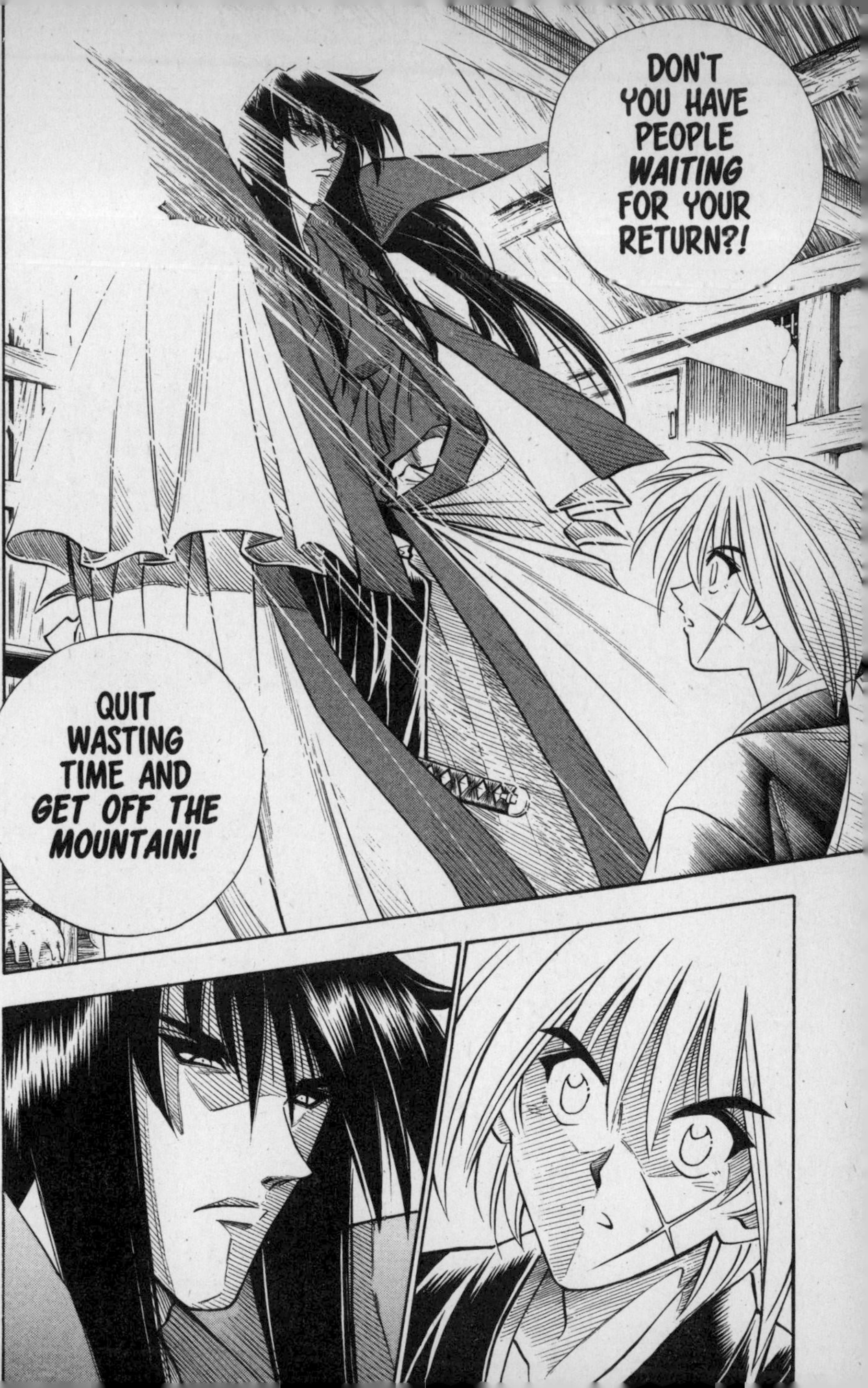
DON'T YOU HAVE PEOPLE WAITING FOR YOUR RETURN?!
QUIT WASTING TIME AND GET OFF THE MOUNTAIN!

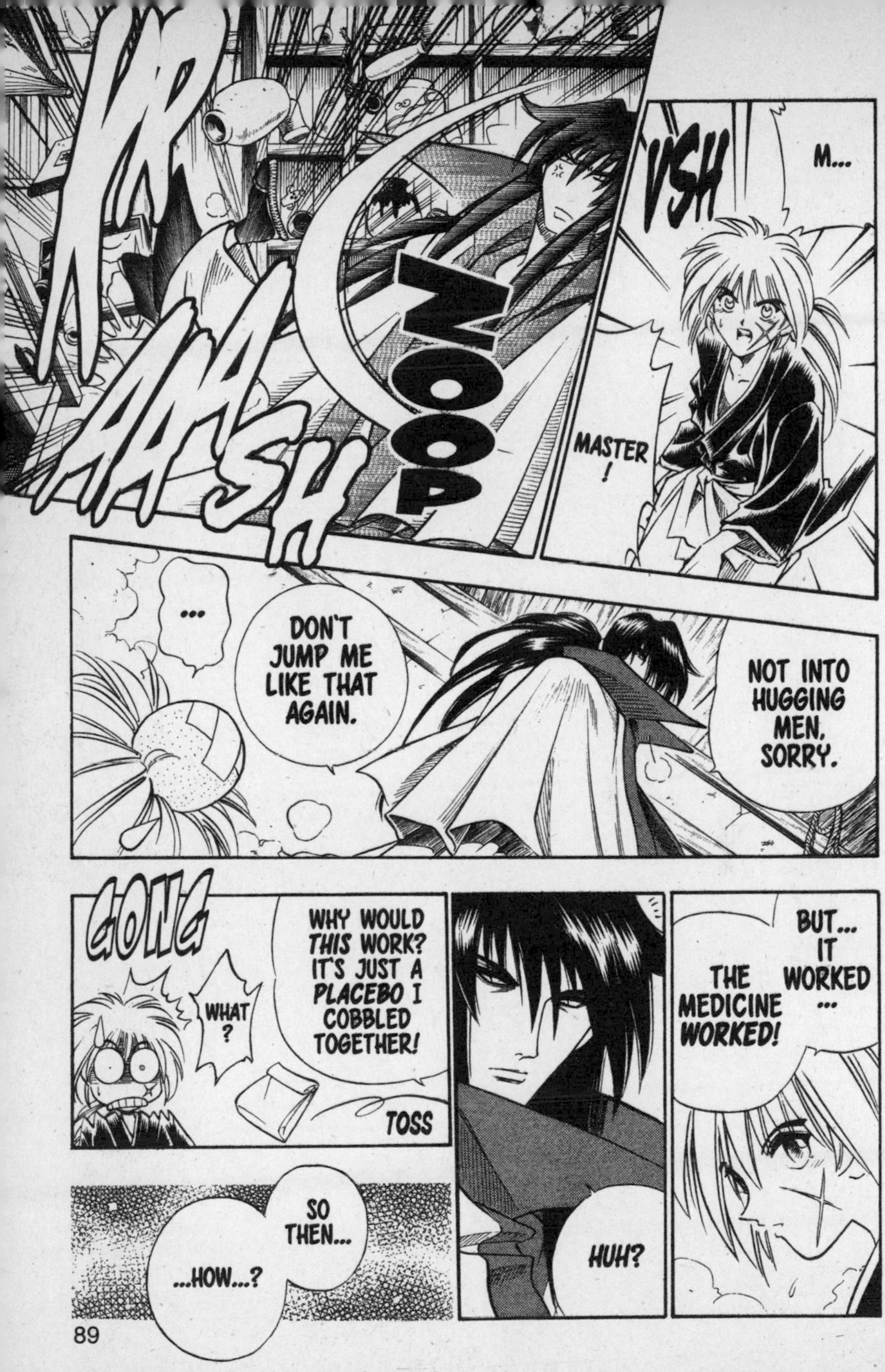
VSH
M...
MASTER!
WHOOP
NOT INTO HUGGING MEN, SORRY.
DON'T JUMP ME LIKE THAT AGAIN.
...
BUT... IT WORKED...
THE MEDICINE WORKED!
HUH?
WHY WOULD *THIS* WORK? IT'S JUST A *PLACEBO* I COBBLED TOGETHER!
GONG
WHAT?
TOSS
SO THEN...
...HOW...?

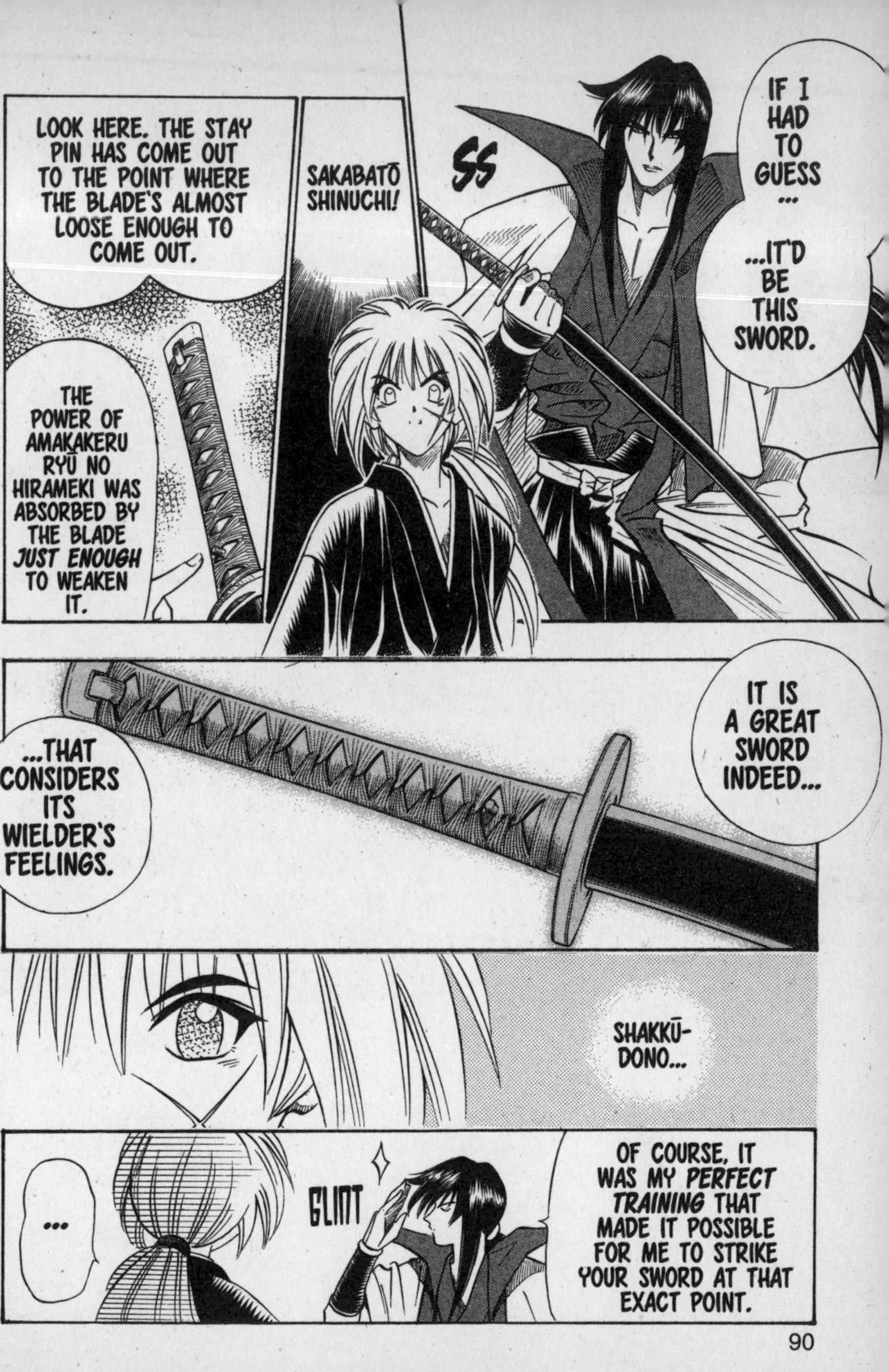
IF I HAD TO GUESS...
...IT'D BE THIS SWORD.
SS
SAKABATŌ SHINUCHI!
LOOK HERE. THE STAY PIN HAS COME OUT TO THE POINT WHERE THE BLADE'S ALMOST LOOSE ENOUGH TO COME OUT.
THE POWER OF AMAKAKERU RYŪ NO HIRAMEKI WAS ABSORBED BY THE BLADE *JUST ENOUGH* TO WEAKEN IT.
IT IS A GREAT SWORD INDEED...
...THAT CONSIDERS ITS WIELDER'S FEELINGS.
SHAKKŪ-DONO...
OF COURSE, IT WAS MY *PERFECT TRAINING* THAT MADE IT POSSIBLE FOR ME TO STRIKE YOUR SWORD AT THAT EXACT POINT.
GLINT
...

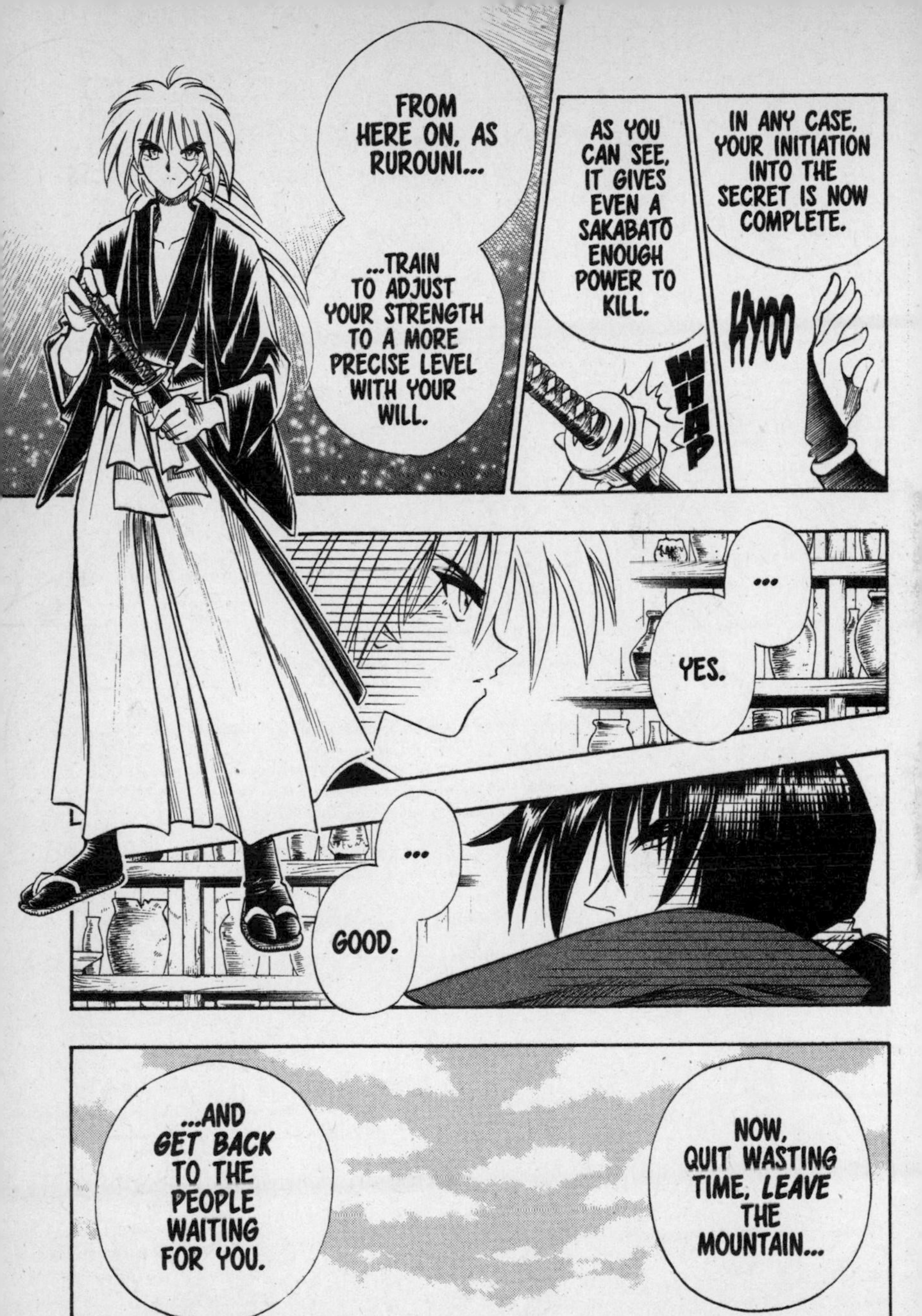
IN ANY CASE, YOUR INITIATION INTO THE SECRET IS NOW COMPLETE.
HYOO
AS YOU CAN SEE, IT GIVES EVEN A SAKABATO ENOUGH POWER TO KILL.
WHAP
...
YES.
...
GOOD.
FROM HERE ON, AS RUROUNI...
...TRAIN TO ADJUST YOUR STRENGTH TO A MORE PRECISE LEVEL WITH YOUR WILL.
NOW, QUIT WASTING TIME, *LEAVE* THE MOUNTAIN...
...AND *GET BACK* TO THE PEOPLE WAITING FOR YOU.

The Secret Life of Characters (32)

—Hiko Seijūrō—

Personality-wise, there's no model. When Watsuki sat down to imagine what sort of guy the "Master" might be, the character at first became this arrogant, twisted guy. As one of my favorites, I actually wanted to give the guy more appearances...but then again, he *is* stronger than Kenshin and, as my editor puts it, "(The Master) is like the joker in a card deck." In other words, he's just too powerful—it's hard to find a place to use him.

This is a little off-topic, but lately Watsuki has found himself fascinated by images of "manliness," and Hiko is one of the first characters to reflect that fascination. The drinking scenes come from Watsuki's own low tolerance for alcohol, and because Watsuki sees a sort of manliness in the image of a man drinking alone (not that Hiko is a drunk). There've been lots of questions lately asking if this Hiko is related to the Hiko Seijūrō in "Crescent Moon of the Warring States," but as Hiten Mitsurugi-ryū is passed on through potential, and not blood, there's no *biologica*l relation, no.

The Hiko Seijūrō of "Crescent Moon" is the model design-wise (of course), but I also threw in a bit of "Hiken Majin Hamerun" from Master Obata's "Arabian Lamp Lamp" (Obata-*shishō*, forgive me!).

In setting the character within the context of "RuroKen," I ended up simplifying his design, such as fixing his hair to be easier to draw. What with his being a completely different type of Hiten Mitsurugi-ryū swordsman, and with the above-mentioned "manliness" as well, his body became a macho one. If there are female fans who liked the face but not so much the body, sorry about that! (Still, if every new character was "just another good-looking guy," how interesting would that be? Watsuki knows *he* wouldn't enjoy it....)

As for the cloak...okay, yes...there's a bit of the American comic "Spawn" in it.

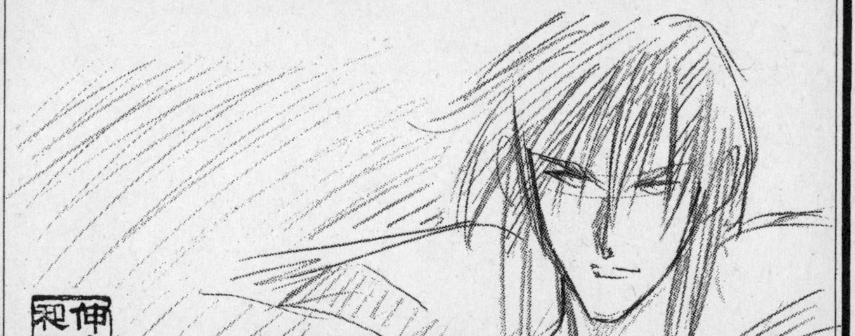
和月伸宏

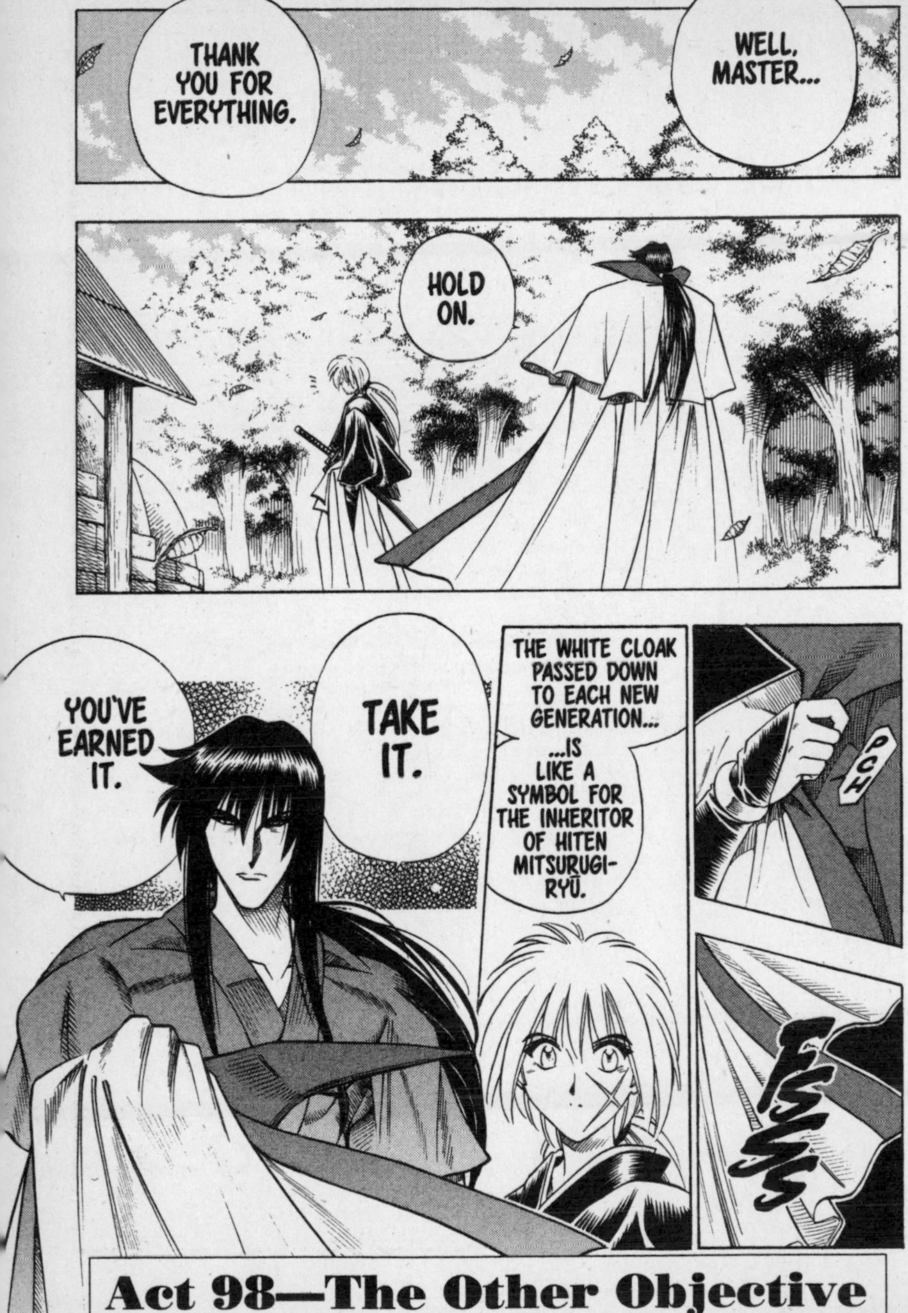
WELL, MASTER...
THANK YOU FOR EVERYTHING.
HOLD ON.
PCH
FSSS
THE WHITE CLOAK PASSED DOWN TO EACH NEW GENERATION...
...IS LIKE A SYMBOL FOR THE INHERITOR OF HITEN MITSURUGI-RYŪ.
TAKE IT.
YOU'VE EARNED IT.

Act 98—The Other Objective

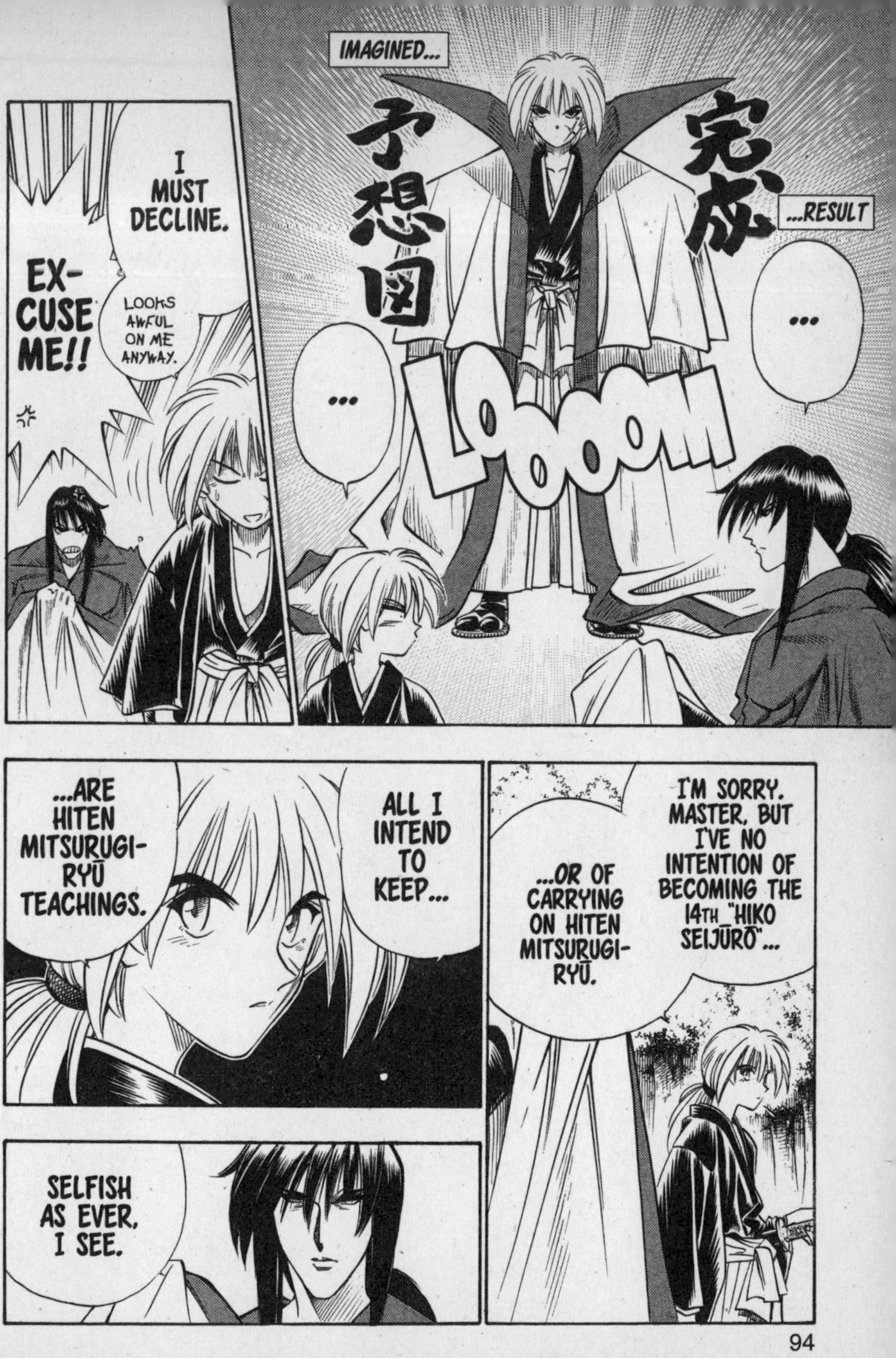
IMAGINED...
予想図
完成
...RESULT
...
LOOOOM
...
I MUST DECLINE.
LOOKS AWFUL ON ME ANYWAY.
EX-CUSE ME!!
I'M SORRY. MASTER, BUT I'VE NO INTENTION OF BECOMING THE 14TH "HIKO SEIJŪRŌ"...
...OR OF CARRYING ON HITEN MITSURUGI-RYŪ.
ALL I INTEND TO KEEP...
...ARE HITEN MITSURUGI-RYŪ TEACHINGS.
SELFISH AS EVER, I SEE.

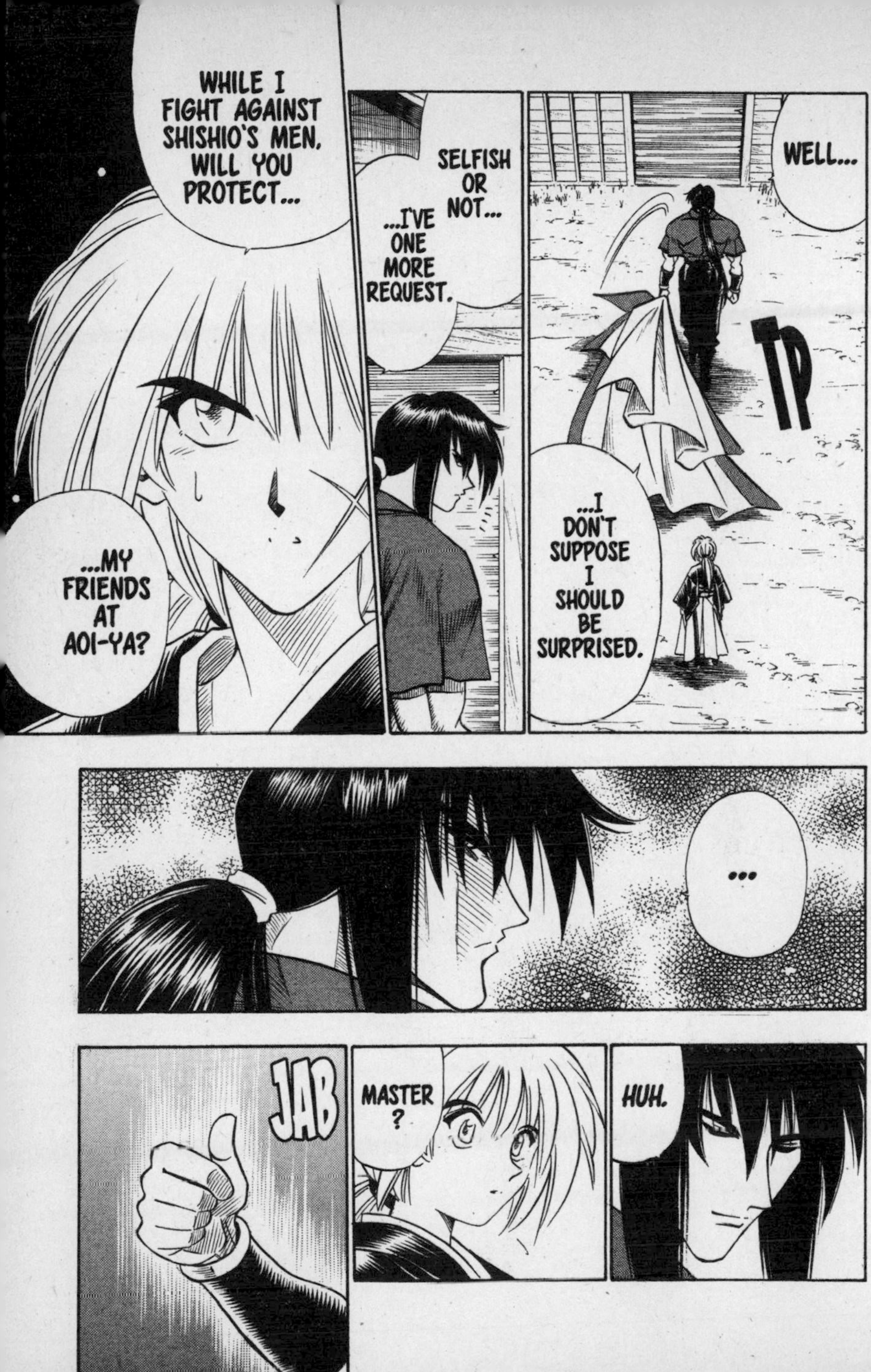
WELL...
TP
...I DON'T SUPPOSE I SHOULD BE SURPRISED.
SELFISH OR NOT...
...I'VE ONE MORE REQUEST.
WHILE I FIGHT AGAINST SHISHIO'S MEN, WILL YOU PROTECT...
...MY FRIENDS AT AOI-YA?
...
HUH.
MASTER?
JAB

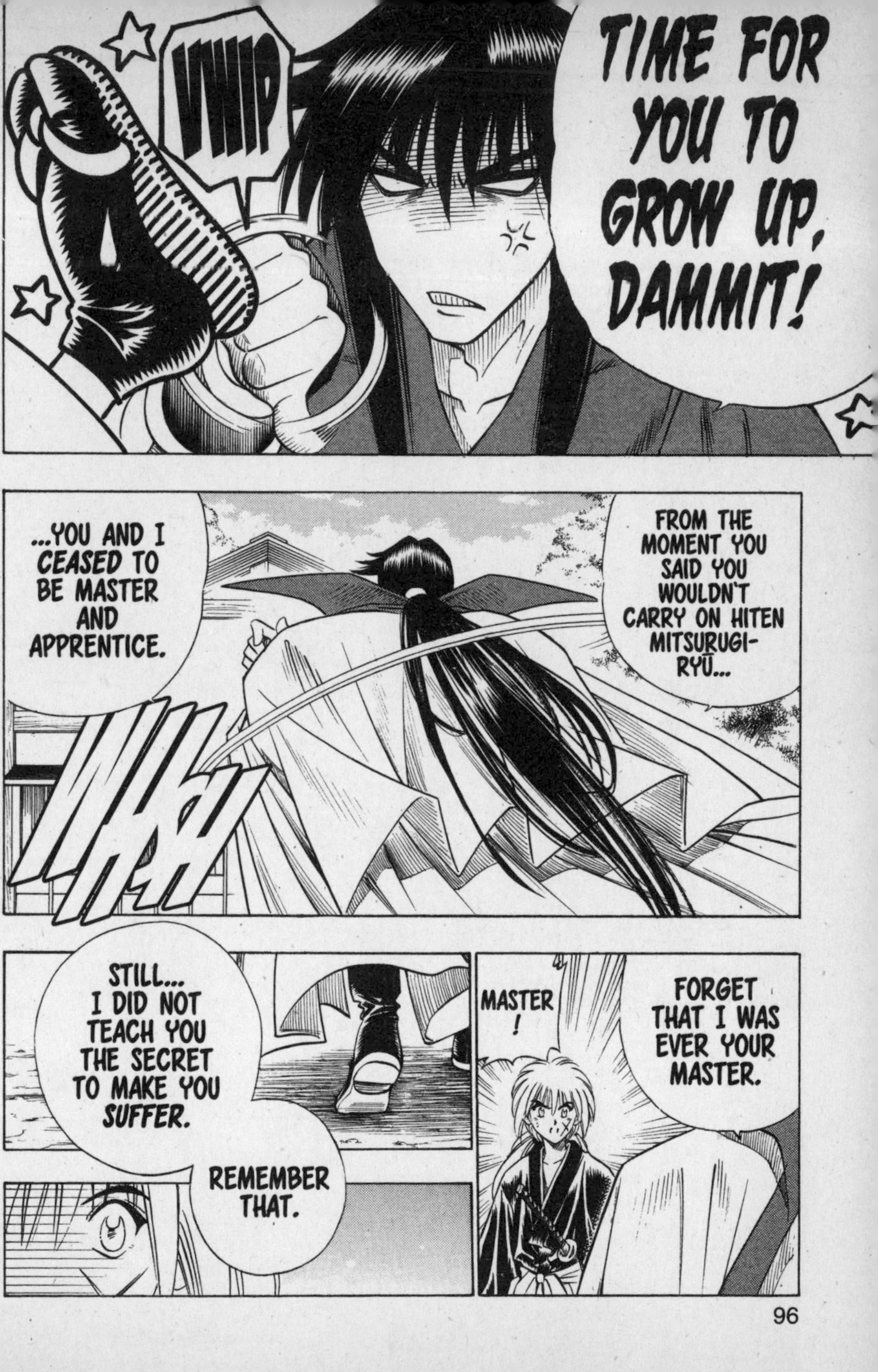
TIME FOR YOU TO GROW UP, DAMMIT!
VWHIP
FROM THE MOMENT YOU SAID YOU WOULDN'T CARRY ON HITEN MITSURUGI-RYŪ...
...YOU AND I *CEASED* TO BE MASTER AND APPRENTICE.
FORGET THAT I WAS EVER YOUR MASTER.
MASTER!
STILL... I DID NOT TEACH YOU THE SECRET TO MAKE YOU *SUFFER*.
REMEMBER THAT.

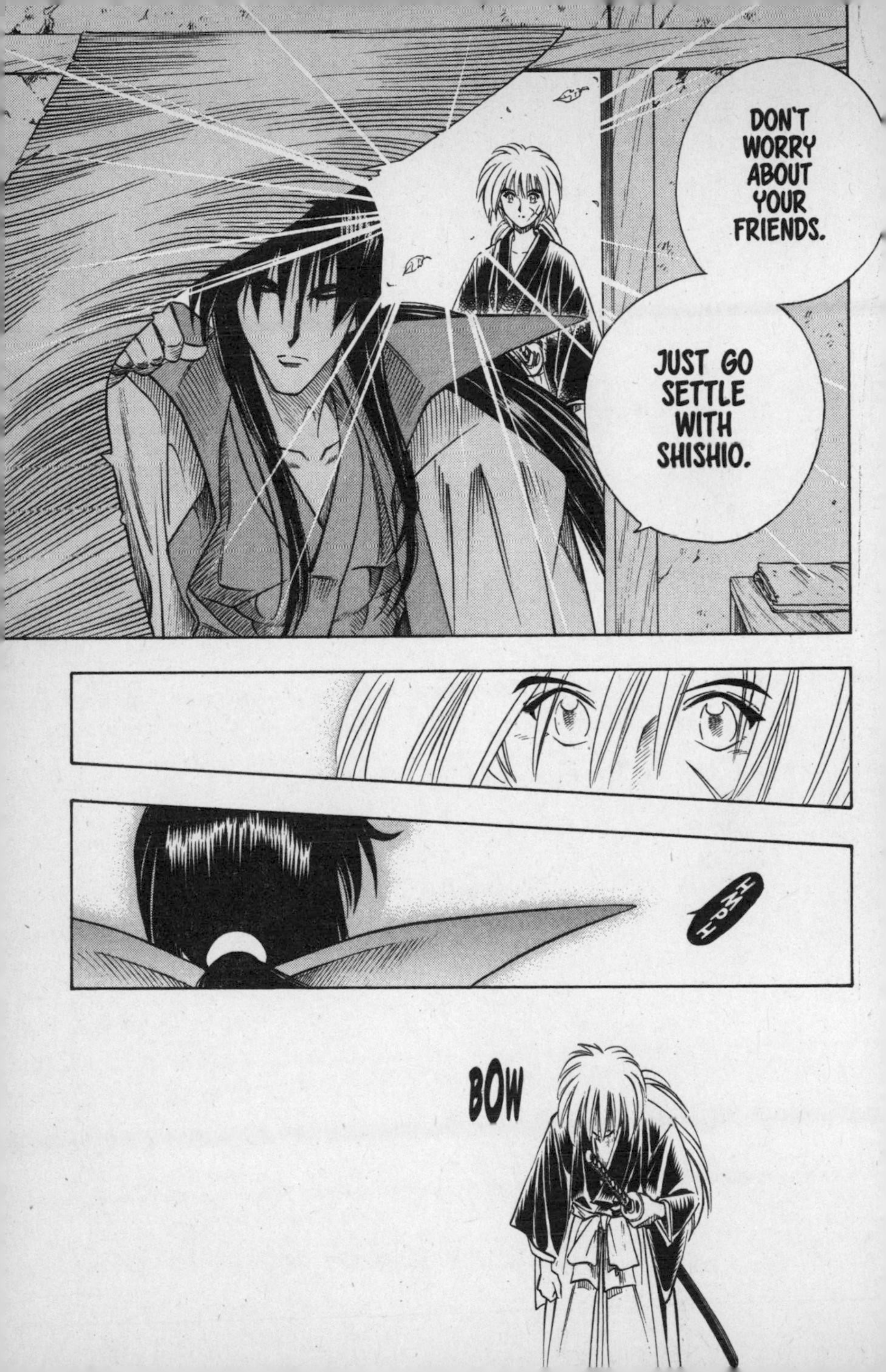
DON'T WORRY ABOUT YOUR FRIENDS.
JUST GO SETTLE WITH SHISHIO.
HMPH
BOW

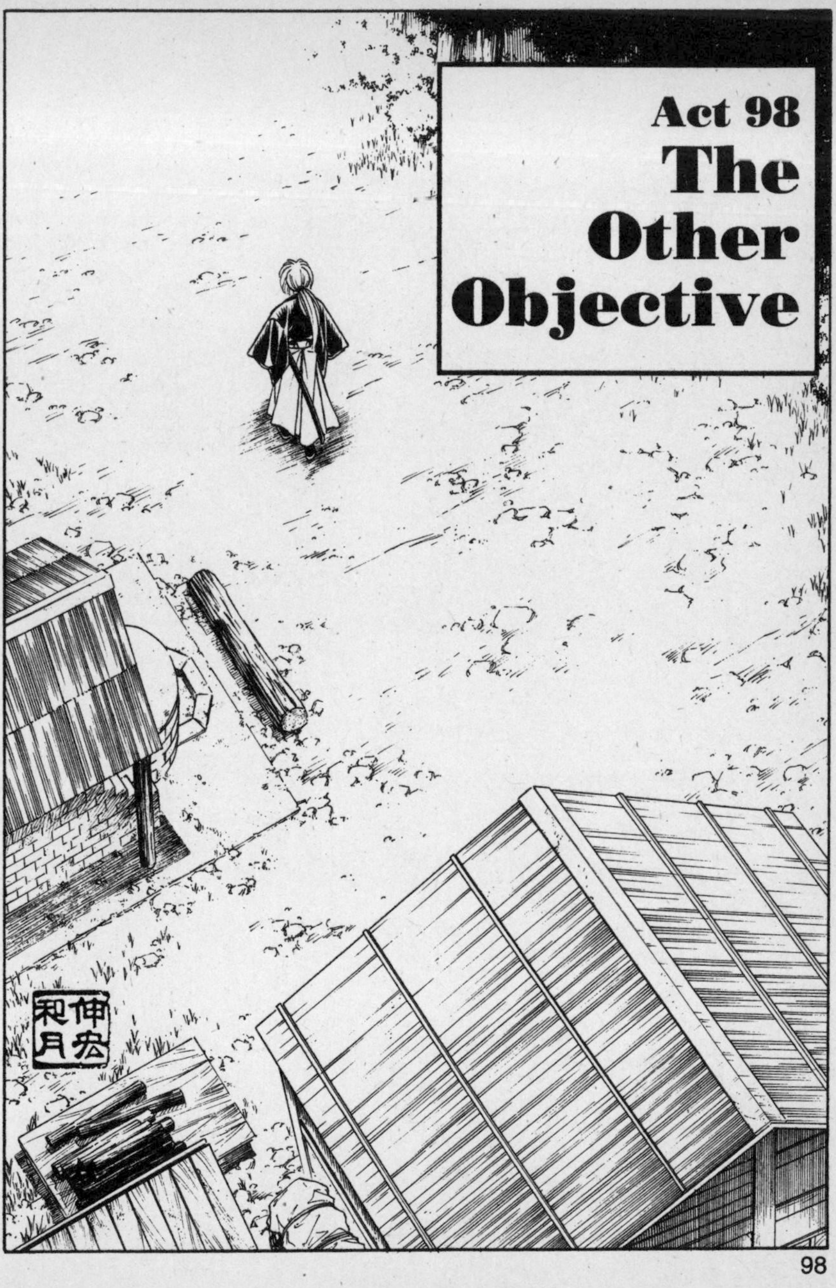
Act 98
The Other Objective
伸宏和月

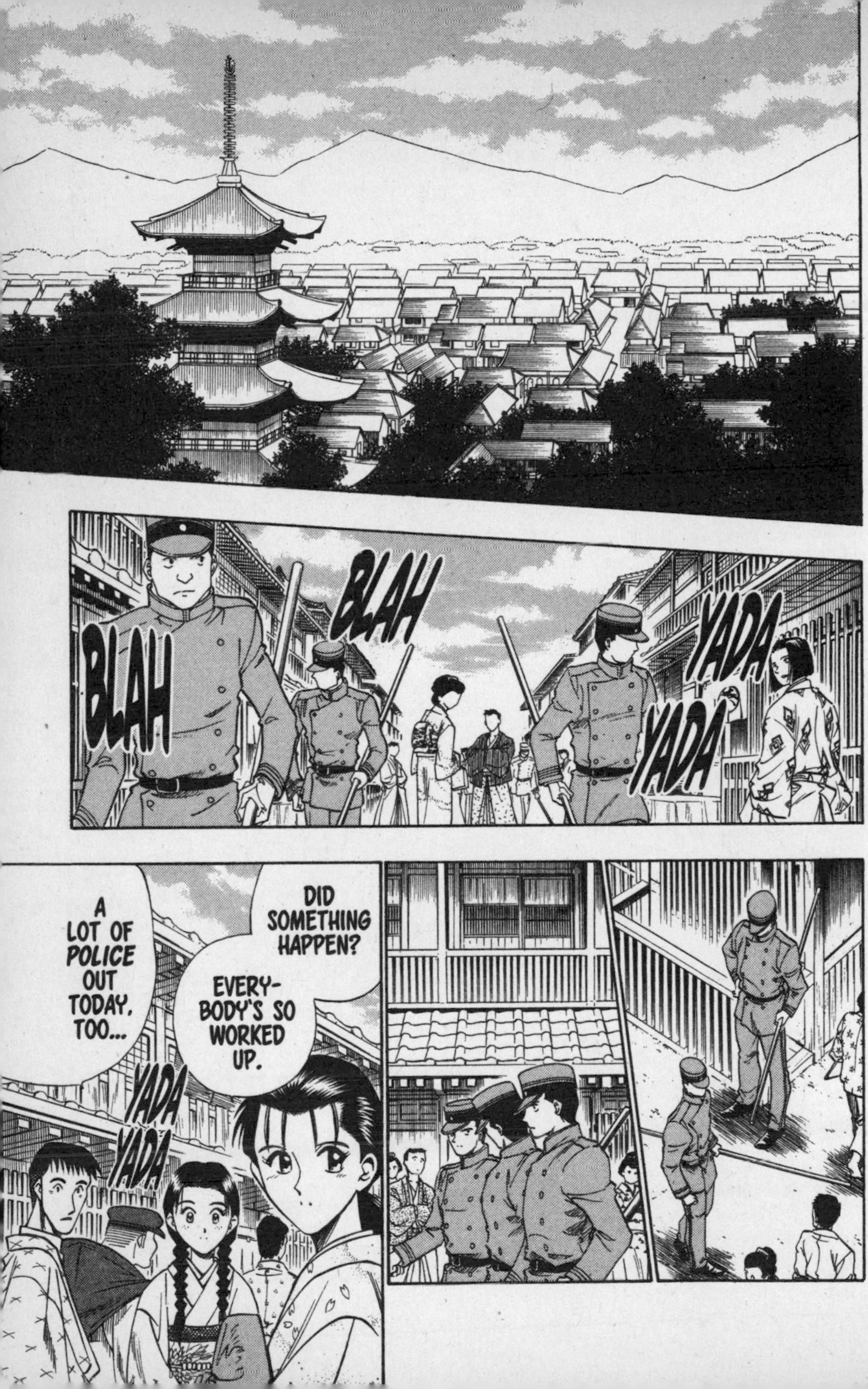
YADA
YADA
BLAH
BLAH
DID SOMETHING HAPPEN?
EVERYBODY'S SO WORKED UP.
A LOT OF POLICE OUT TODAY, TOO...
YADA
YADA

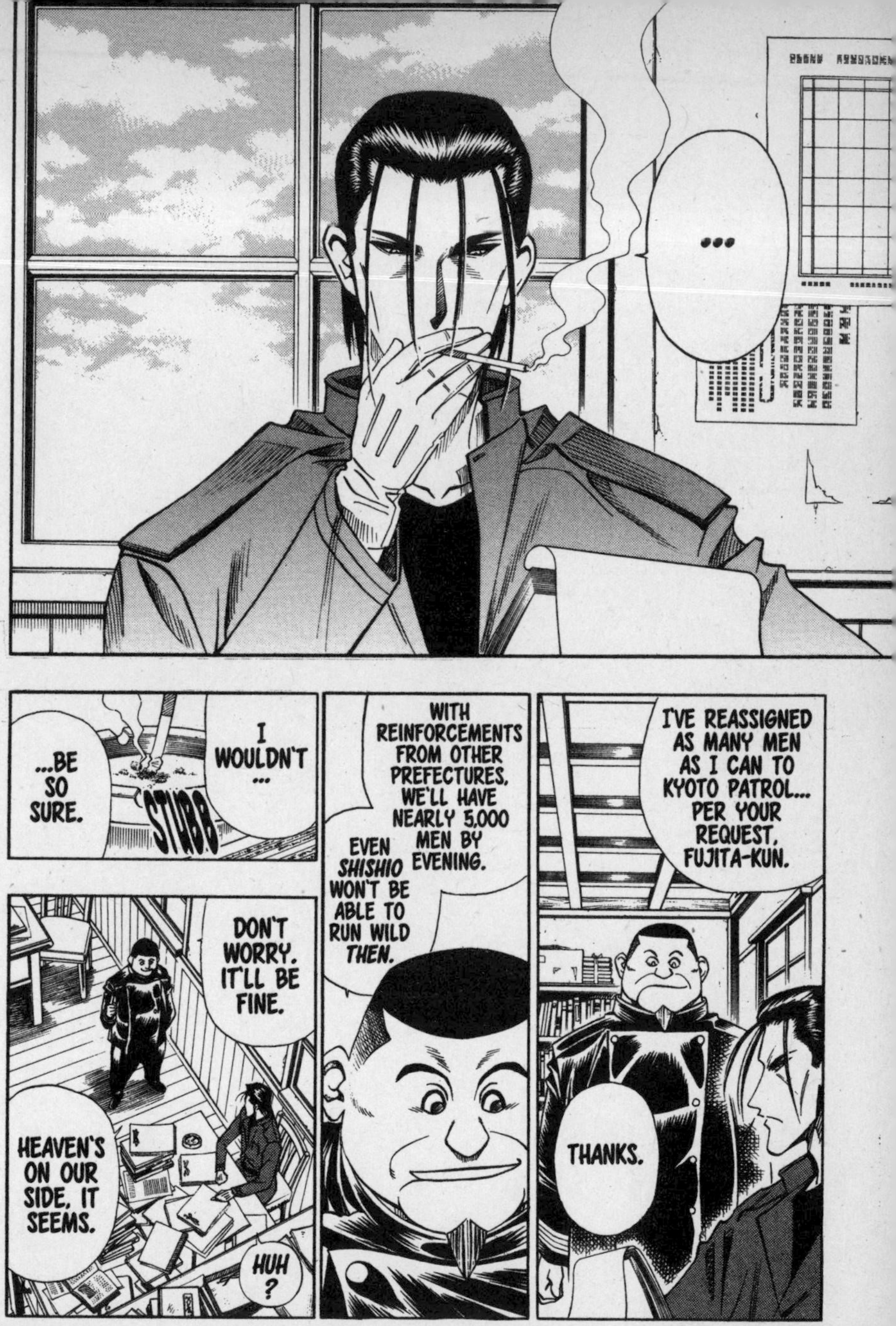
...
I'VE REASSIGNED AS MANY MEN AS I CAN TO KYOTO PATROL... PER YOUR REQUEST, FUJITA-KUN.
THANKS.
WITH REINFORCEMENTS FROM OTHER PREFECTURES, WE'LL HAVE NEARLY 5,000 MEN BY EVENING.
EVEN SHISHIO WON'T BE ABLE TO RUN WILD THEN.
I WOULDN'T ...
...BE SO SURE.
STUBB
DON'T WORRY. IT'LL BE FINE.
HEAVEN'S ON OUR SIDE, IT SEEMS.
HUH?

READ THIS WAY

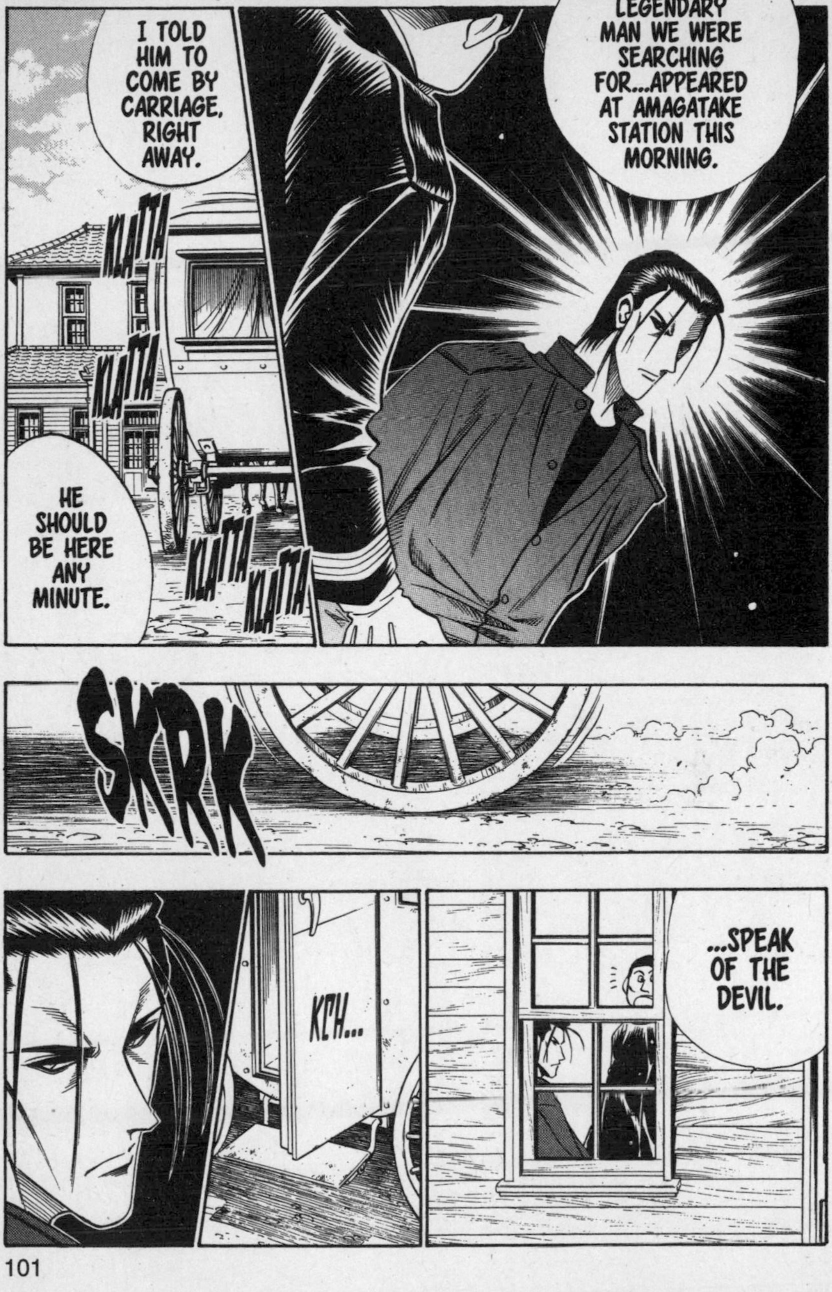
THAT... LEGENDARY MAN WE WERE SEARCHING FOR...APPEARED AT AMAGATAKE STATION THIS MORNING.
I TOLD HIM TO COME BY CARRIAGE, RIGHT AWAY.
KLATTA
KLATTA
HE SHOULD BE HERE ANY MINUTE.
KLATTA
KLATTA
SKRK
...SPEAK OF THE DEVIL.
KCH...

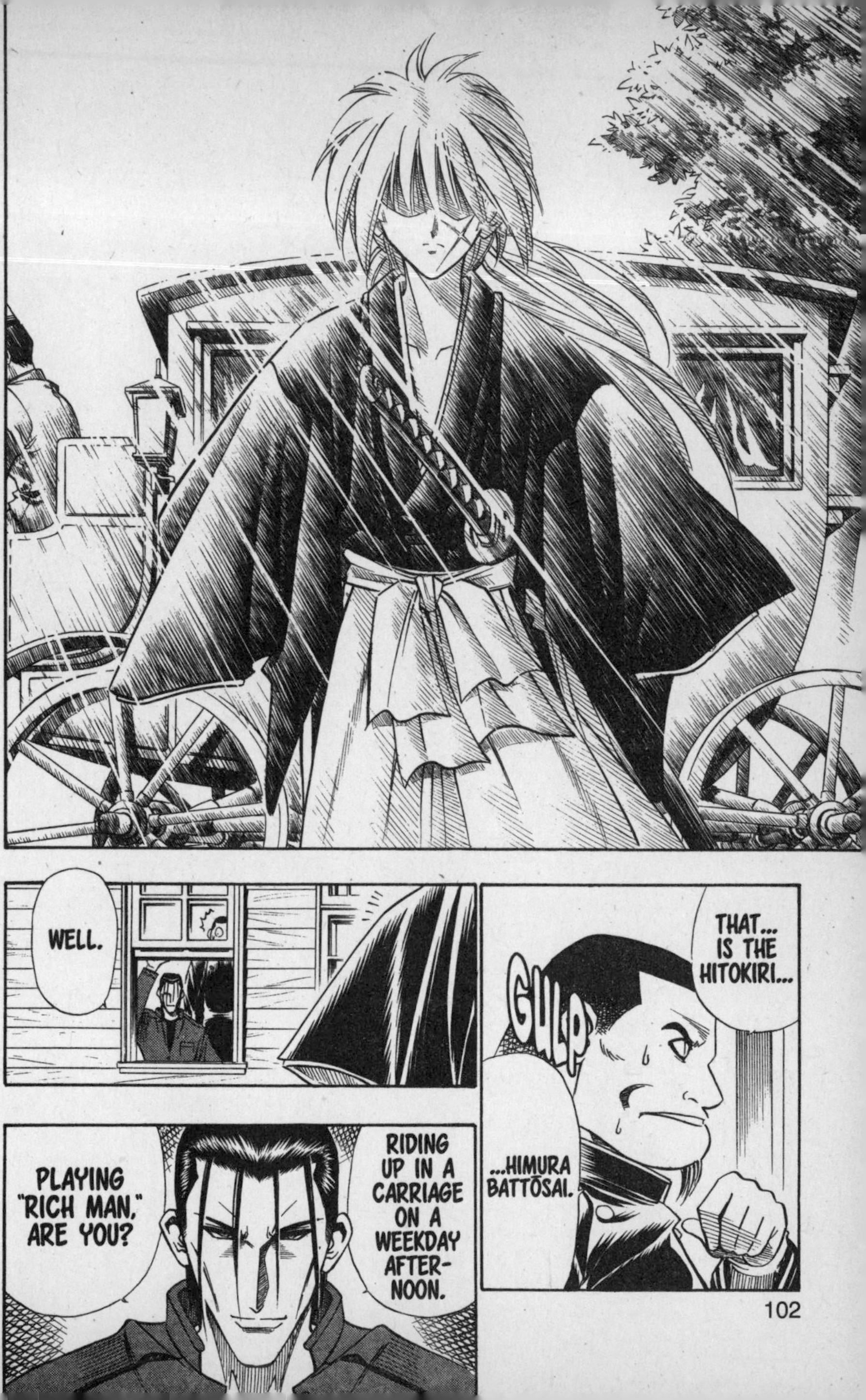
THAT... IS THE HITOKIRI...
GULP
...HIMURA BATTŌSAI.
WELL.
RIDING UP IN A CARRIAGE ON A WEEKDAY AFTER-NOON.
PLAYING "RICH MAN," ARE YOU?

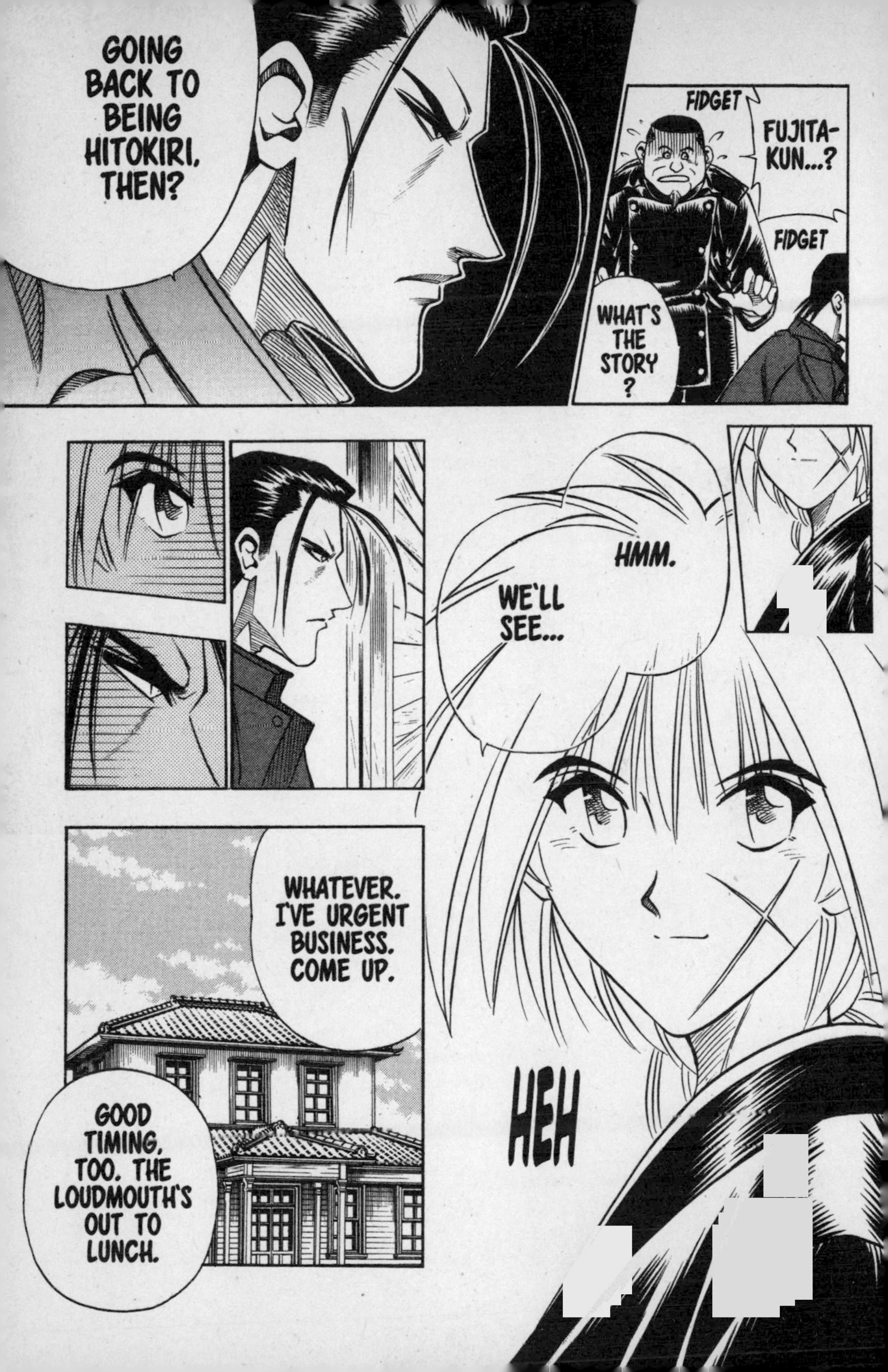
FIDGET
FUJITA-KUN...?
FIDGET
WHAT'S THE STORY?
GOING BACK TO BEING HITOKIRI, THEN?
HMM.
WE'LL SEE...
HEH
WHATEVER. I'VE URGENT BUSINESS. COME UP.
GOOD TIMING, TOO. THE LOUDMOUTH'S OUT TO LUNCH.

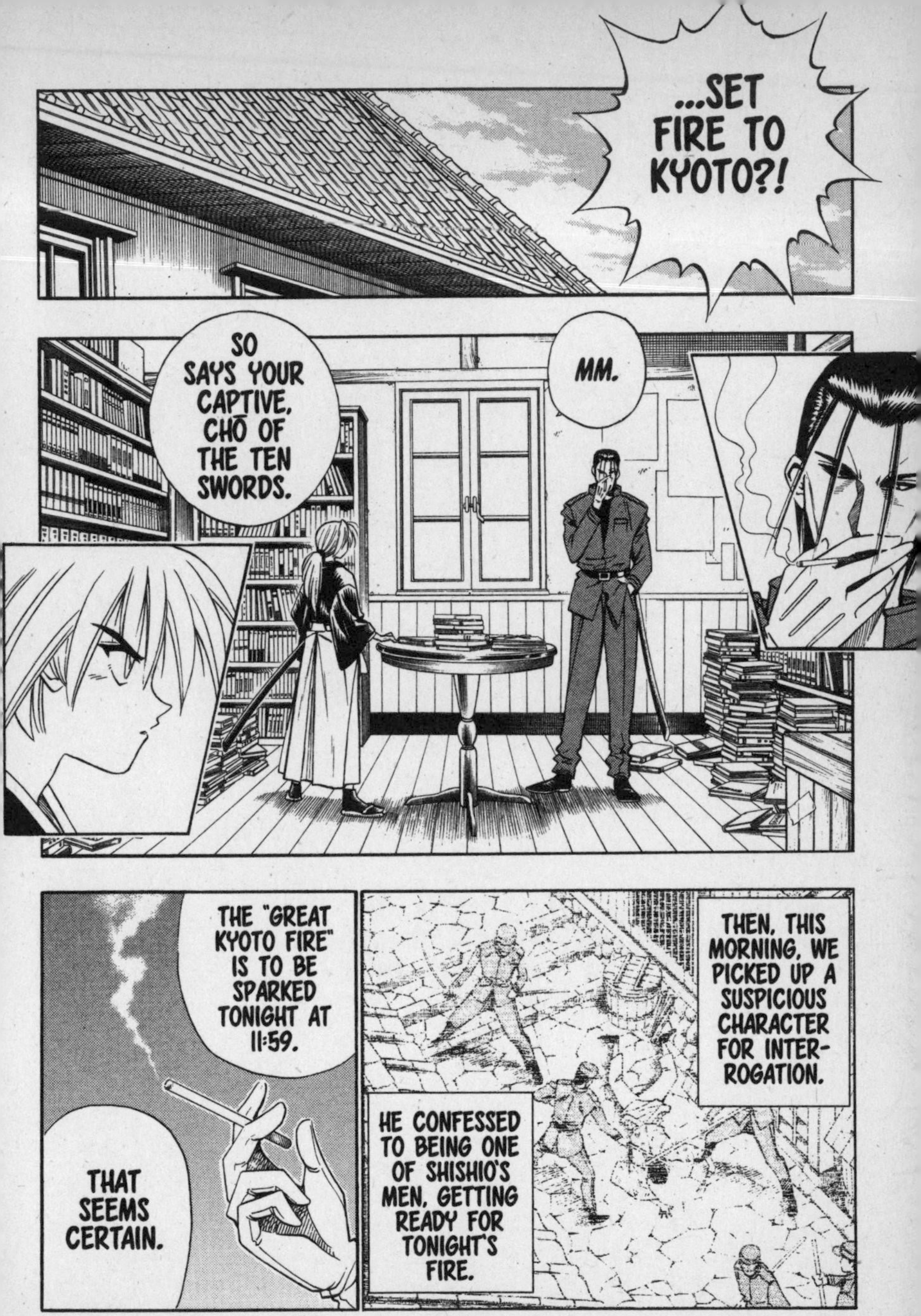
...SET FIRE TO KYOTO?!
SO SAYS YOUR CAPTIVE, CHŌ OF THE TEN SWORDS.
MM.
THEN, THIS MORNING, WE PICKED UP A SUSPICIOUS CHARACTER FOR INTER-ROGATION.
HE CONFESSED TO BEING ONE OF SHISHIO'S MEN, GETTING READY FOR TONIGHT'S FIRE.
THE "GREAT KYOTO FIRE" IS TO BE SPARKED TONIGHT AT 11:59.
THAT SEEMS CERTAIN.

READ THIS WAY

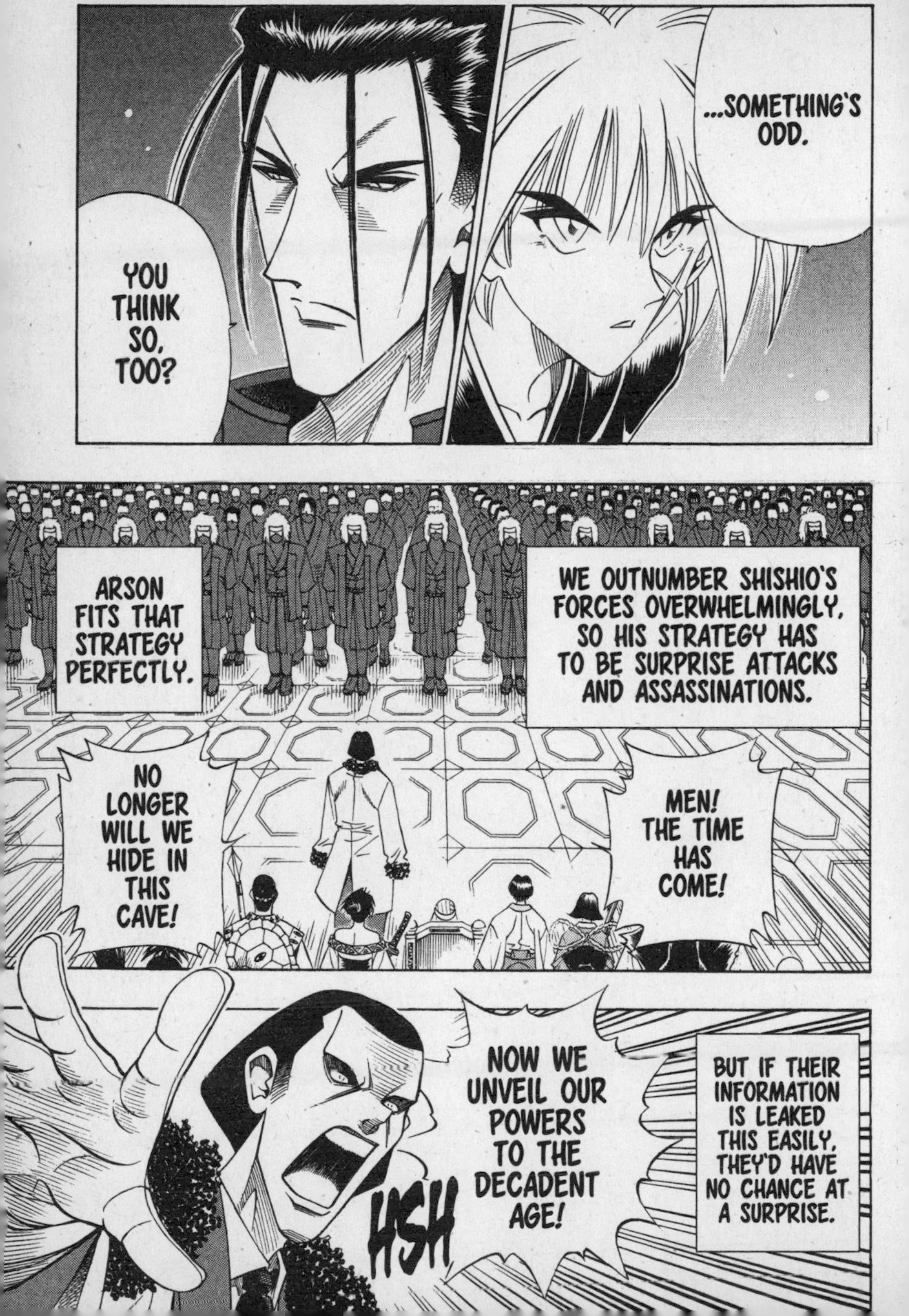

...SOMETHING'S ODD.
YOU THINK SO, TOO?
WE OUTNUMBER SHISHIO'S FORCES OVERWHELMINGLY, SO HIS STRATEGY HAS TO BE SURPRISE ATTACKS AND ASSASSINATIONS.
ARSON FITS THAT STRATEGY PERFECTLY.
MEN! THE TIME HAS COME!
NO LONGER WILL WE HIDE IN THIS CAVE!
BUT IF THEIR INFORMATION IS LEAKED THIS EASILY, THEY'D HAVE NO CHANCE AT A SURPRISE.
NOW WE UNVEIL OUR POWERS TO THE DECADENT AGE!
HSH

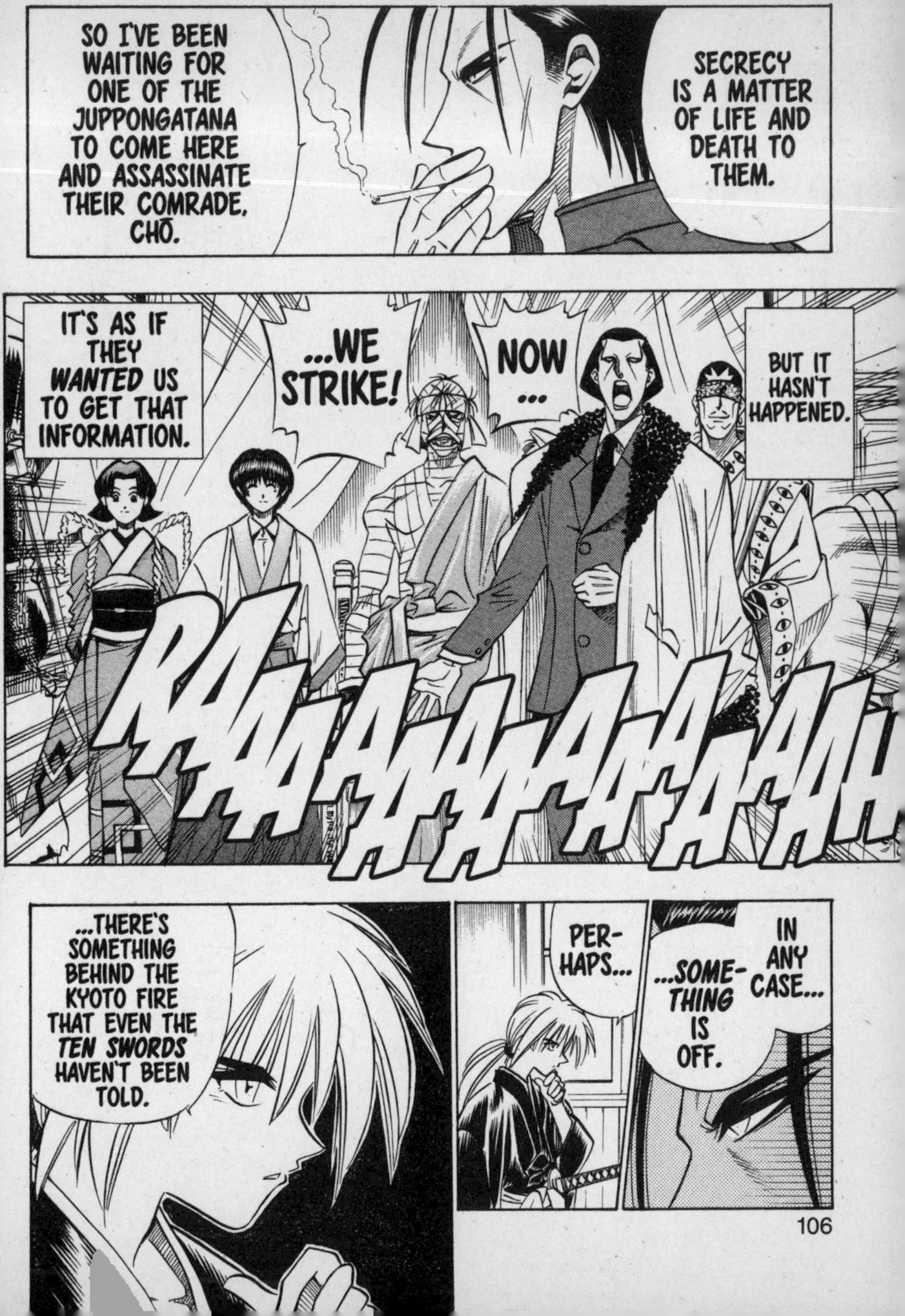
SECRECY IS A MATTER OF LIFE AND DEATH TO THEM.
SO I'VE BEEN WAITING FOR ONE OF THE JUPPONGATANA TO COME HERE AND ASSASSINATE THEIR COMRADE, CHŌ.
BUT IT HASN'T HAPPENED.
NOW ...
...WE STRIKE!
IT'S AS IF THEY *WANTED* US TO GET THAT INFORMATION.
RAAAAAAAAAAH
IN ANY CASE...
...SOME-THING IS OFF.
PER-HAPS...
...THERE'S SOMETHING BEHIND THE KYOTO FIRE THAT EVEN THE *TEN SWORDS* HAVEN'T BEEN TOLD.

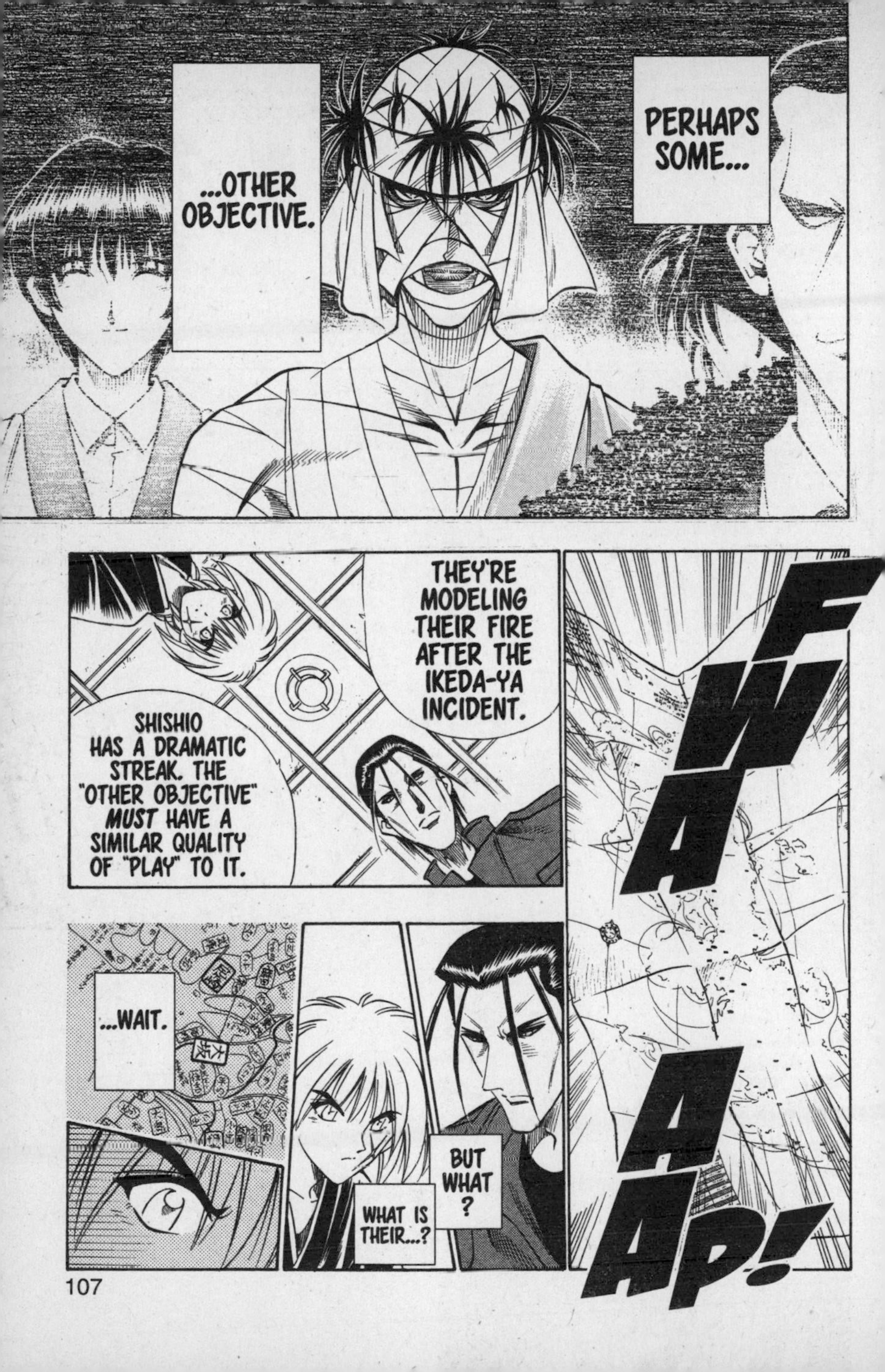
PERHAPS SOME...
...OTHER OBJECTIVE.
FWAAAAP!
THEY'RE MODELING THEIR FIRE AFTER THE IKEDA-YA INCIDENT.
SHISHIO HAS A DRAMATIC STREAK. THE "OTHER OBJECTIVE" *MUST* HAVE A SIMILAR QUALITY OF "PLAY" TO IT.
BUT WHAT?
WHAT IS THEIR...?
...WAIT.

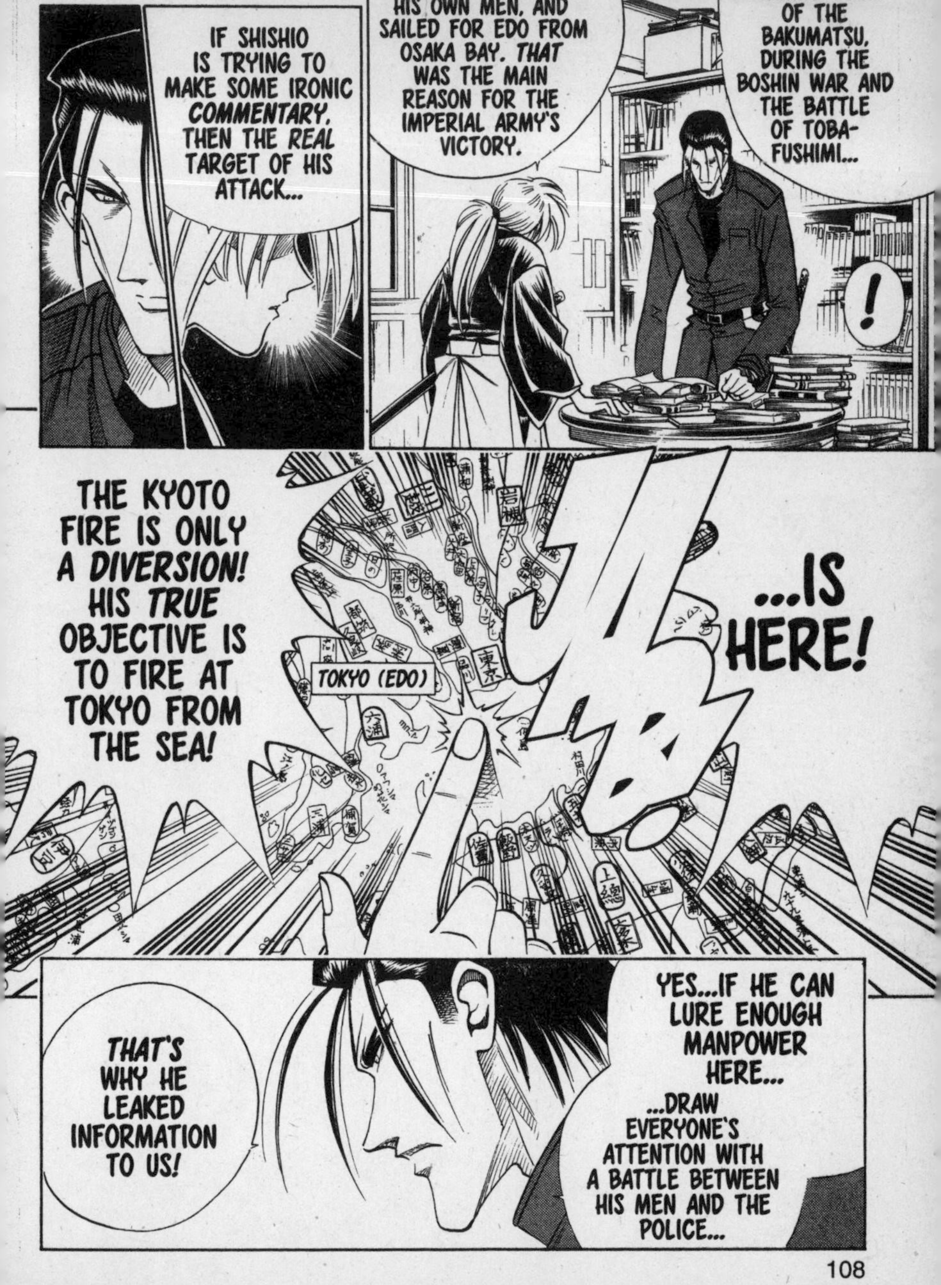
SAITŌ...AT THE TURNING POINT OF THE BAKUMATSU, DURING THE BOSHIN WAR AND THE BATTLE OF TOBA-FUSHIMI...
...SHŌGUN TOKUGAWA YOSHINOBU DECEIVED HIS OWN MEN, AND SAILED FOR EDO FROM OSAKA BAY. THAT WAS THE MAIN REASON FOR THE IMPERIAL ARMY'S VICTORY.
!
IF SHISHIO IS TRYING TO MAKE SOME IRONIC COMMENTARY, THEN THE REAL TARGET OF HIS ATTACK...
...IS HERE!
TOKYO (EDO)
THE KYOTO FIRE IS ONLY A DIVERSION! HIS TRUE OBJECTIVE IS TO FIRE AT TOKYO FROM THE SEA!
YES...IF HE CAN LURE ENOUGH MANPOWER HERE...
...DRAW EVERYONE'S ATTENTION WITH A BATTLE BETWEEN HIS MEN AND THE POLICE...
THAT'S WHY HE LEAKED INFORMATION TO US!

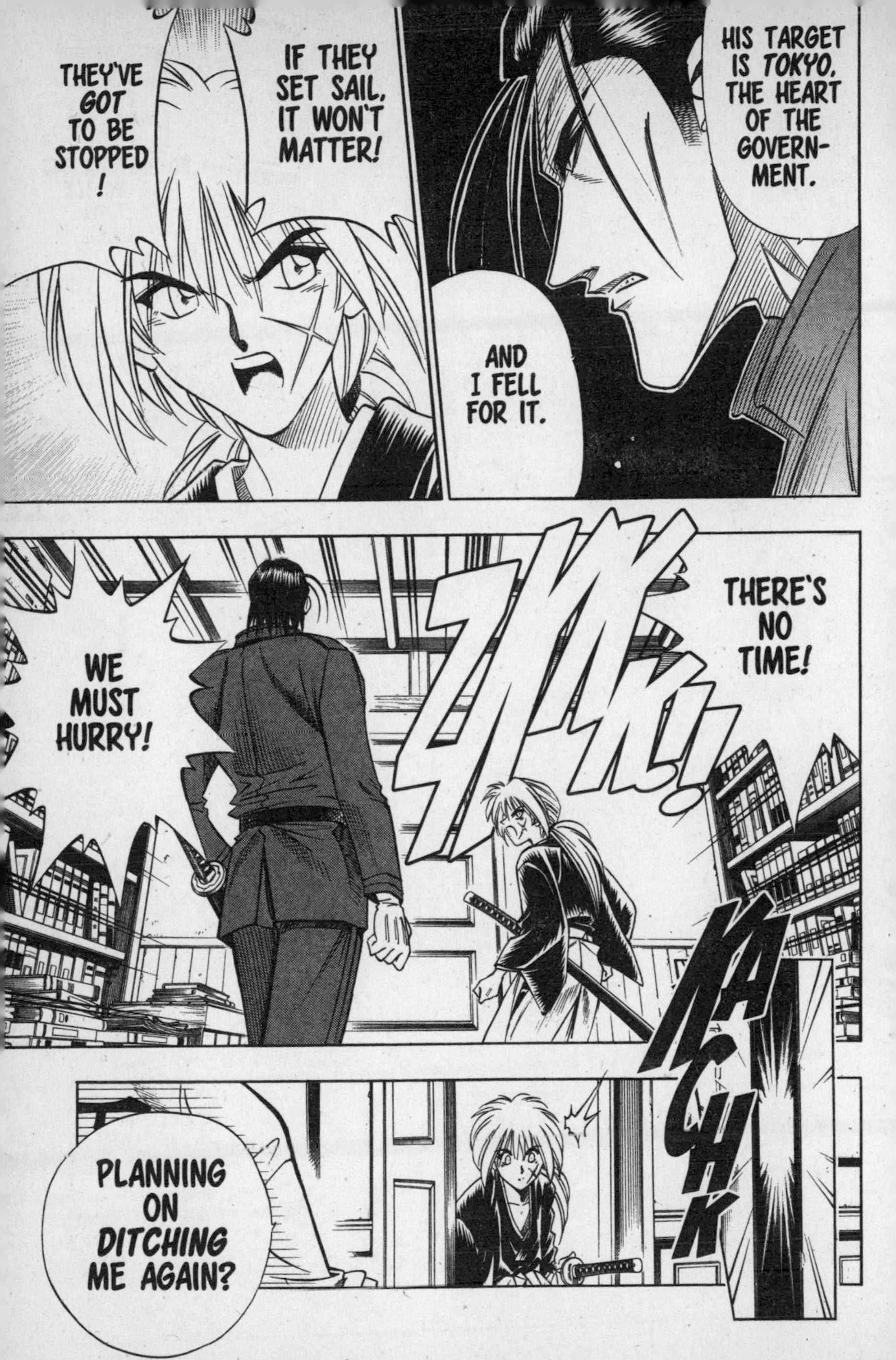
HIS TARGET IS *TOKYO*, THE HEART OF THE GOVERNMENT.
AND I FELL FOR IT.
IF THEY SET SAIL, IT WON'T MATTER!
THEY'VE *GOT* TO BE STOPPED!
THERE'S NO TIME!
ZAK!
WE MUST HURRY!
KACHIK
PLANNING ON *DITCHING* ME AGAIN?

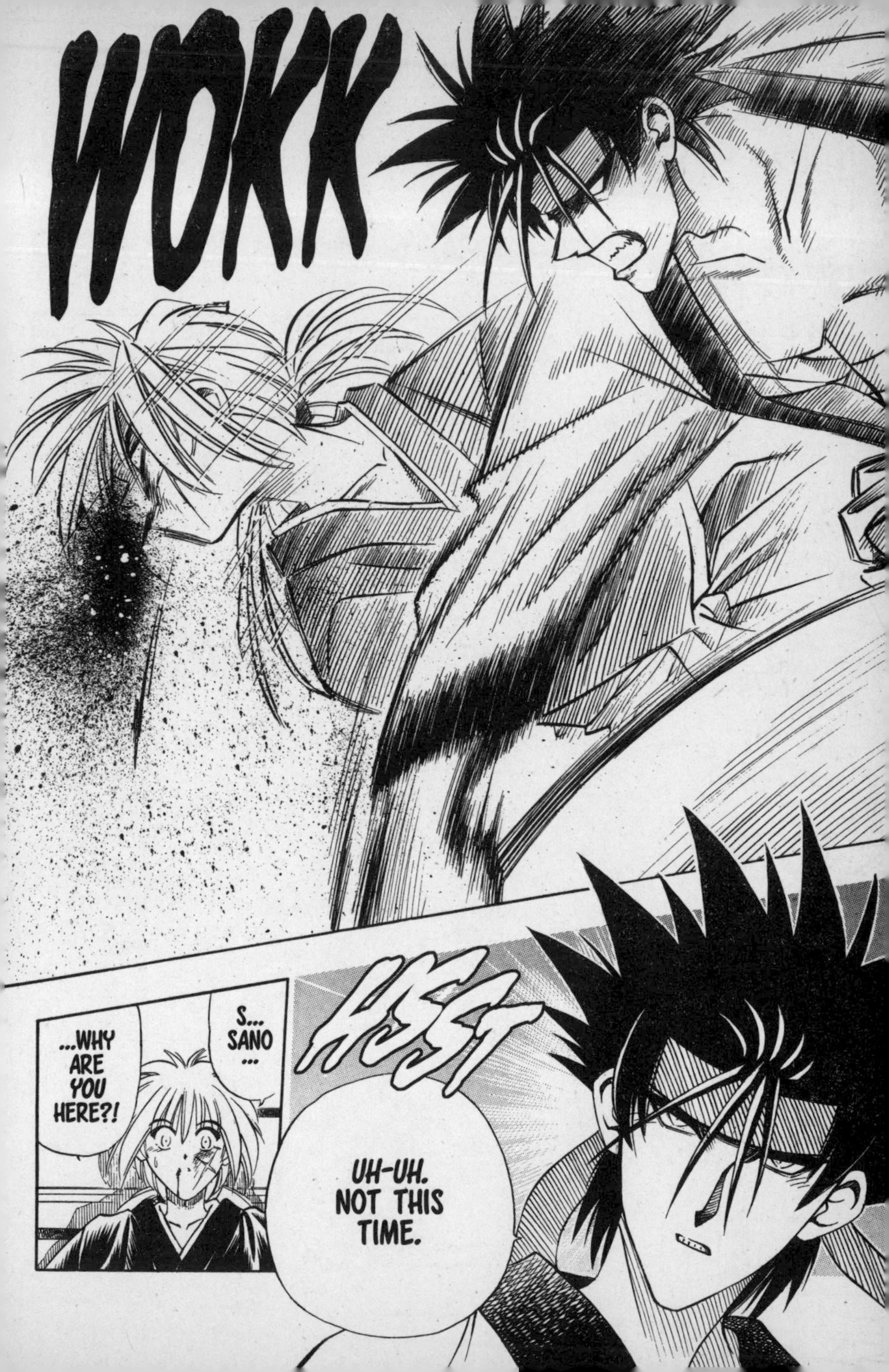
WOKK
HEY
S... SANO ...
...WHY ARE YOU HERE?!
UH-UH. NOT THIS TIME.

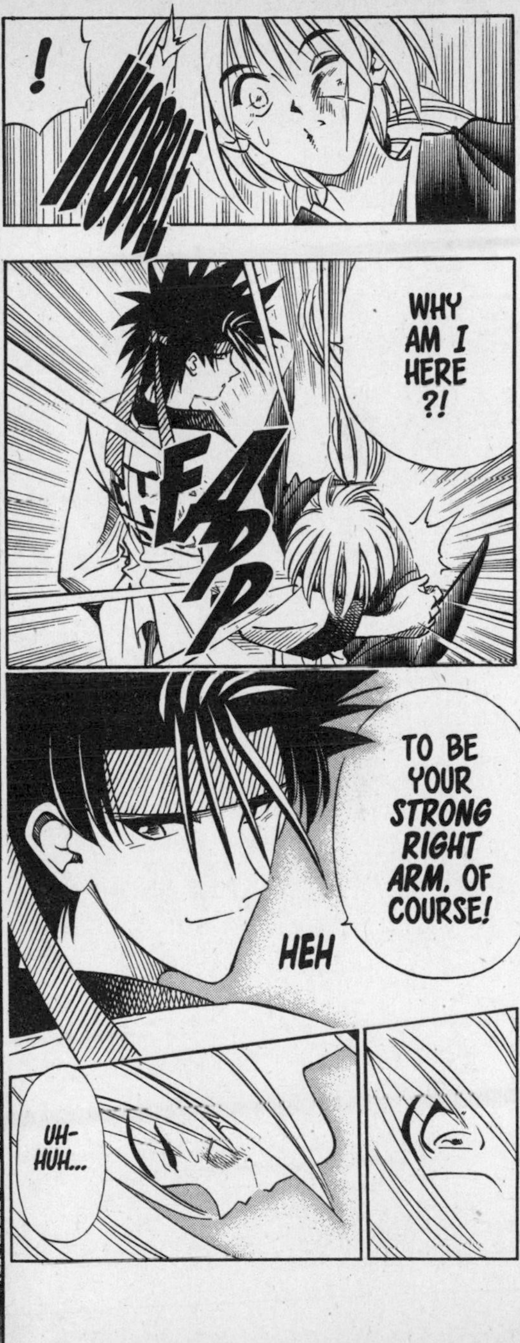
!
WOBBLE
WHY AM I HERE?!
TO BE YOUR STRONG RIGHT ARM, OF COURSE!
HEH
UH-HUH...

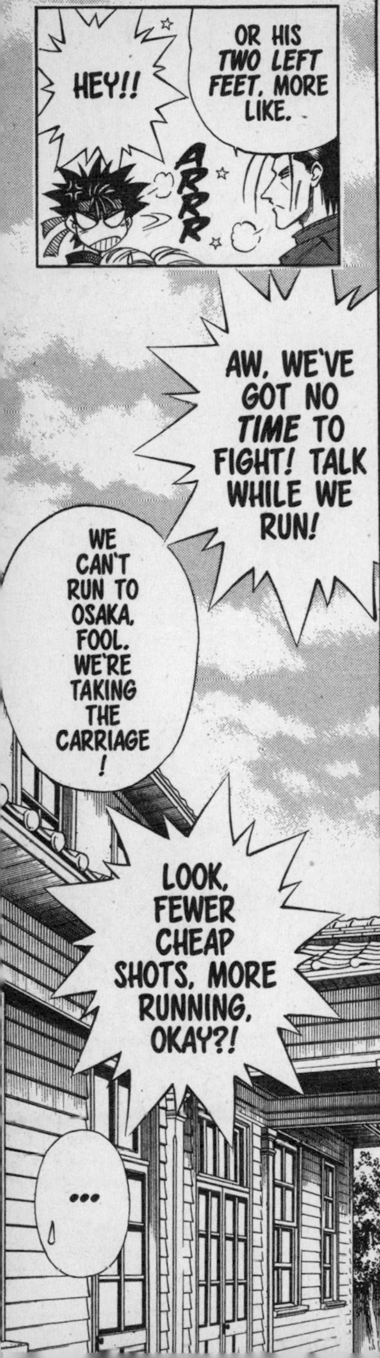
OR HIS TWO LEFT FEET, MORE LIKE.
HEY!!
ARRR
AW, WE'VE GOT NO TIME TO FIGHT! TALK WHILE WE RUN!
WE CAN'T RUN TO OSAKA, FOOL. WE'RE TAKING THE CARRIAGE!
LOOK, FEWER CHEAP SHOTS, MORE RUNNING, OKAY?!
...

Rurouni Kenshin

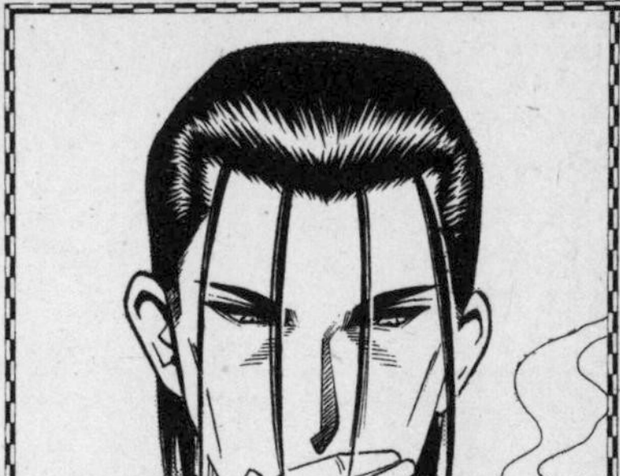

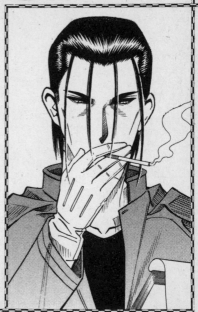

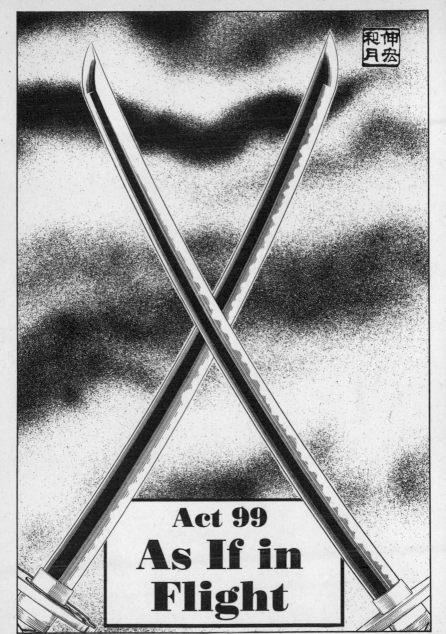

Act 99
As If in Flight

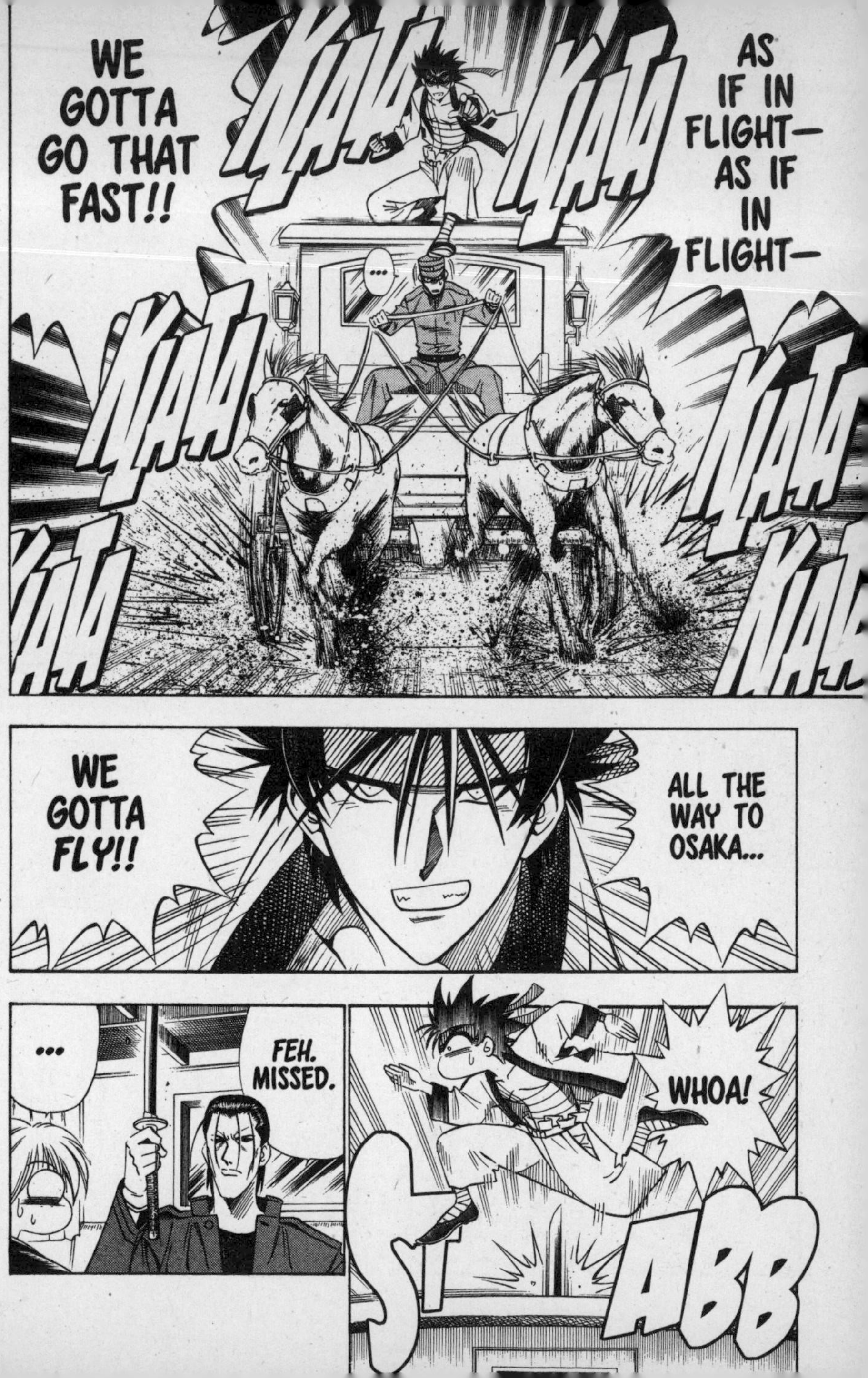
AS IF IN FLIGHT— AS IF IN FLIGHT—
...
WE GOTTA GO THAT FAST!!
ALL THE WAY TO OSAKA...
WE GOTTA FLY!!
WHOA!
FEH. MISSED.
...

READ THIS WAY

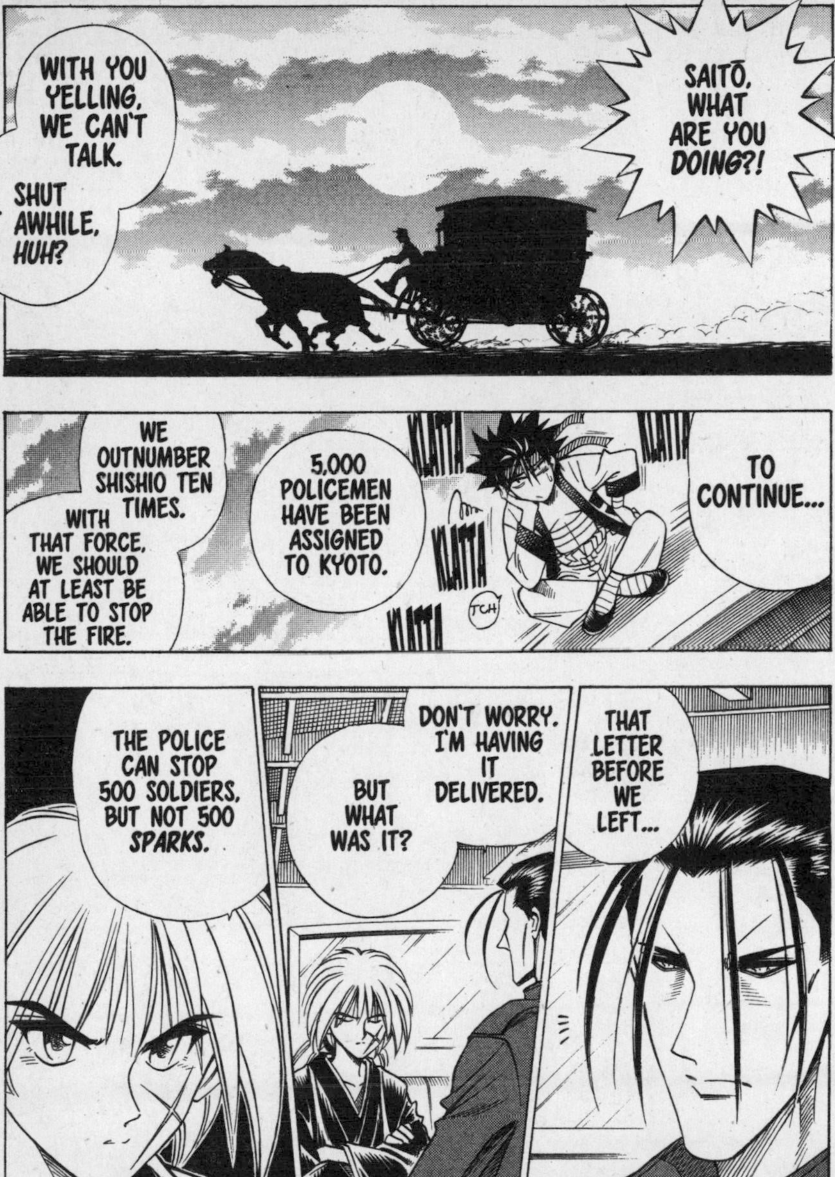

SAITŌ, WHAT ARE YOU DOING?!
WITH YOU YELLING, WE CAN'T TALK.
SHUT IT AWHILE, HUH?
TO CONTINUE...
KLATTA
KLATTA
TCH
5,000 POLICEMEN HAVE BEEN ASSIGNED TO KYOTO.
WE OUTNUMBER SHISHIO TEN TIMES.
WITH THAT FORCE, WE SHOULD AT LEAST BE ABLE TO STOP THE FIRE.
THAT LETTER BEFORE WE LEFT...
DON'T WORRY. I'M HAVING IT DELIVERED.
BUT WHAT WAS IT?
THE POLICE CAN STOP 500 SOLDIERS, BUT NOT 500 SPARKS.

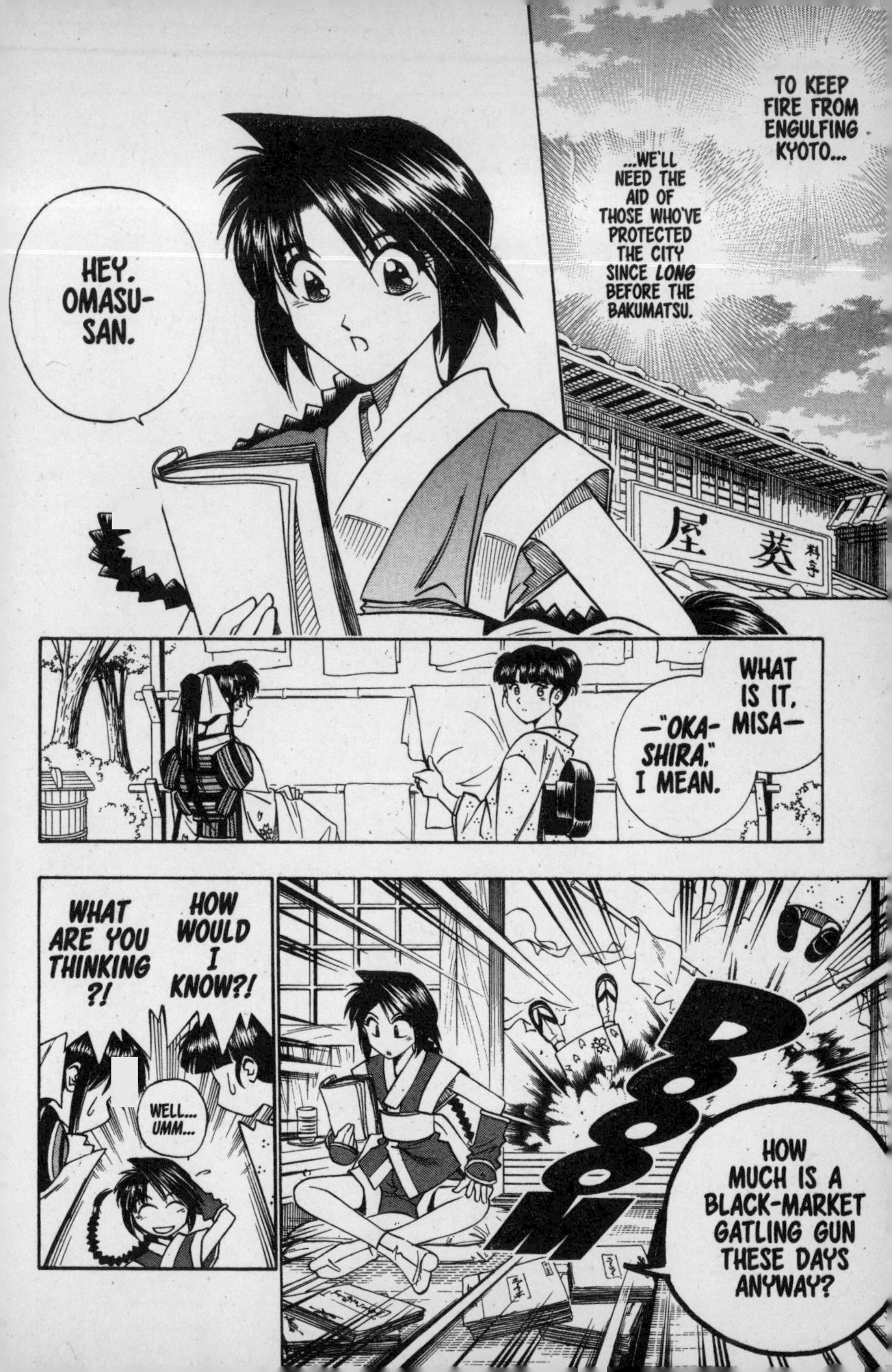
TO KEEP FIRE FROM ENGULFING KYOTO...
...WE'LL NEED THE AID OF THOSE WHO'VE PROTECTED THE CITY SINCE *LONG* BEFORE THE BAKUMATSU.
料亭 葵屋
HEY. OMASU-SAN.
WHAT IS IT, MISA—
—"OKASHIRA," I MEAN.
BOOOM
HOW MUCH IS A BLACK-MARKET GATLING GUN THESE DAYS ANYWAY?
HOW WOULD I KNOW?!
WHAT ARE YOU THINKING?!
WELL... UMM...

READ THIS WAY

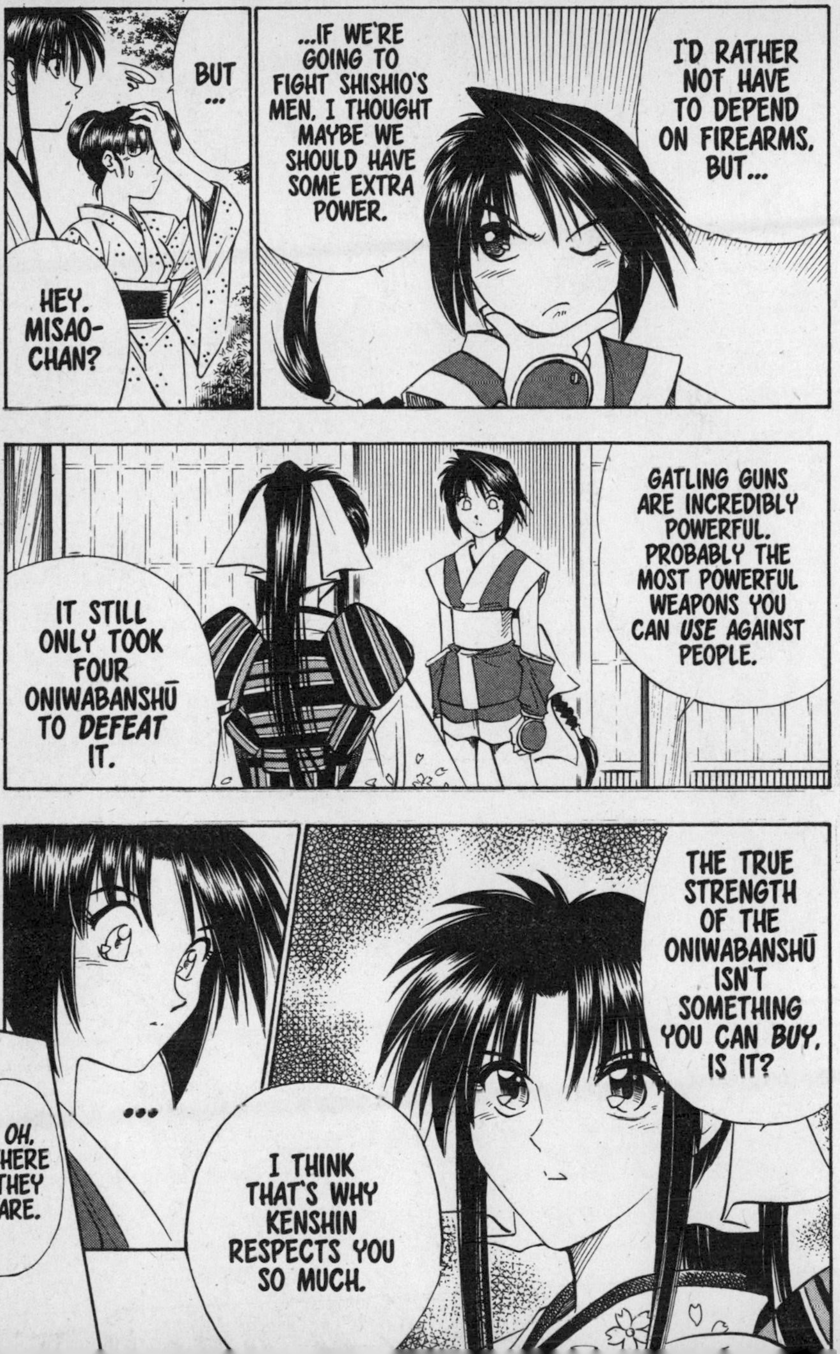
I'D RATHER NOT HAVE TO DEPEND ON FIREARMS, BUT...
...IF WE'RE GOING TO FIGHT SHISHIO'S MEN, I THOUGHT MAYBE WE SHOULD HAVE SOME EXTRA POWER.
BUT ...
HEY. MISAO-CHAN?
GATLING GUNS ARE INCREDIBLY POWERFUL. PROBABLY THE MOST POWERFUL WEAPONS YOU CAN USE AGAINST PEOPLE.
IT STILL ONLY TOOK FOUR ONIWABANSHŪ TO DEFEAT IT.
THE TRUE STRENGTH OF THE ONIWABANSHŪ ISN'T SOMETHING YOU CAN BUY, IS IT?
...
I THINK THAT'S WHY KENSHIN RESPECTS YOU SO MUCH.
OH, THERE THEY ARE.

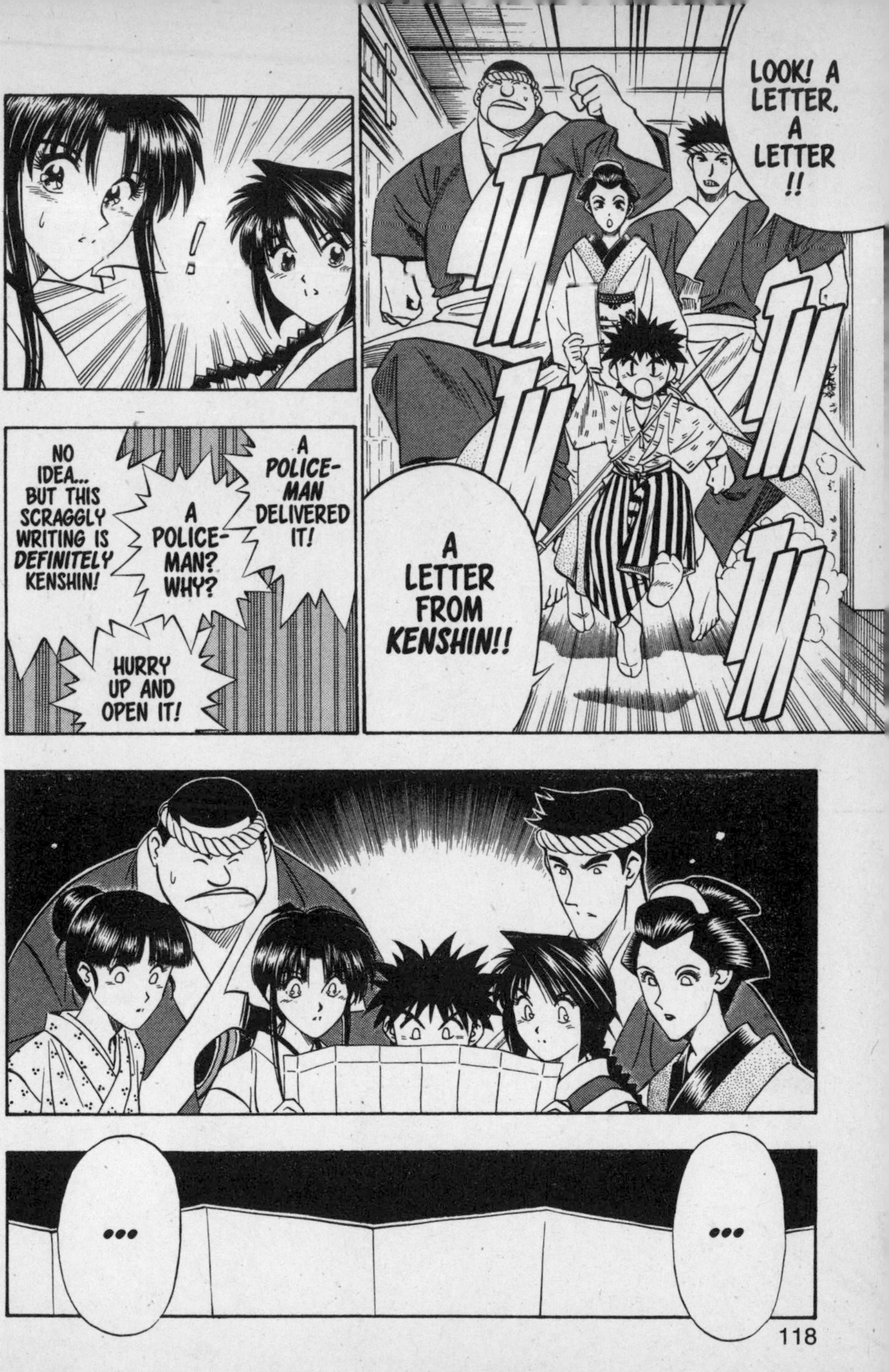
LOOK! A LETTER, A LETTER !!
A LETTER FROM KENSHIN!!
!
A POLICE-MAN DELIVERED IT!
A POLICE-MAN? WHY?
NO IDEA... BUT THIS SCRAGGLY WRITING IS DEFINITELY KENSHIN!
HURRY UP AND OPEN IT!
...
...

READ THIS WAY

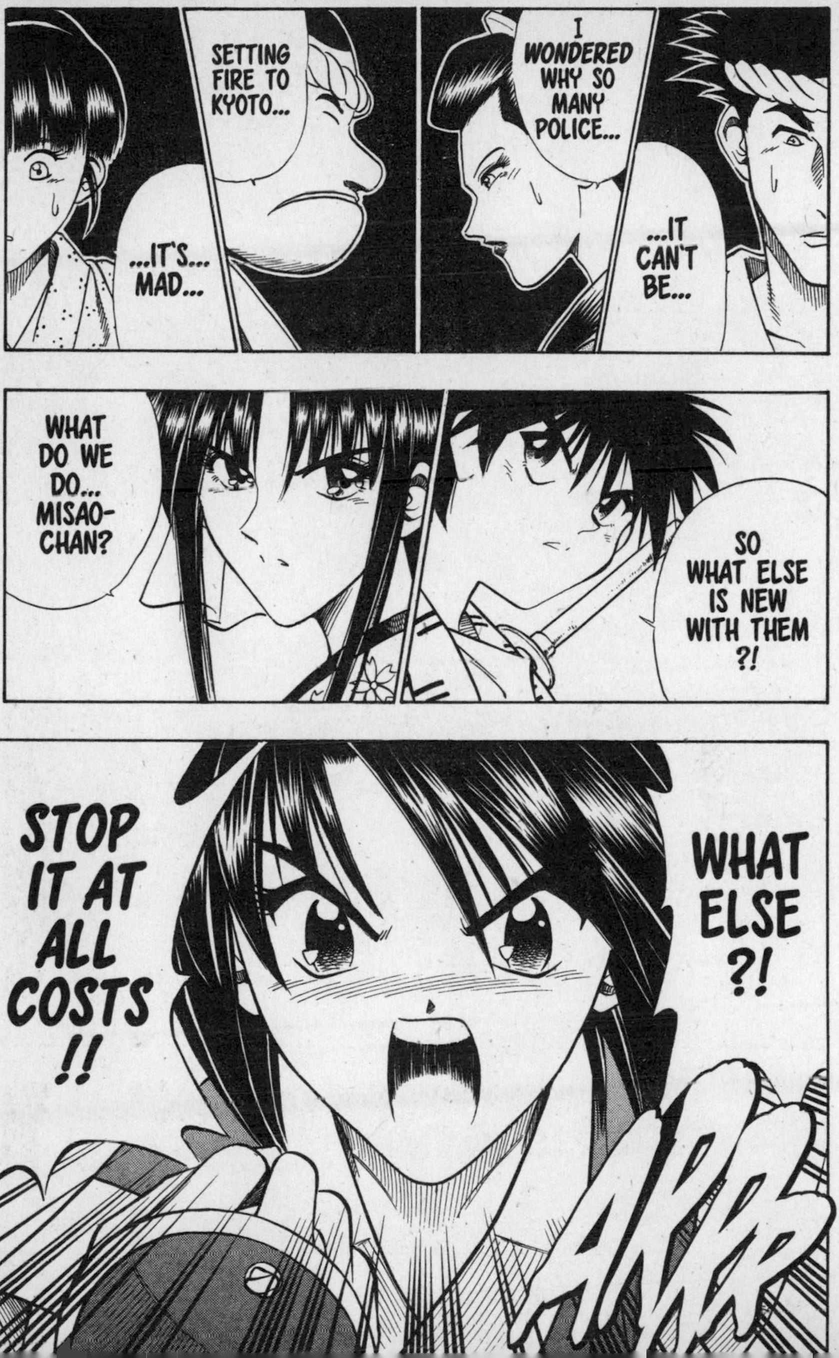
I WONDERED WHY SO MANY POLICE...
...IT CAN'T BE...
SETTING FIRE TO KYOTO...
...IT'S... MAD...
SO WHAT ELSE IS NEW WITH THEM ?!
WHAT DO WE DO... MISAO-CHAN?
WHAT ELSE ?!
STOP IT AT ALL COSTS !!

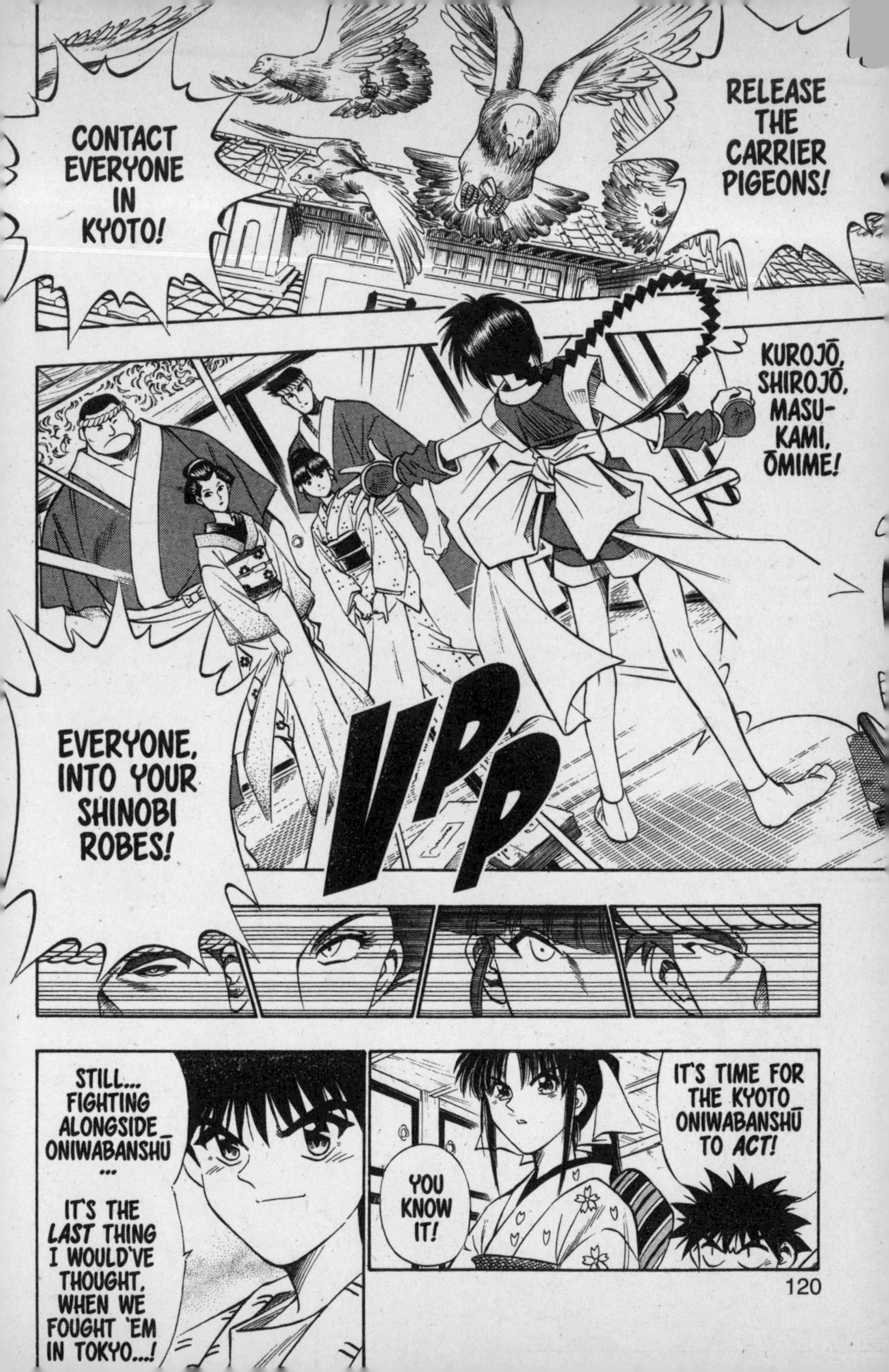
RELEASE THE CARRIER PIGEONS!
CONTACT EVERYONE IN KYOTO!
KUROJŌ, SHIROJŌ, MASU-KAMI, ŌMIME!
EVERYONE, INTO YOUR SHINOBI ROBES!
VIPP
IT'S TIME FOR THE KYOTO ONIWABANSHŪ TO *ACT*!
YOU KNOW IT!
STILL... FIGHTING ALONGSIDE ONIWABANSHŪ...
IT'S THE *LAST* THING I WOULD'VE THOUGHT, WHEN WE FOUGHT 'EM IN TOKYO...!

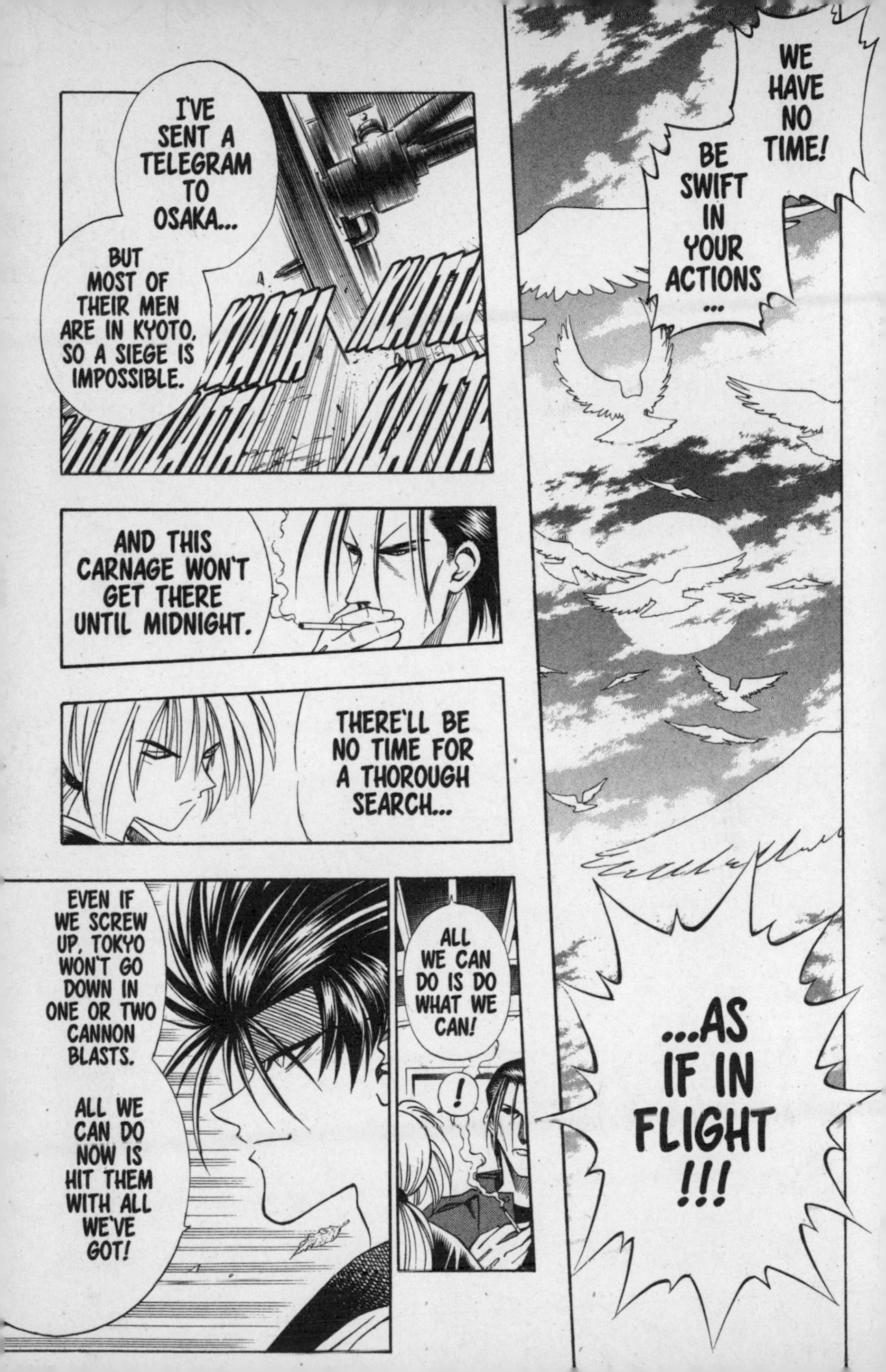
WE HAVE NO TIME!
BE SWIFT IN YOUR ACTIONS...
...AS IF IN FLIGHT!!!
I'VE SENT A TELEGRAM TO OSAKA...
BUT MOST OF THEIR MEN ARE IN KYOTO, SO A SIEGE IS IMPOSSIBLE.
AND THIS CARNAGE WON'T GET THERE UNTIL MIDNIGHT.
THERE'LL BE NO TIME FOR A THOROUGH SEARCH...
ALL WE CAN DO IS DO WHAT WE CAN!
!
EVEN IF WE SCREW UP, TOKYO WON'T GO DOWN IN ONE OR TWO CANNON BLASTS.
ALL WE CAN DO NOW IS HIT THEM WITH ALL WE'VE GOT!

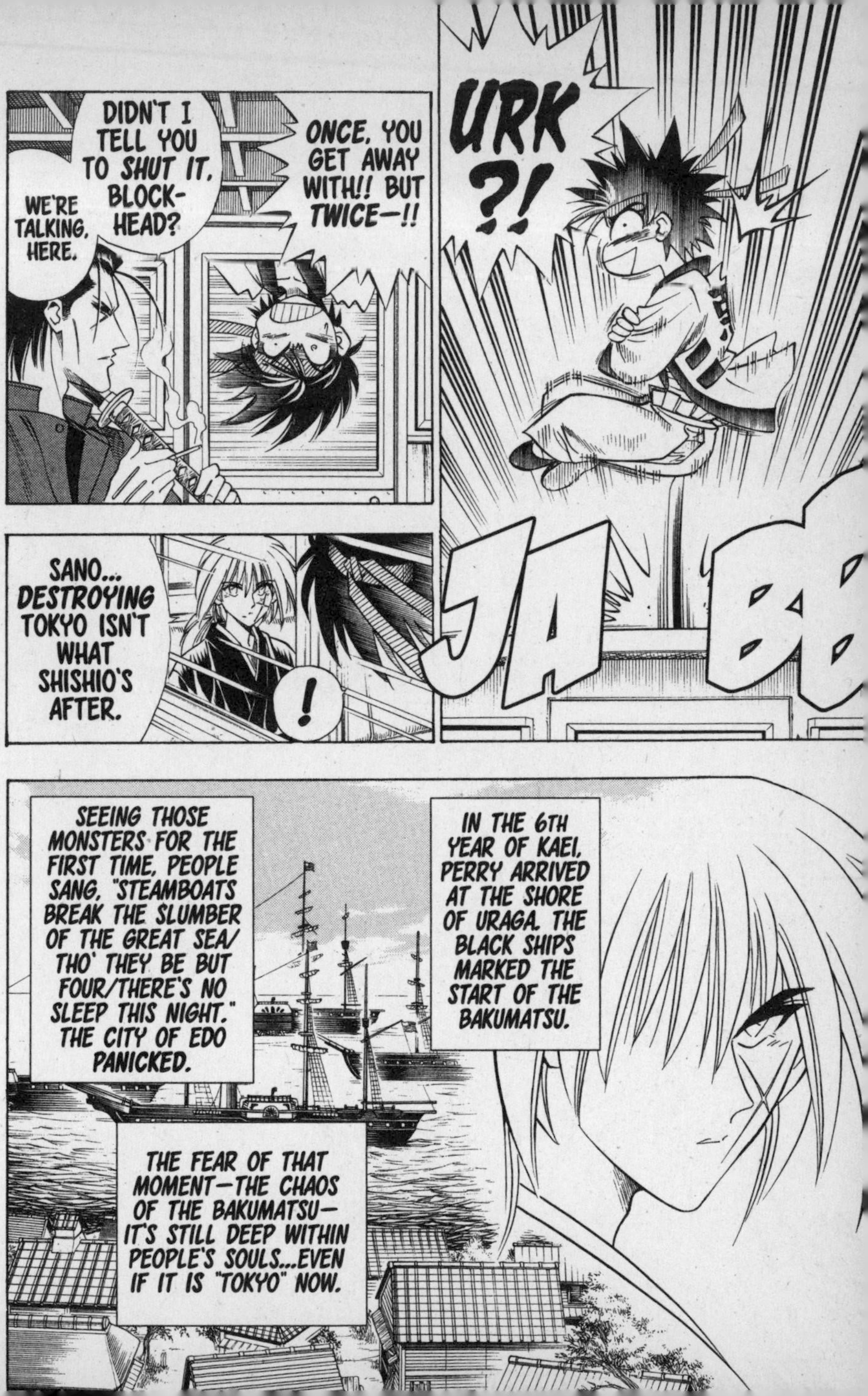
URK
?!
JA
ONCE, YOU GET AWAY WITH!! BUT TWICE—!!
DIDN'T I TELL YOU TO SHUT IT, BLOCK-HEAD?
WE'RE TALKING, HERE.
!
SANO... DESTROYING TOKYO ISN'T WHAT SHISHIO'S AFTER.
IN THE 6TH YEAR OF KAEI, PERRY ARRIVED AT THE SHORE OF URAGA. THE BLACK SHIPS MARKED THE START OF THE BAKUMATSU.
SEEING THOSE MONSTERS FOR THE FIRST TIME, PEOPLE SANG, "STEAMBOATS BREAK THE SLUMBER OF THE GREAT SEA/ THO' THEY BE BUT FOUR/THERE'S NO SLEEP THIS NIGHT." THE CITY OF EDO PANICKED.
THE FEAR OF THAT MOMENT—THE CHAOS OF THE BAKUMATSU—IT'S STILL DEEP WITHIN PEOPLE'S SOULS...EVEN IF IT IS "TOKYO" NOW.

READ THIS WAY

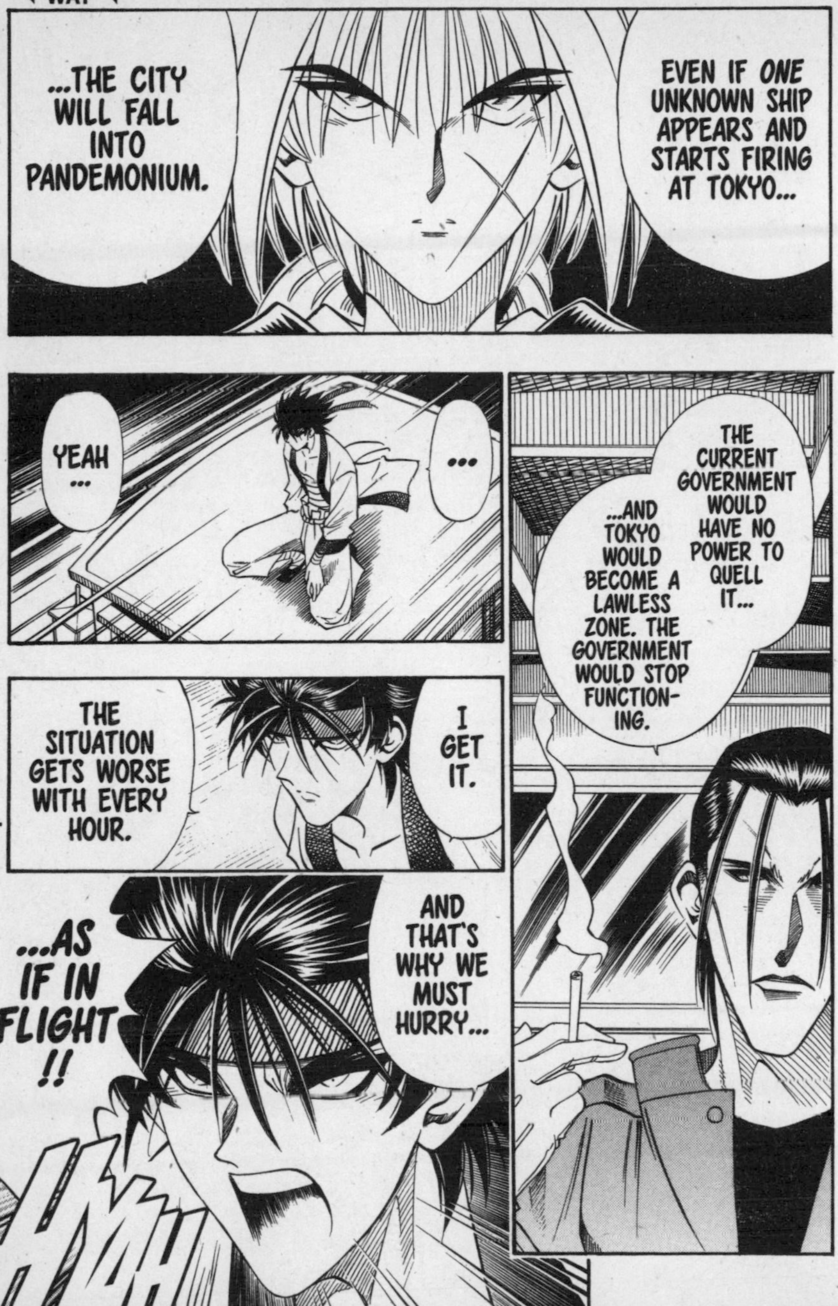
EVEN IF *ONE* UNKNOWN SHIP APPEARS AND STARTS FIRING AT TOKYO...
...THE CITY WILL FALL INTO PANDEMONIUM.
THE CURRENT GOVERNMENT WOULD HAVE NO POWER TO QUELL IT...
...AND TOKYO WOULD BECOME A LAWLESS ZONE. THE GOVERNMENT WOULD STOP FUNCTION-ING.
...
YEAH ...
I GET IT.
THE SITUATION GETS WORSE WITH EVERY HOUR.
AND THAT'S WHY WE MUST HURRY...
...AS IF IN FLIGHT !!
HAH

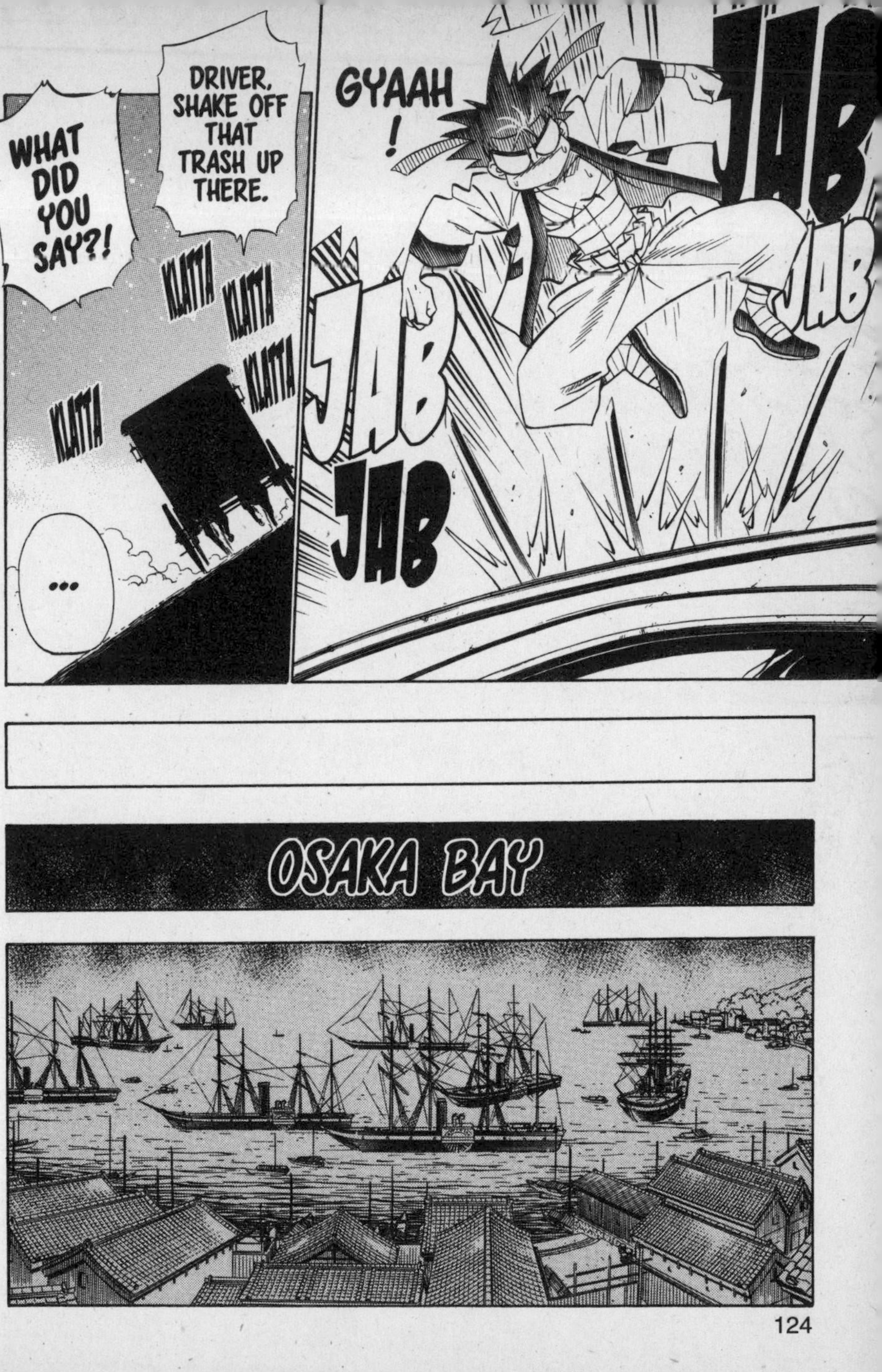
GYAAH !
JAB
JAB
JAB
JAB
DRIVER, SHAKE OFF THAT TRASH UP THERE.
WHAT DID YOU SAY?!
KLATTA
KLATTA
KLATTA
KLATTA
...
OSAKA BAY

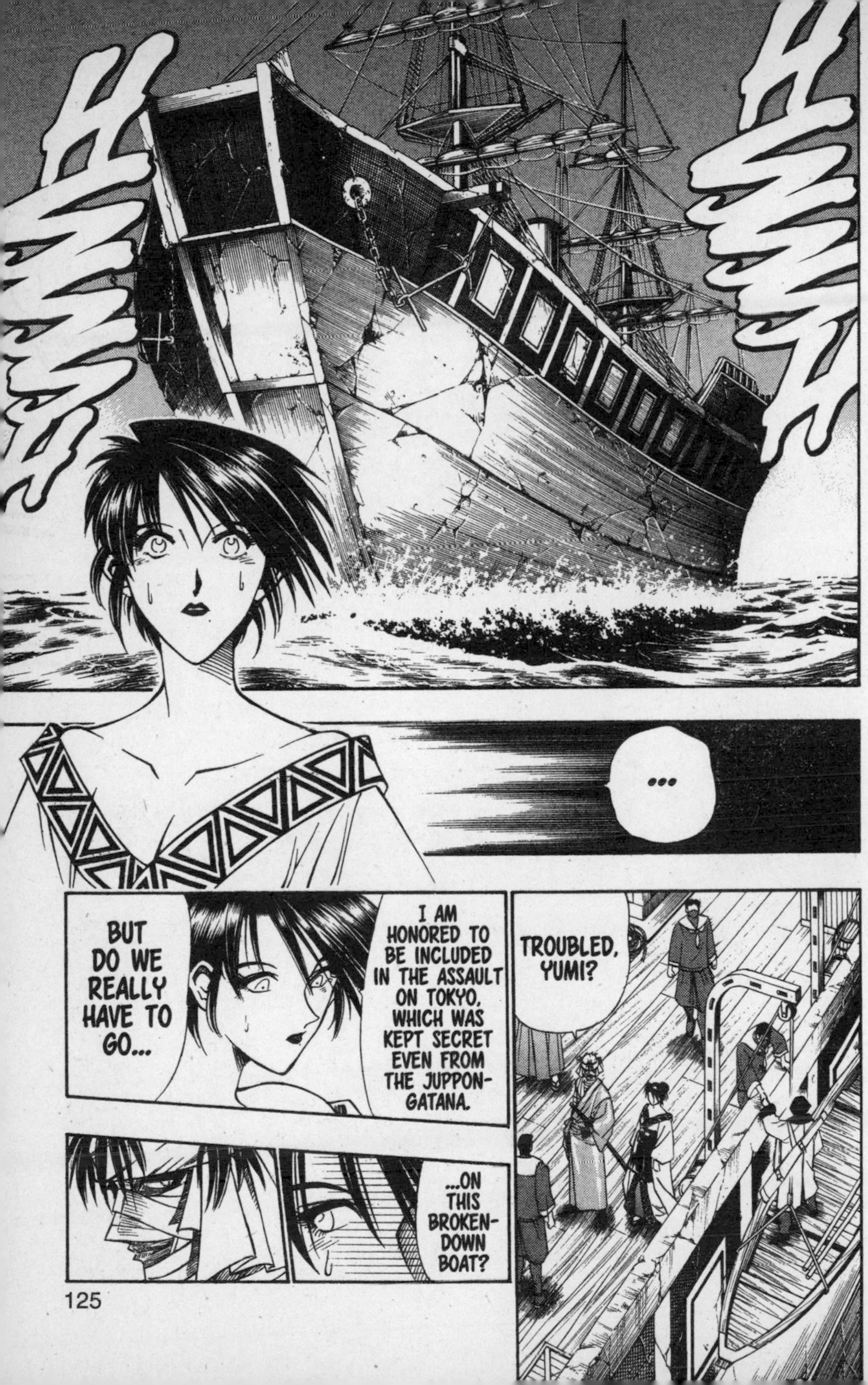
...
TROUBLED, YUMI?
I AM HONORED TO BE INCLUDED IN THE ASSAULT ON TOKYO, WHICH WAS KEPT SECRET EVEN FROM THE JUPPON-GATANA.
BUT DO WE REALLY HAVE TO GO...
...ON THIS BROKEN-DOWN BOAT?

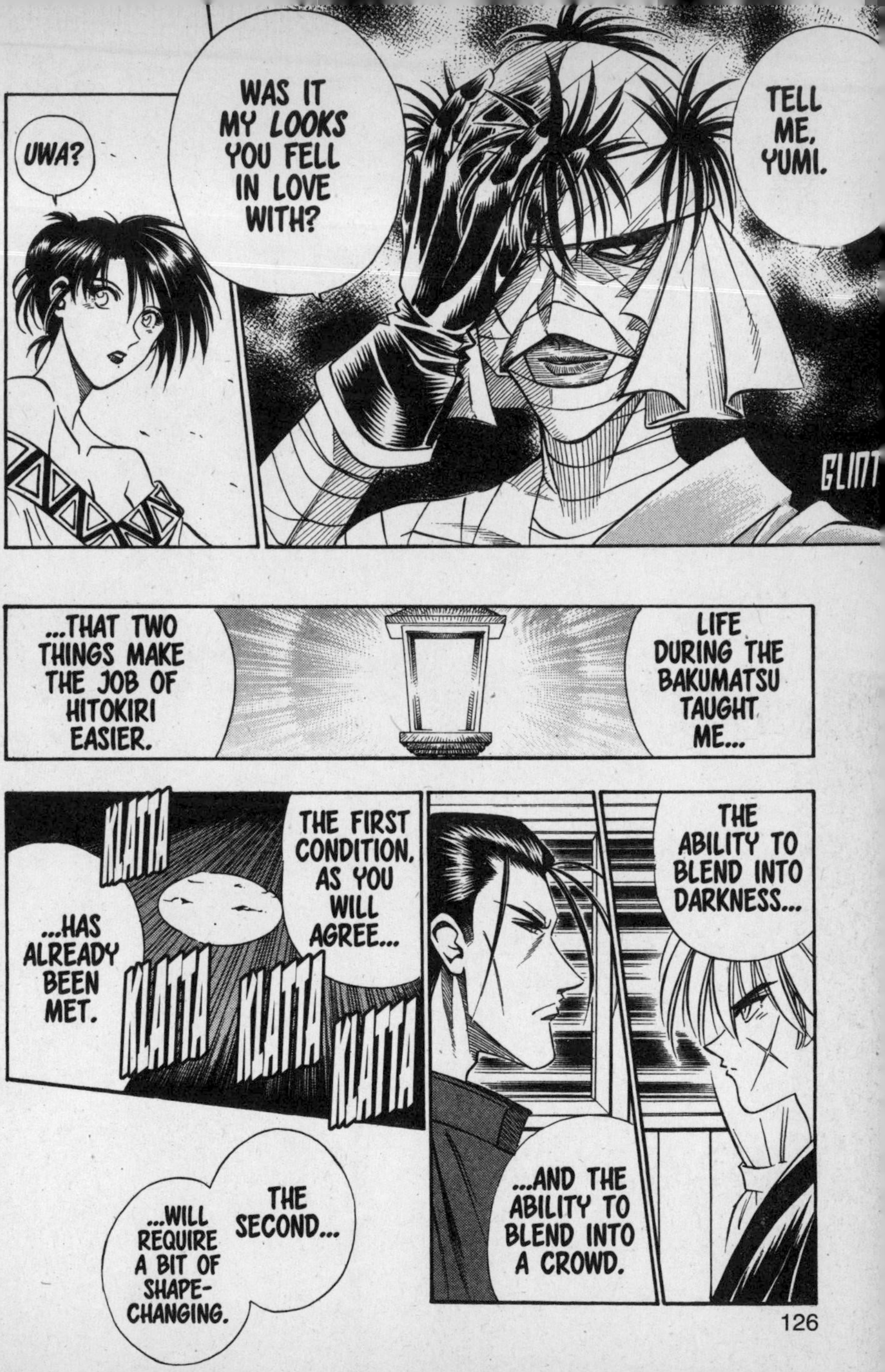
TELL ME, YUMI.
WAS IT MY LOOKS YOU FELL IN LOVE WITH?
UWA?
GLINT
LIFE DURING THE BAKUMATSU TAUGHT ME...
...THAT TWO THINGS MAKE THE JOB OF HITOKIRI EASIER.
THE ABILITY TO BLEND INTO DARKNESS...
...AND THE ABILITY TO BLEND INTO A CROWD.
THE FIRST CONDITION, AS YOU WILL AGREE...
KLATTA
KLATTA
KLATTA
KLATTA
...HAS ALREADY BEEN MET.
THE SECOND...
...WILL REQUIRE A BIT OF SHAPE-CHANGING.

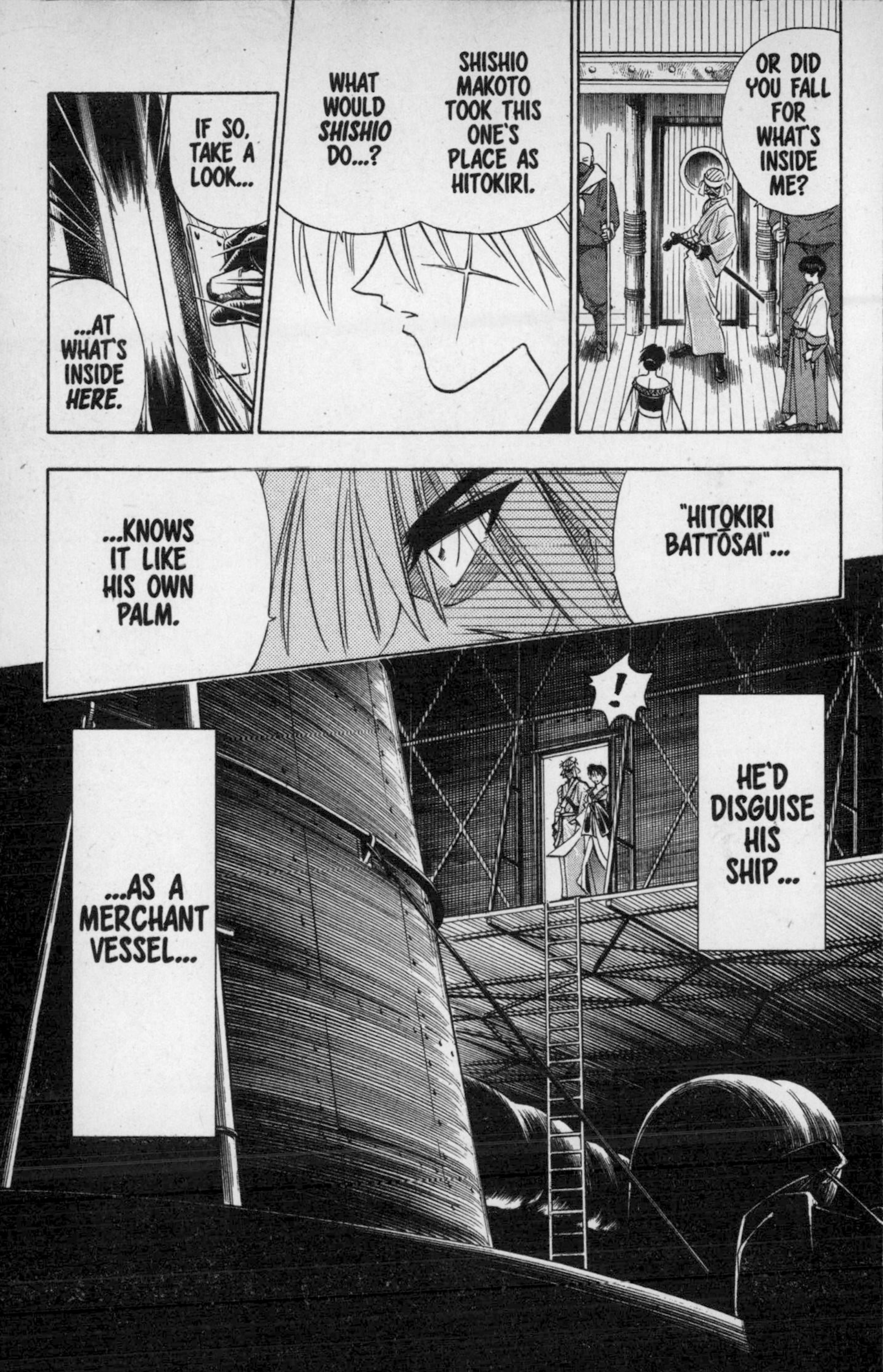
OR DID YOU FALL FOR WHAT'S INSIDE ME?
SHISHIO MAKOTO TOOK THIS ONE'S PLACE AS HITOKIRI.
WHAT WOULD SHISHIO DO...?
IF SO, TAKE A LOOK...
...AT WHAT'S INSIDE HERE.
"HITOKIRI BATTŌSAI"...
...KNOWS IT LIKE HIS OWN PALM.
!
HE'D DISGUISE HIS SHIP...
...AS A MERCHANT VESSEL...

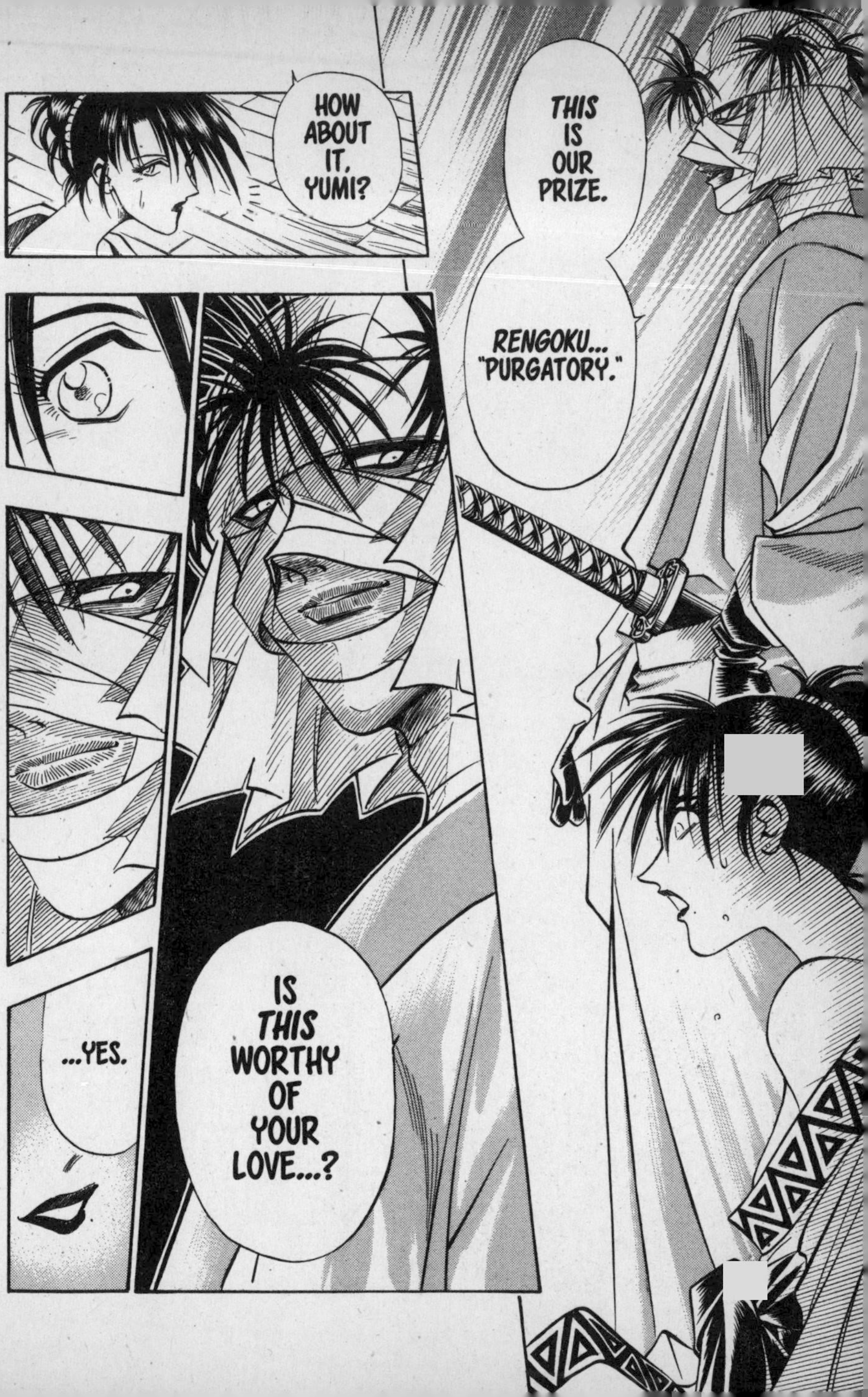
THIS IS OUR PRIZE.
RENGOKU... "PURGATORY."
HOW ABOUT IT, YUMI?
IS THIS WORTHY OF YOUR LOVE...?
...YES.

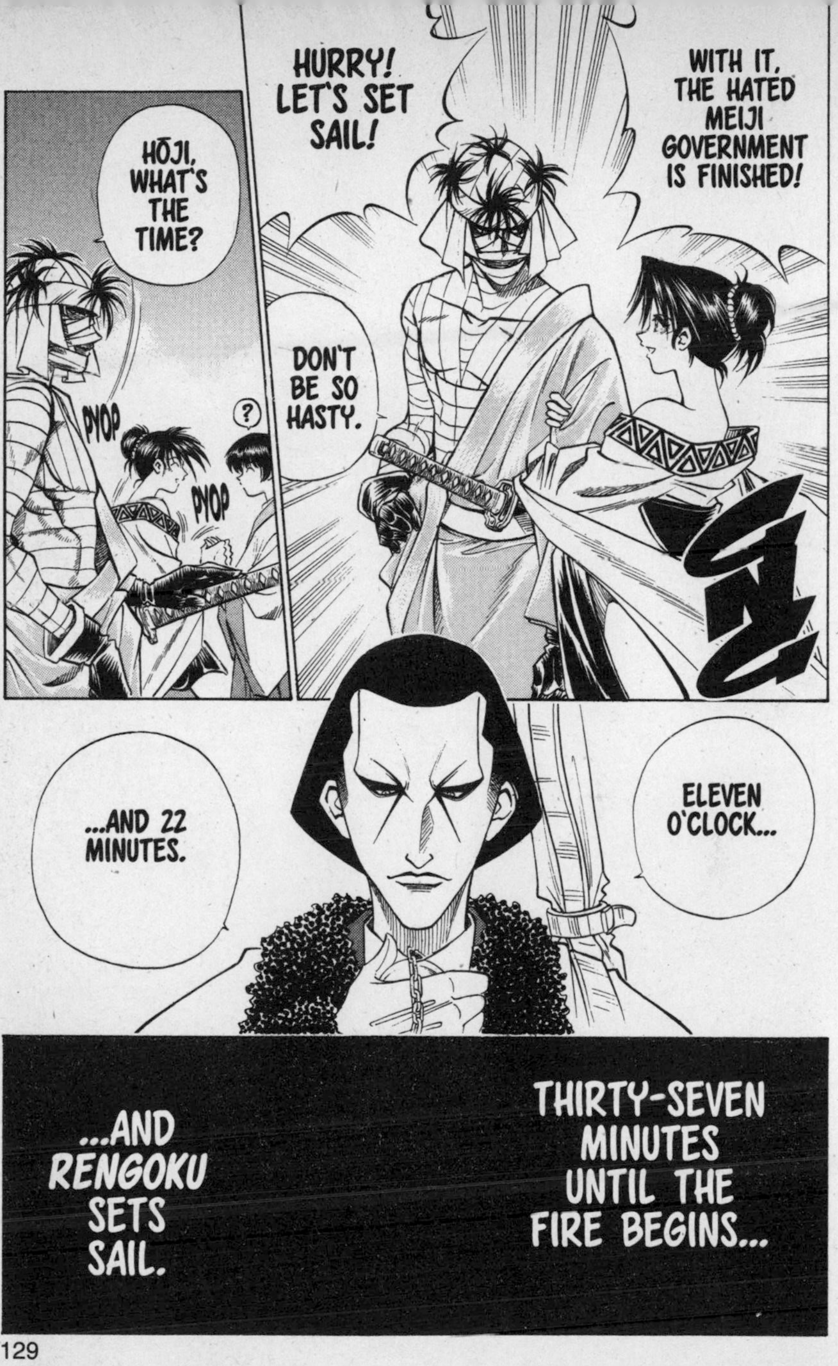
WITH IT, THE HATED MEIJI GOVERNMENT IS FINISHED!
HURRY! LET'S SET SAIL!
DON'T BE SO HASTY.
HŌJI, WHAT'S THE TIME?
PYOP
PYOP
?
ELEVEN O'CLOCK...
...AND 22 MINUTES.
THIRTY-SEVEN MINUTES UNTIL THE FIRE BEGINS...
...AND RENGOKU SETS SAIL.

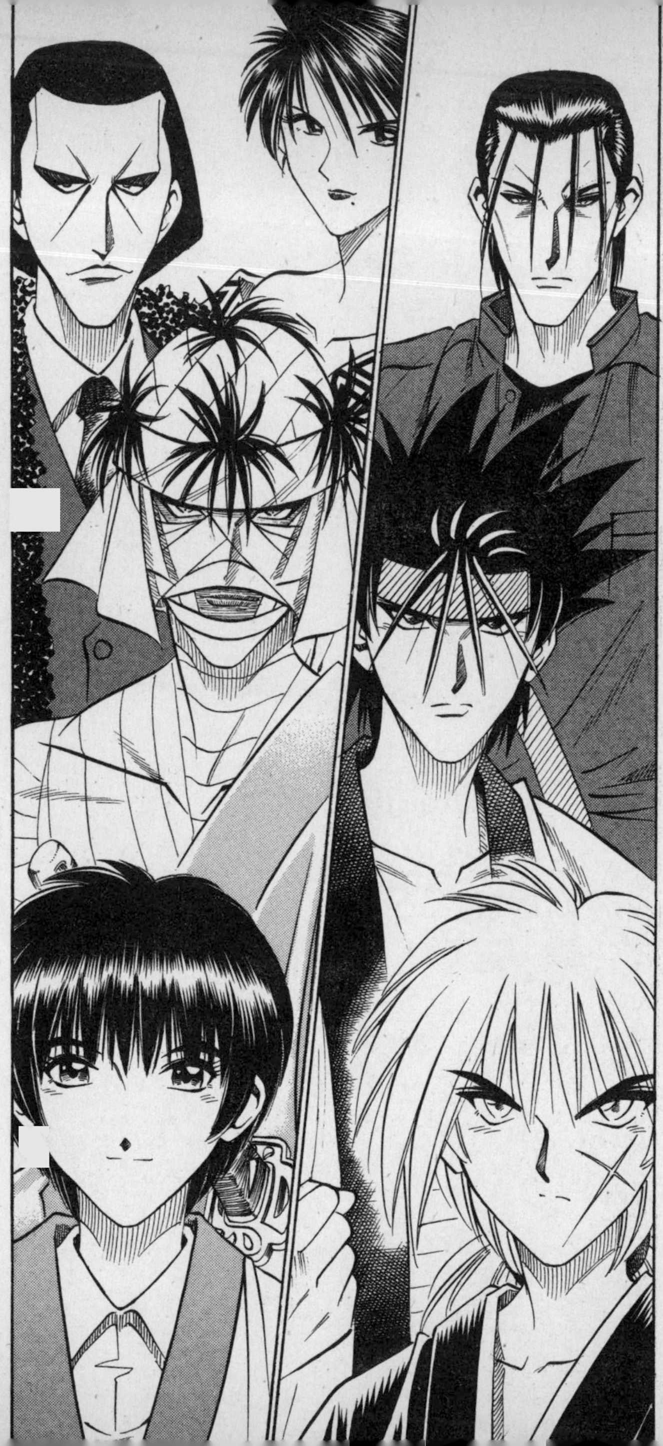

THIRTY-SEVEN MINUTES UNTIL...

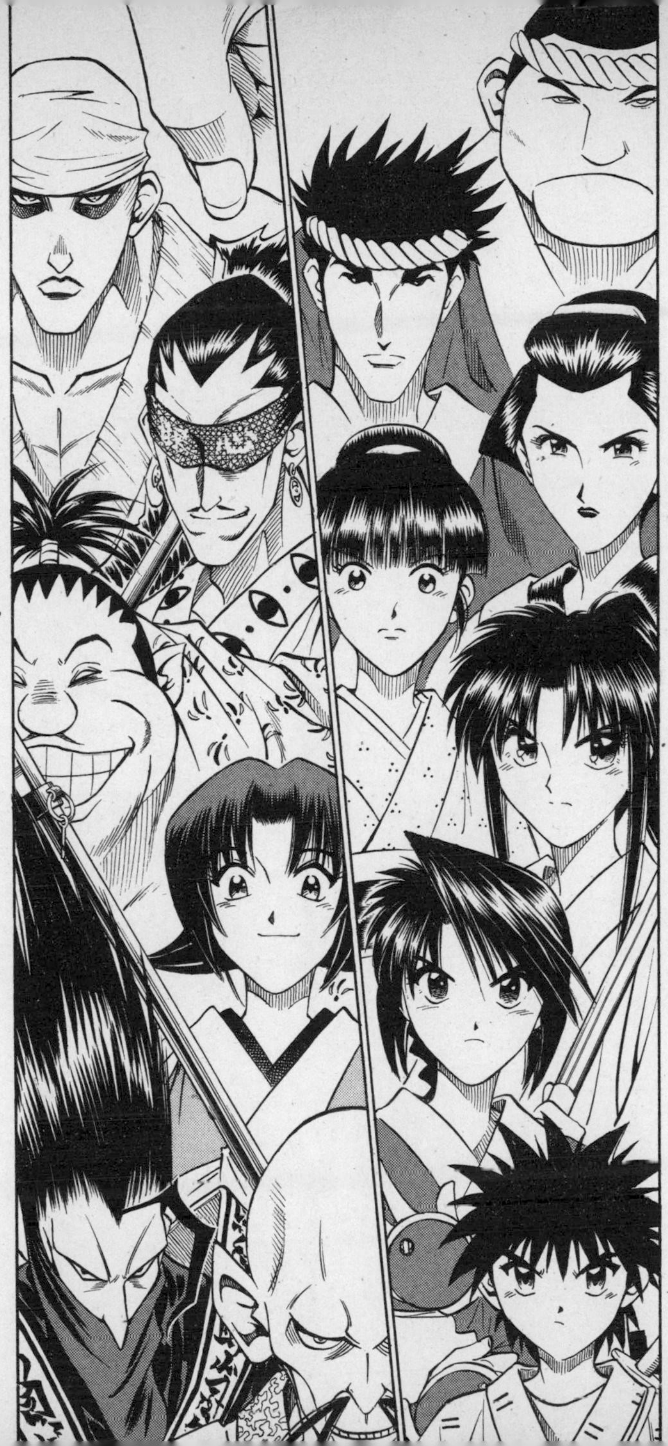
...IT ALL
COMES
TOGETHER.

Rurouni Kenshin

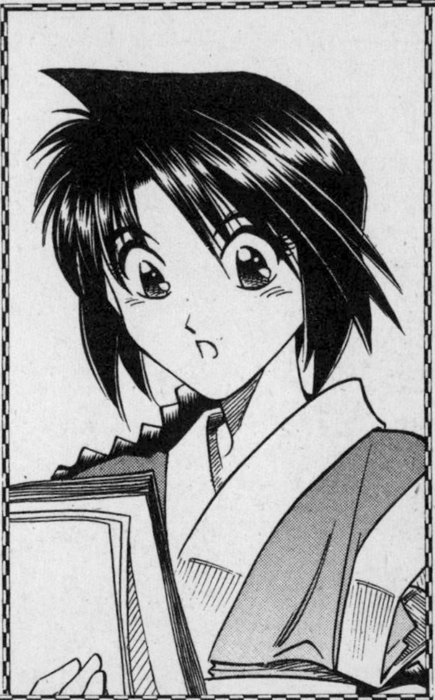

Act 1
The Great Kyoto Fire (Part I)

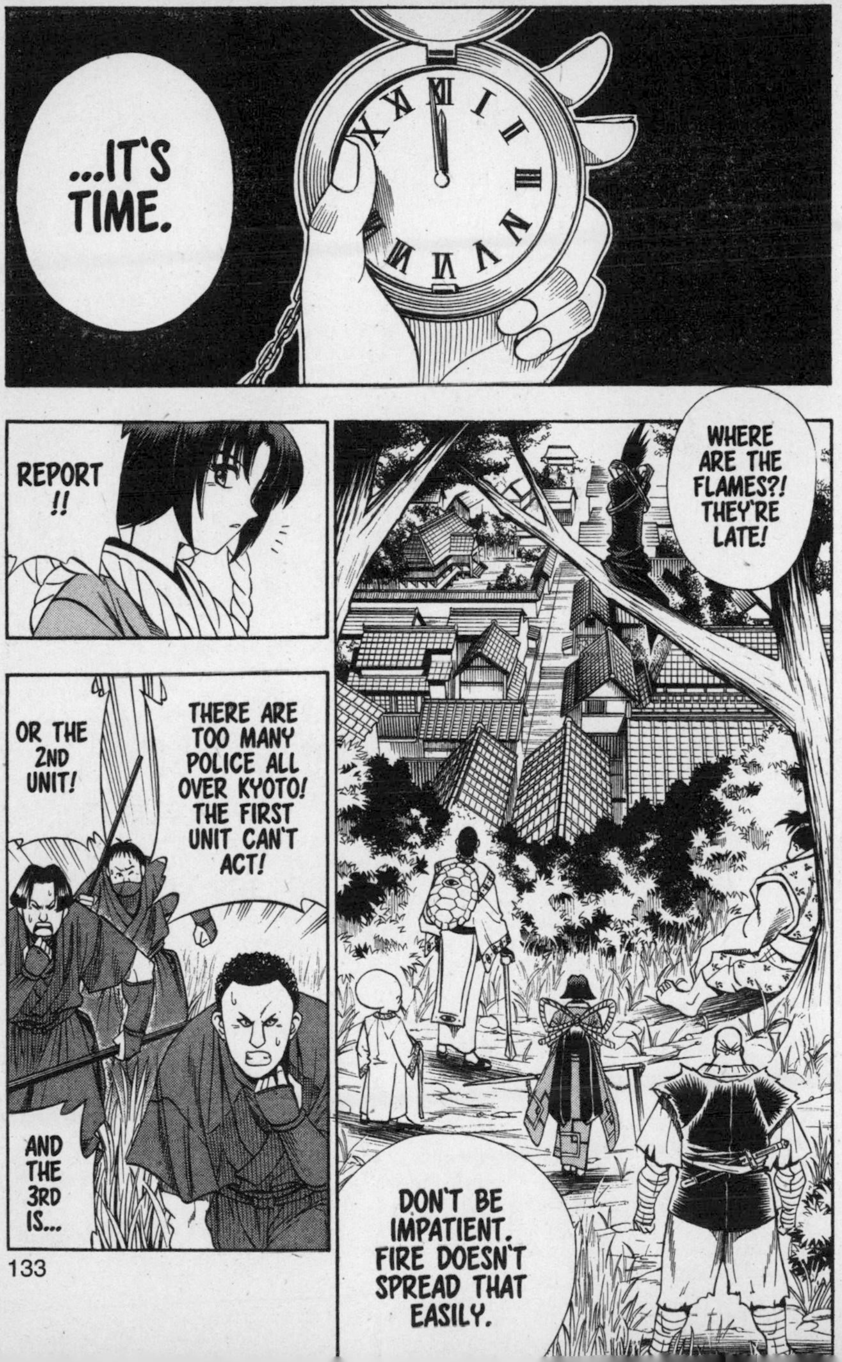

...IT'S TIME.
WHERE ARE THE FLAMES?! THEY'RE LATE!
DON'T BE IMPATIENT. FIRE DOESN'T SPREAD THAT EASILY.
REPORT !!
THERE ARE TOO MANY POLICE ALL OVER KYOTO! THE FIRST UNIT CAN'T ACT!
OR THE 2ND UNIT!
AND THE 3RD IS...

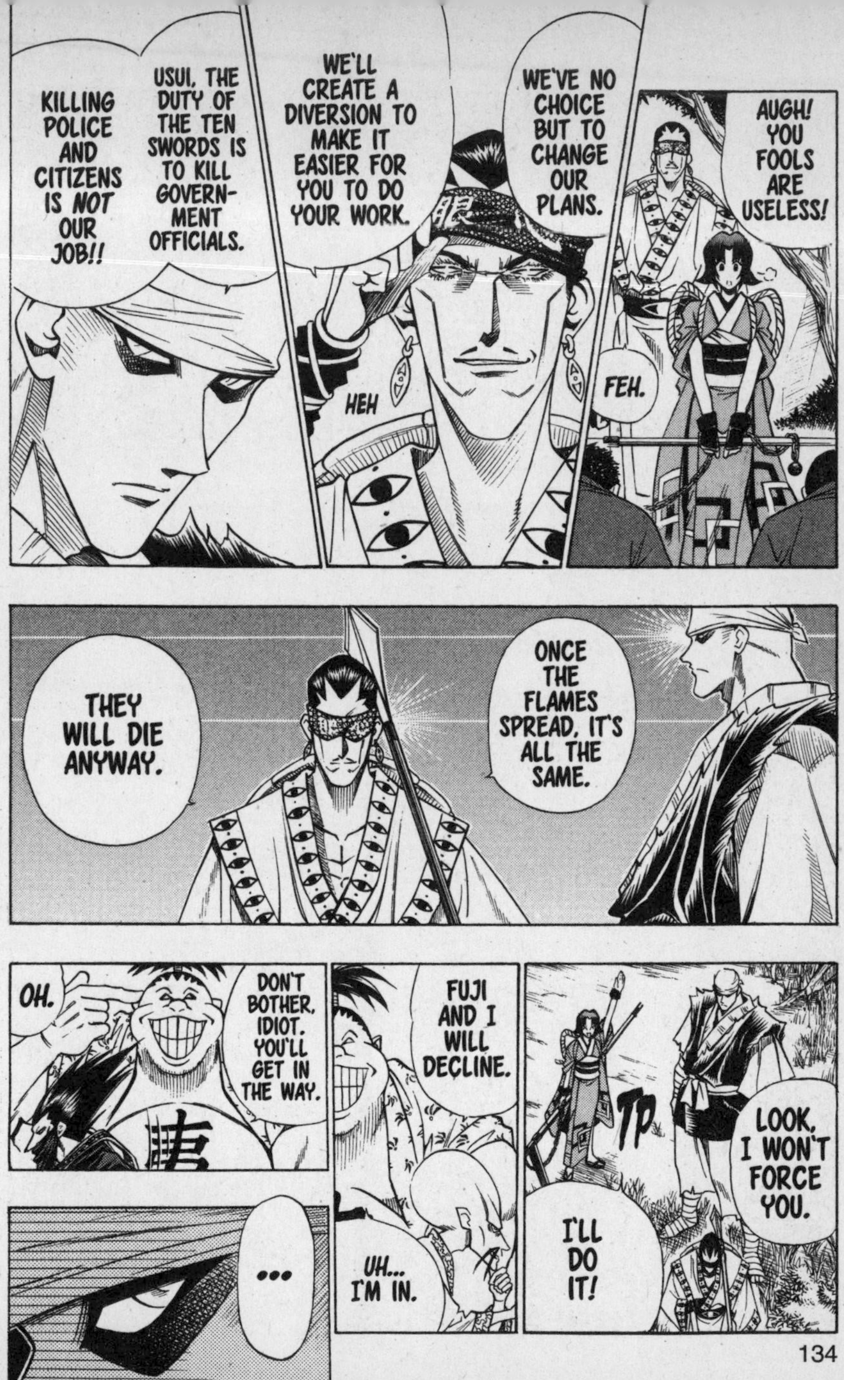
AUGH! YOU FOOLS ARE USELESS!
FEH.
WE'VE NO CHOICE BUT TO CHANGE OUR PLANS.
WE'LL CREATE A DIVERSION TO MAKE IT EASIER FOR YOU TO DO YOUR WORK.
HEH
USUI, THE DUTY OF THE TEN SWORDS IS TO KILL GOVERNMENT OFFICIALS.
KILLING POLICE AND CITIZENS IS *NOT* OUR JOB!!
ONCE THE FLAMES SPREAD, IT'S ALL THE SAME.
THEY WILL DIE ANYWAY.
LOOK, I WON'T FORCE YOU.
TP
I'LL DO IT!
FUJI AND I WILL DECLINE.
UH... I'M IN.
DON'T BOTHER, IDIOT. YOU'LL GET IN THE WAY.
OH.
...

Act 100

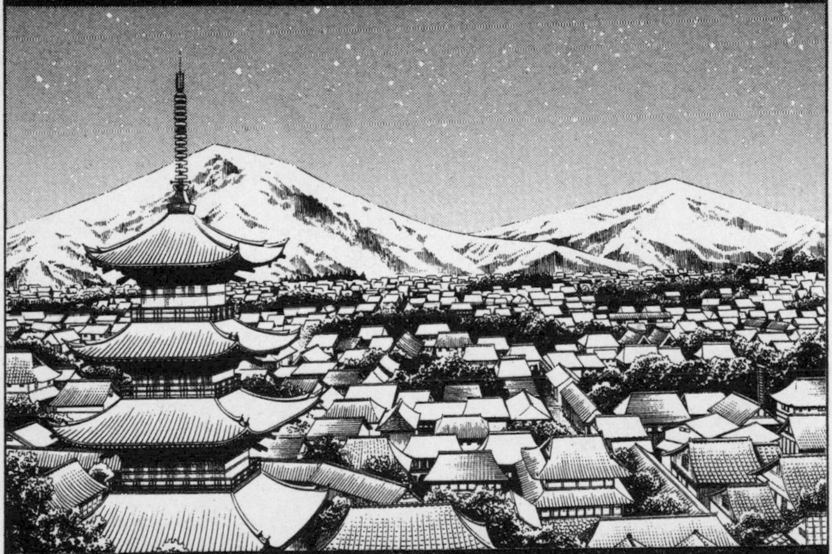

The Great Kyoto Fire (Part I)

伸宏和月

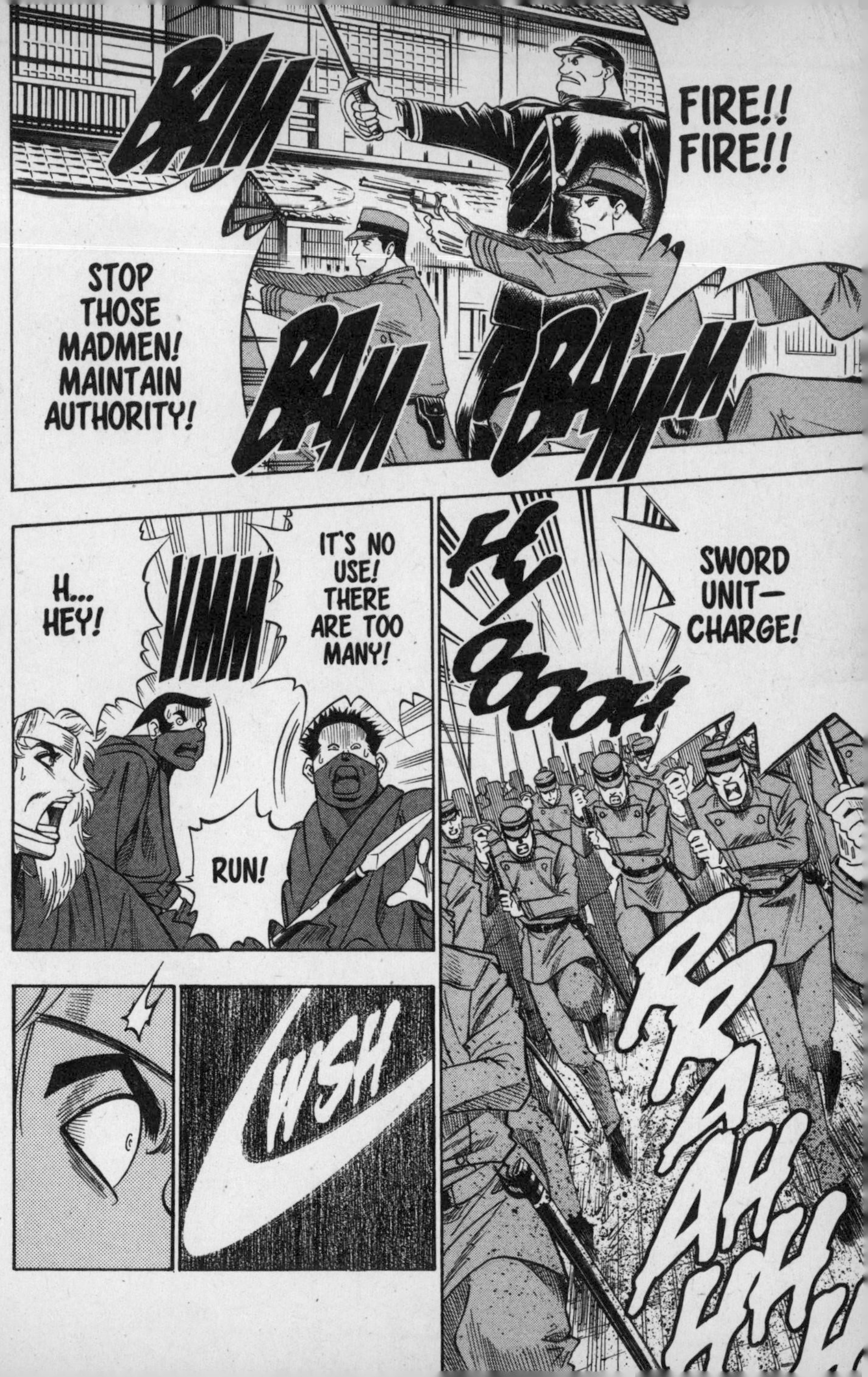
FIRE!! FIRE!!
BAM
STOP THOSE MADMEN! MAINTAIN AUTHORITY!
BAM
BAM
SWORD UNIT—CHARGE!
HEY OOOOH
RAAAH
IT'S NO USE! THERE ARE TOO MANY!
VMMM
H... HEY!
RUN!
WSH

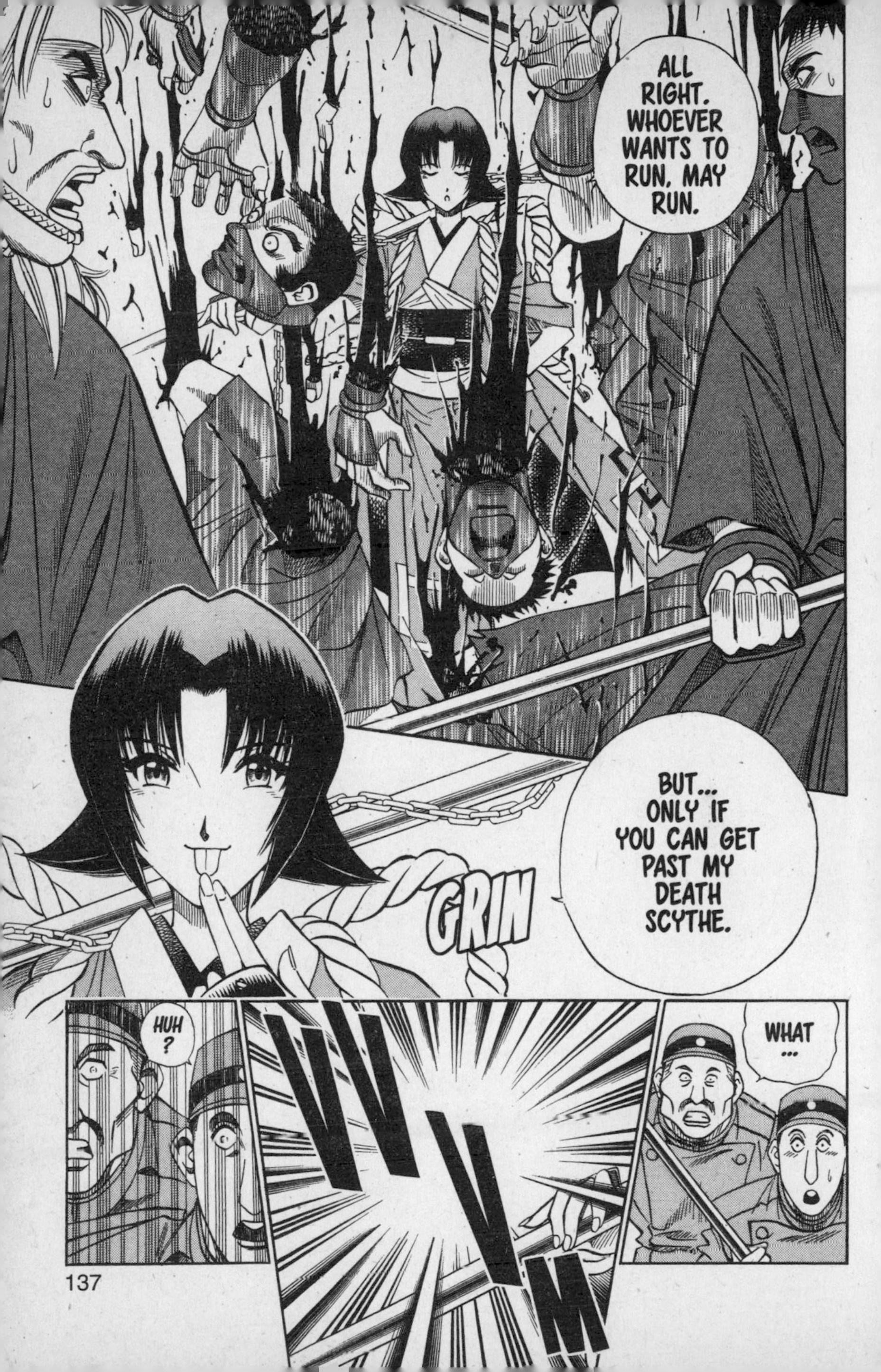
ALL RIGHT. WHOEVER WANTS TO RUN, MAY RUN.
BUT... ONLY IF YOU CAN GET PAST MY DEATH SCYTHE.
GRIN
WHAT ...
VVVM
HUH ?

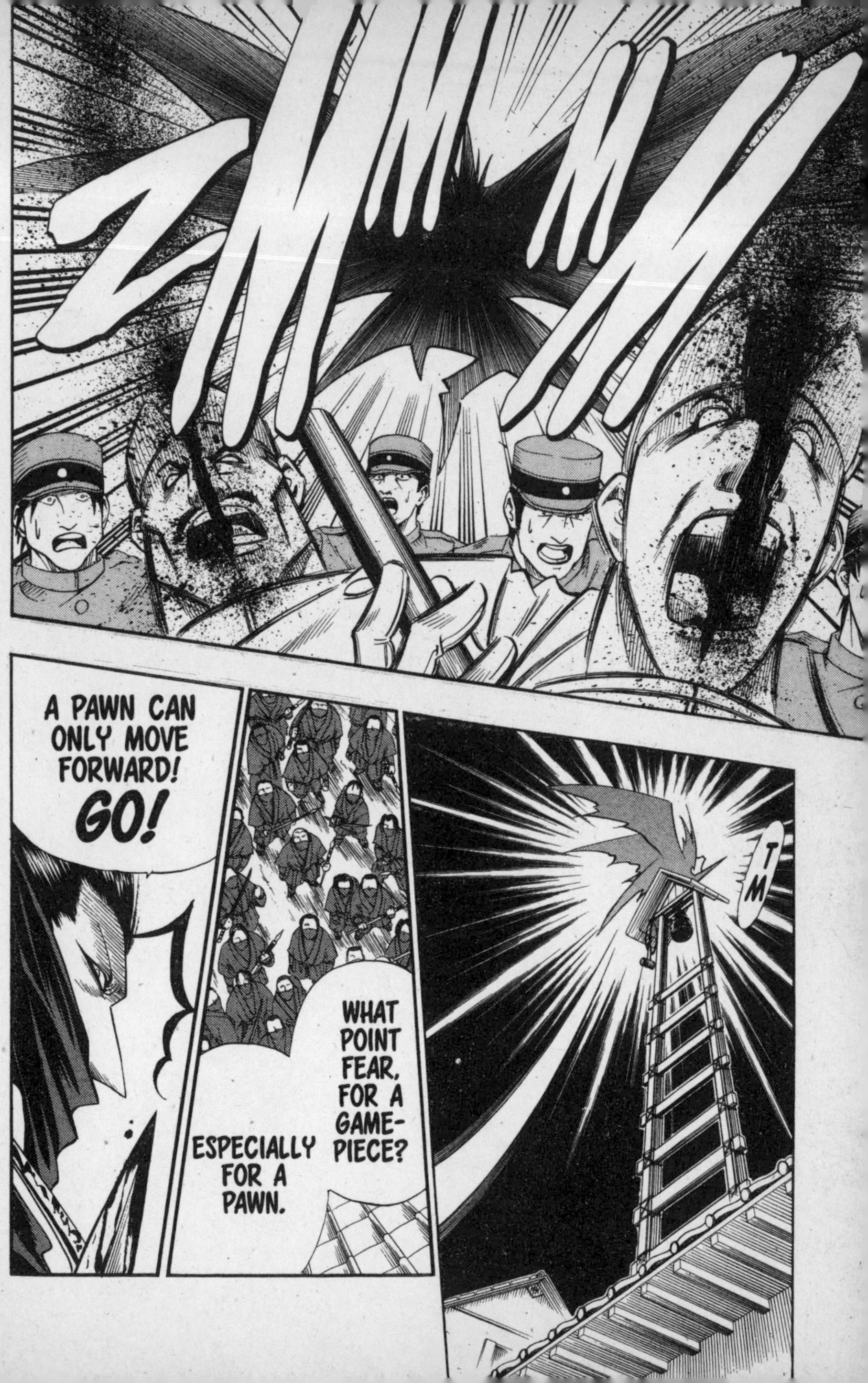
TM
WHAT POINT FEAR, FOR A GAME-PIECE?
ESPECIALLY FOR A PAWN.
A PAWN CAN ONLY MOVE FORWARD! GO!

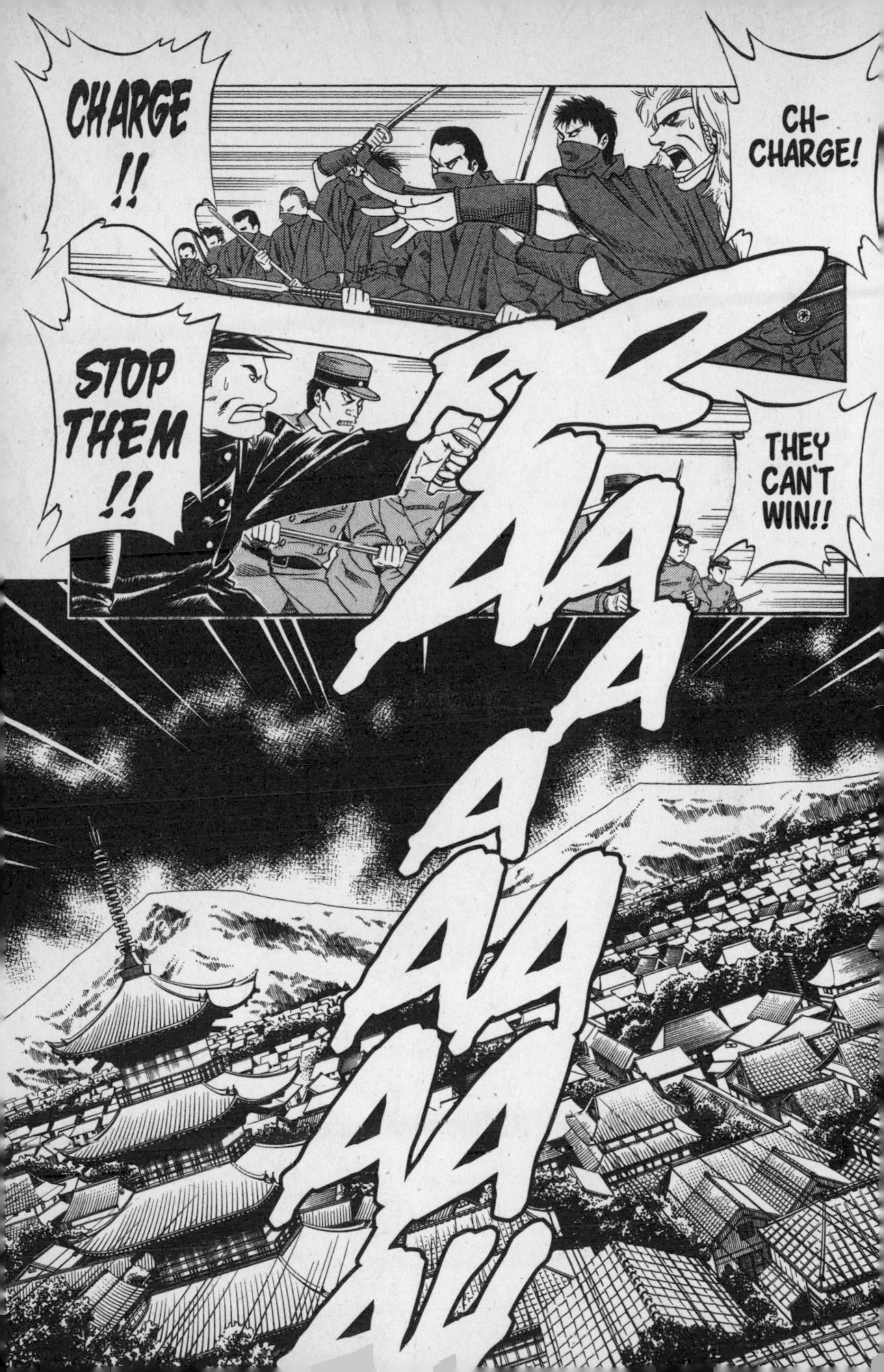
CH- CHARGE!
CHARGE!!
THEY CAN'T WIN!!
STOP THEM!!

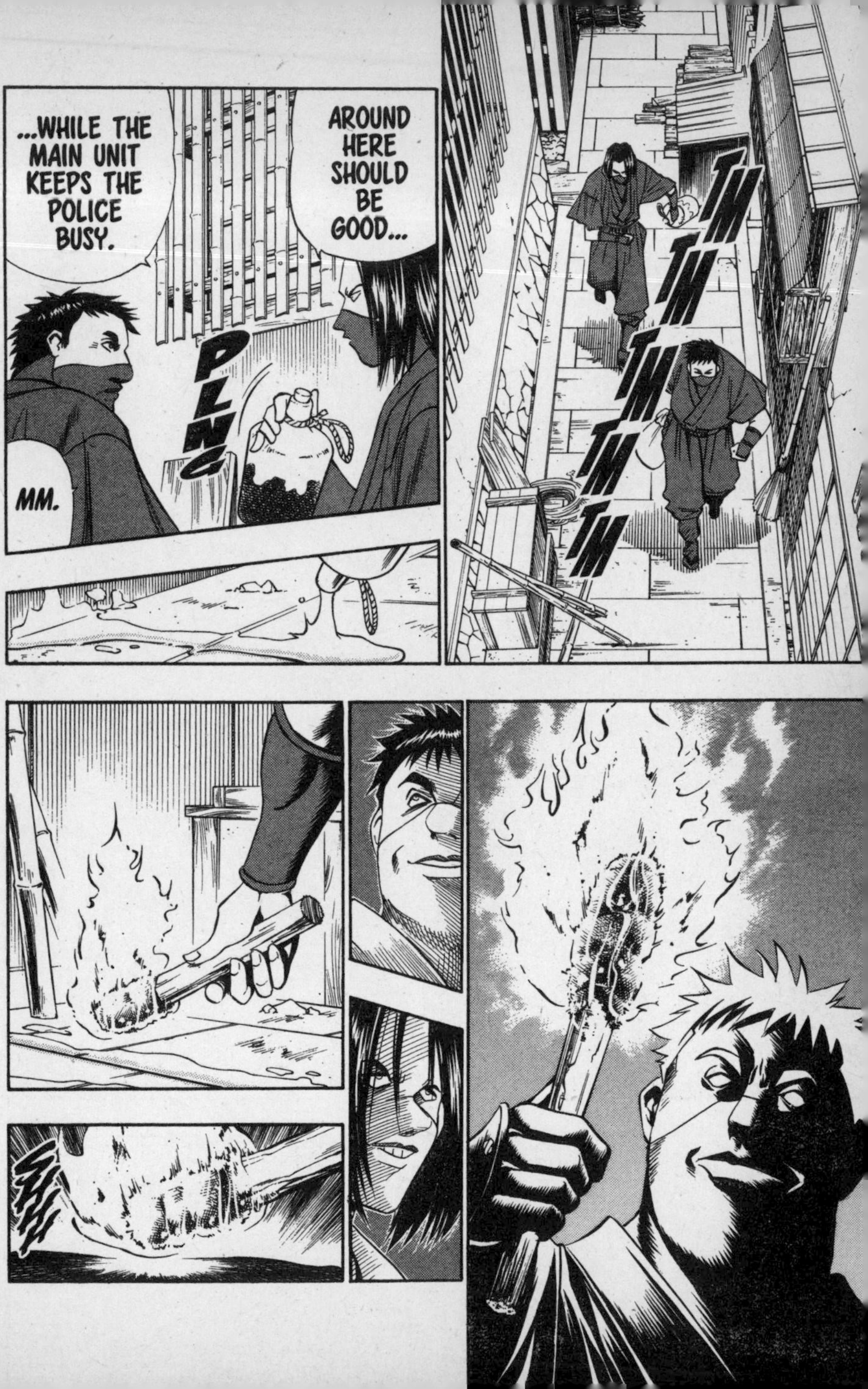
TH TH TH TH TH TH
AROUND HERE SHOULD BE GOOD...
...WHILE THE MAIN UNIT KEEPS THE POLICE BUSY.
PLNG
MM.

READ THIS WAY

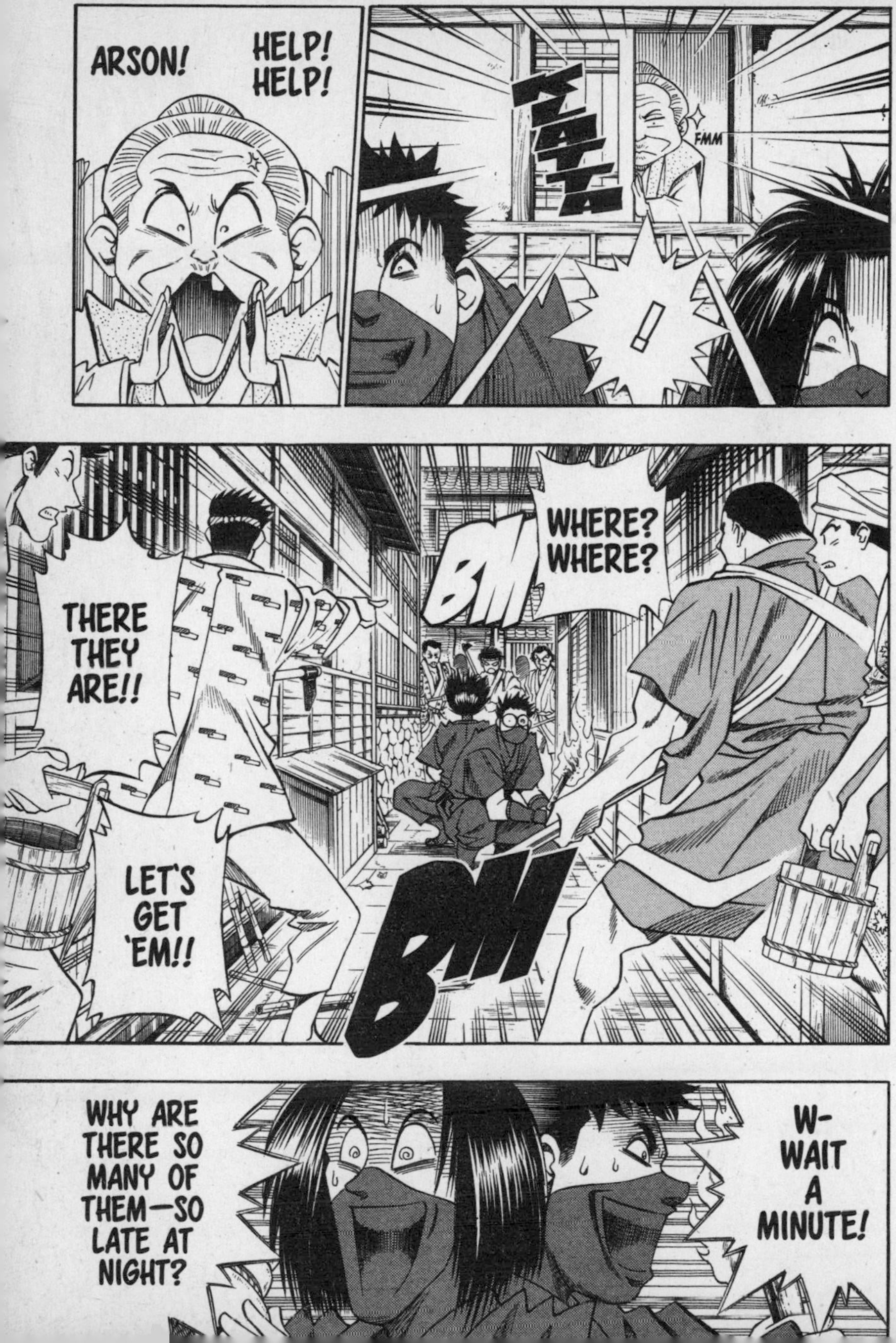
FMM
!
HELP! HELP!
ARSON!
WHERE? WHERE?
BAM
THERE THEY ARE!!
LET'S GET 'EM!!
BAM
W-WAIT A MINUTE!
WHY ARE THERE SO MANY OF THEM—SO LATE AT NIGHT?

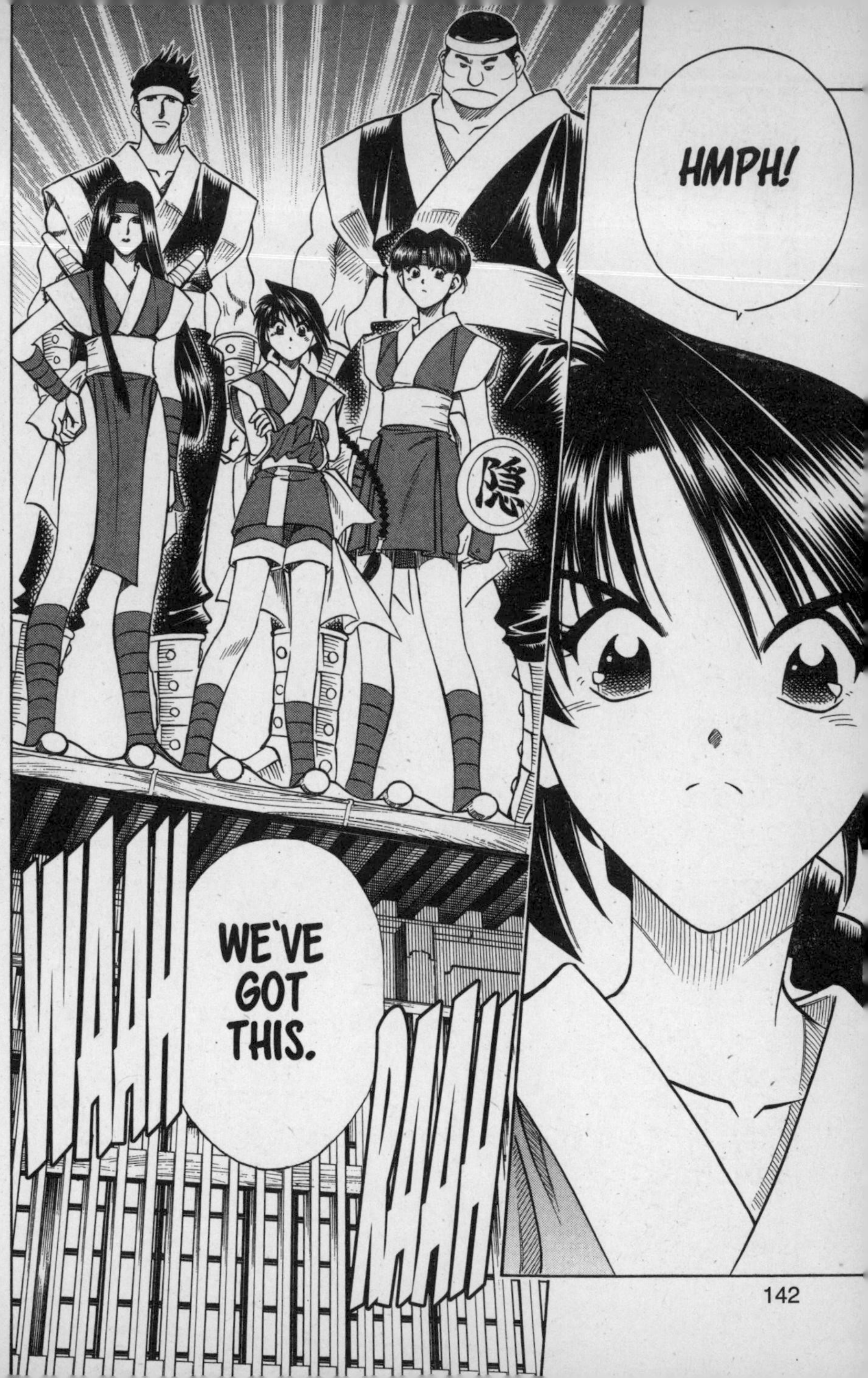
HMPH!
隠
WE'VE GOT THIS.

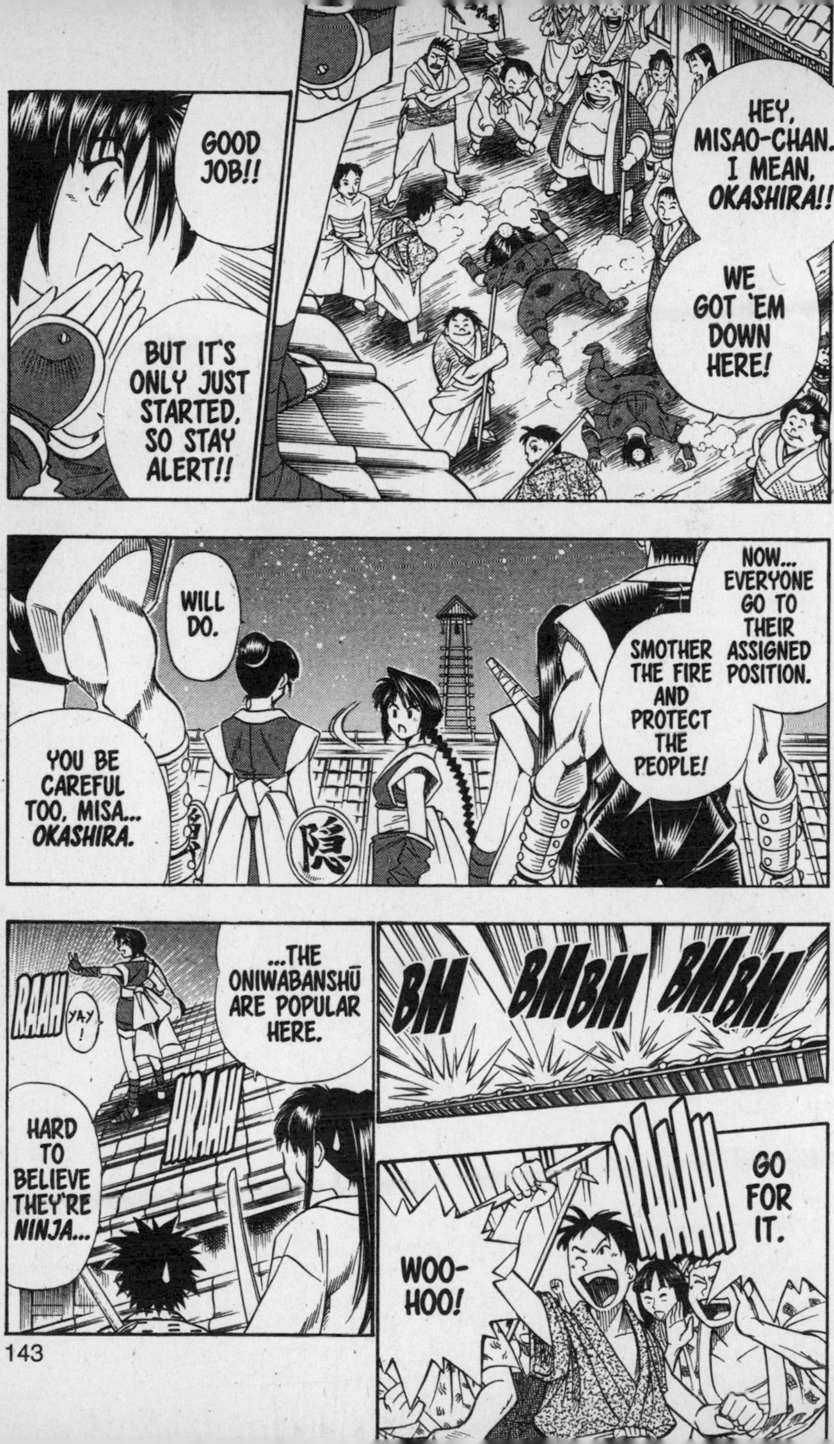
HEY, MISAO-CHAN... I MEAN, OKASHIRA!!
WE GOT 'EM DOWN HERE!
GOOD JOB!!
BUT IT'S ONLY JUST STARTED, SO STAY ALERT!!
NOW... EVERYONE GO TO THEIR ASSIGNED POSITION.
SMOTHER THE FIRE AND PROTECT THE PEOPLE!
WILL DO.
隠
YOU BE CAREFUL TOO, MISA... OKASHIRA.
BM BMBM BMBM
GO FOR IT.
WOO-HOO!
RAAH
YAY!
HRAAH
...THE ONIWABANSHŪ ARE POPULAR HERE.
HARD TO BELIEVE THEY'RE NINJA...

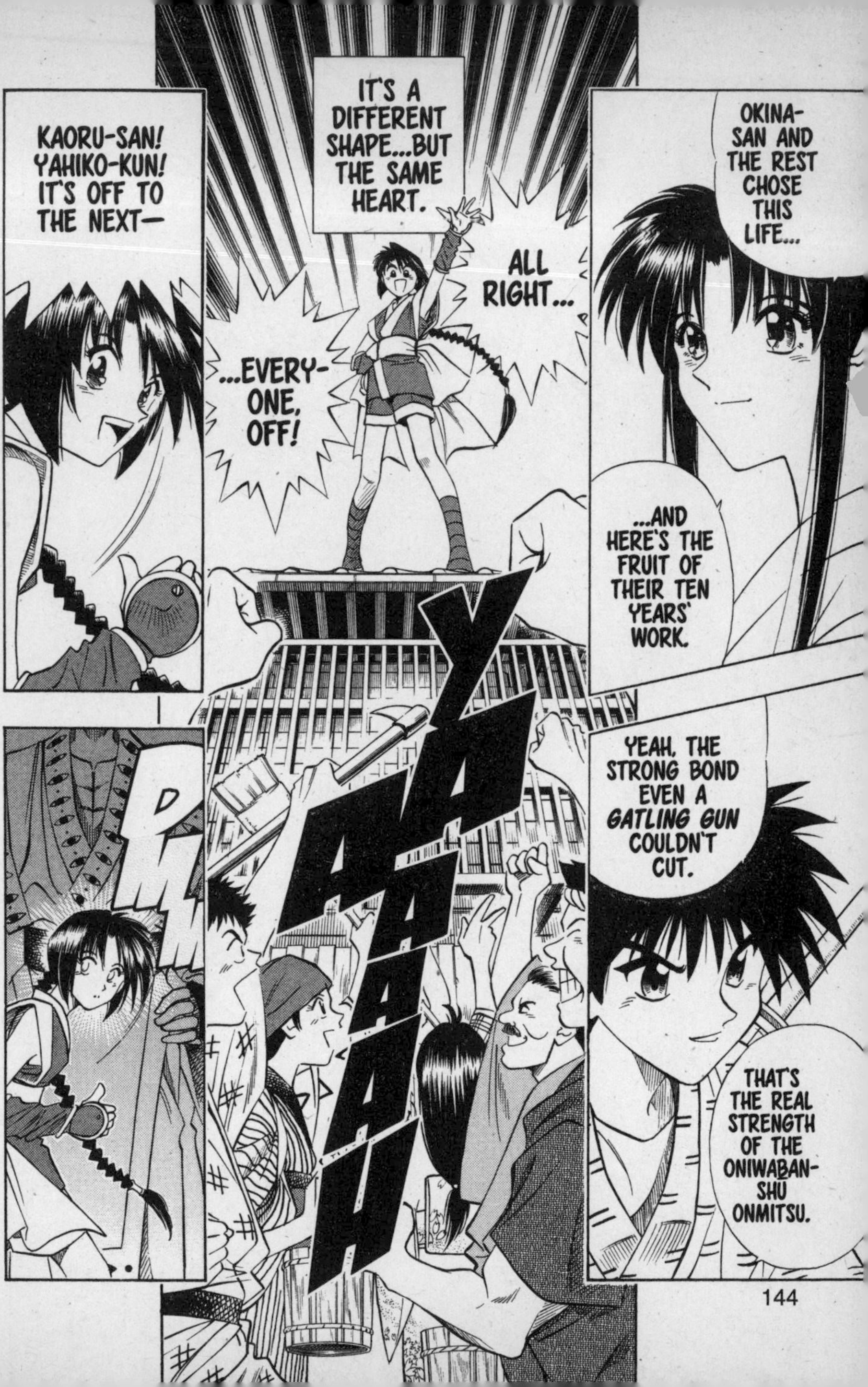

OKINA-SAN AND THE REST CHOSE THIS LIFE...
...AND HERE'S THE FRUIT OF THEIR TEN YEARS' WORK.
YEAH, THE STRONG BOND EVEN A *GATLING GUN* COULDN'T CUT.
THAT'S THE REAL STRENGTH OF THE ONIWABANSHŪ ONMITSU.
IT'S A DIFFERENT SHAPE...BUT THE SAME HEART.
ALL RIGHT...
...EVERYONE, OFF!
KAORU-SAN! YAHIKO-KUN! IT'S OFF TO THE NEXT—

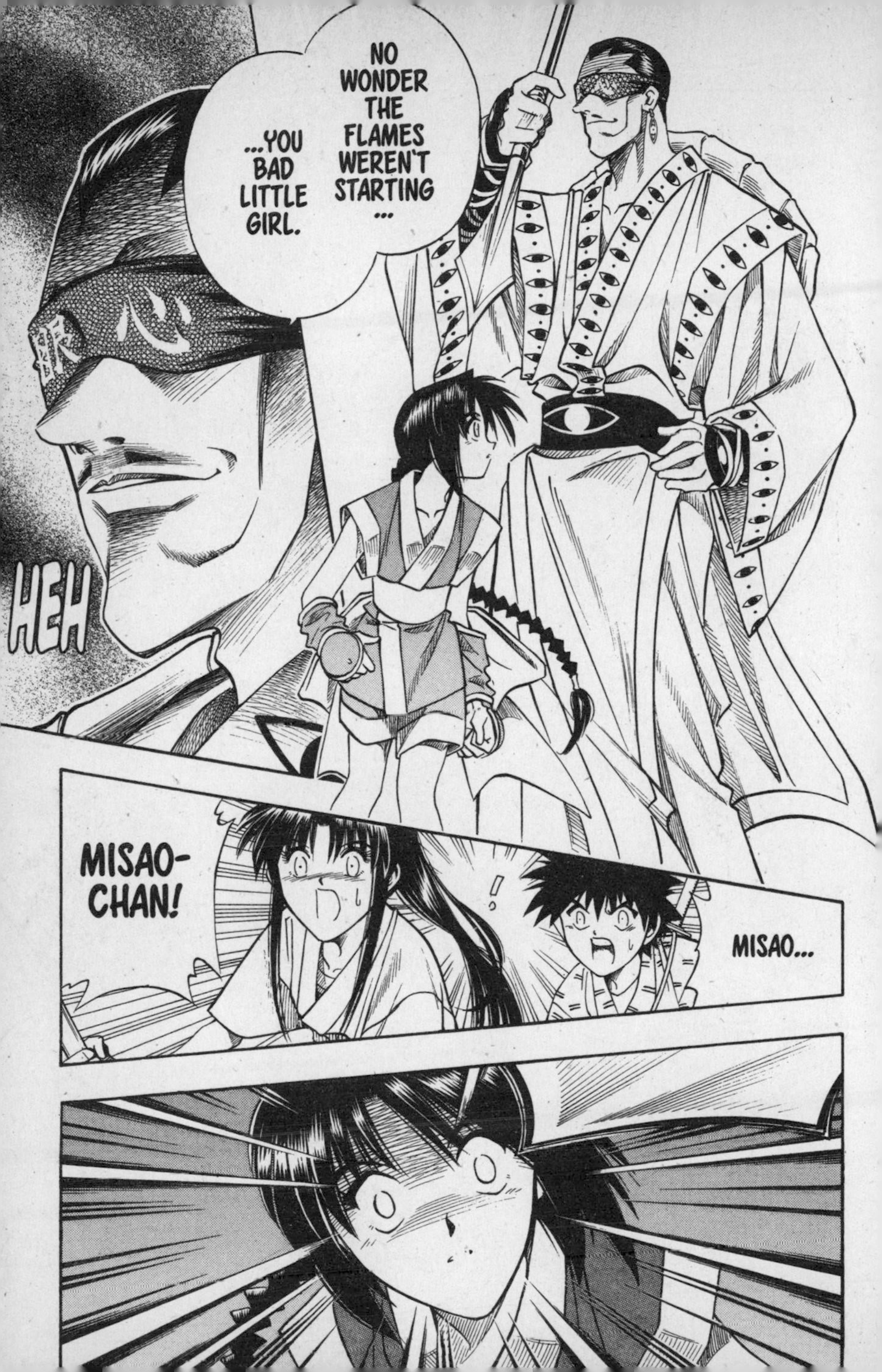
NO WONDER THE FLAMES WEREN'T STARTING...
...YOU BAD LITTLE GIRL.
HEH
MISAO...
!
MISAO-CHAN!

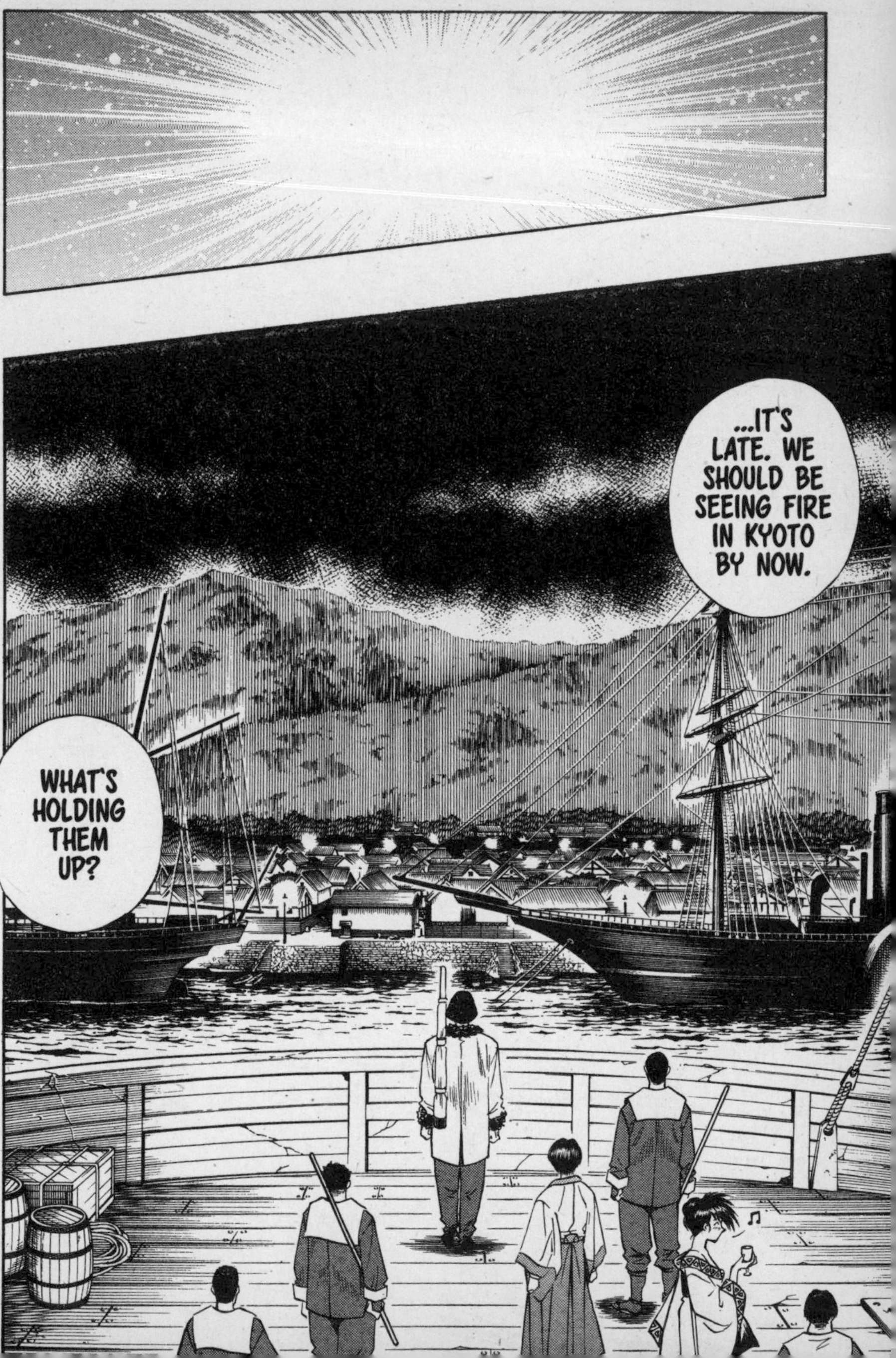
...IT'S LATE. WE SHOULD BE SEEING FIRE IN KYOTO BY NOW.
WHAT'S HOLDING THEM UP?

READ THIS WAY

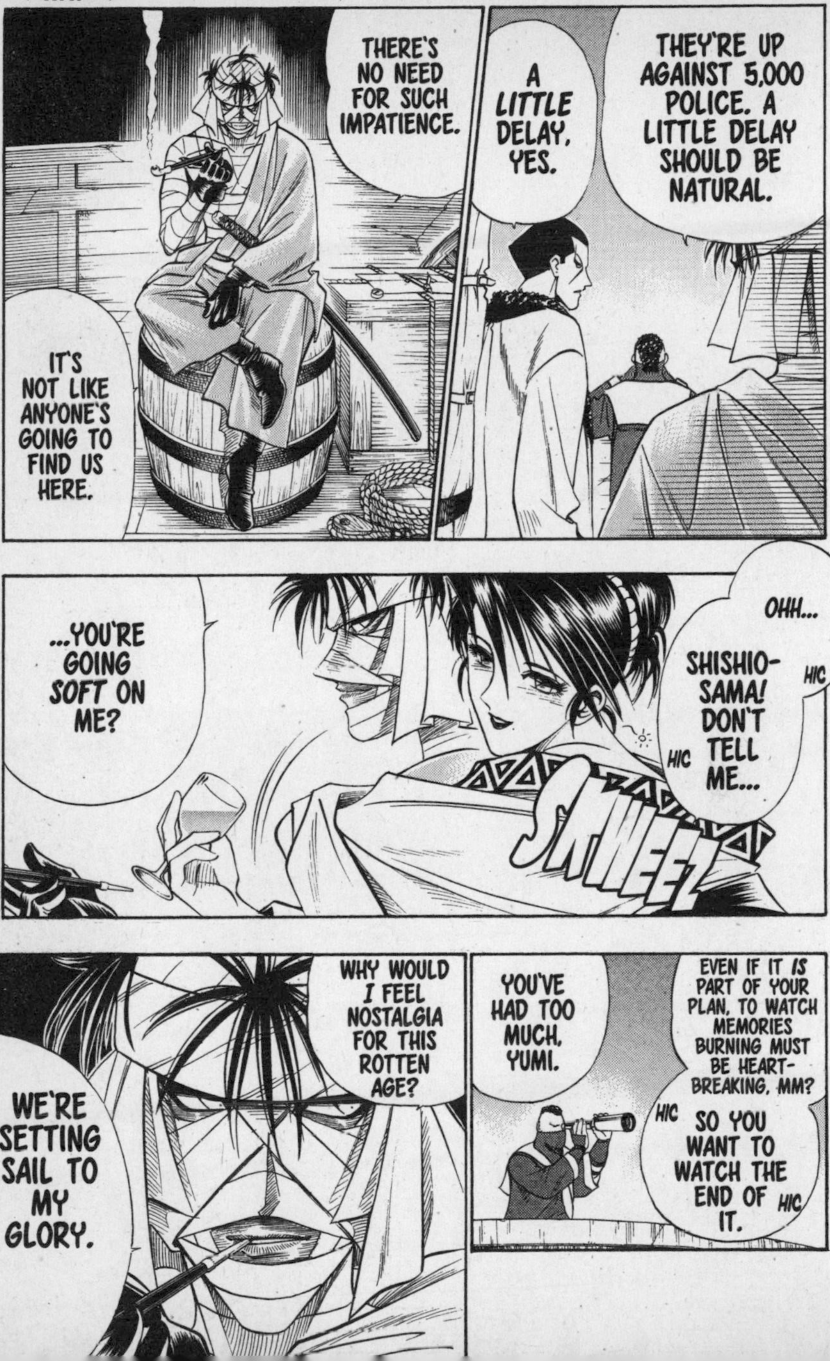

THEY'RE UP AGAINST 5,000 POLICE. A LITTLE DELAY SHOULD BE NATURAL.
A *LITTLE* DELAY, YES.
THERE'S NO NEED FOR SUCH IMPATIENCE.
IT'S NOT LIKE ANYONE'S GOING TO FIND US HERE.
OHH...
HIC
SHISHIO-SAMA! DON'T TELL ME...
HIC
SKWEEZ
...YOU'RE GOING *SOFT* ON ME?
EVEN IF IT *IS* PART OF YOUR PLAN, TO WATCH MEMORIES BURNING MUST BE HEART-BREAKING, MM?
HIC
SO YOU WANT TO WATCH THE END OF IT.
HIC
YOU'VE HAD TOO MUCH, YUMI.
WHY WOULD *I* FEEL NOSTALGIA FOR THIS ROTTEN AGE?
WE'RE SETTING SAIL TO MY GLORY.

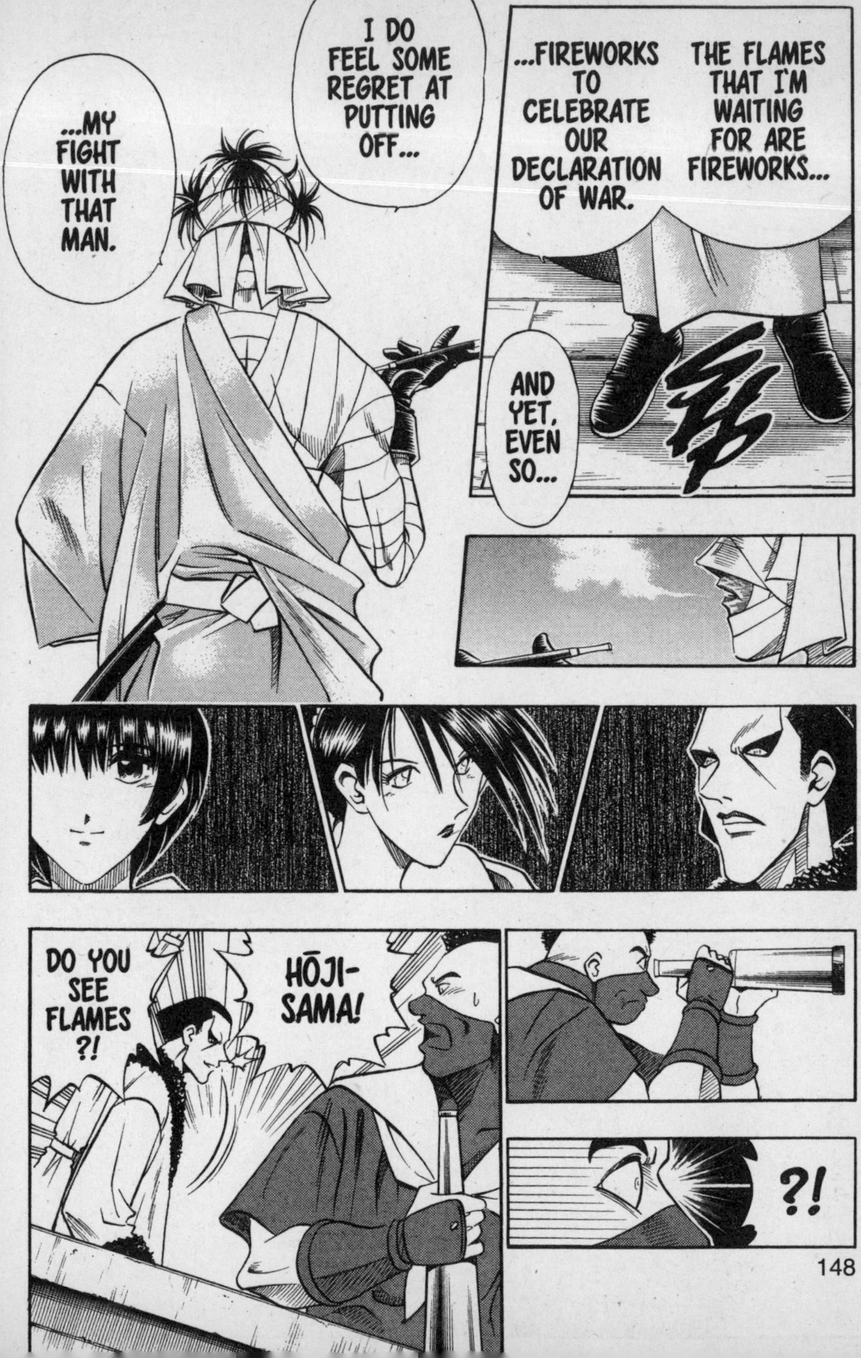
THE FLAMES THAT I'M WAITING FOR ARE FIREWORKS...
...FIREWORKS TO CELEBRATE OUR DECLARATION OF WAR.
AND YET, EVEN SO...
I DO FEEL SOME REGRET AT PUTTING OFF...
...MY FIGHT WITH THAT MAN.
?!
HŌJI-SAMA!
DO YOU SEE FLAMES ?!

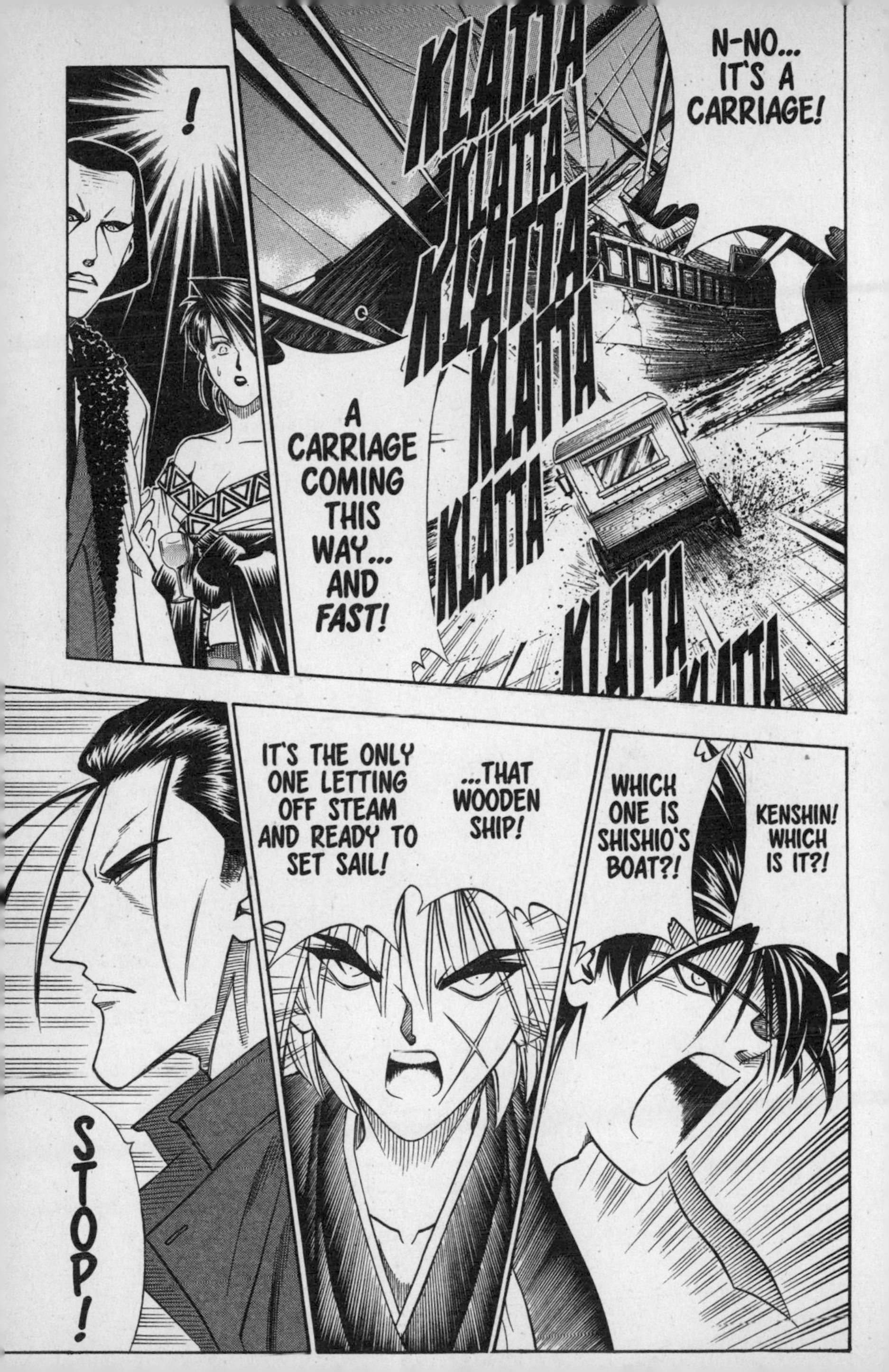
N-NO... IT'S A CARRIAGE!
KLATTA KLATTA KLATTA KLATTA KLATTA
A CARRIAGE COMING THIS WAY... AND FAST!
KLATTA
KLATTA KLATTA
!
KENSHIN! WHICH IS IT?!
WHICH ONE IS SHISHIO'S BOAT?!
...THAT WOODEN SHIP!
IT'S THE ONLY ONE LETTING OFF STEAM AND READY TO SET SAIL!
STOP!

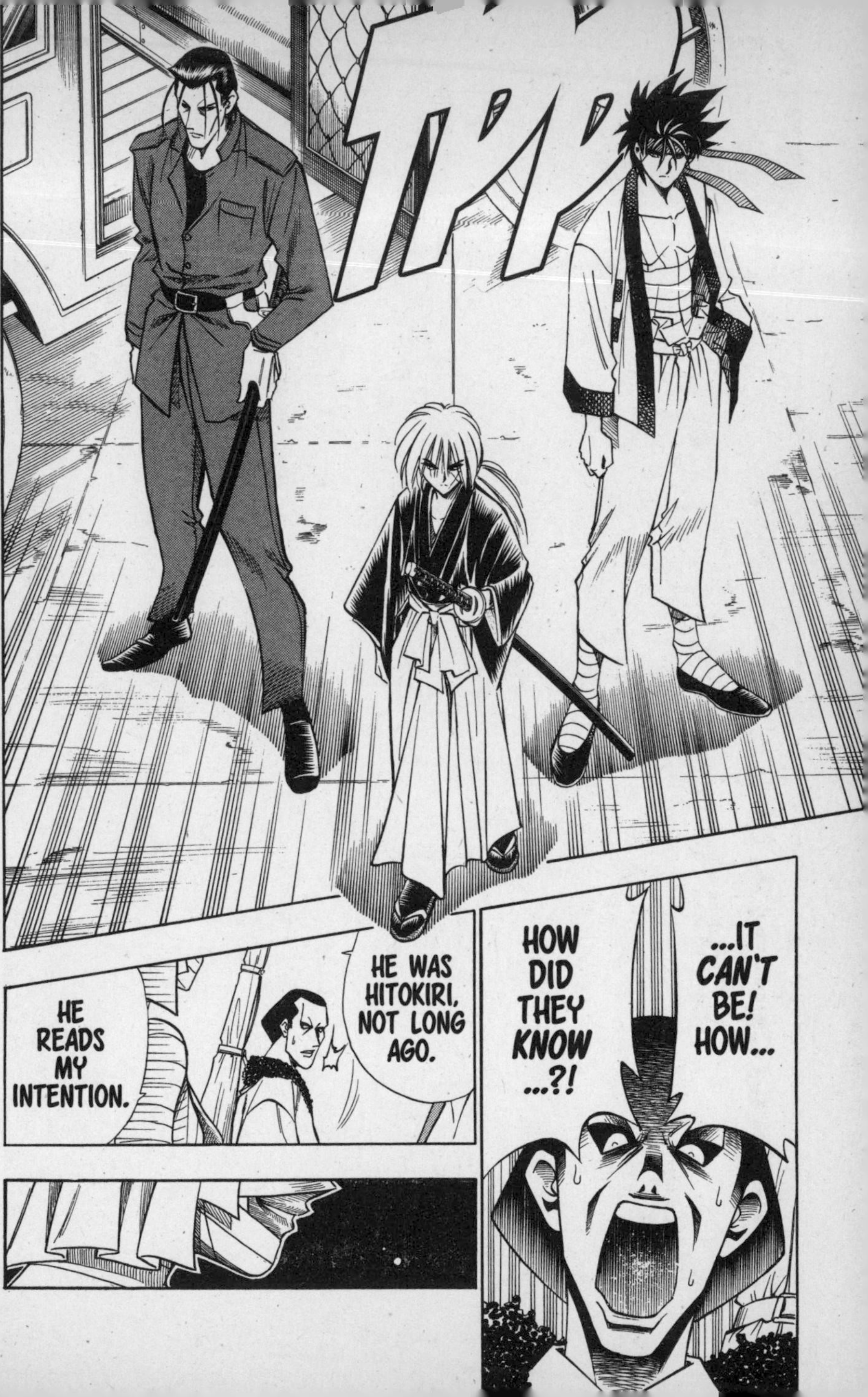
...IT CAN'T BE! HOW...
HOW DID THEY KNOW ...?!
HE WAS HITOKIRI, NOT LONG AGO.
HE READS MY INTENTION.

READ THIS WAY

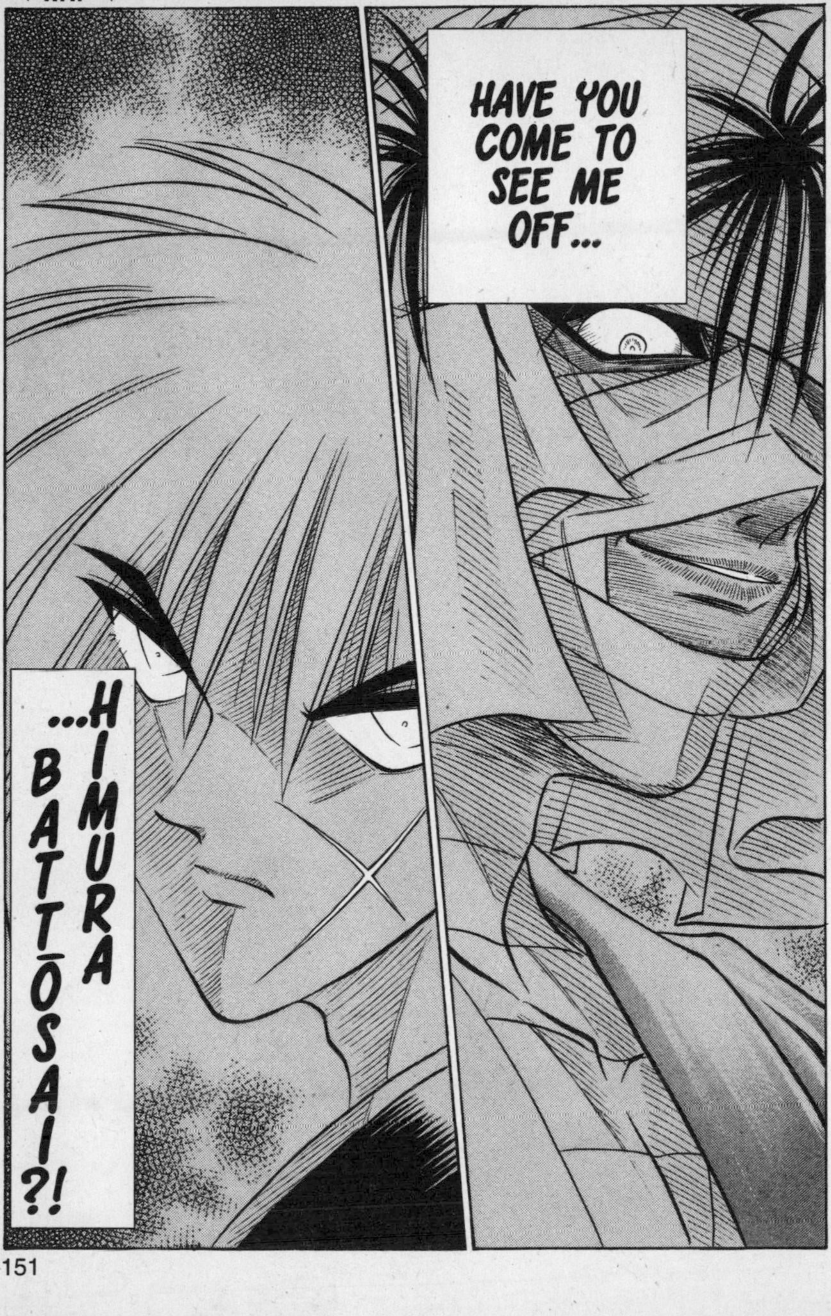
HAVE YOU COME TO SEE ME OFF...
...HIMURA BATTŌSAI?!

Rurouni Kenshin

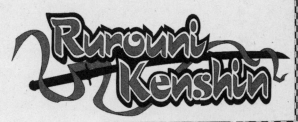

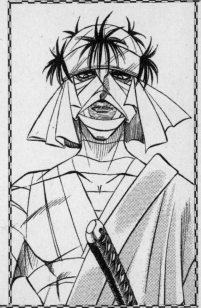

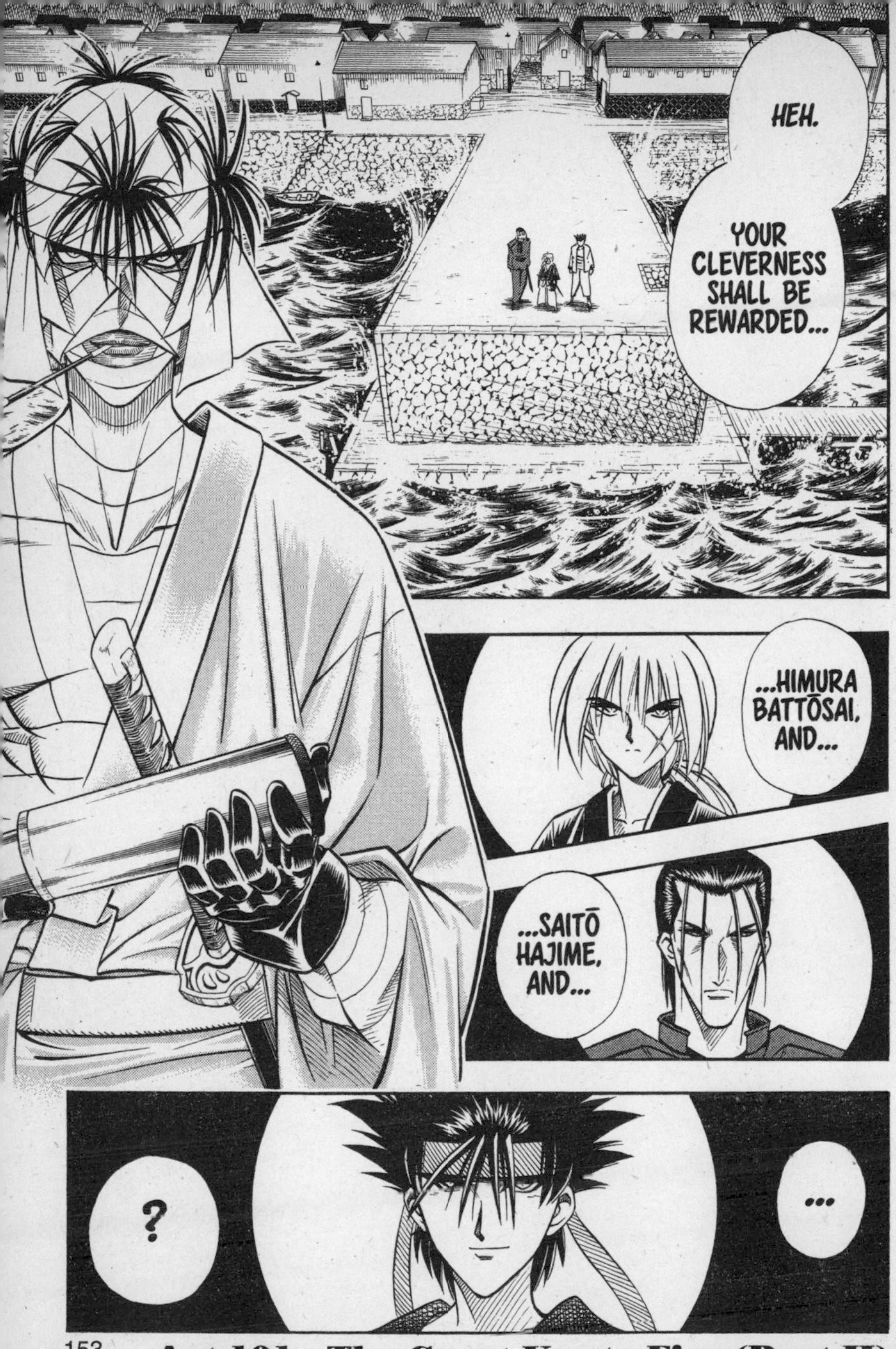
HEH.
YOUR CLEVERNESS SHALL BE REWARDED...
...HIMURA BATTŌSAI, AND...
...SAITŌ HAJIME, AND...
...
?

Act 101—The Great Kyoto Fire (Part II)

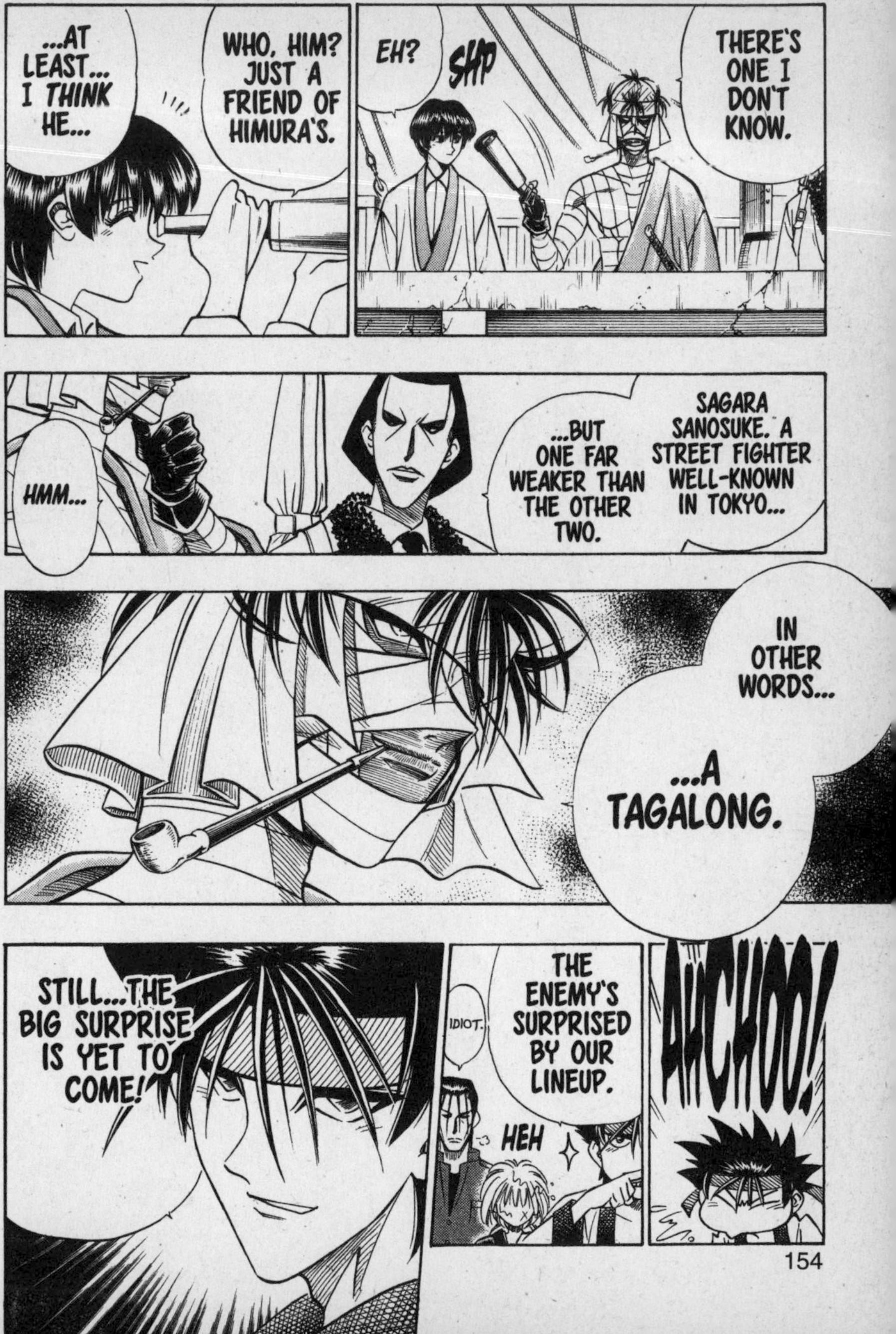
THERE'S ONE I DON'T KNOW.
SHP
EH?
WHO, HIM? JUST A FRIEND OF HIMURA'S.
...AT LEAST... I THINK HE...
SAGARA SANOSUKE. A STREET FIGHTER WELL-KNOWN IN TOKYO...
...BUT ONE FAR WEAKER THAN THE OTHER TWO.
HMM...
IN OTHER WORDS...
...A TAGALONG.
AHCHOO!
THE ENEMY'S SURPRISED BY OUR LINEUP.
IDIOT.
HEH
STILL... THE BIG SURPRISE IS YET TO COME!

Act 101
The Great Kyoto Fire (Part II)

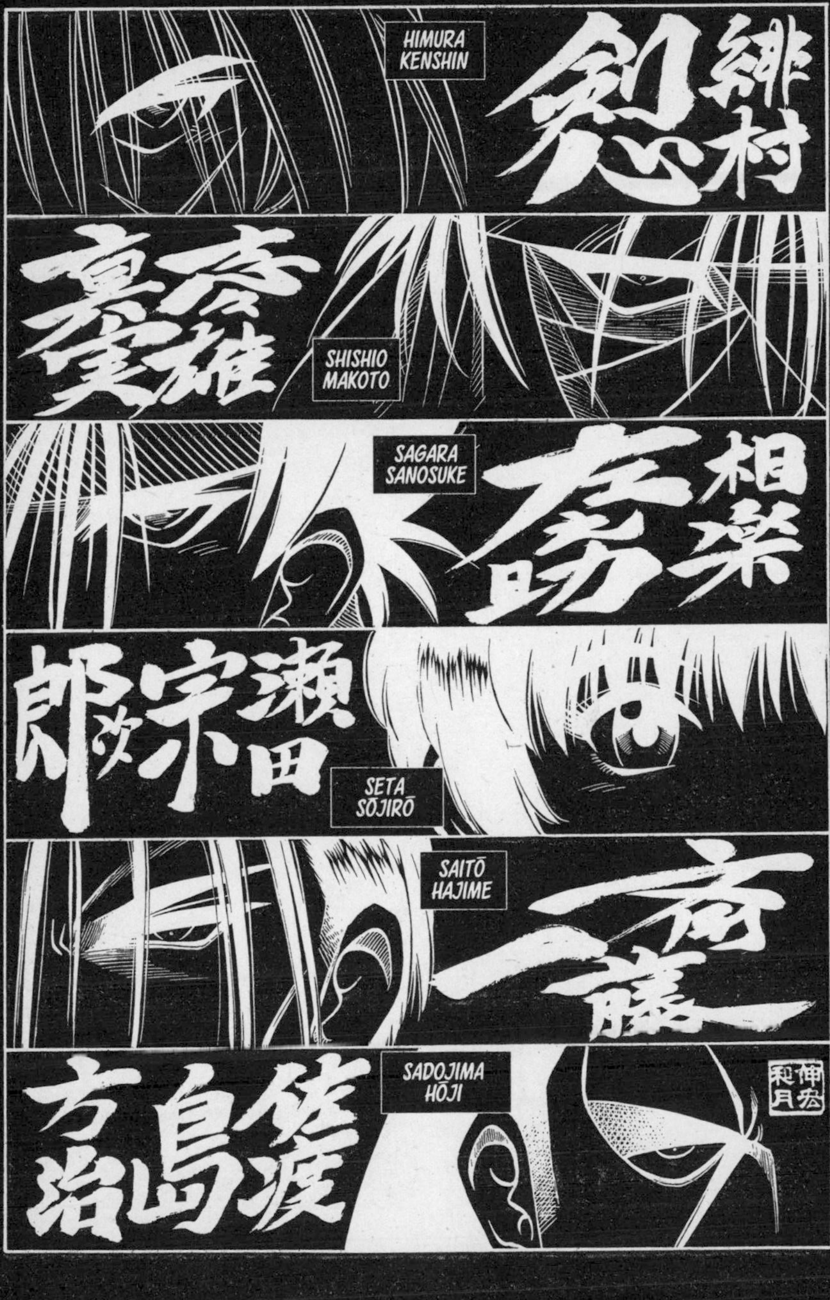

緋村剣心
HIMURA KENSHIN
SHISHIO MAKOTO
相楽左之助
SAGARA SANOSUKE
瀬田宗次郎
SETA SŌJIRŌ
斎藤一
SAITŌ HAJIME
佐渡島方治
SADOJIMA HŌJI

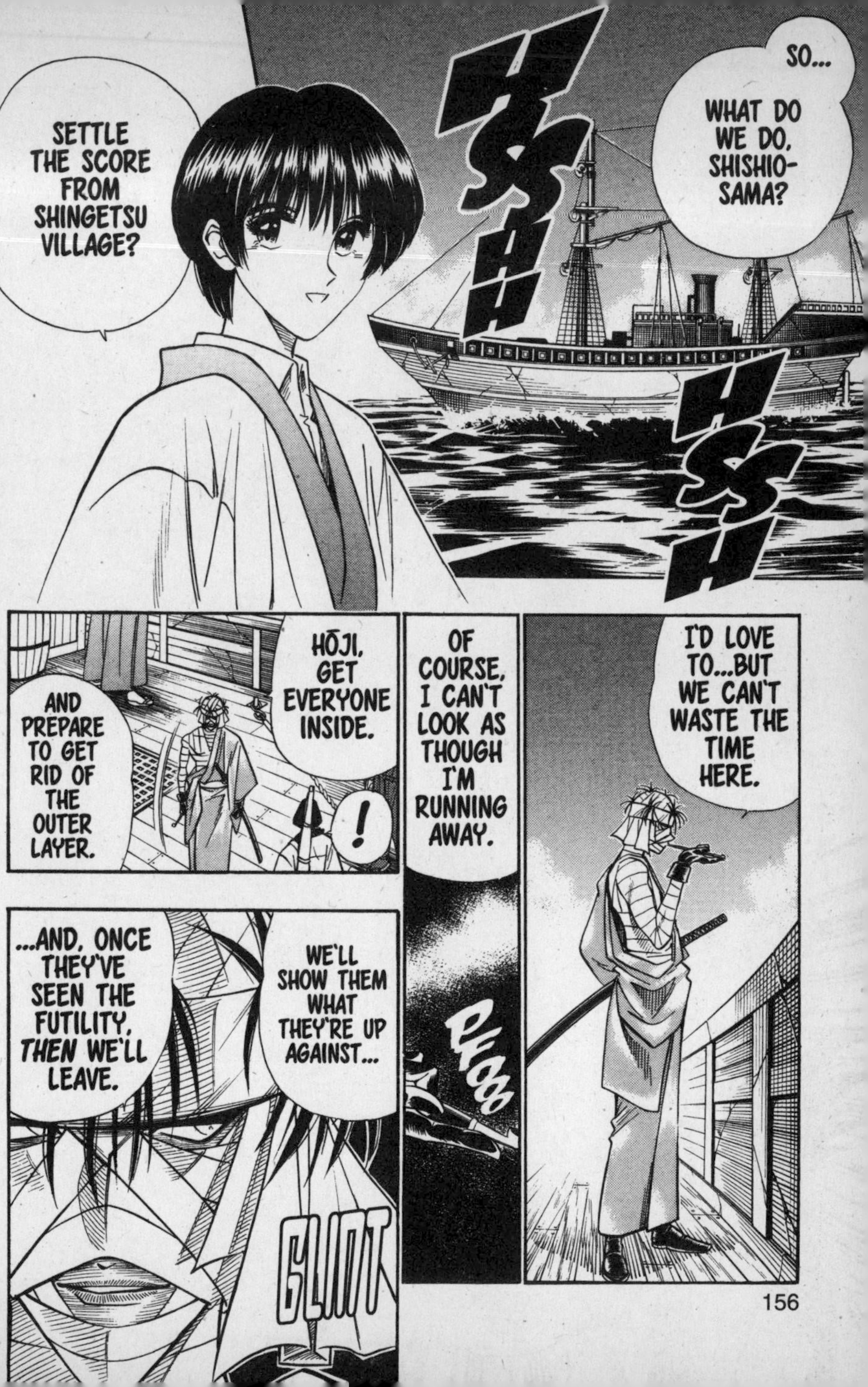
SO...
WHAT DO WE DO, SHISHIO-SAMA?
SETTLE THE SCORE FROM SHINGETSU VILLAGE?
I'D LOVE TO...BUT WE CAN'T WASTE THE TIME HERE.
OF COURSE, I CAN'T LOOK AS THOUGH I'M RUNNING AWAY.
HŌJI, GET EVERYONE INSIDE.
AND PREPARE TO GET RID OF THE OUTER LAYER.
!
WE'LL SHOW THEM WHAT THEY'RE UP AGAINST...
...AND, ONCE THEY'VE SEEN THE FUTILITY, *THEN* WE'LL LEAVE.
GLINT

READ THIS WAY

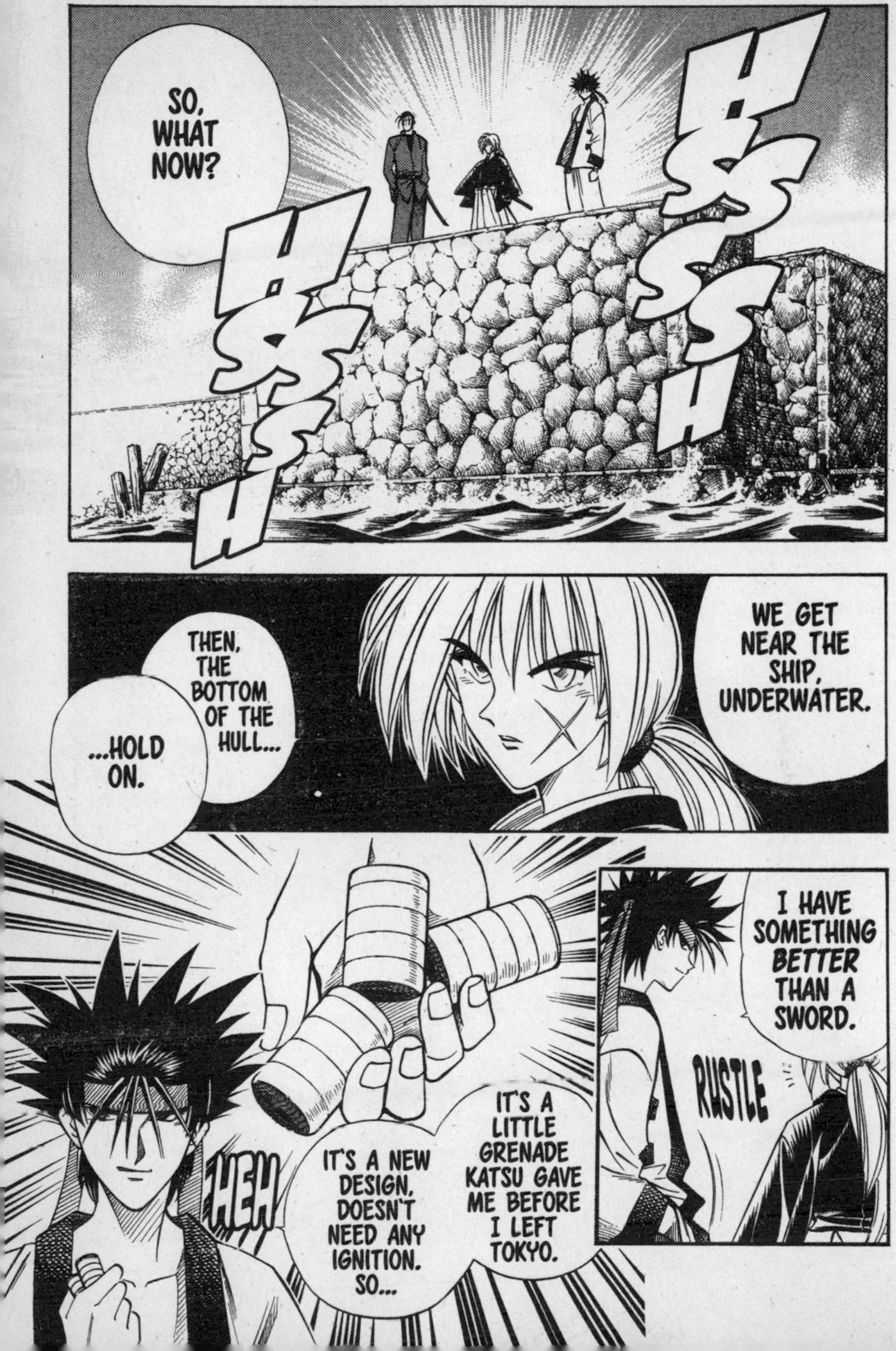
HSSSH
SO, WHAT NOW?
HSSSH
WE GET NEAR THE SHIP, UNDERWATER.
THEN, THE BOTTOM OF THE HULL...
...HOLD ON.
I HAVE SOMETHING BETTER THAN A SWORD.
RUSTLE
IT'S A LITTLE GRENADE KATSU GAVE ME BEFORE I LEFT TOKYO.
IT'S A NEW DESIGN, DOESN'T NEED ANY IGNITION. SO...
HEH

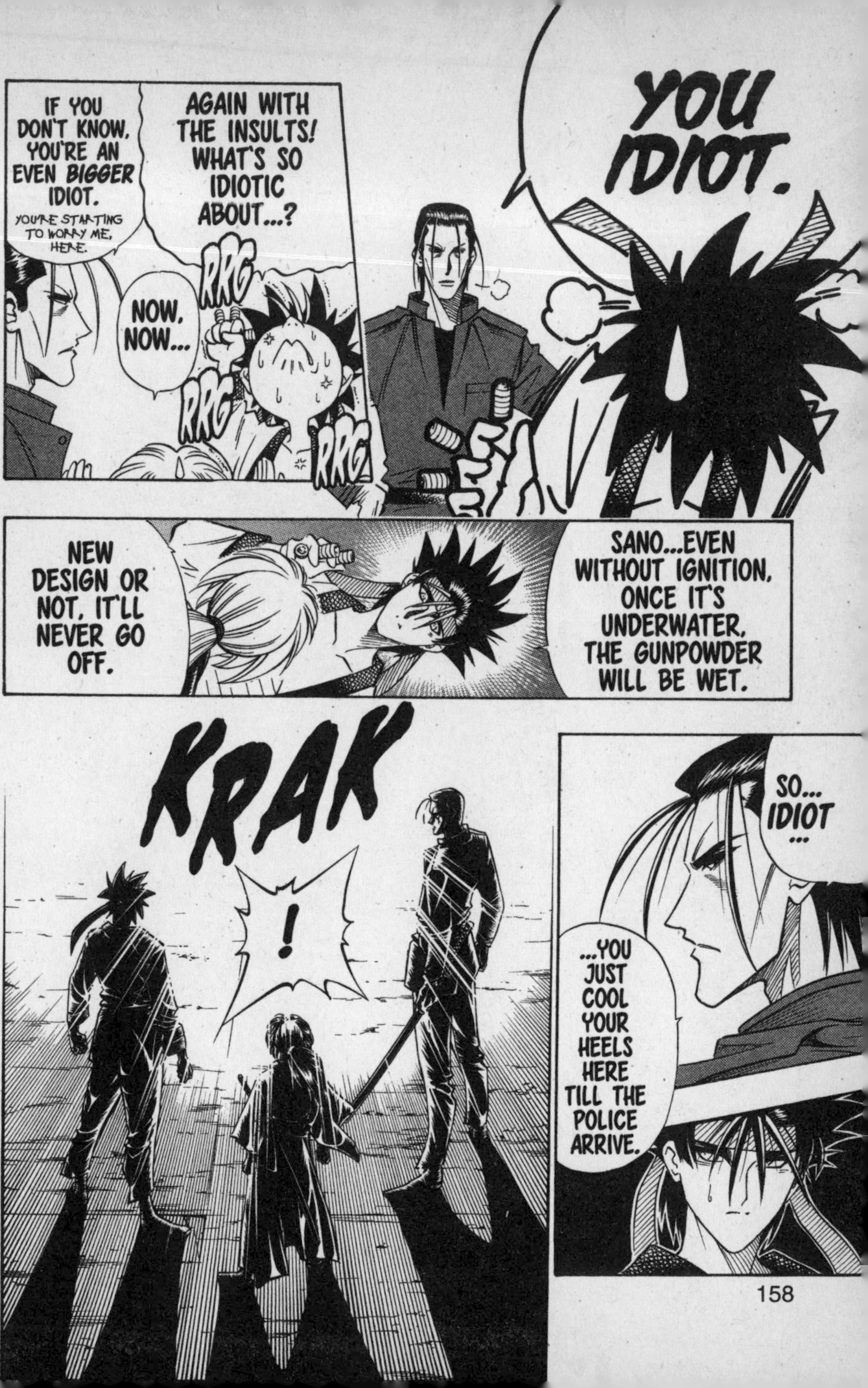
YOU IDIOT.
AGAIN WITH THE INSULTS! WHAT'S SO IDIOTIC ABOUT...?
IF YOU DON'T KNOW, YOU'RE AN EVEN BIGGER IDIOT.
YOU'RE STARTING TO WORRY ME, HERE.
RRG
NOW, NOW...
RRG
RRG
SANO...EVEN WITHOUT IGNITION, ONCE IT'S UNDERWATER, THE GUNPOWDER WILL BE WET.
NEW DESIGN OR NOT, IT'LL NEVER GO OFF.
SO... IDIOT...
...YOU JUST COOL YOUR HEELS HERE TILL THE POLICE ARRIVE.
KRAK
!

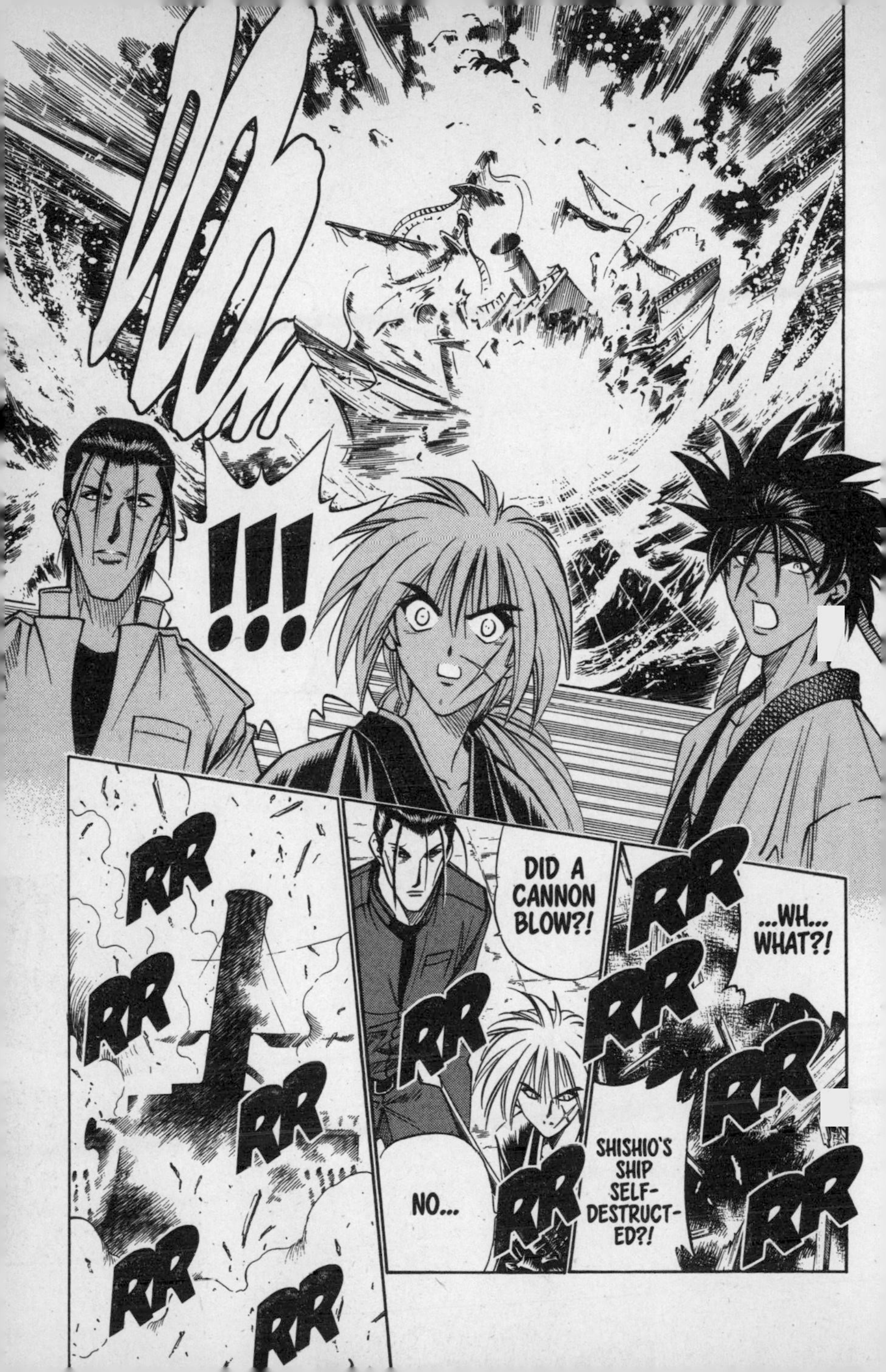
!!!
RR
RR
RR
RR
RR
RR
...WH... WHAT?!
SHISHIO'S SHIP SELF-DESTRUCTED?!
RR
RR
DID A CANNON BLOW?!
NO...
RR
RR
RR
RR
RR
RR

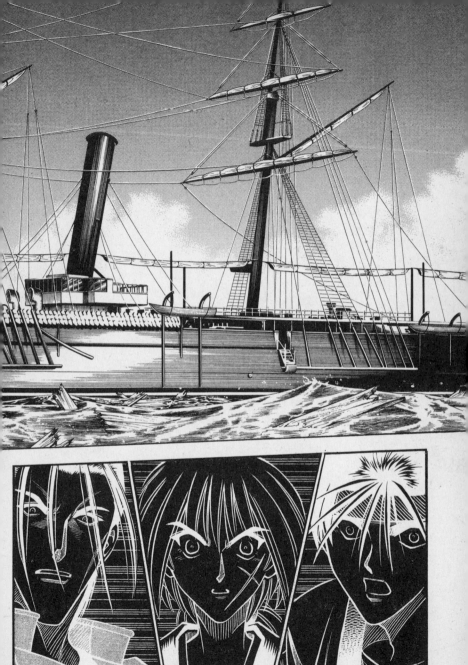

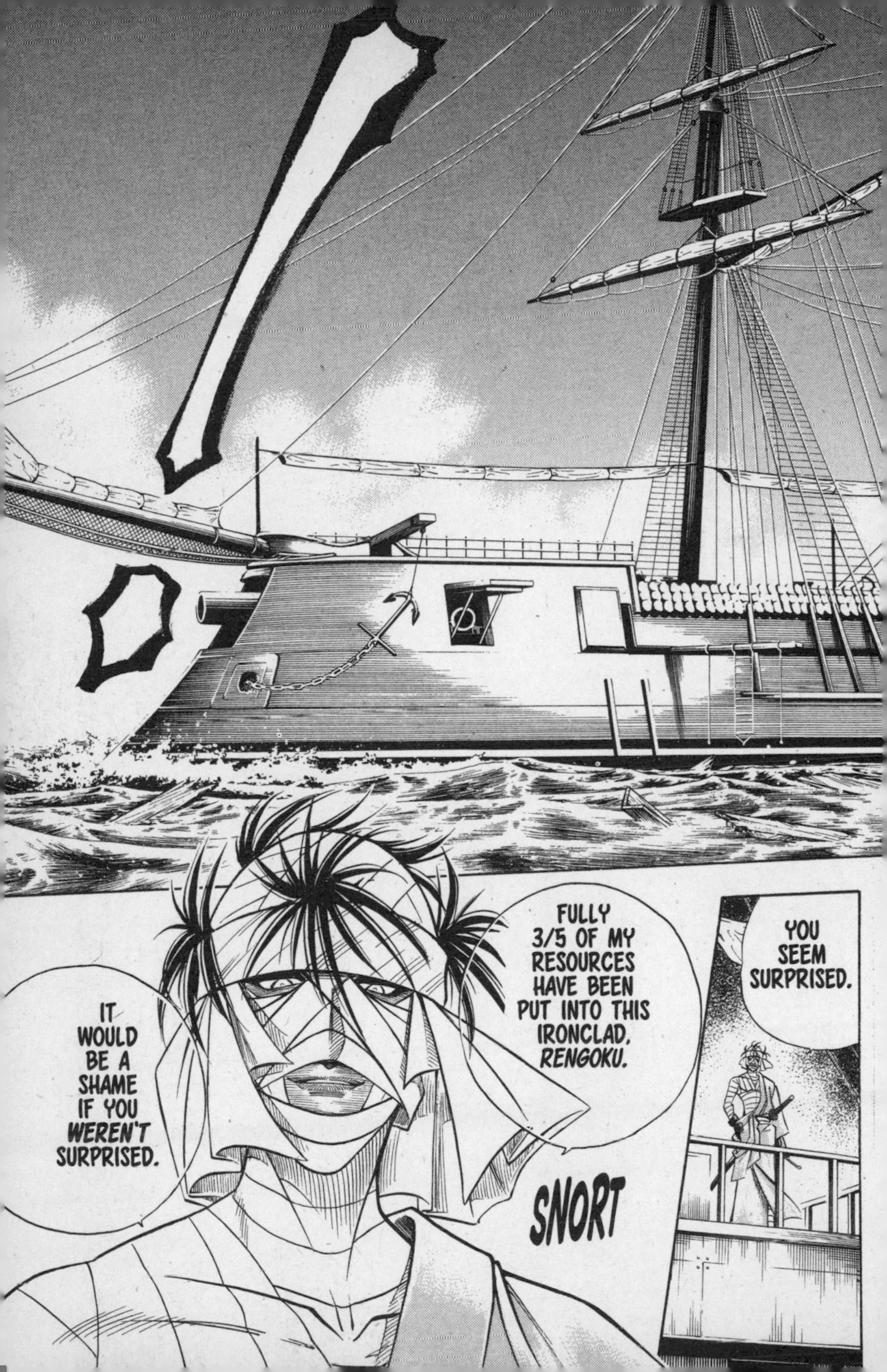
YOU SEEM SURPRISED.
FULLY 3/5 OF MY RESOURCES HAVE BEEN PUT INTO THIS IRONCLAD, RENGOKU.
SNORT
IT WOULD BE A SHAME IF YOU WEREN'T SURPRISED.

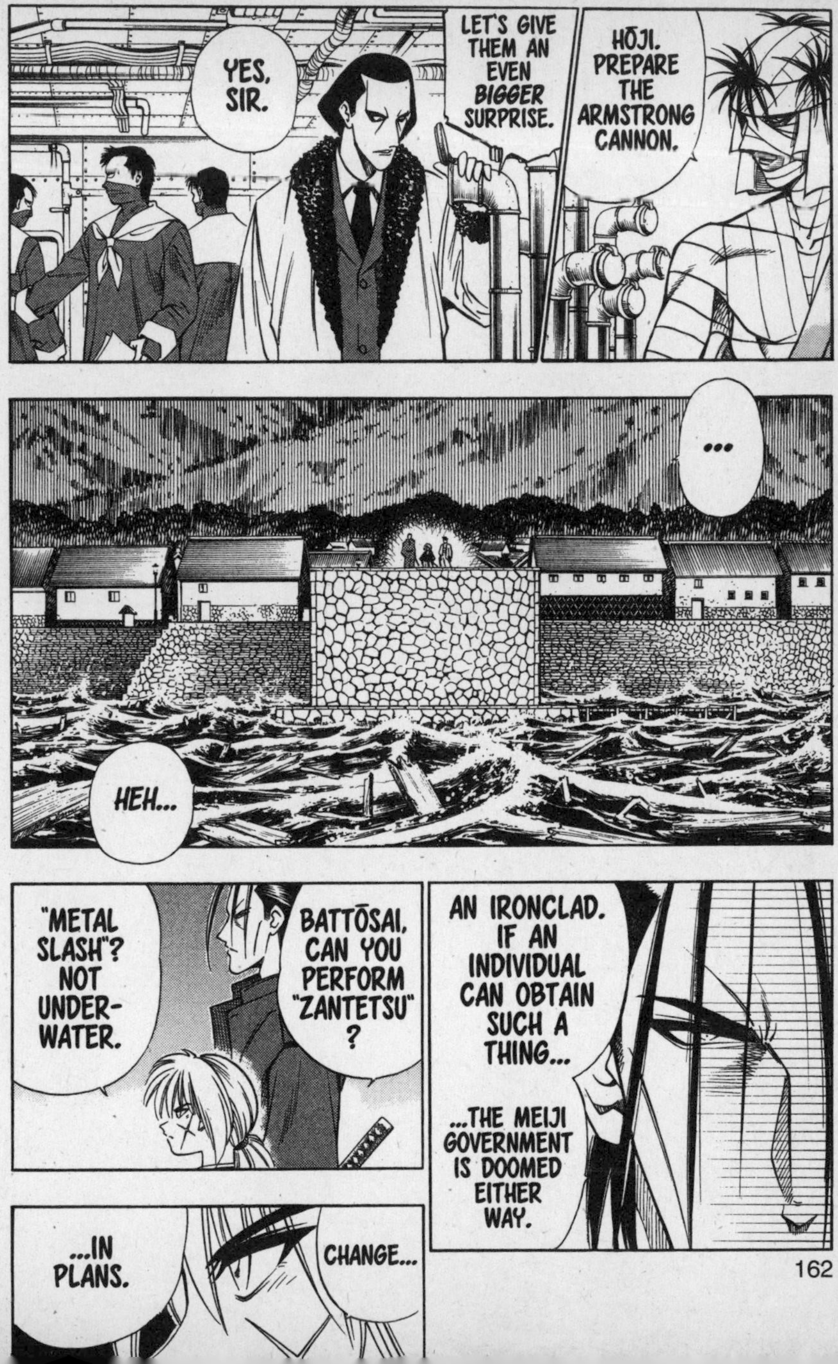
HŌJI. PREPARE THE ARMSTRONG CANNON.
LET'S GIVE THEM AN EVEN BIGGER SURPRISE.
YES, SIR.
...
HEH...
AN IRONCLAD. IF AN INDIVIDUAL CAN OBTAIN SUCH A THING...
...THE MEIJI GOVERNMENT IS DOOMED EITHER WAY.
BATTŌSAI, CAN YOU PERFORM "ZANTETSU"?
"METAL SLASH"? NOT UNDER-WATER.
CHANGE...
...IN PLANS.

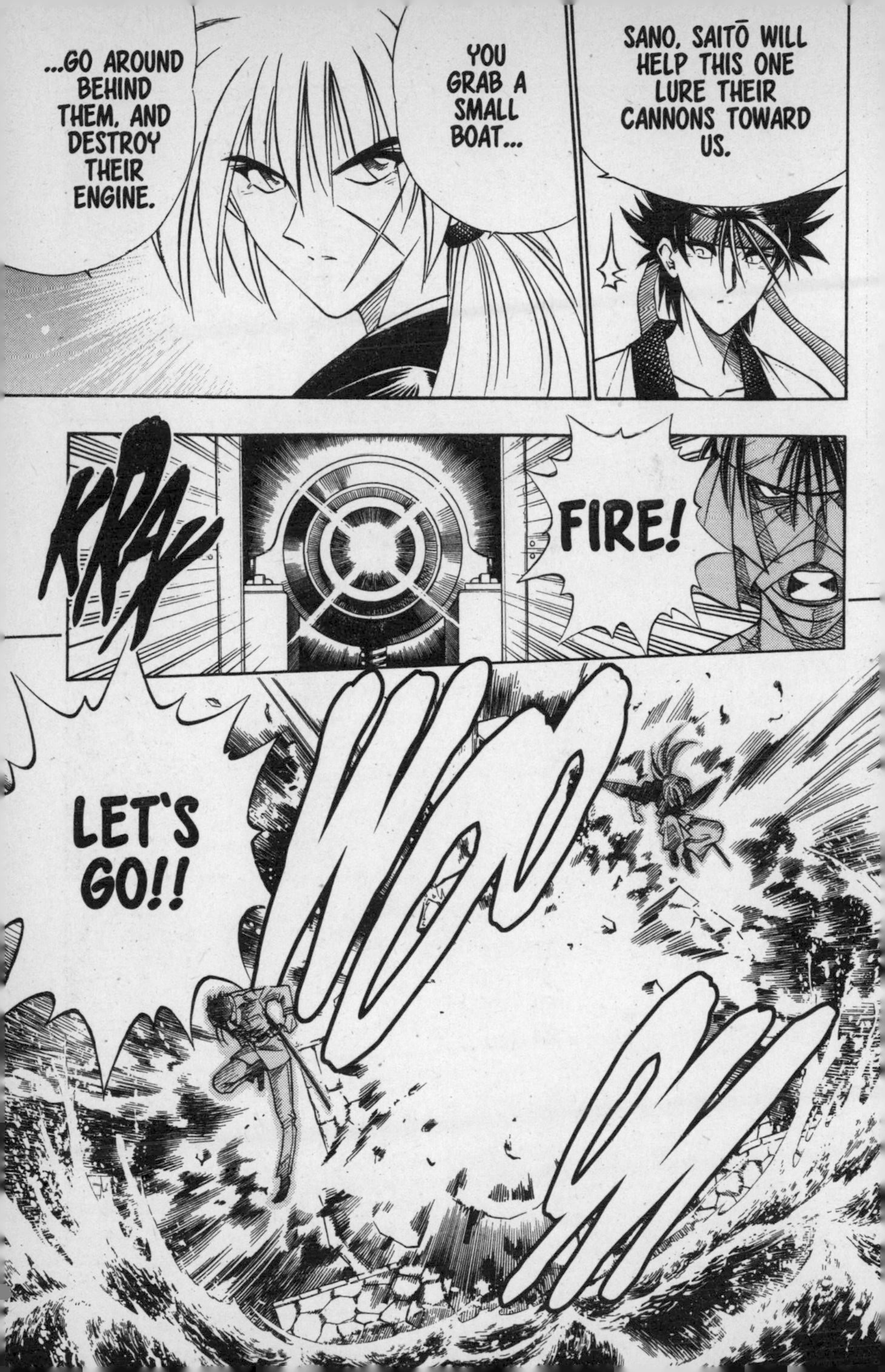
SANO, SAITŌ WILL HELP THIS ONE LURE THEIR CANNONS TOWARD US.
YOU GRAB A SMALL BOAT...
...GO AROUND BEHIND THEM, AND DESTROY THEIR ENGINE.
FIRE!
LET'S GO!!

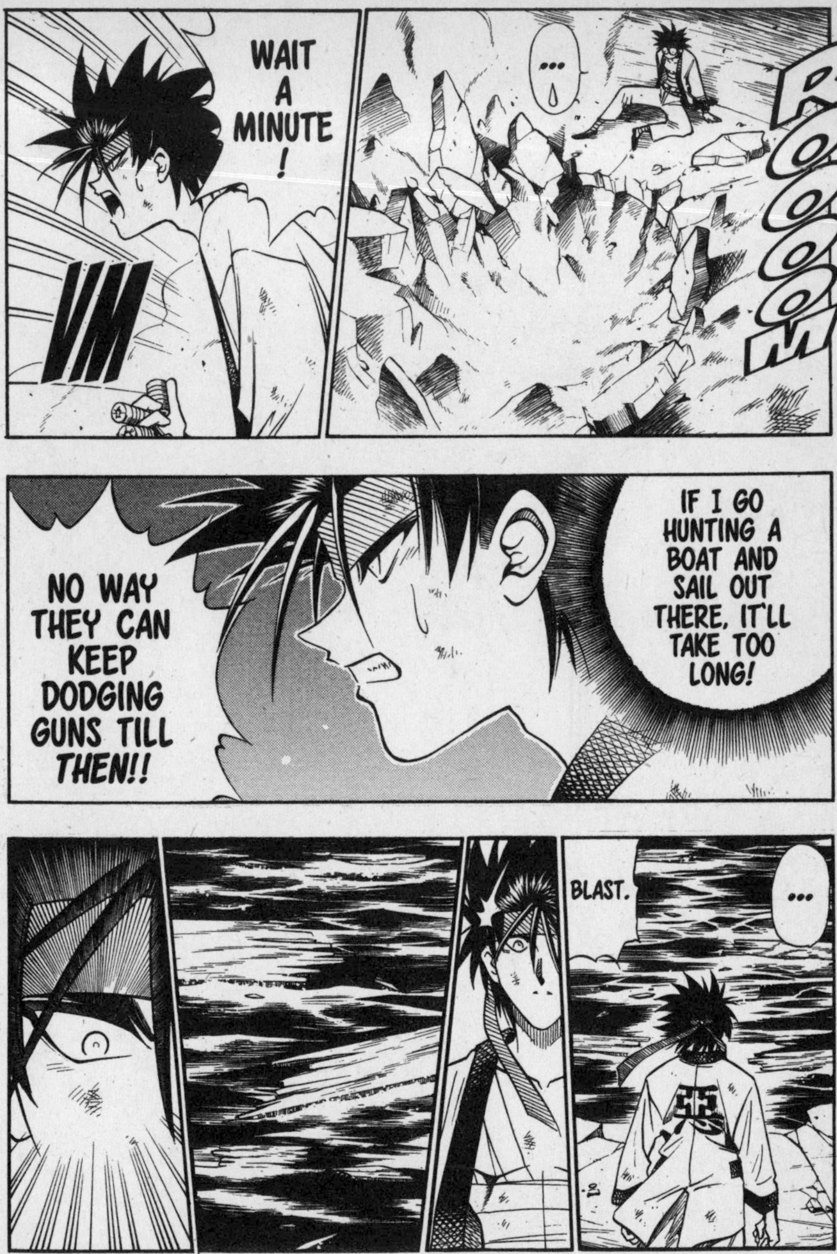
ROOOOOOM
...
WAIT A MINUTE!
VM
IF I GO HUNTING A BOAT AND SAIL OUT THERE, IT'LL TAKE TOO LONG!
NO WAY THEY CAN KEEP DODGING GUNS TILL THEN!!
...
BLAST.

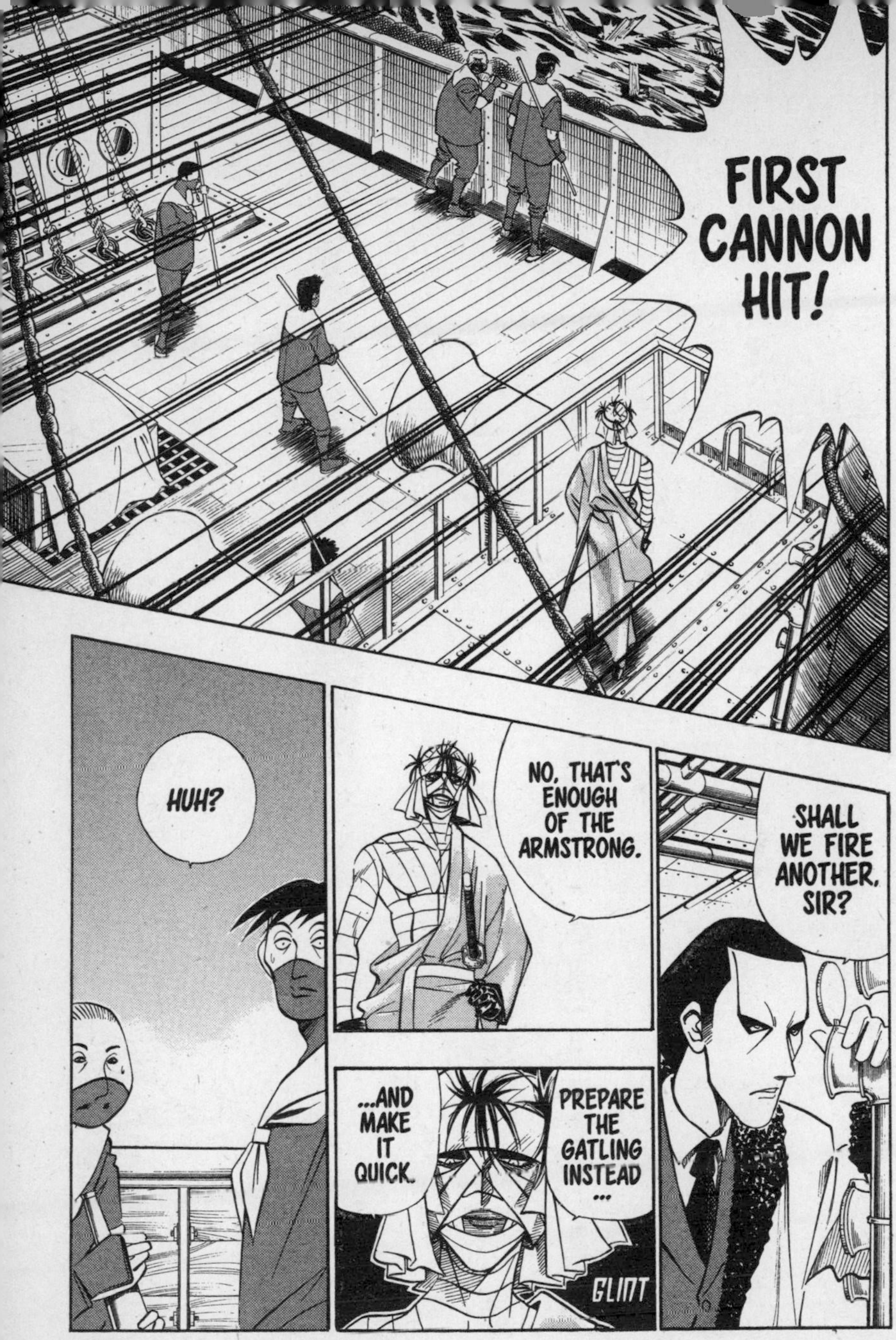
FIRST CANNON HIT!
SHALL WE FIRE ANOTHER, SIR?
NO, THAT'S ENOUGH OF THE ARMSTRONG.
HUH?
PREPARE THE GATLING INSTEAD ...
...AND MAKE IT QUICK.
GLINT

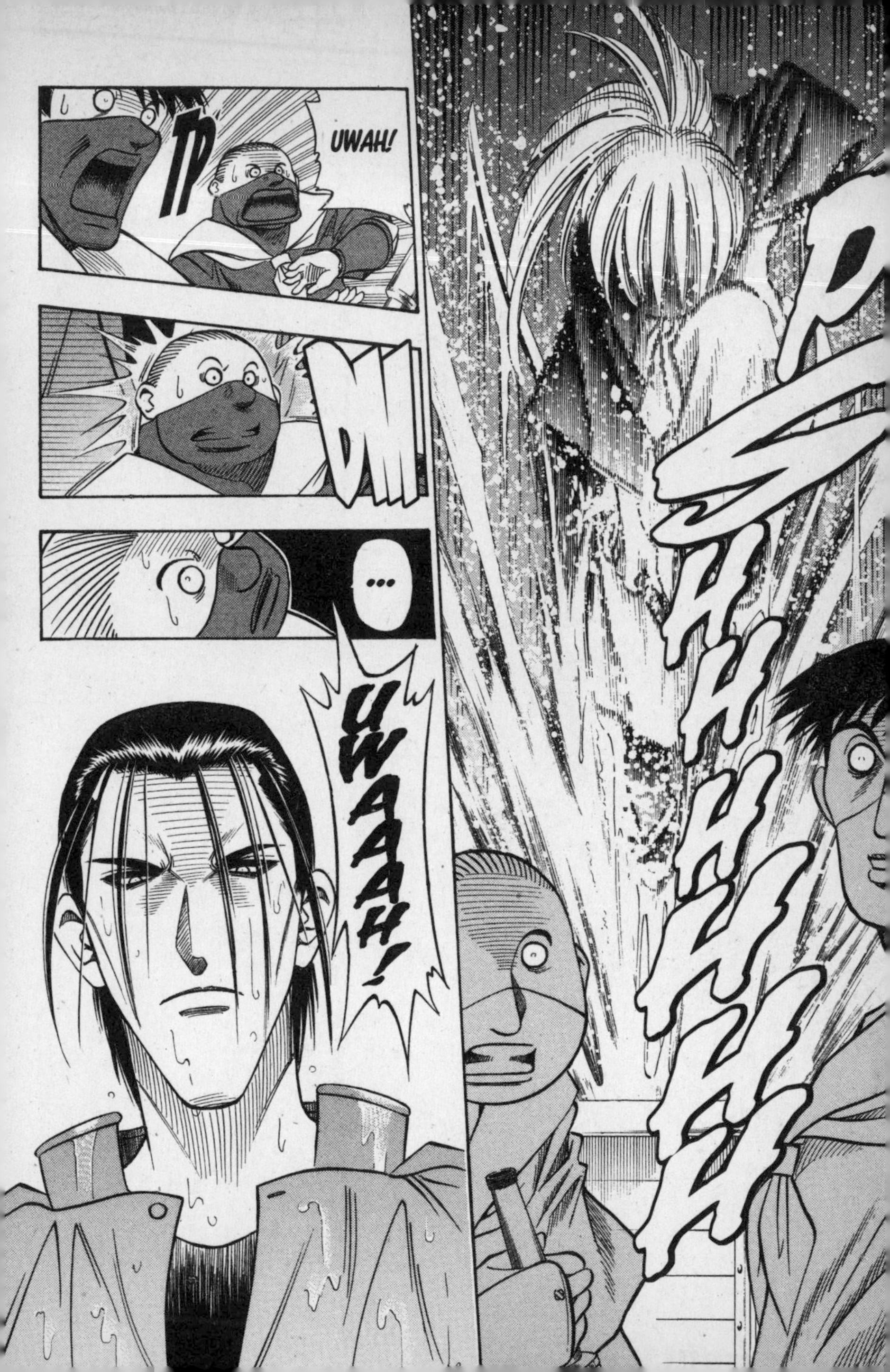
PSHHHHHHH
TP
UWAH!
DM
...
UWAAAH!

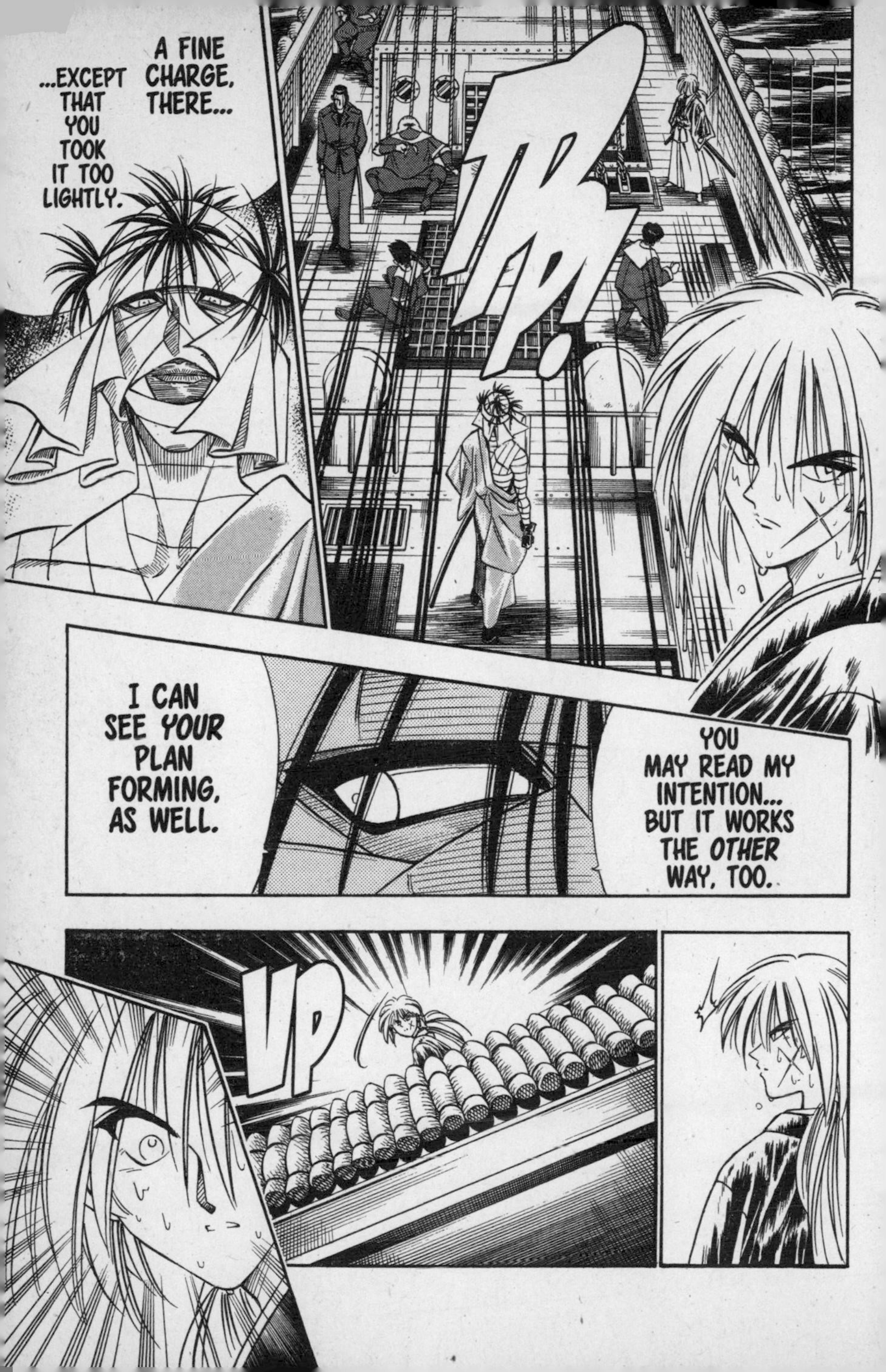
TA!
A FINE CHARGE, THERE...
...EXCEPT THAT YOU TOOK IT TOO LIGHTLY.
YOU MAY READ MY INTENTION... BUT IT WORKS THE *OTHER* WAY, TOO.
I CAN SEE *YOUR* PLAN FORMING, AS WELL.
VP

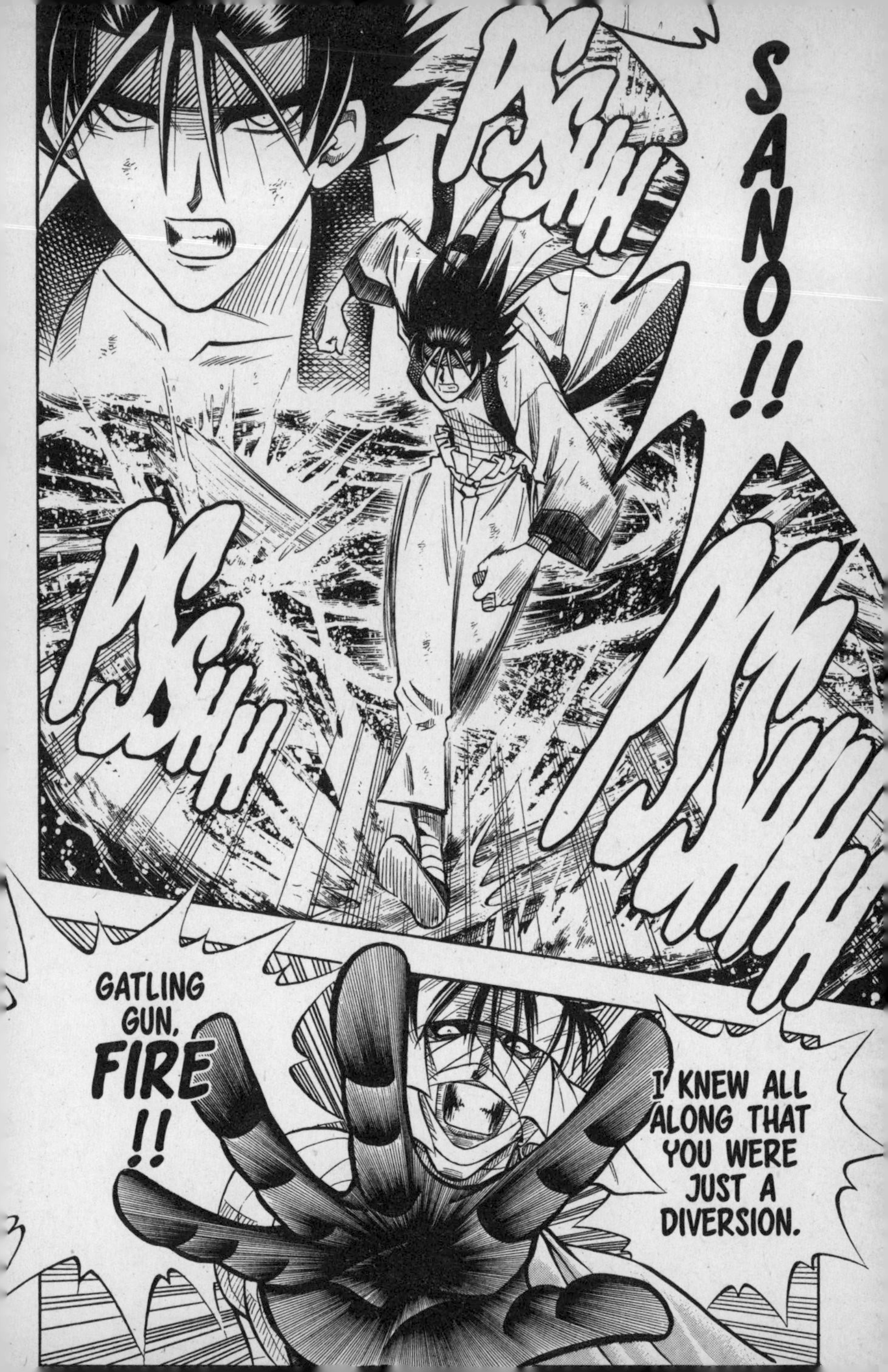
SANO!!
I KNEW ALL ALONG THAT YOU WERE JUST A DIVERSION.
GATLING GUN, FIRE!!

READ THIS WAY

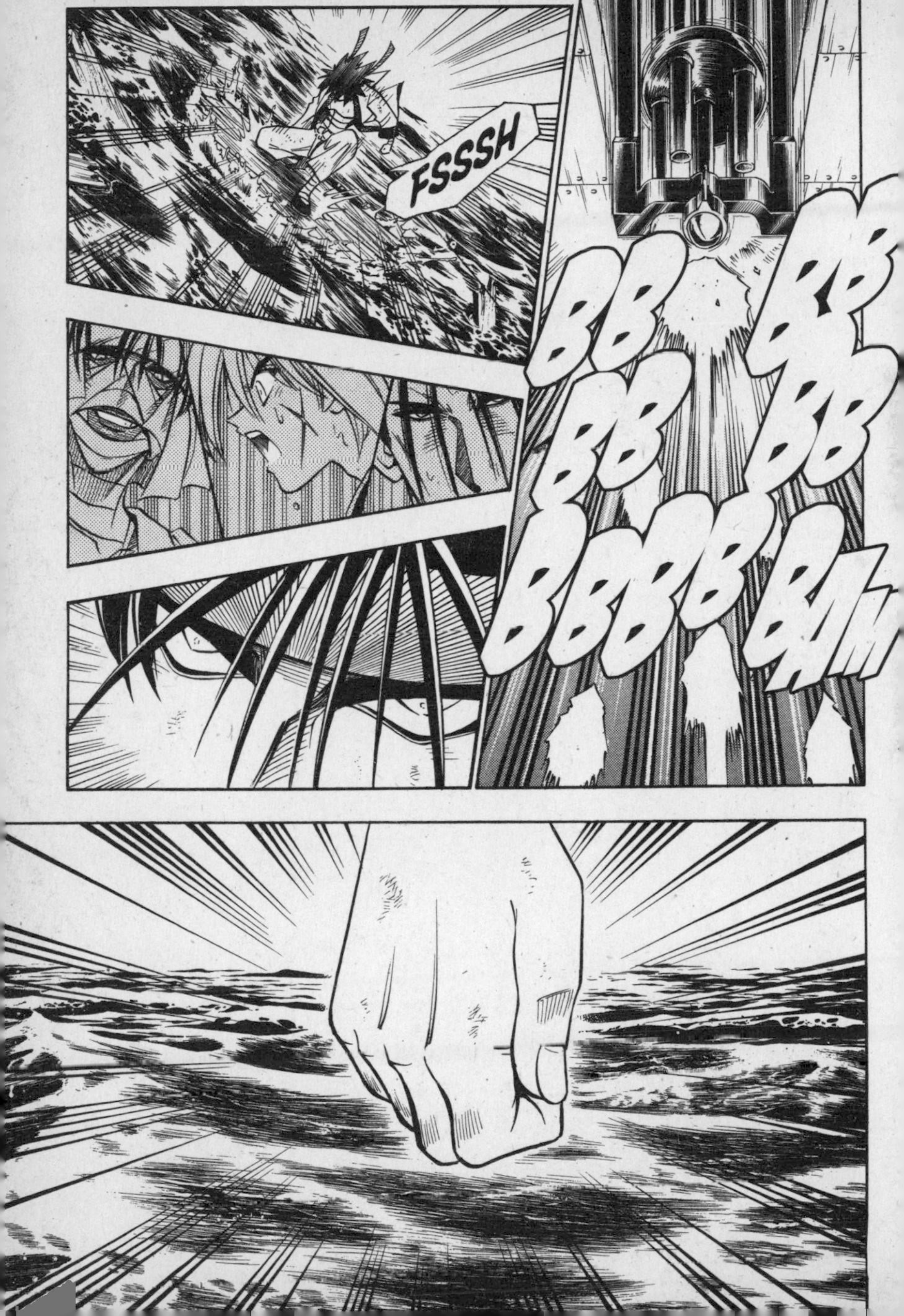
BB BB BBBB BB BB BAM
FSSSH

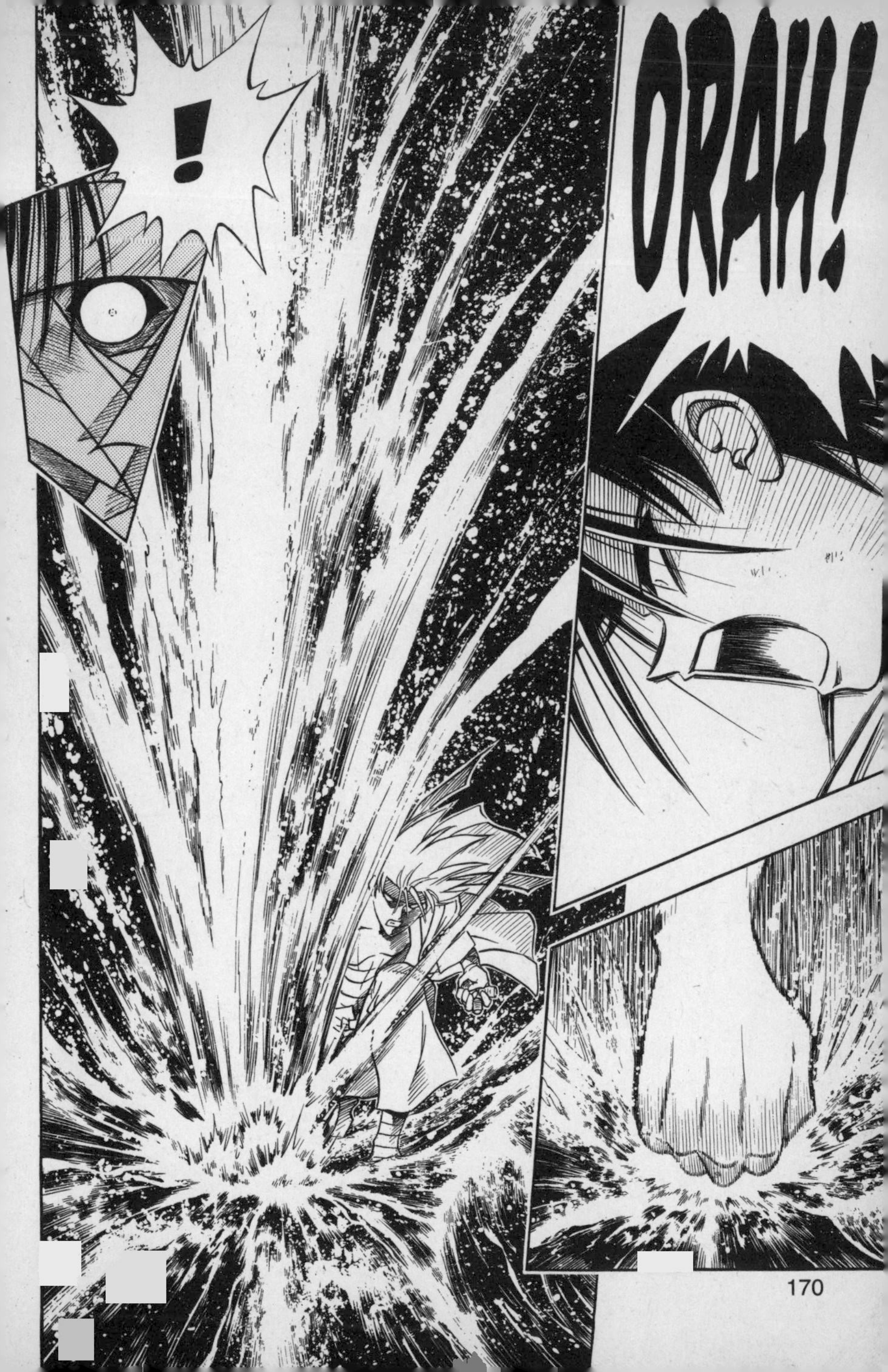
ORAH!
!

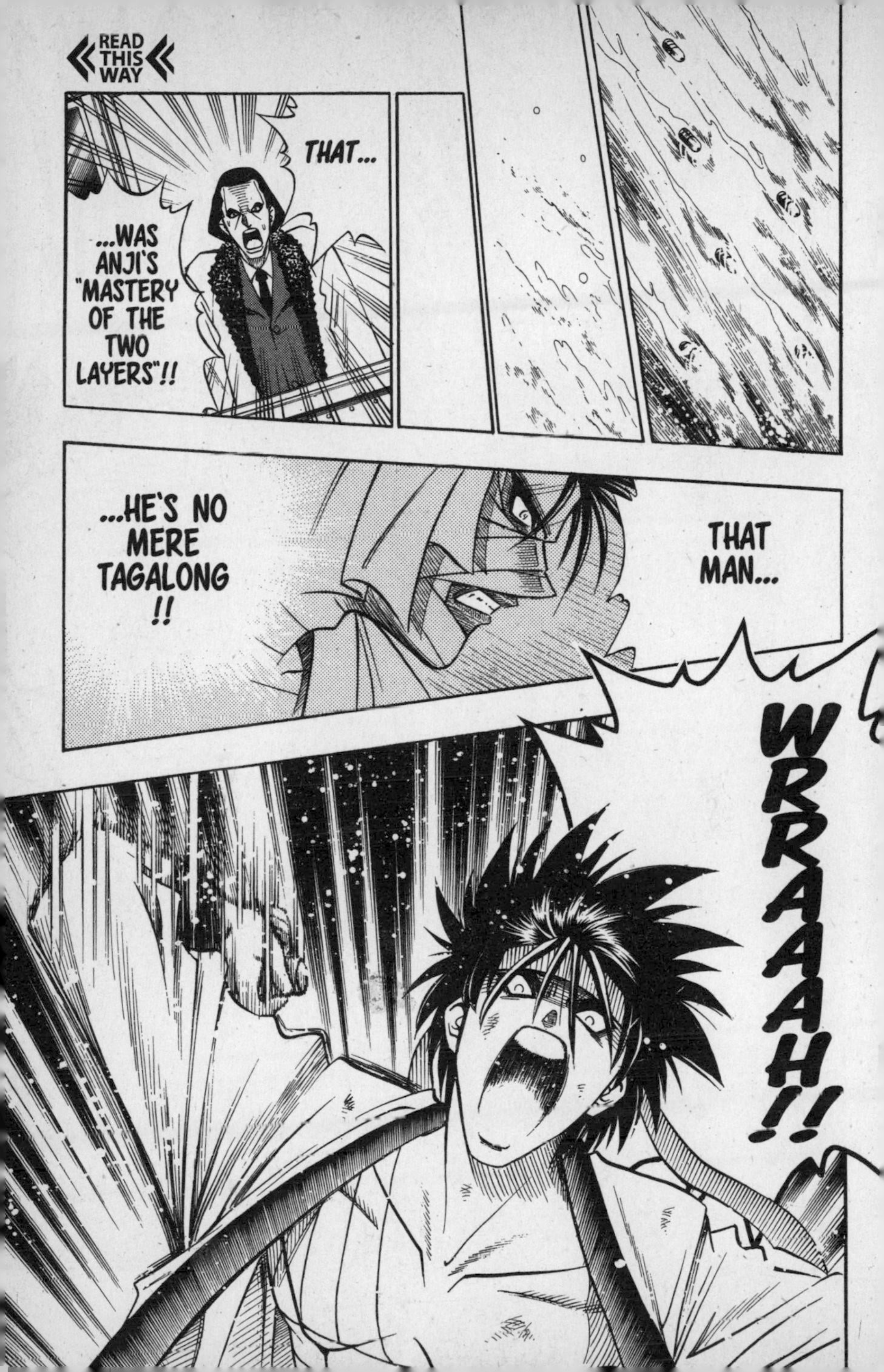
READ THIS WAY
THAT...
...WAS ANJI'S "MASTERY OF THE TWO LAYERS"!!
THAT MAN...
...HE'S NO MERE TAGALONG!!
WRRAAAAH!!

Rurouni Kenshin

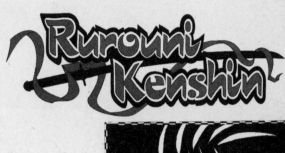

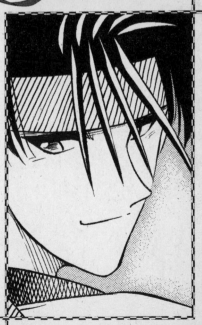

Act 102
The Great Kyoto Fire (Part III)

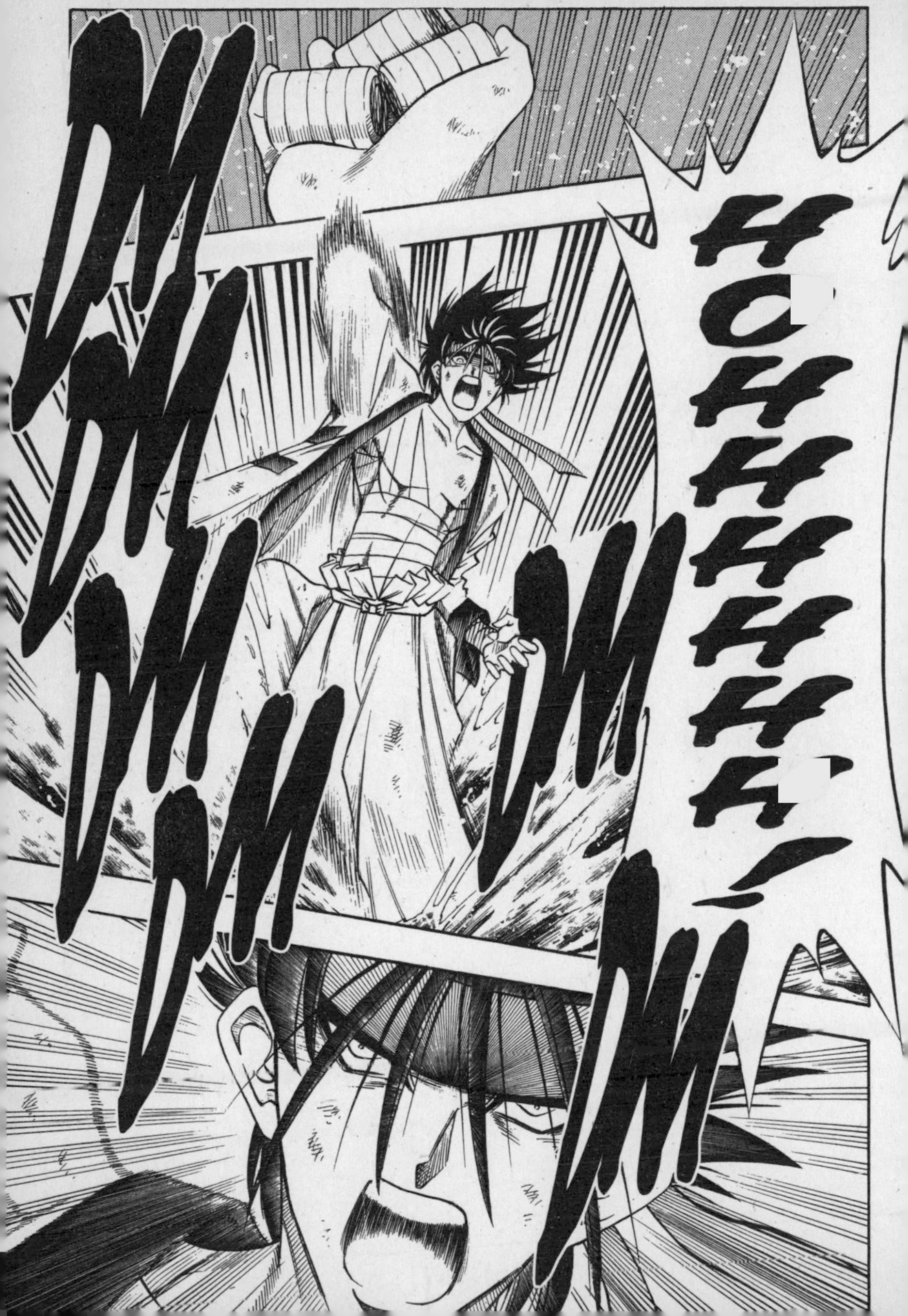
HOHHHHHH!

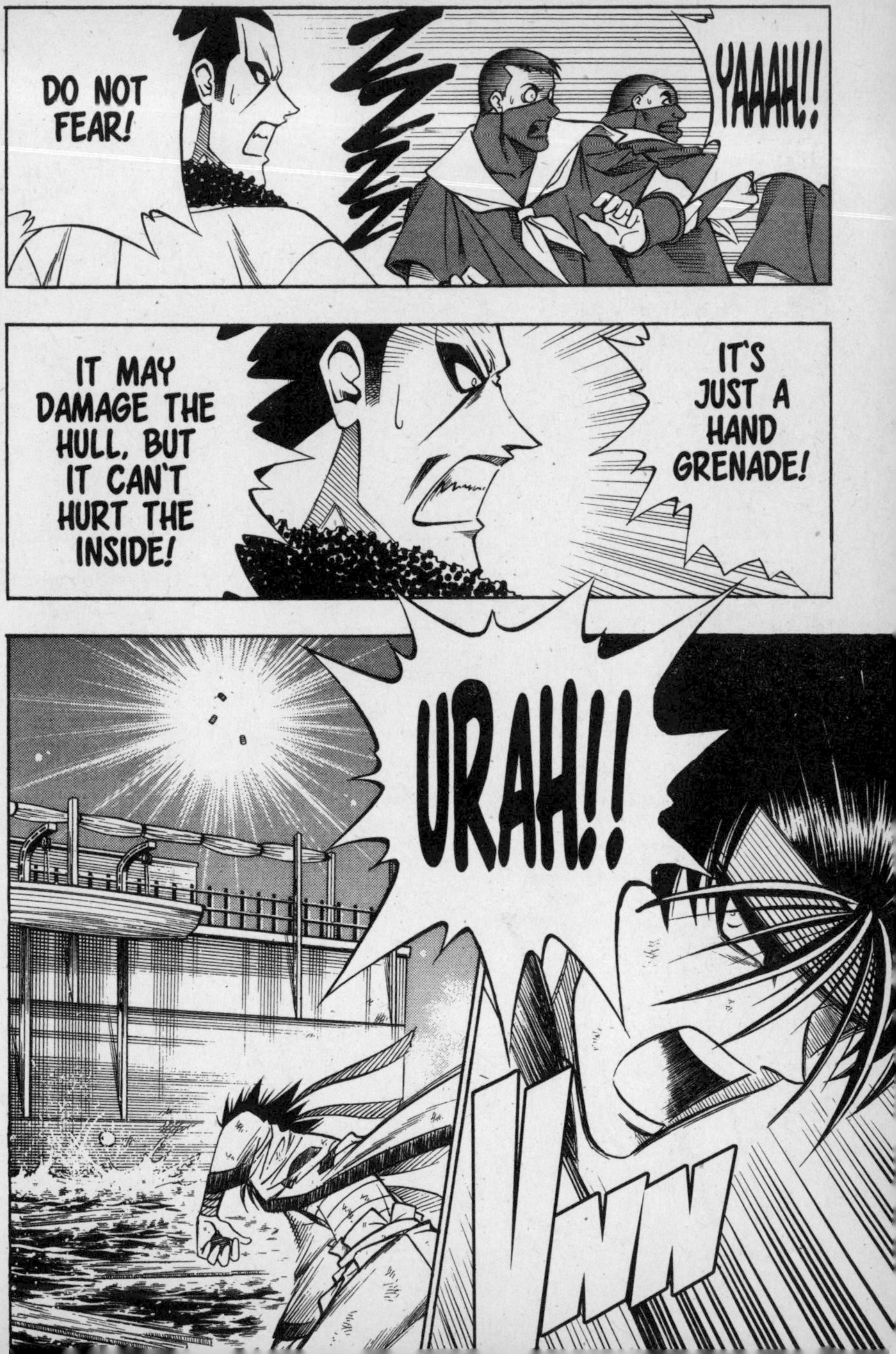
YAAAH!!
DO NOT FEAR!
IT'S JUST A HAND GRENADE!
IT MAY DAMAGE THE HULL, BUT IT CAN'T HURT THE INSIDE!
URAH!!

READ THIS WAY

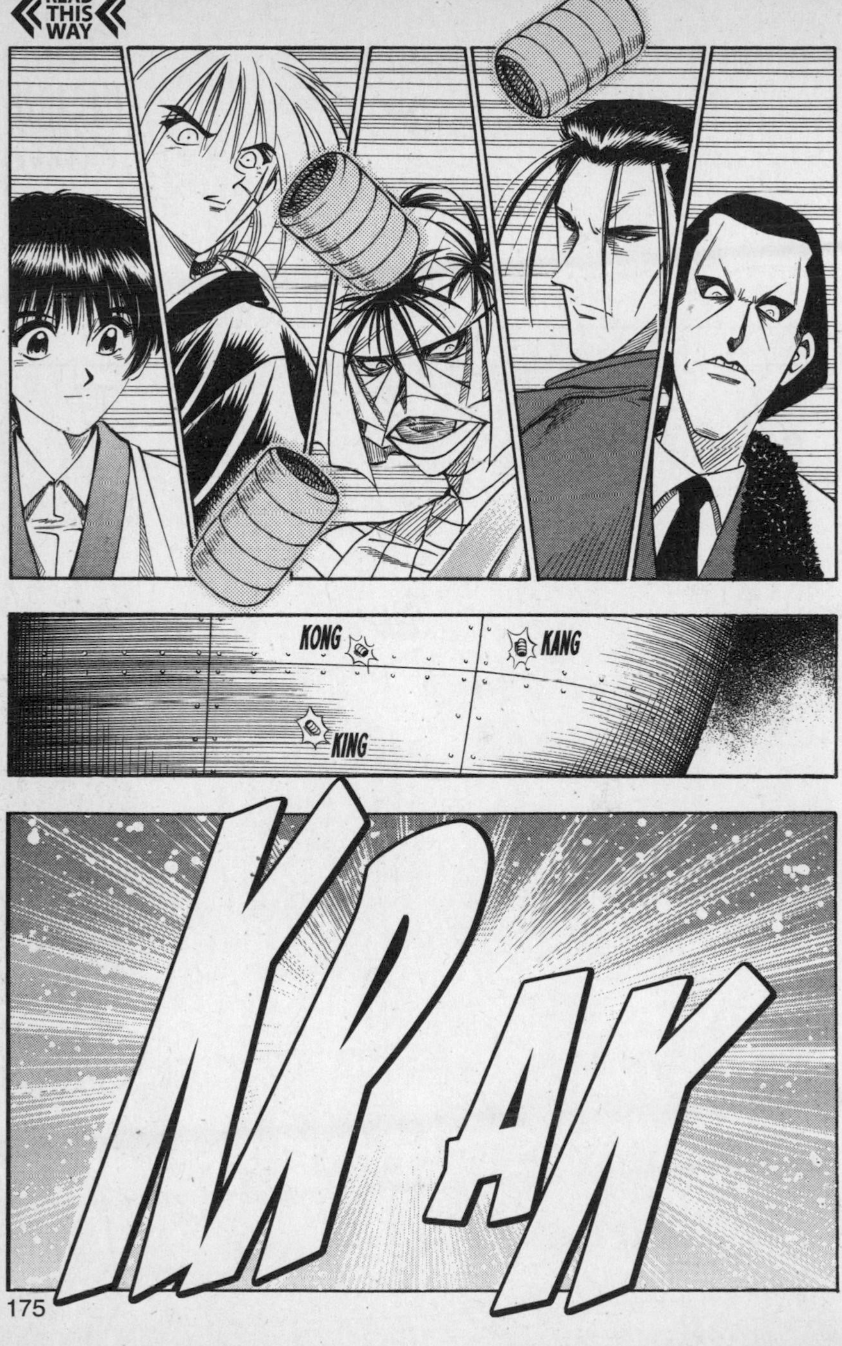
KANG
KONG
KING
KRAK

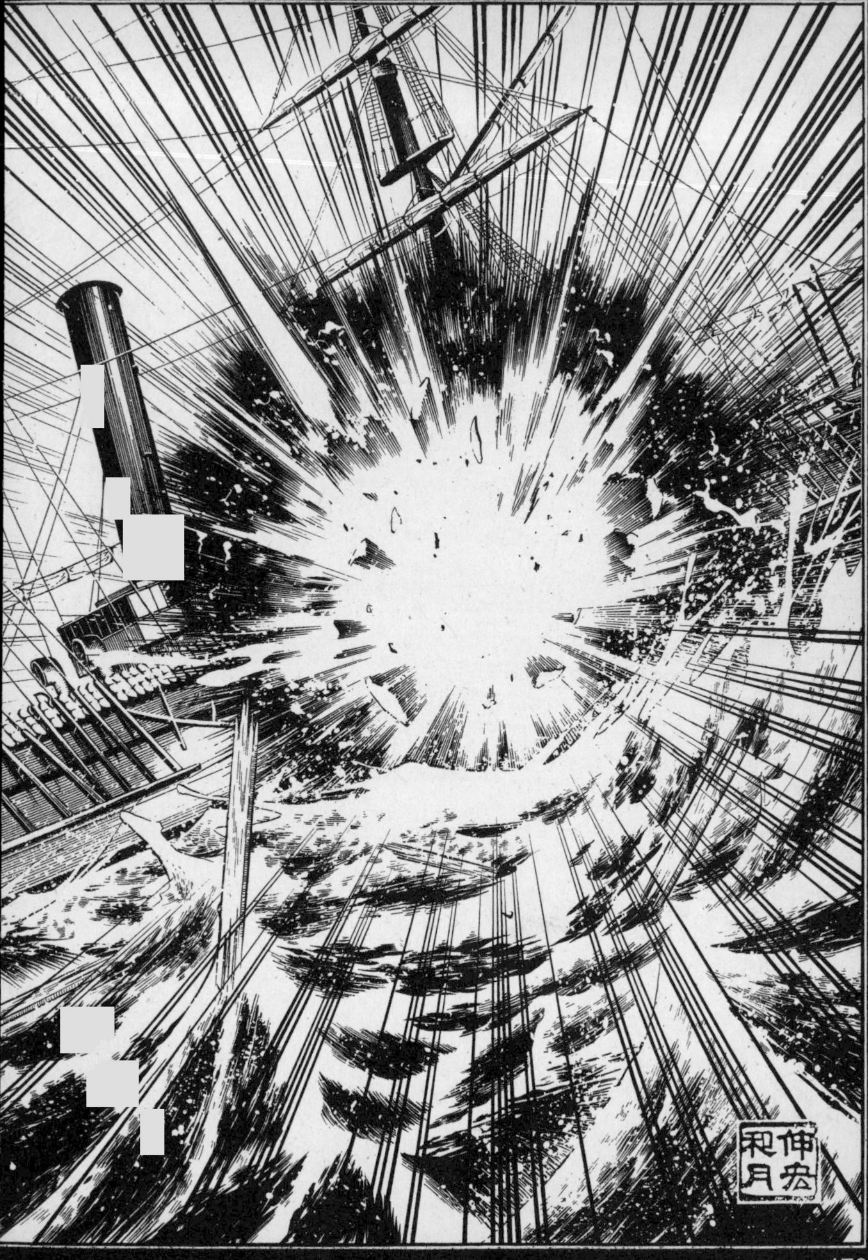
伸宏
和月

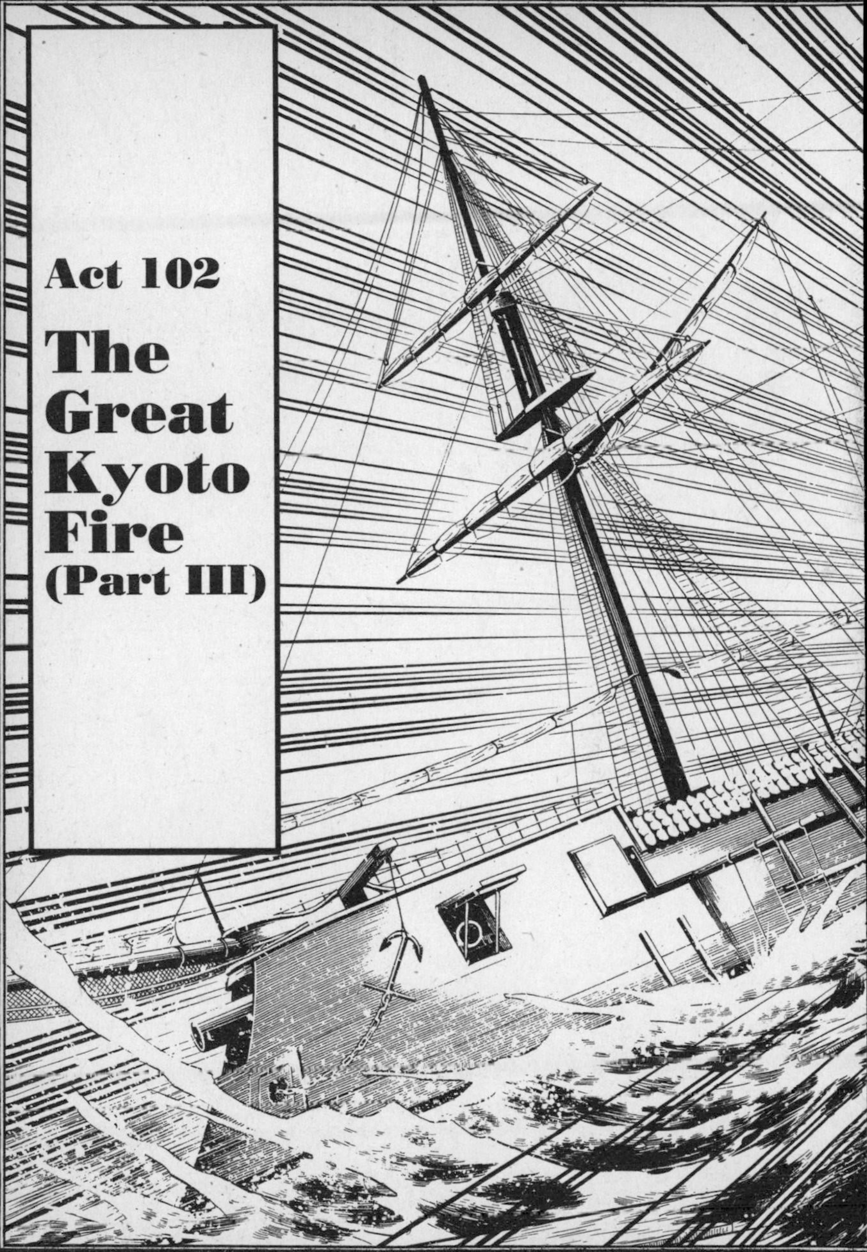
Act 102
The Great Kyoto Fire
(Part III)

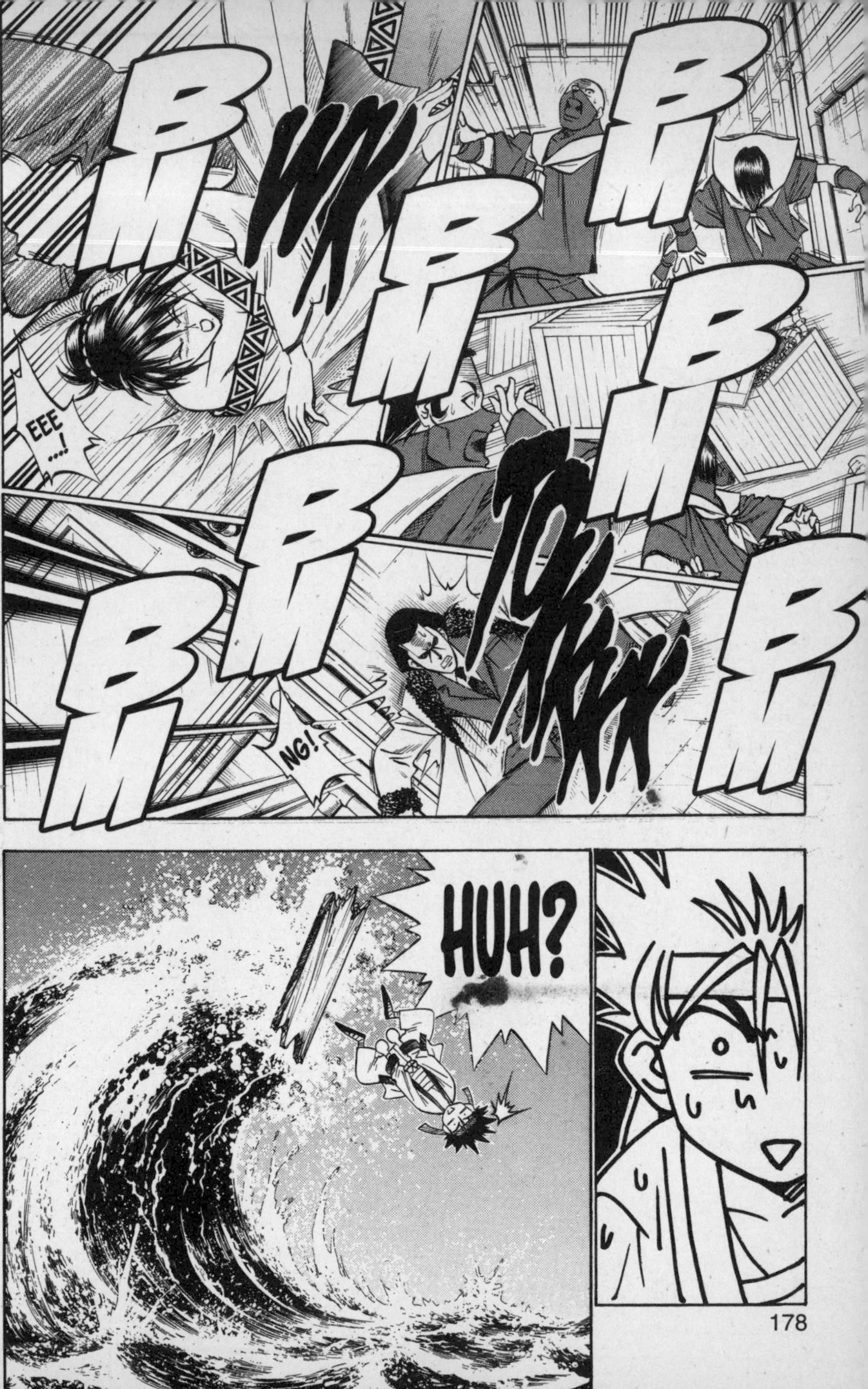
BAM
BAM
BAM
BAM
EEE ...!
BAM
BAM
BAM
NG!
HUH?

READ THIS WAY

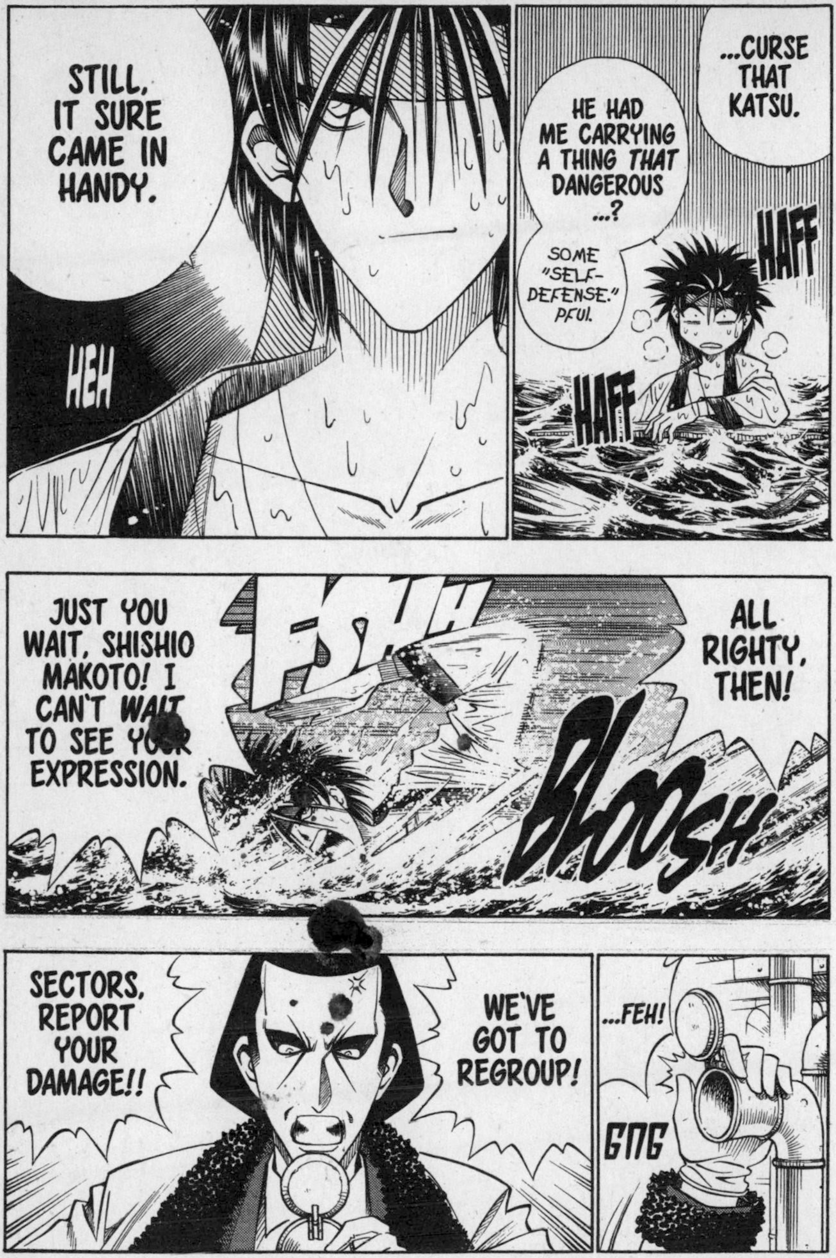
...CURSE THAT KATSU.
HE HAD ME CARRYING A THING THAT DANGEROUS ...?
SOME "SELF-DEFENSE." PFUI.
HAFF
HAFF
STILL, IT SURE CAME IN HANDY.
HEH
ALL RIGHTY, THEN!
BLOOSH
JUST YOU WAIT, SHISHIO MAKOTO! I CAN'T WAIT TO SEE YOUR EXPRESSION.
...FEH!
GNG
WE'VE GOT TO REGROUP!
SECTORS, REPORT YOUR DAMAGE!!

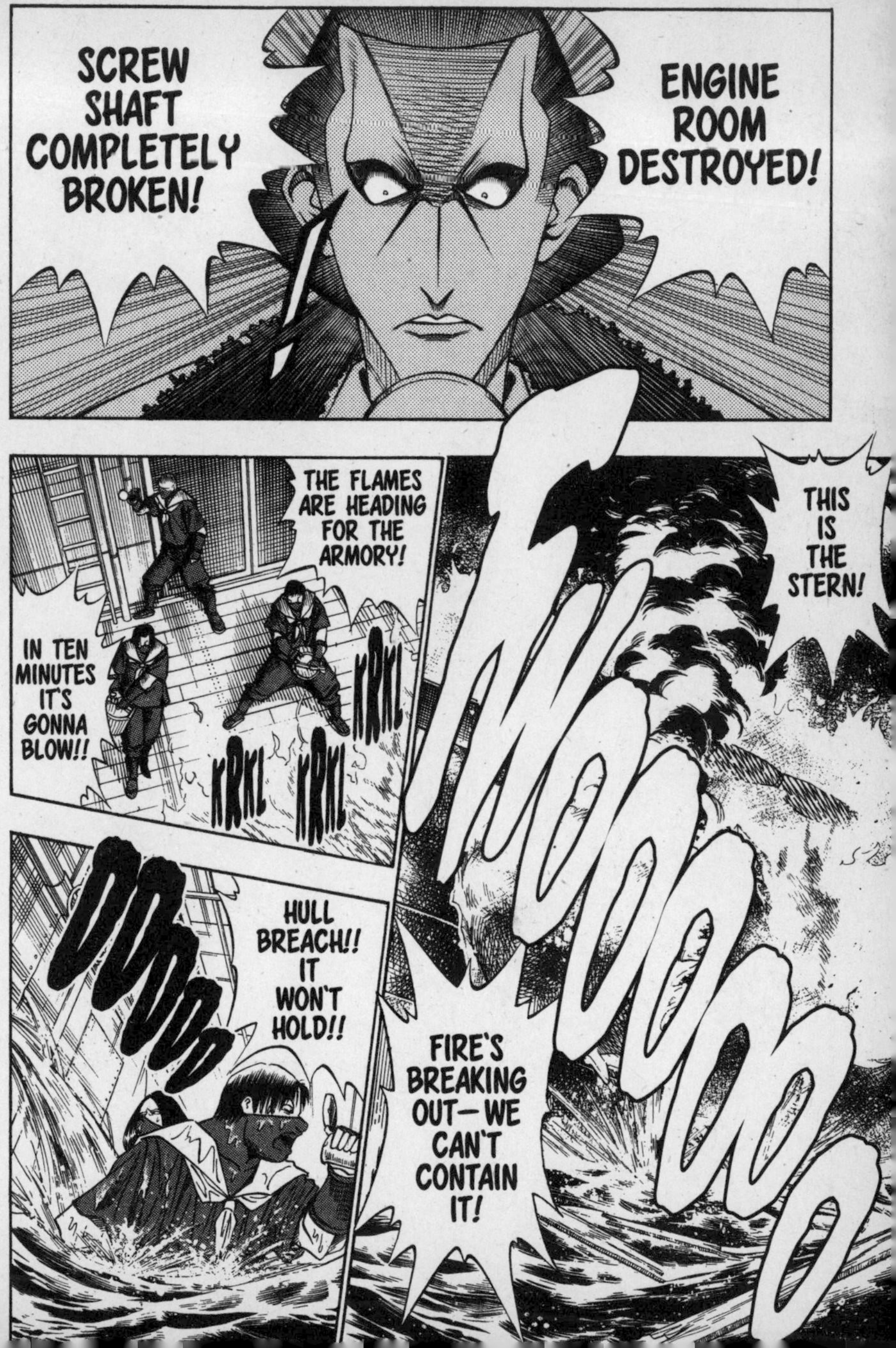
ENGINE ROOM DESTROYED!
SCREW SHAFT COMPLETELY BROKEN!
THIS IS THE STERN!
FIRE'S BREAKING OUT—WE CAN'T CONTAIN IT!
THE FLAMES ARE HEADING FOR THE ARMORY!
IN TEN MINUTES IT'S GONNA BLOW!!
KRKL
KRKL
KRKL
HULL BREACH!! IT WON'T HOLD!!

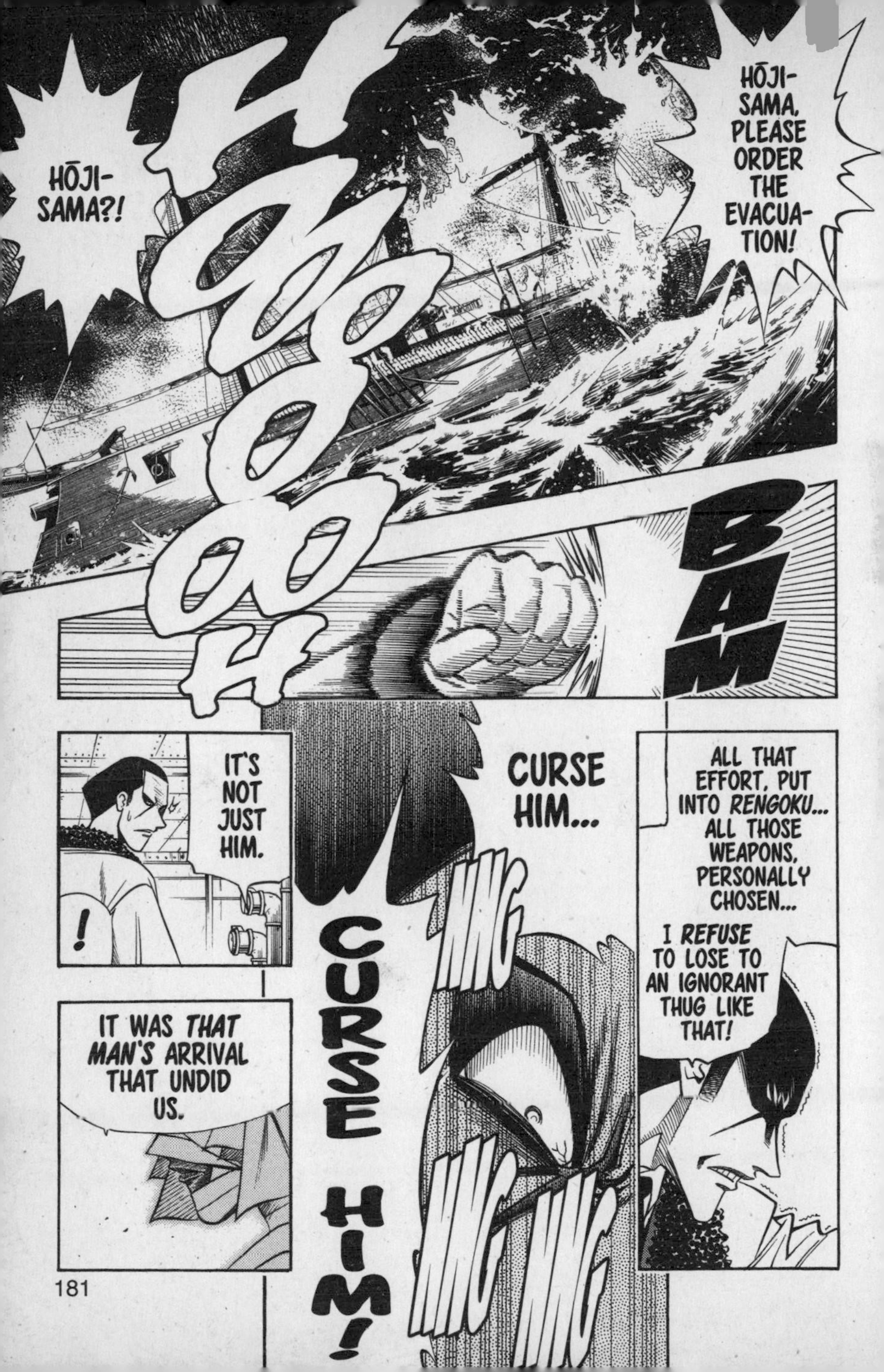
HŌJI-SAMA, PLEASE ORDER THE EVACUATION!
HŌJI-SAMA?!
BAM
ALL THAT EFFORT, PUT INTO *RENGOKU*... ALL THOSE WEAPONS, PERSONALLY CHOSEN...
I *REFUSE* TO LOSE TO AN IGNORANT THUG LIKE THAT!
CURSE HIM...
NNG
NNG NNG
CURSE HIM!
IT'S NOT JUST HIM.
!
IT WAS *THAT MAN'S* ARRIVAL THAT UNDID US.

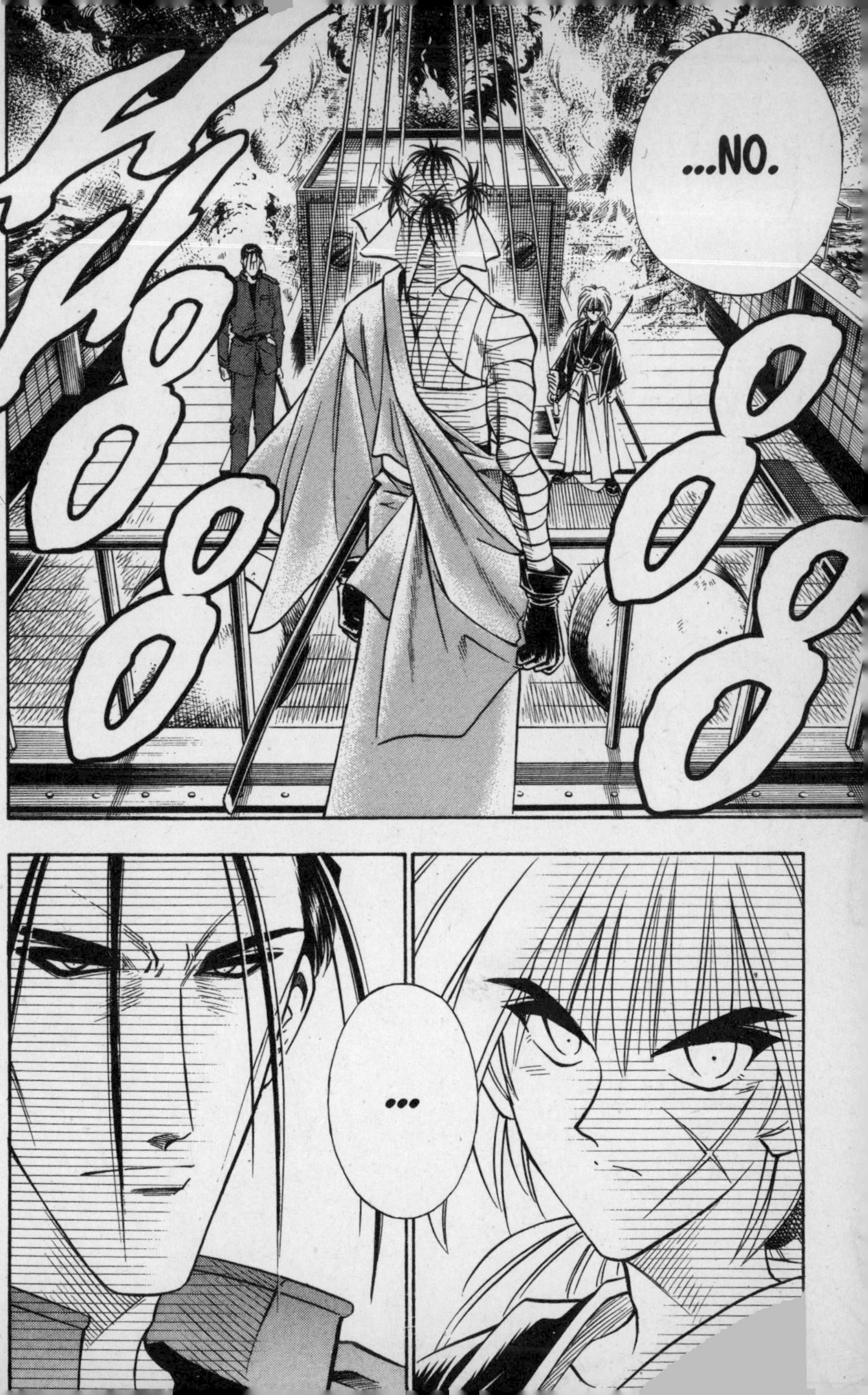
...NO.
...

READ THIS WAY

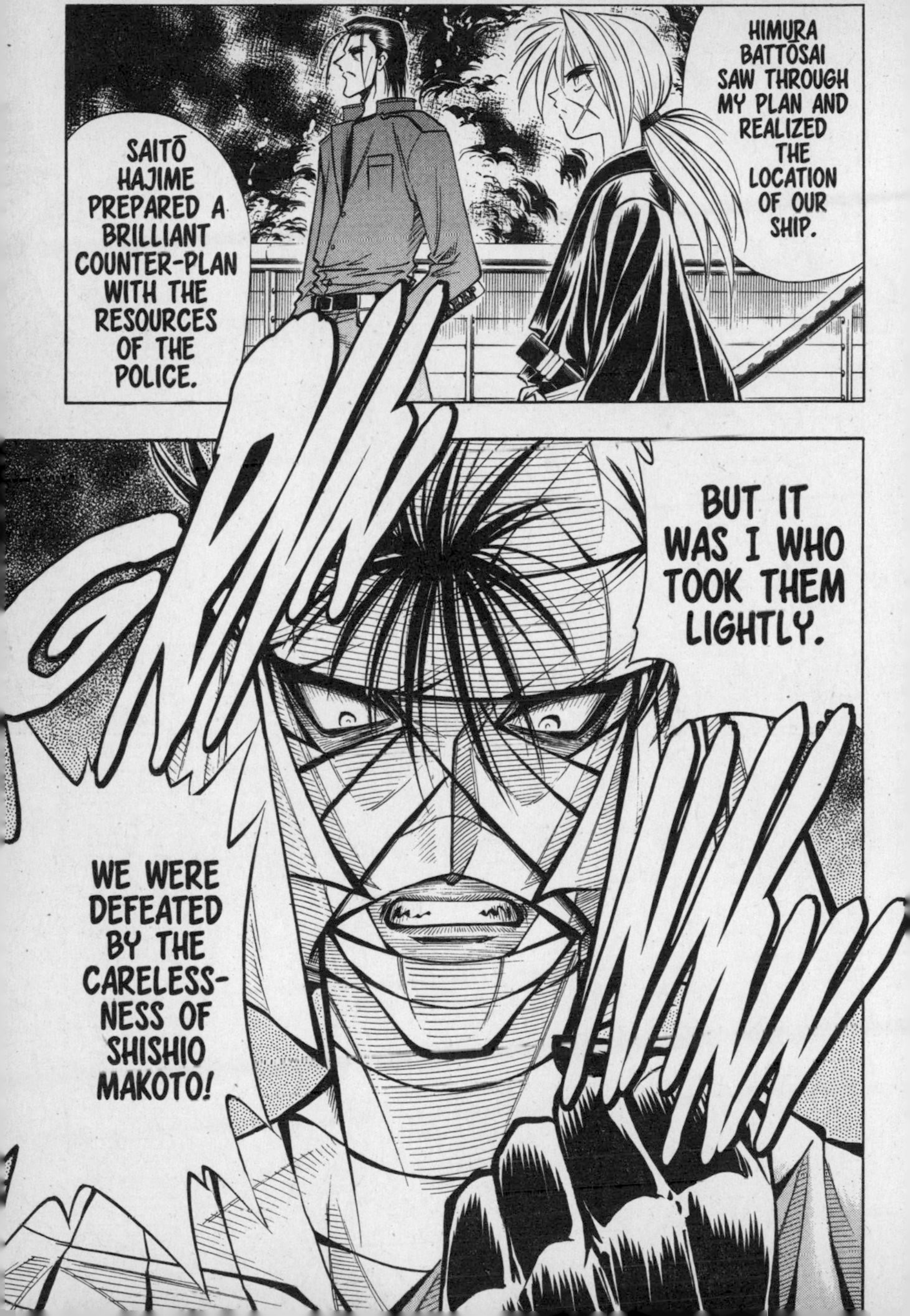
HIMURA BATTŌSAI SAW THROUGH MY PLAN AND REALIZED THE LOCATION OF OUR SHIP.
SAITŌ HAJIME PREPARED A BRILLIANT COUNTER-PLAN WITH THE RESOURCES OF THE POLICE.
BUT IT WAS I WHO TOOK THEM LIGHTLY.
WE WERE DEFEATED BY THE CARELESS-NESS OF SHISHIO MAKOTO!

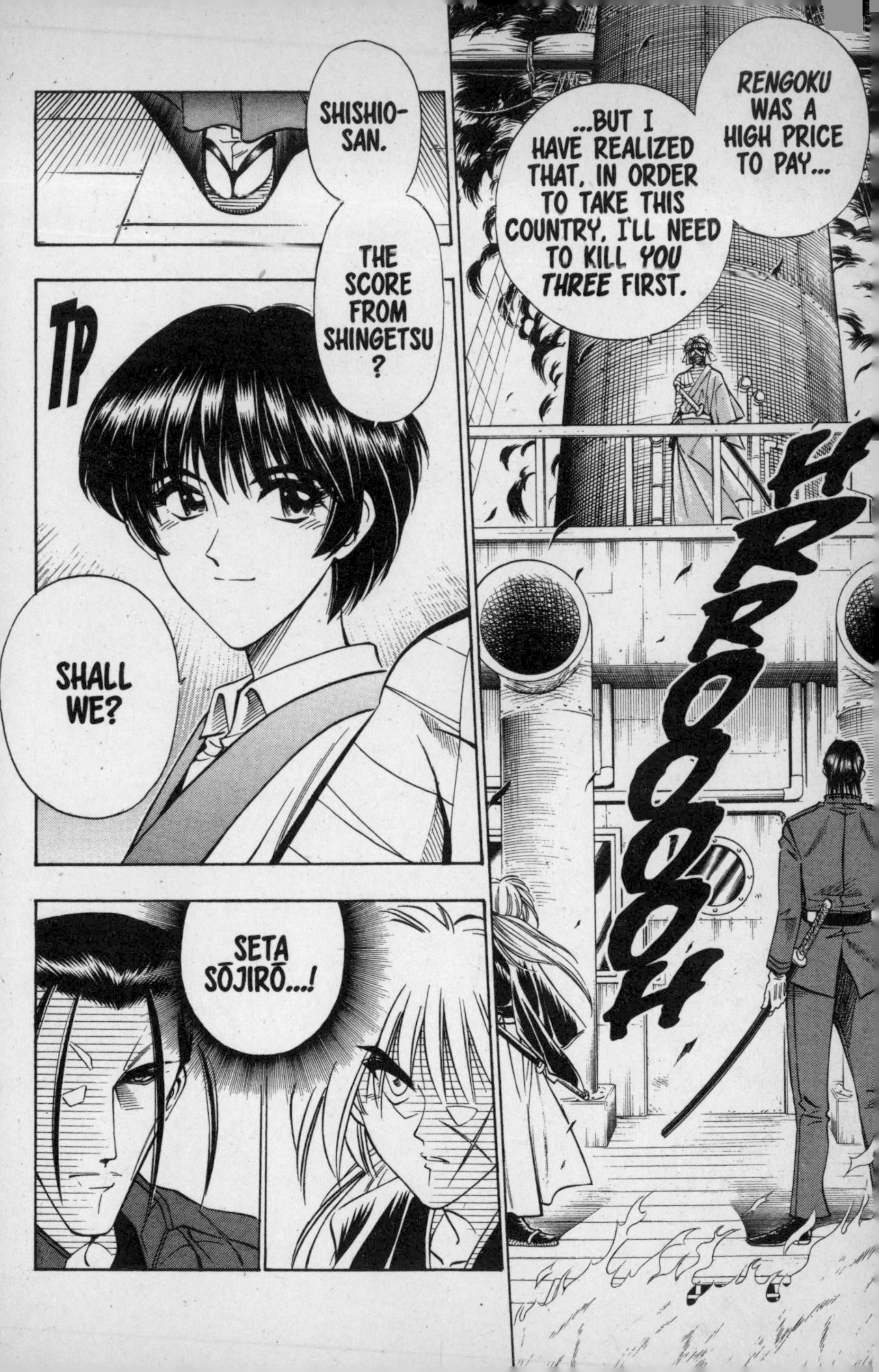
RENGOKU WAS A HIGH PRICE TO PAY...
...BUT I HAVE REALIZED THAT, IN ORDER TO TAKE THIS COUNTRY, I'LL NEED TO KILL *YOU THREE* FIRST.
HRROOOOOM
SHISHIO-SAN.
THE SCORE FROM SHINGETSU?
TP
SHALL WE?
SETA SŌJIRŌ...!

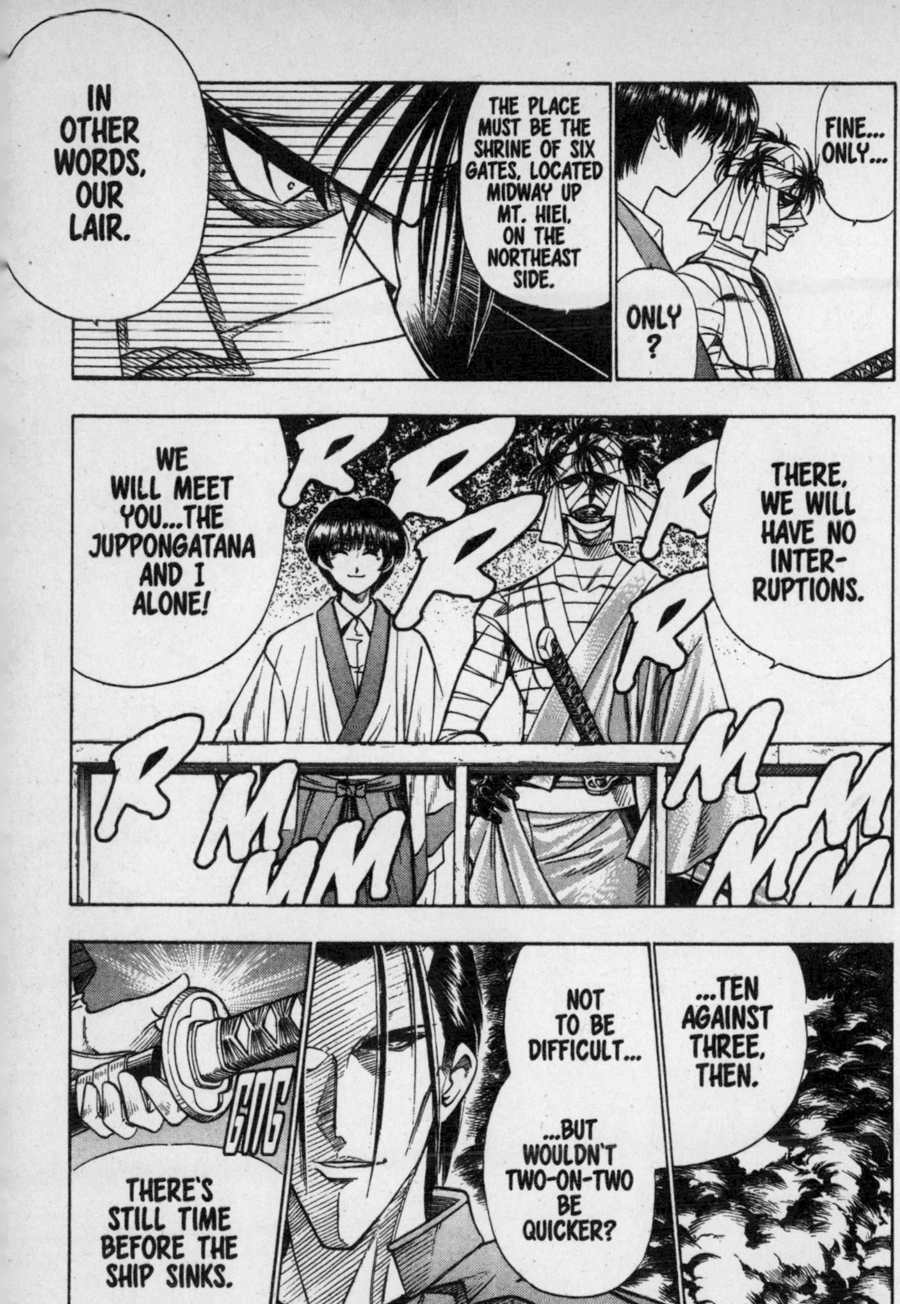
FINE... ONLY...
ONLY ?
THE PLACE MUST BE THE SHRINE OF SIX GATES, LOCATED MIDWAY UP MT. HIEI, ON THE NORTHEAST SIDE.
IN OTHER WORDS, OUR LAIR.
THERE, WE WILL HAVE NO INTER-RUPTIONS.
WE WILL MEET YOU...THE JUPPONGATANA AND I ALONE!
RRRRR
MMMMMM
...TEN AGAINST THREE, THEN.
NOT TO BE DIFFICULT...
...BUT WOULDN'T TWO-ON-TWO BE QUICKER?
THERE'S STILL TIME BEFORE THE SHIP SINKS.

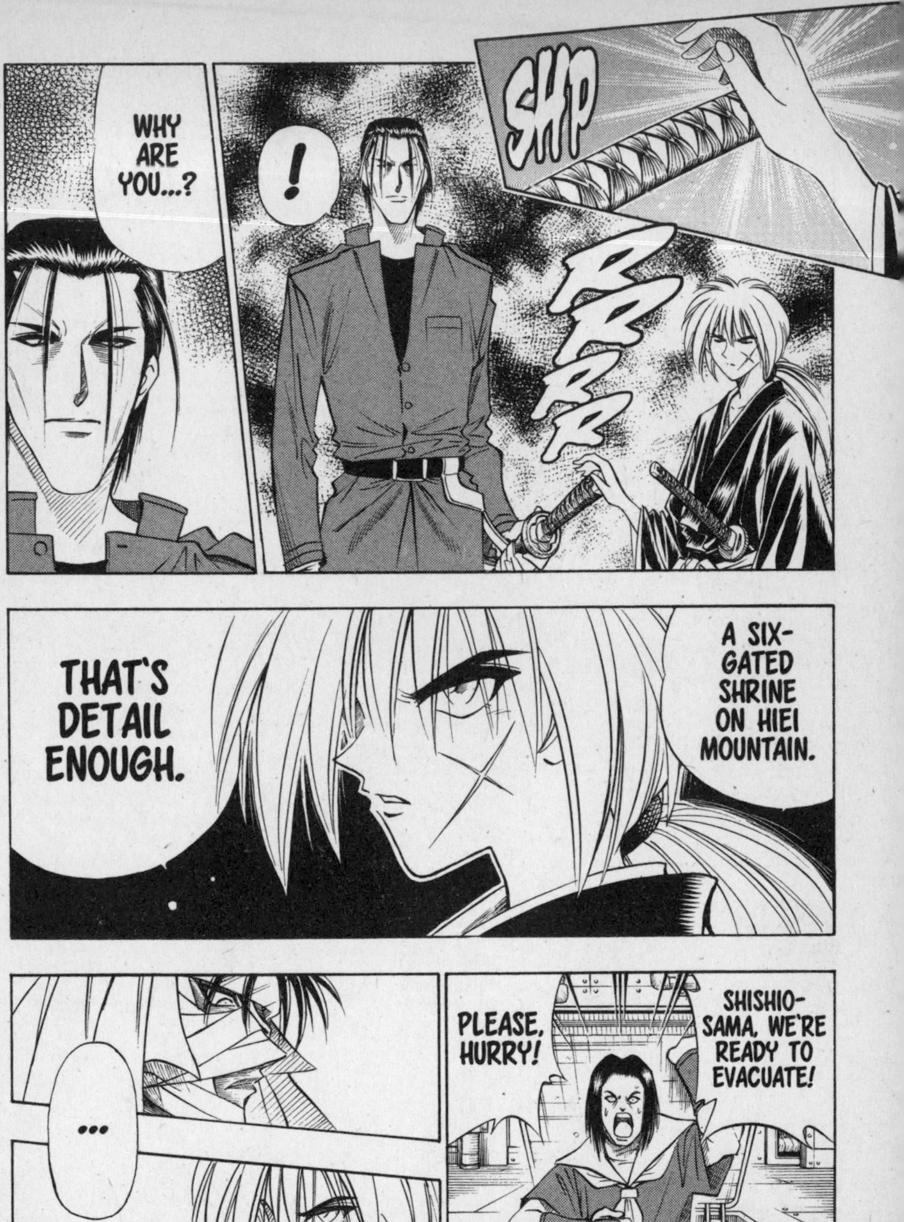
SHP
!
WHY ARE YOU...?
A SIX-GATED SHRINE ON HIEI MOUNTAIN.
THAT'S DETAIL ENOUGH.
SHISHIO-SAMA, WE'RE READY TO EVACUATE!
PLEASE, HURRY!
...

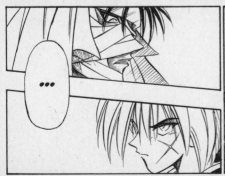

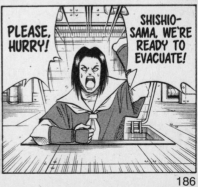

READ THIS WAY

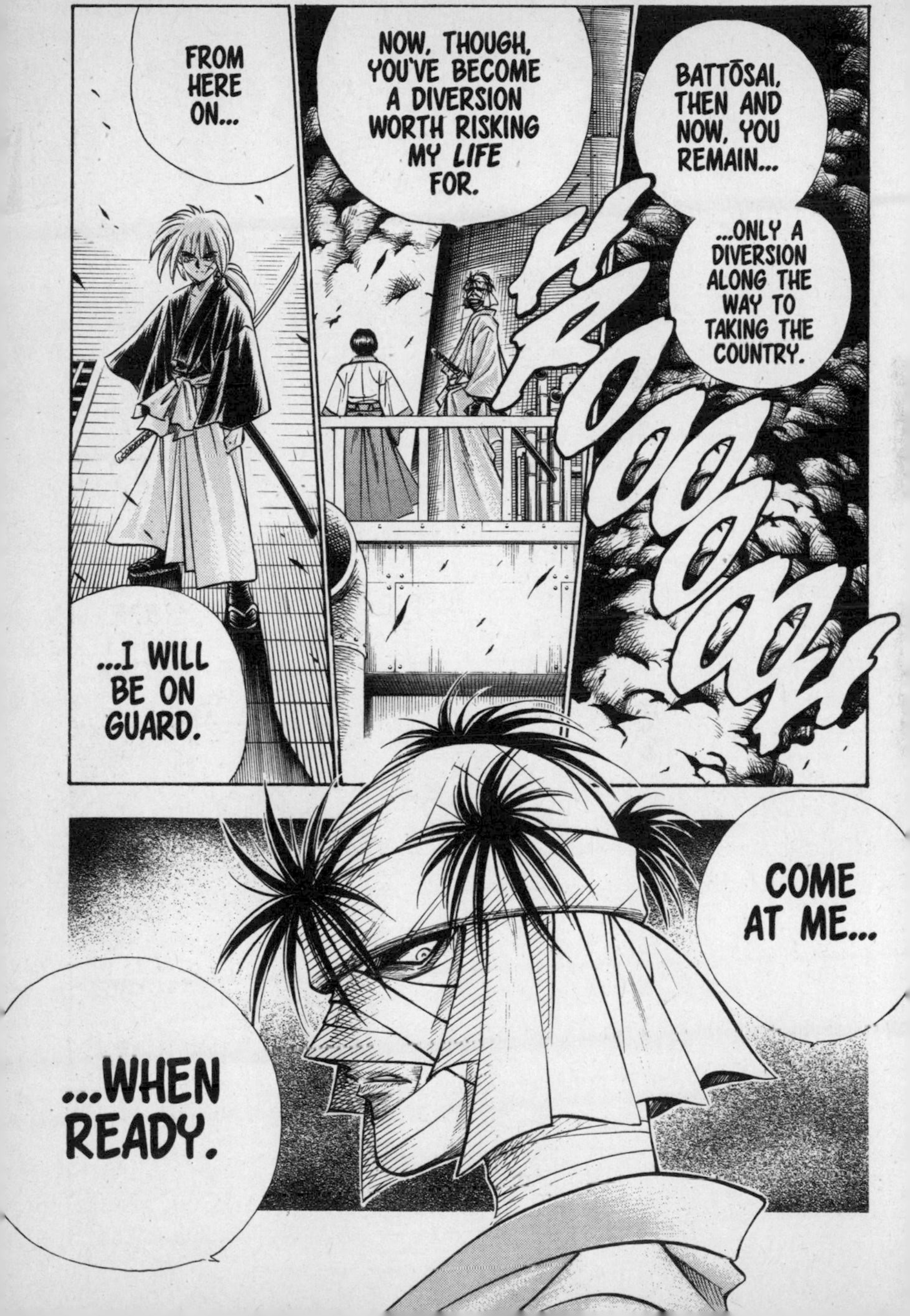
BATTŌSAI, THEN AND NOW, YOU REMAIN...
...ONLY A DIVERSION ALONG THE WAY TO TAKING THE COUNTRY.
NOW, THOUGH, YOU'VE BECOME A DIVERSION WORTH RISKING MY *LIFE* FOR.
FROM HERE ON...
...I WILL BE ON GUARD.
COME AT ME...
...WHEN READY.

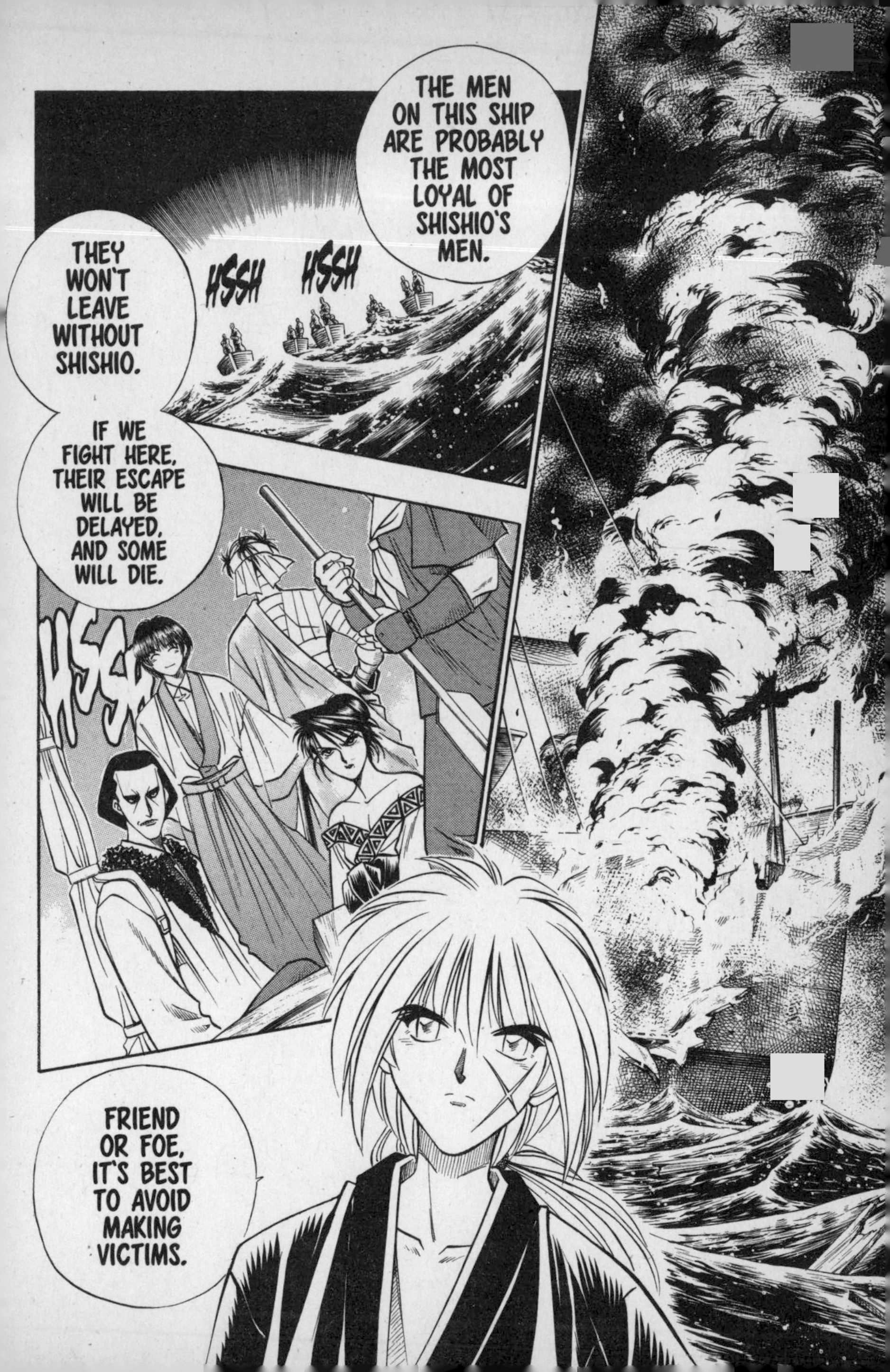
THE MEN ON THIS SHIP ARE PROBABLY THE MOST LOYAL OF SHISHIO'S MEN.
HSSH
HSSH
THEY WON'T LEAVE WITHOUT SHISHIO.
IF WE FIGHT HERE, THEIR ESCAPE WILL BE DELAYED, AND SOME WILL DIE.
FRIEND OR FOE, IT'S BEST TO AVOID MAKING VICTIMS.

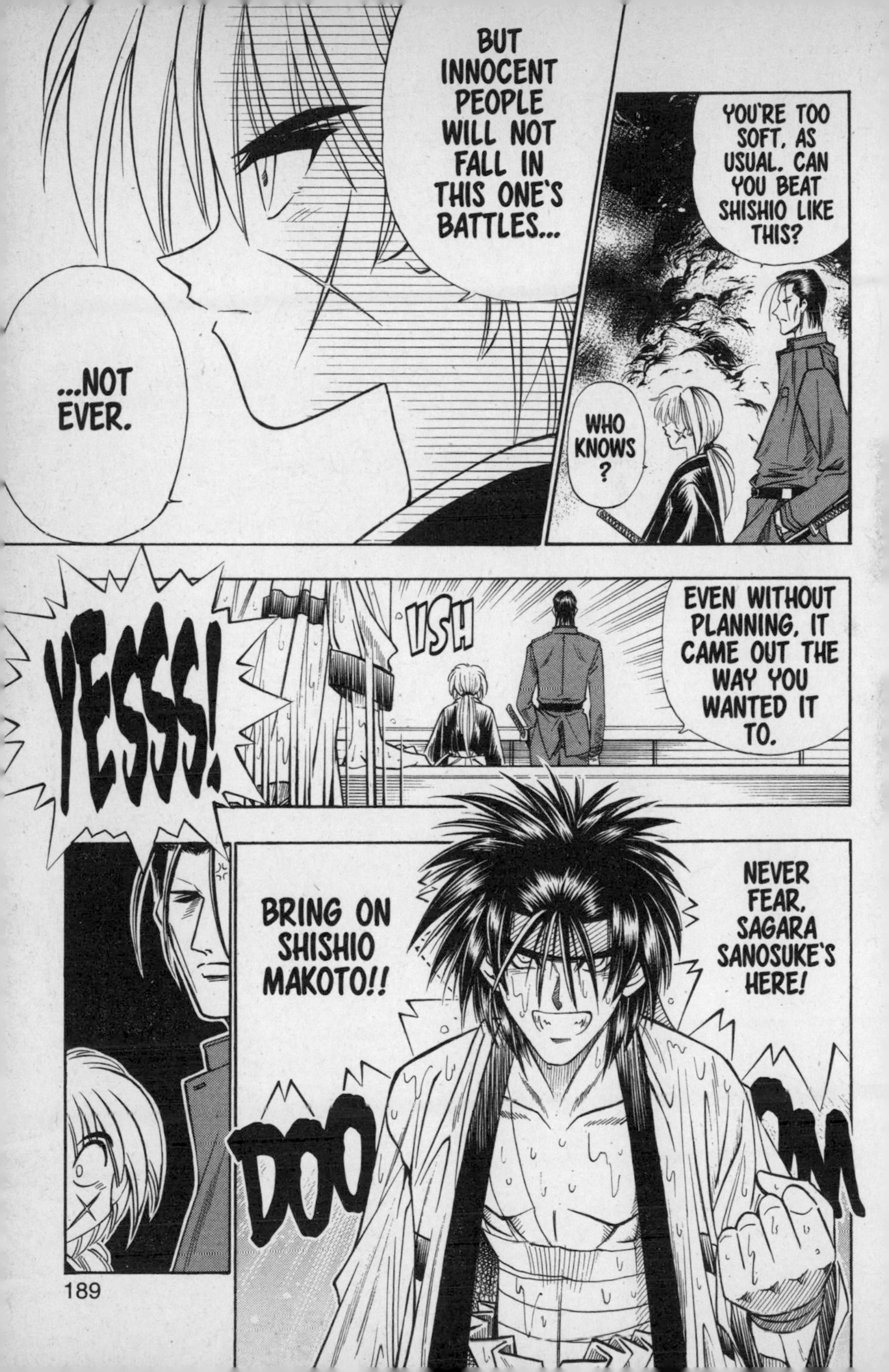

YOU'RE TOO SOFT, AS USUAL. CAN YOU BEAT SHISHIO LIKE THIS?
WHO KNOWS?
BUT INNOCENT PEOPLE WILL NOT FALL IN THIS ONE'S BATTLES...
...NOT EVER.
EVEN WITHOUT PLANNING, IT CAME OUT THE WAY YOU WANTED IT TO.
USH
YESSS!
NEVER FEAR, SAGARA SANOSUKE'S HERE!
BRING ON SHISHIO MAKOTO!!
DOO
OM

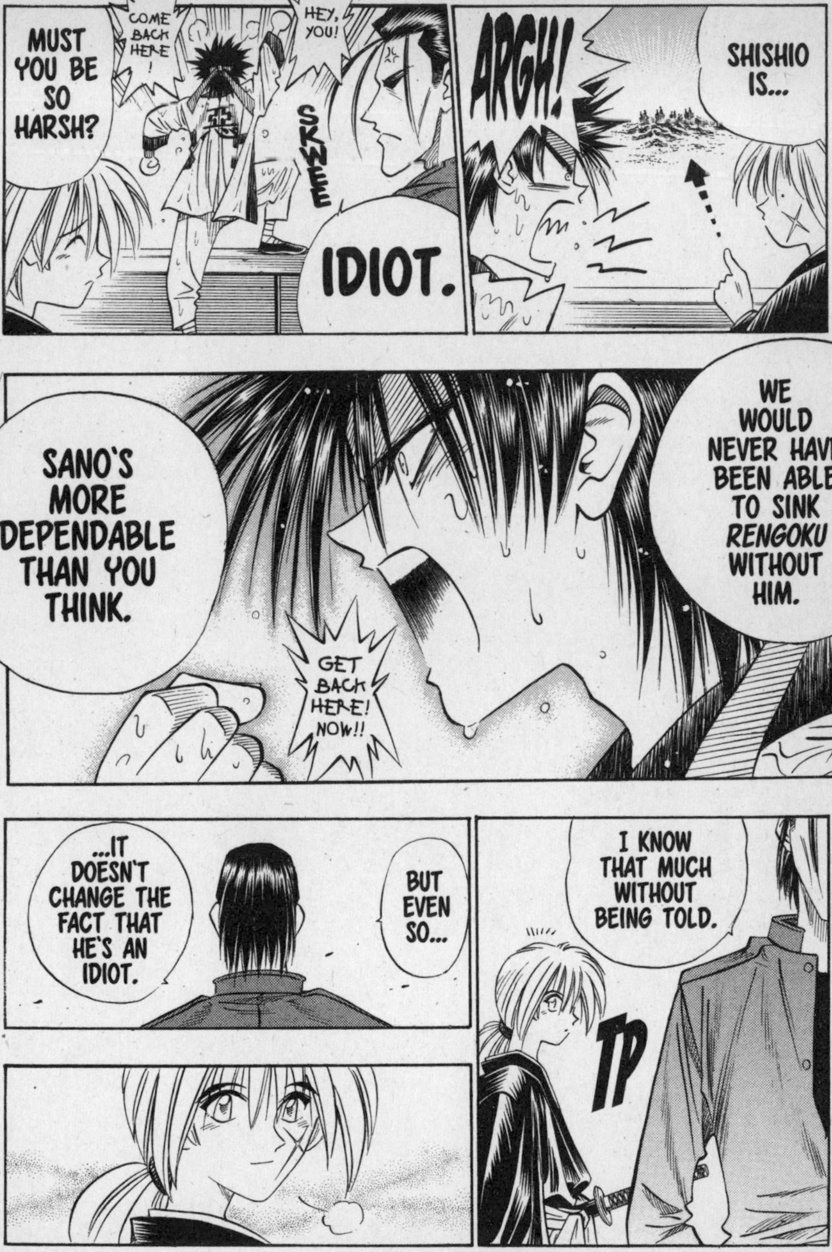
SHISHIO IS...
ARGH!
HEY, YOU!
COME BACK HERE!
MUST YOU BE SO HARSH?
SKWEE
IDIOT.
WE WOULD NEVER HAVE BEEN ABLE TO SINK *RENGOKU* WITHOUT HIM.
SANO'S MORE DEPENDABLE THAN YOU THINK.
GET BACK HERE! NOW!!
I KNOW THAT MUCH WITHOUT BEING TOLD.
TP
BUT EVEN SO...
...IT DOESN'T CHANGE THE FACT THAT HE'S AN IDIOT.

READ THIS WAY

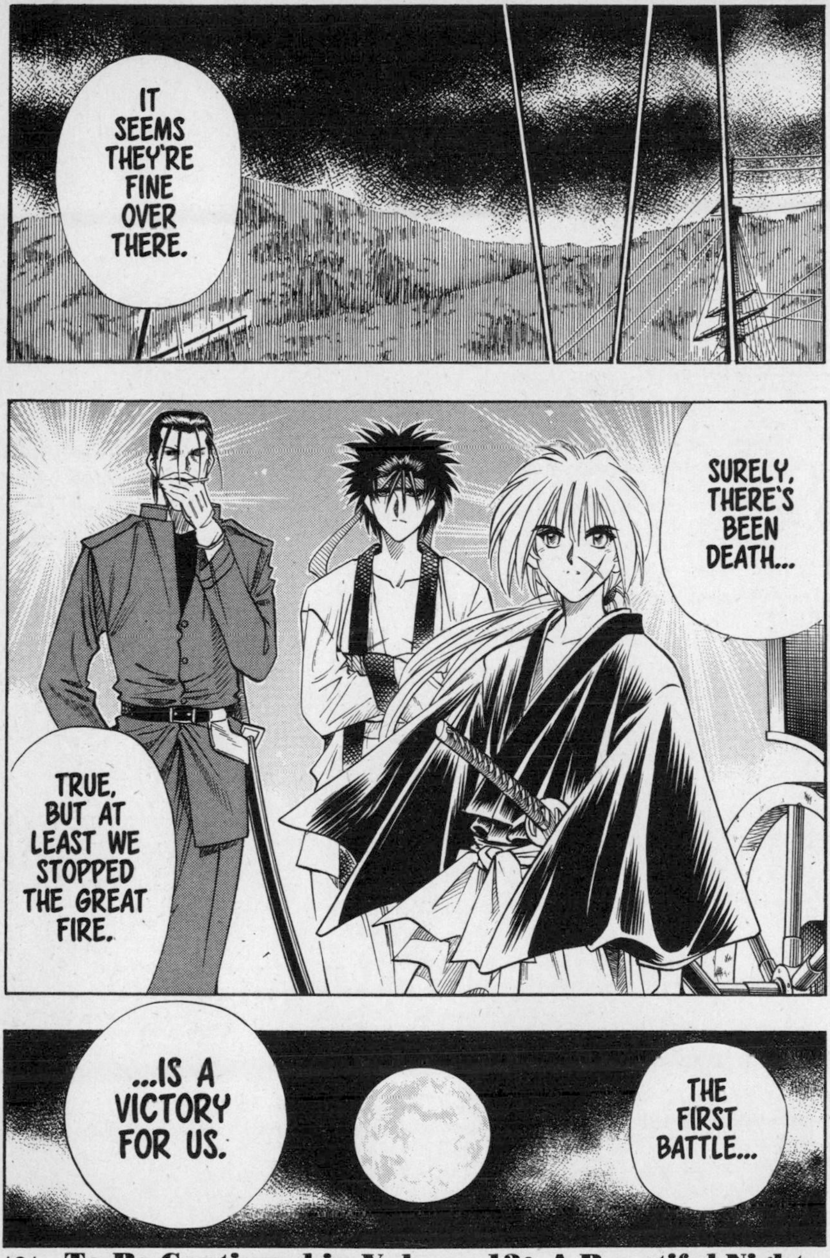
IT SEEMS THEY'RE FINE OVER THERE.
SURELY, THERE'S BEEN DEATH...
TRUE, BUT AT LEAST WE STOPPED THE GREAT FIRE.
THE FIRST BATTLE...
...IS A VICTORY FOR US.

 To Be Continued in Volume 13: A Beautiful Night

GLOSSARY of the RESTORATION

*A brief guide to select Japanese terms used in **Rurouni Kenshin**. Note that, both here and within the story itself, all names are Japanese style—i.e., last or "family" name first, with personal or "given" name following. This is both because **Kenshin** is a "period" story, as well as to decrease confusion—if we were to take the example of Kenshin's sakabatô and "reverse" the format of the historically established assassin-name "Hitokiri Battôsai," for example, it would make little sense to then call him "Battôsai Himura."*

Ishin Shishi
Loyalist or pro-Imperialist **patriots** who fought to restore the Emperor to his ancient seat of power

Juppongatana
Written with the characters for "ten" and "swords," Shishio's **Juppongatana** are literally that—the ten "swords" or generals he plans to use in his overthrow of Japan

Kamiya Kasshin-ryû
Sword-arts or **kenjutsu** school established by Kaoru's father, who rejected the ethics of **Satsujin-ken** for **Katsujin-ken**

katana
Traditional Japanese longsword (curved, single-edge, worn cutting-edge up) of the samurai. Used primarily for slashing; can be wielded either one- or two-handed.

Katsujin-ken
"Swords that give life"; the sword-arts style developed over ten years by Kaoru's father and founding principle of **Kamiya Kasshin-ryû**

Kawakami Gensai
Real-life, historical inspiration for the character of **Himura Kenshin**

kenjutsu
The art of fencing; sword arts; kendô

Bakumatsu
Final, chaotic days of the Tokugawa regime

-chan
Honorific. Can be used either as a diminutive (e.g., with a small child—"Little Hanako or Kentarô"), or with those who are grown, to indicate affection ("My dear...")

dojo
Martial-arts training hall

-dono
Honorific. Even more respectful than **–san**; the effect in modern-day Japanese conversation would be along the lines of "Milord So-and-So." As used by Kenshin, it indicates both respect and humility.

Edo
Capital city of the **Tokugawa Bakufu**; renamed **Tokyo** ("Eastern Capital") after the Meiji Restoration

Himura Kenshin
Kenshin's "real" name, revealed to Kaoru only at her urging

Hiten Mitsurugi-ryû
Kenshin's sword technique, used more for defense than offense. An "ancient style that pits one against many," it requires exceptional speed and agility to master.

hitokiri
An assassin. Famous swordsmen of the period were sometimes thus known to adopt "professional" names—**Kawakami Gensai**, for example, was also known as "Hitokiri Gensai."

-sama
Honorific. The respectful equivalent of **-san**, **-sama** is used primarily in addressing persons of much higher rank than one's self...or, in a romantic sense, in addressing those upon whom one is crushing, wicked hard.

-san
Honorific. Carries the meaning of "Mr.," "Ms.," "Miss," etc., but used more extensively in Japanese than its English equivalent (note that even an enemy may be addressed as "**-san**").

Satsujin-ken
"Swords that give death"; a style of swordsmanship rejected by Kaoru's father

Shinsengumi
"True to the old ways and risking their lives to preserve the old **shōgunate** system," the popular view of the Shinsengumi ("newly elected group") was that of swordsmen as charismatic as they were skilled. Of note: Thanks to the popularity of the NHK drama of the same name, several historical sites in Japan are reportedly enjoying record attendance levels of late.

shōgun
Feudal military ruler of Japan

shōgunate
See **Tokugawa Bakufu**

Tokugawa Bakufu
Military feudal government which dominated Japan from 1603 to 1867

Tokyo
The renaming of "**Edo**" to "**Tokyo**" is a marker of the start of the **Meiji Restoration**

Wolves of Mibu
Nickname for the **Shinsengumi**, so called because of the town (Mibu) where they were first stationed

yatsuhashi
A traditional Japanese sweet and a Kyoto speciality

-kun
Honorific. Used in the modern day among male students, or those who grew up together, but another usage—the one you're more likely to find in *Rurouni Kenshin*—is the "superior-to-inferior" form, intended as a way to emphasize a difference in status or rank, as well as to indicate familiarity or affection.

kunoichi
Female ninja. In that they are not referred to as simply "*onmitsu*" (ninja), their special name suggests their relative scarcity

loyalists
Those who supported the return of the Emperor to power; **Ishin Shishi**

Meiji Restoration
1853-1868; culminated in the collapse of the **Tokugawa Bakufu** and the restoration of imperial rule. So called after Emperor Meiji, whose chosen name was written with the characters for "culture and enlightenment."

patriots
Another term for **Ishin Shishi**... and when used by Sano, not a flattering one

rurouni
Wanderer, vagabond

ryūshōsen
Sometimes translated as "Soaring-Dragon Flash," the **ryūshōsen** of Kenshin's Hiten Mitsurugi school is one of his special moves, and is also known as "Dragon Flight"

ryūkansen
Also translatable as "Winding-Dragon Flash," Kenshin's Hiten Mitsurugi school special move **ryūkansen** is given in here as "Dragon-Spiral Strike"

sakabatō
Reversed-edge sword (the dull edge on the side the sharp should be, and vice versa); carried by Kenshin as a symbol of his resolution never to kill again

IN THE NEXT VOLUME...

The Great Kyoto Fire behind them (and casualties relatively few), Kenshin and the others must weigh their next move carefully. The Kyoto-based spy group Oniwabanshû may be trustworthy, but their leader—Shinomori Aoshi—is not. Elsewhere, the monomaniacal madman, Shishio Makoto, makes plans for what is not only practical to his long-range goals, but for also his own, personal pleasure: a one-on-one, to-the-death battle to the finish....

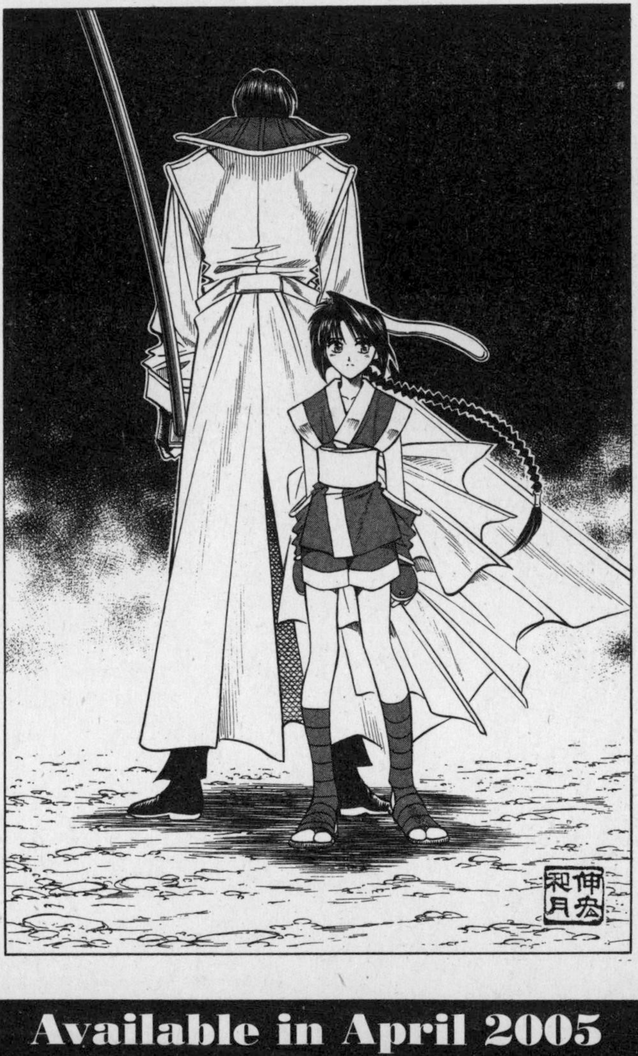
伸宏
和月

Available in April 2005

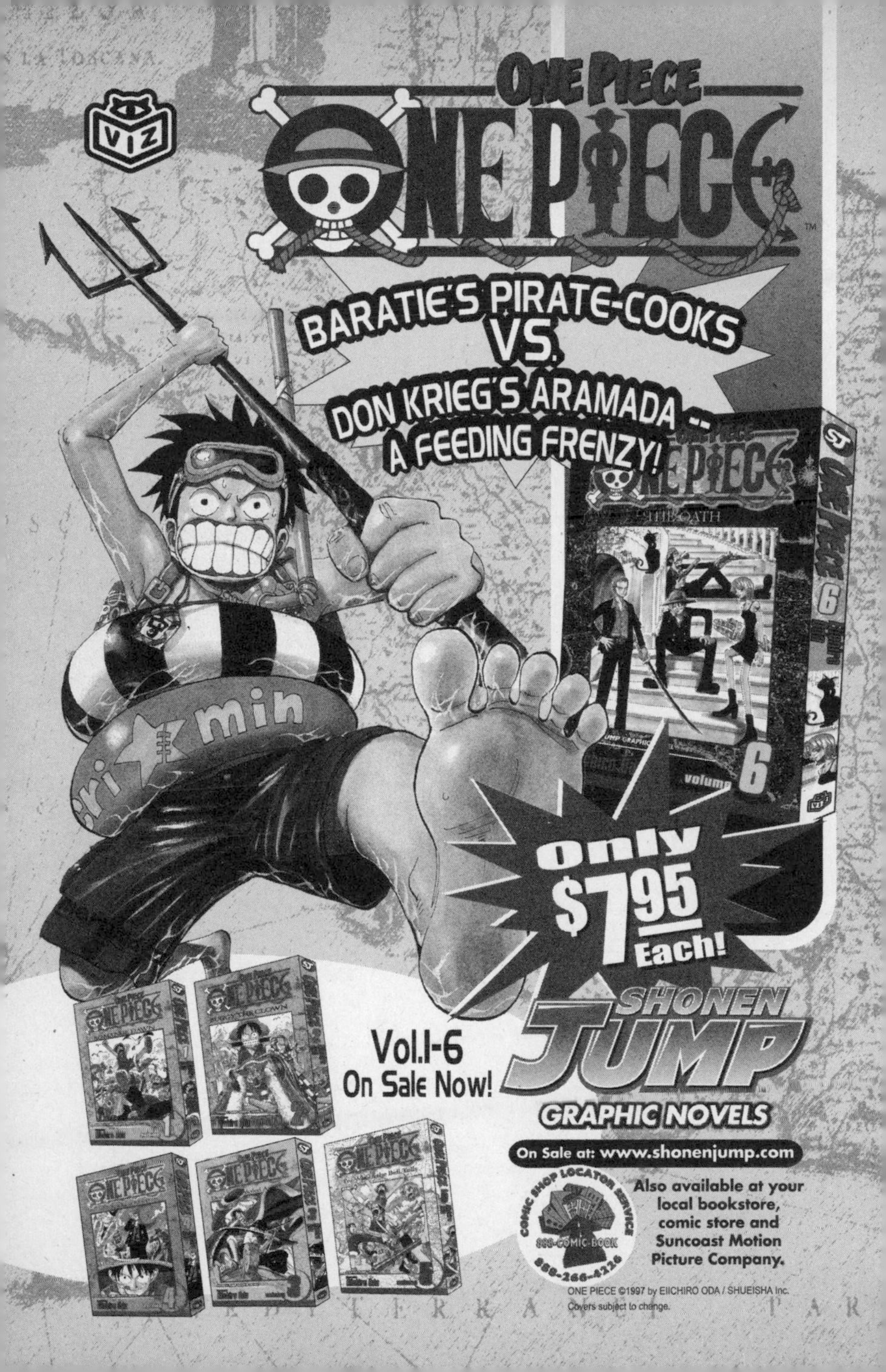
VIZ
ONE PIECE
ONE PIECE
BARATIE'S PIRATE-COOKS
VS.
DON KRIEG'S ARAMADA --
A FEEDING FRENZY!
Only
$7.95
Each!
SHONEN JUMP
GRAPHIC NOVELS
Vol.1-6
On Sale Now!
On Sale at: www.shonenjump.com
COMIC SHOP LOCATOR SERVICE
888-COMIC-BOOK
888-266-4226
Also available at your
local bookstore,
comic store and
Suncoast Motion
Picture Company.
ONE PIECE ©1997 by EIICHIRO ODA / SHUEISHA Inc.
Covers subject to change.

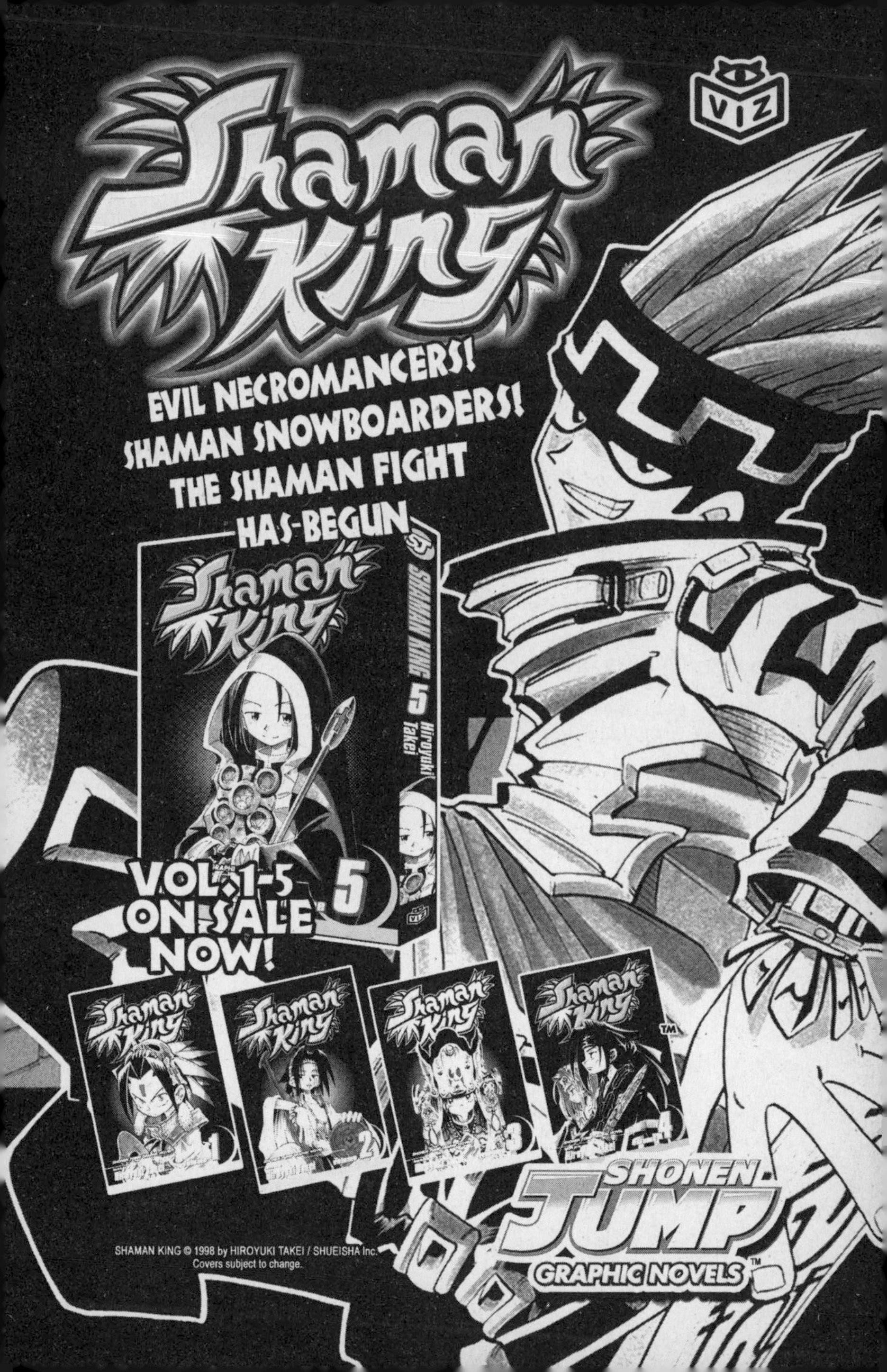

Shaman King
VIZ
EVIL NECROMANCERS!
SHAMAN SNOWBOARDERS!
THE SHAMAN FIGHT
HAS BEGUN
SHAMAN KING 5 Hiroyuki Takei
VOL. 1-5
ON SALE
NOW!
SHONEN JUMP
GRAPHIC NOVELS
SHAMAN KING © 1998 by HIROYUKI TAKEI / SHUEISHA Inc.
Covers subject to change.

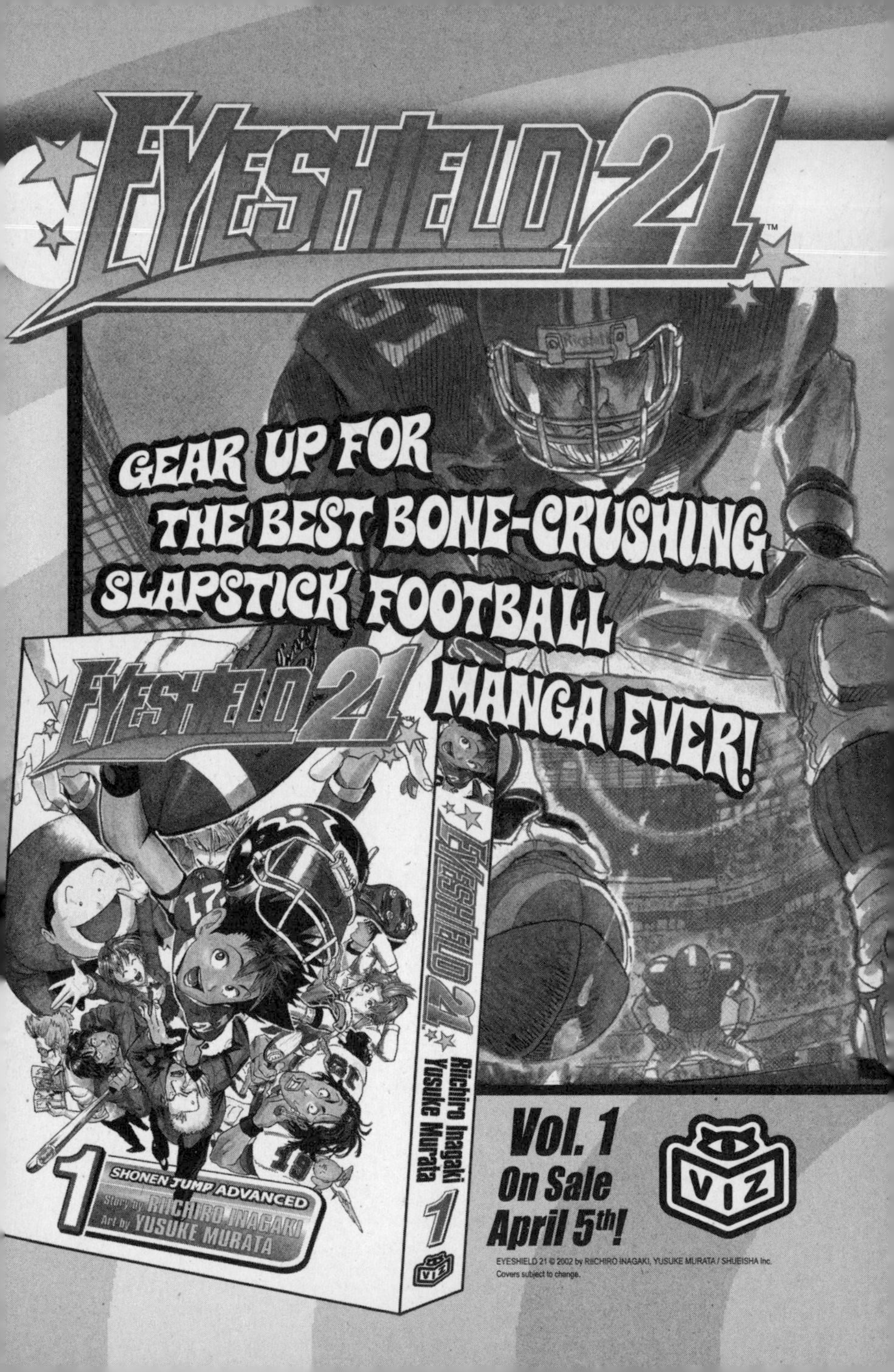
EYESHIELD 21™
GEAR UP FOR
THE BEST BONE-CRUSHING
SLAPSTICK FOOTBALL
MANGA EVER!
EYESHIELD 21
1
SHONEN JUMP ADVANCED
Story by RIICHIRO INAGAKI
Art by YUSUKE MURATA
EYESHIELD 21 Riichiro Inagaki Yusuke Murata 1
VIZ
Vol. 1
On Sale
April 5th!
VIZ
EYESHIELD 21 © 2002 by RIICHIRO INAGAKI, YUSUKE MURATA / SHUEISHA Inc.
Covers subject to change.

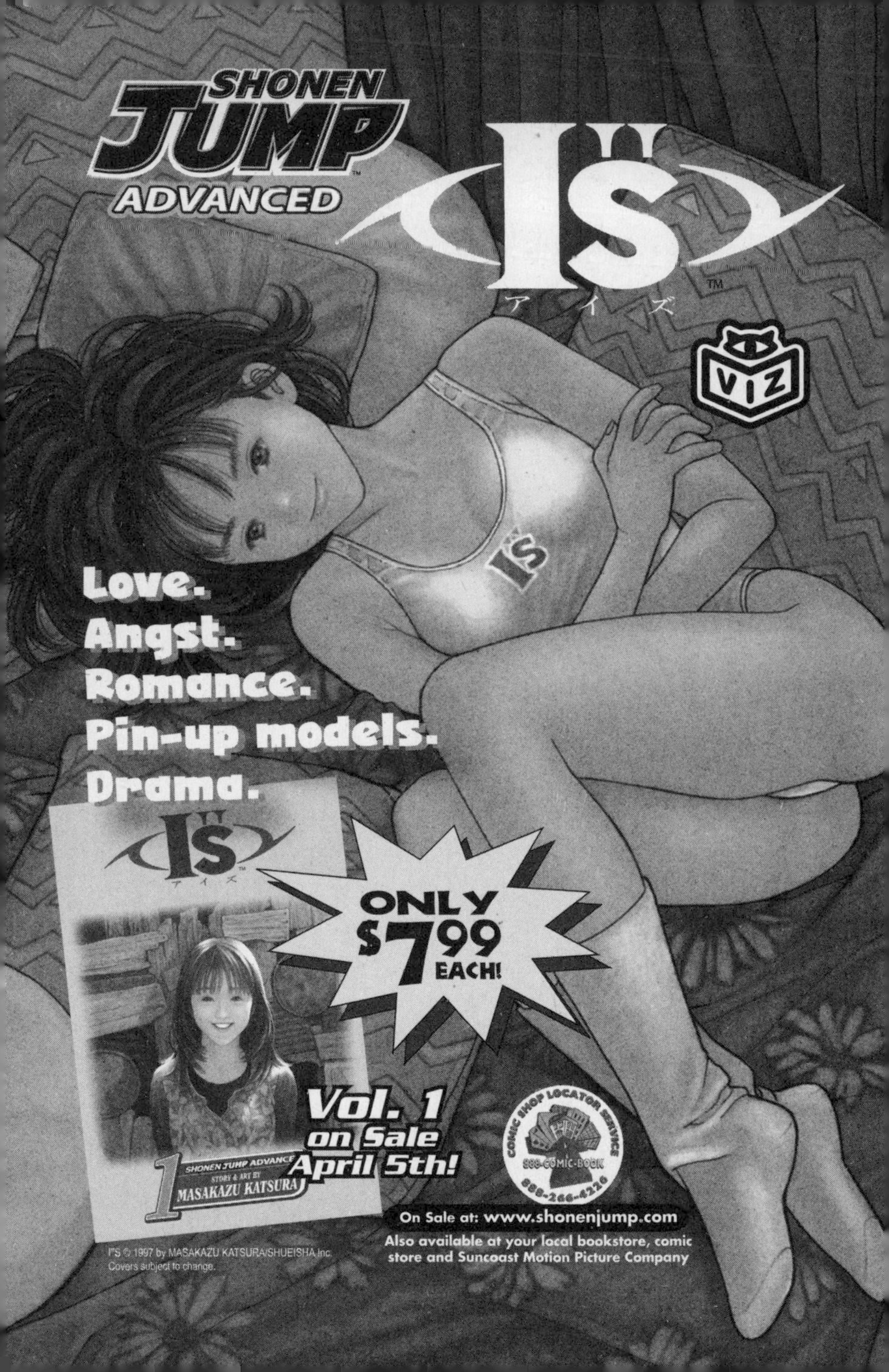